a bibliography of the work of Carl Van Vechten

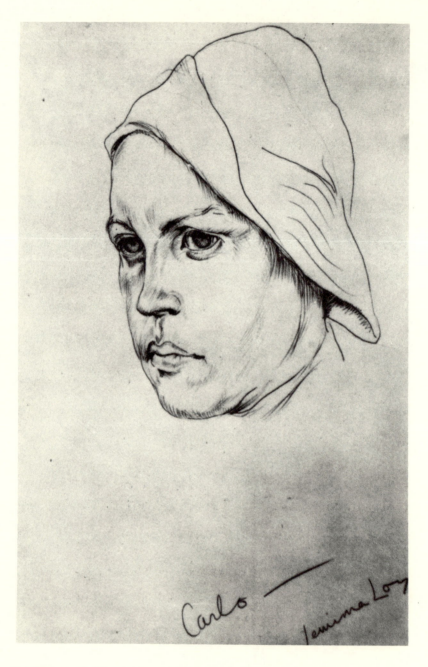

Frontispiece: Carl Van Vechten, 1913, drawing by Mina Loy

a bibliography of the work of Carl Van Vechten

COMPILED BY
BRUCE
KELLNER

GREENWOOD PRESS
WESTPORT, CONNECTICUT • LONDON, ENGLAND

Z 8926
K44

Library of Congress Cataloging in Publication Data

Kellner, Bruce.
  A bibliography of the work of Carl Van Vechten.

  Includes index.
  1. Van Vechten, Carl, 1880-1964—Bibliography.
I. Title.
Z8926.K44   [PS3543.3.A653]   016.813'5'2   79-8409
ISBN 0-313-20767-4

Library of Congress Catalog Card Number: 79-8409
ISBN: 0-313-20767-4

First published in 1980

Greenwood Press
A division of Congressional Information Service, Inc.
51 Riverside Avenue, Westport, Connecticut 06880

Printed in the United States of America

10 9 8 7 6 5 4 3 2 1

I have been a good boy,
    wed to peace and study.
I shall have an old age,
    ribald, coarse, and bloody.

          —marginalia

CONTENTS

Illustrations		ix
Photographs		xi
Coda to an Overture		xiii
A.	Books and Pamphlets	3
B.	Books and Pamphlets Edited or with Introductions	60
C.	Contributions to Books and Pamphlets	82
D.	Contributions to Periodicals	106
E.	Contributions to Newspapers	118
F.	Ephemera and Miscellanea	169
G.	Photography	184
H.	Biography, Bibliography, and Criticism	217
I.	Collections	244
Index		249

ILLUSTRATIONS

Frontispiece
Carl Van Vechten, 1913

Following page 59

Ex Libris: Carl Van Vechten's bookplate
The Tiger in the House
The Blind Bow Boy by Robert Locher
The Blind Bow Boy by Alastair
The Tattooed Countess
Nigger Heaven
Peter Whiffle: His Life and Works
Spider Boy
Parties
Sacred and Profane Memories

PHOTOGRAPHS

Following page 183

Grandmother Ilona Van Vechten
Ina Claire
Ettie and Carrie Stettheimer
Philadelphia Cheese Shop
Artificial Cave by Antoni Gaudí, Parque Guell, Barcelona
Domingo Ortega, El Soto
Fania Marinoff
Strongman in Chains, Place de la Bastille, Paris
Columbus Circle, New York City
Wystan Hugh Auden
Alicia Markova's Hand
Private Herbert Coburn, U.S. Army; Seaman Andy Mann,
  U.S. Navy; Seaman J. H. Keller, Canadian Navy—at the
  Stage Door Canteen
Watching a Parade in Harlem
A Harlem Madonna
Sandy Campbell and Donald Windham
Christopher Isherwood
Isak Dinesen, the Baroness Karen Blixen
Pierre Olaf in *La Plume De Ma Tante*

CODA TO AN OVERTURE

When Scott Cunningham prepared his first bibliography in 1924, Carl Van Vechten supplied an introduction, called "Overture in the form of a funeral march." "Tombs, tombs, on every hand," Van Vechten lightly lamented, "some of the mounds desolate and uncared for, a few out of which flowers have struggled upward." Half a dozen substantial volumes still lay ahead of him, as well as many essays and reviews in periodicals, and a whole new career in photography. When Klaus Jonas prepared a second bibliography, in 1955, Van Vechten referred to its entries as "stepping stones toward a 75th year celebration." Another decade of remarkable activity ensued before his death in 1964. My copies of these two studies are dogeared and worn from the hard use required of them in this third, rather more complete, bibliography.

I have attempted to record Van Vechten's entire output: his novels and collections of essays already cataloged by my predecessors but with fully descriptive accounts of them and of their variations from one printing to another because of the interest of scholars in revision and of bibliophiles in bindings; the bulk of his newspaper work because of its historical interest as an index to musical and theatrical taste during the period of its composition; his photography because of its own artistic significance. I also have recorded attendant criticism and biographical studies as well as a record of sources and collections.

All bibliographers must gratefully pillage the work of Donald Gallup, whose Pound and Eliot bibliographies have established precedents of inarguable excellence. It is my good fortune that Donald Gallup is literary trustee for the estate of Carl Van Vechten as well as curator of American literature in the Beinecke Rare Book and Manuscript Library at Yale University. His assistance and cooperation have never flagged, not, indeed, during the twenty-five years we have met or corresponded over various literary matters. I am grateful to him for his generosity in time and of spirit.

I am also indebted to the staff of the Beinecke Library; to the Manuscript and Archives Division of the New York Public Library, with special thanks to Michael Nash, annex archivist; to the staff of Ganser Library, at Millersville State College where I teach, for its cheerful patience and persistence; to the Philadelphia Museum of Art; to William Koshland of Alfred A. Knopf, Inc., for making publication records available to me and for permission to reproduce dust jackets and other illustrations; and to Joseph Solomon, representing the estate of Carl Van Vechten, for permission to reproduce photographs.

Minor services often make major contributions, thanks to Sandy Campbell, Jerald Ketchum, Frank Paluka, Bruce Parker, James Ringo, Dennis E. Robison, Richard Rutledge, Milton Saul, Richard Stoddard, Joanne Trautmann, Robert A. Wilson. Finally, I would like to thank my son, Hans, and my daughter, Kate, for helping me with the details of filing and alphabetizing.

My greatest debt, however, is to my friend, Paul Padgette. Without his meticulous records and continued interest, this bibliography would be far less complete. He began collecting materials for an annotated bibliography in 1964, at the time of Van Vechten's death, but for various practical considerations—my own proximity to Yale and the New York Public Library, for example—I undertook the project. Its completion was possible only through Paul Padgette's constant cooperation, and I am deeply grateful to him.

During the 1975-76 academic year I was given a research grant, and in 1977 I was granted a sabbatical leave of absence from Millersville State College to complete the research for this bibliography. It is heartening to know that a most esoteric project can be cheerfully encouraged, even in times of economic restrictions.

When I was torn between one breakdown in materials over another, Donald Gallup averred that every bibliographer had to choose how to best handle the requirements of his own subject. Accordingly, there are substantial differences between my divisions and those customarily followed. Further, I have devised a method of description based on the Rupert Hart-Davis Soho Bibliographies, on John Carter's always useful *ABC for Book Collectors* (Knopf, 1953), and my own best hunch. The latter grew, in spirit at least, from Donald Gallup's admirable monograph, *On Contemporary Bibliography* (University of Texas Press, 1970), which deserves attention from any bibliographer. I have listed all English language editions of a volume—beginning with those issued in the United States—before proceeding to foreign language versions, regardless of publication dates. I have cross-referenced all reprintings by including in brackets [ ] at the conclusion of the entries my own corresponding numbers, and for many entries I have indicated those publications which contain substantial quotations. My descriptive phraseology is conventional whenever possible, and I have avoided specifying outré variations: *red*, whether scarlet or crimson or tomato, is simply *red; rule*, whether swelled or not, is simply *rule*, although I have indicated dark or light, thick or thin, wide or narrow, as necessary. All edges may be considered trimmed and unstained and all end-papers may be assumed as white unless otherwise specified. Missing information from an entry in Section A or B was unavailable; entries in Section C are deliberately truncated; moreover, the detailing of the publication history is purposely more complete for Van Vechten's own books than for those to which he contributed. I have given full attention to bindings and to dust jackets because Van Vechten usually had a hand in their design (as the number of dummies—accepted as well as rejected—in his collection suggests). Early on, Alfred A. Knopf, Inc., began to use a line of a particular design— ⎍⎍⎍⎍⎍⎍⎍⎍ —in Van Vechten's books that I have not discovered in any other volumes issued under the Borzoi imprint; whenever it appears, I have referred to it as *CVV rule* or *CVV border*. Finally, I have identified those few items I have not seen, and I have indicated the source of information and the degree to which the items may be apocryphal.

Section A contains all books and pamphlets in all editions, printings, states, and translations, the contents of which are solely Van Vechten's work. It also accounts for manuscript versions of them, when appropriate.

Section B contains books and pamphlets for which Van Vechten served as editor or for which he prepared prefaces or introductions or to which he was the major contributor.

Section C contains books and pamphlets with contributions by Carl Van Vechten as well as contributions by others, usually under circumstances in which he was not directly involved. This convenient division—between B and C—which occurs in the Klaus Jonas bibliography, I find preferable to a single section because of the marked difference in materials.

Section D contains periodical and other magazine writings.

Section E contains Van Vechten's newspaper work, a section separate from D because of the number of entries. Moreover, because they run more or less consecutively—one term of employment following another—I have listed entries for each newspaper separately, even though some articles from the *New York Times*, for example, followed some in the *Evening Globe*. Some of these articles exist only in Van Vechten's scrapbooks: his first essay about Gertrude Stein, for example, appeared only once, in an early Monday morning edition, on the financial page, and is not included in the microfilm copies of the *New York Times*; his Sunday editorial about *The Darktown Follies*, perhaps the first serious or extensive consideration of what he called "The Negro Theatre," is simply missing from the only extant version of the *New York Press,* a microfilm copy in the New York Public Library. A few articles have conflicting dates, when, for example, they appeared in both a late evening and early morning edition. In these instances, I have used Van Vechten's scrapbook dating for practical reasons. I have not included minor squibs and fillers unless they have some marked historical interest. (The fact that Caruso was going to sing in a particular opera on 10 February is hardly sacrosanct when a review of the performance occurred on 11 February.) A catalog of such useless information might swell Van Vechten's contributions by about a third.

Section F contains ephemera, many entries which might qualify elsewhere in another bibliographer's opinion. In most instances, however, the materials in this section were not only printed as ephemera—dust jacket blurbs, short program notes, endorsements for books by others—but written as ephemera. Van Vechten's squibs for his own books, included here, are cross-referenced with the books themselves, of course.

Section G contains a fairly complete catalog of photographic subjects and a fairly complete list of reproductions. When a subject was photographed more than once—Eugene O'Neill, for example, was photographed by Van Vechten in 1932, 1933, 1936, 1945, and 1953—I have listed the earliest date, unless the only published photograph comes from a later sitting, in which case I have listed that date. I have not accounted for the various geographical locations in various parts of the world which Van Vechten photographed extensively, nor have I made any attempt to account for photographs of paintings, flowers, clouds, the 1939 World's Fair, apartment house doormen identified only by their first names, strangers at Coney Island, the Cloisters, Harlem, the Bowery, or Macy's annual Thanksgiving Day parade—although some of these include some of his most interesting work. In the case of the Stage Door Canteen, which Van Vechten photographed extensively as an historical document, I have listed several subjects he photographed individually, but I have not listed dozens of service people in dozens of group shots. I have made no attempt to catalog the difference between black-and-white and color photographs. Van Vechten began to photograph in color in 1939, and the majority of his subjects exist in both black-and-white and in Kodachrome after that date.

Section H contains biographical, bibliographical, and critical studies, including individual reviews of Van Vechten's books, interviews, photographic exhibitions, and obituaries.

Section I accounts for various literary and photographic collections of Van Vechten's work and of the work of others which he established.

An index, as the University of Chicago Press's guide to indexing wisely observes, should not be a concordance. The index to this bibliography, therefore, is selective. It lists major titles by Van Vechten and titles with which he was significantly associated. It lists the names of all individuals as subjects and the names of all significant individuals as authors. It does not include the titles of newspaper articles—most of which were the inventions of editors, in any case—nor of essays. It does not list the names of minor reviewers peripherally connected with Van Vechten's career. It does not list photographic subjects, since the section devoted to photography is itself a more than sufficient index. Further, the bracketed [   ] cross-referencings of photographs and essays should serve the same ends as a more elaborate index and, at the same time, avoid redundancy.

For these foregoing divisions and decisions, and for the inevitable errors and omissions associated with any bibliographical work, I assume responsibility, defending the former and apologizing for the latter.

One of the happiest aspects of preparing this bibliography was my knowledge that it would be outdated even before publication: Charles Scribner's Sons will add Carl Van Vechten to its extension of the University of Minnesota *American Writers* monograph series in the near future; Paul Padgette is presently editing a volume of Van Vechten's dance photographs; *Opera News* will observe Van Vechten's centenary by publishing his essay on Enrico Caruso—previously available only in a Yiddish translation—in the spring of 1980; at about the same time, Dance Horizons will re-issue *The Dance Writings of Carl Van Vechten*, this time in paperback; Hollywood is turning *Spider Boy* into a movie; Alec Wilder is rumored to be turning *The Tattooed Countess* into an opera; and, in this age of instant reprints, AMS Press has announced new editions of three Van Vechten novels.

All of which is at least as exhausting as it is exhaustive. Why such a complete catalog for the work of a largely forgotten figure? Lincoln Kirstein said it best, in his eulogy for Carl Van Vechten, and, later, in print: "He was an important artist and history will admit it."

17 June 1979

a bibliography of the work of Carl Van Vechten

A.
BOOKS AND
PAMPHLETS

A 1 <u>Five Old English Ditties</u> 1904

Five Old English Ditties | WITH MUSIC BY | CARL VAN VECHTEN | [rule] |
Pious Selinda - - - - - William Congreve. | Apelle's Song - - - - - John
Lyly. | Sabina Wakes - - - - - William Congreve. | A Lenten Ditty - - - -
- F. C. | The Petition - - - - - William Congreve. | [rule] | PUBLISHED
FOR THE AUTHOR BY N. NELSON, CHICAGO | COPYRIGHT 1904 BY CARL VAN VECHTEN

6 leaves. 35 X 28 cm.

[1] title; [2] blank; [3-10] text; [11-12] blank. Folded sheets to make
12 pages.

Maroon paper wrapper, lettered on front in gold to duplicate the title
page, minus publisher and copyright.

100 copies printed, October 1904, none for sale.

Contents: [as on title page]

    Originally titled "Love Songs of a Philanderer" and dedicated in the
manuscript to Anna Elizabeth Snyder who later became Van Vechten's
first wife, these five songs are among a group of musical compositions weitten over a period of about five years. The "love songs"
were published privately at a cost of $30 to Van Vechten. Two sets
of manuscripts are included among the other compositions, with a
specific instruction that none of them is ever to be published.
The collection includes "I sit by the house," words by Francis Denis
Campau, a boyhood friend, 21 December 1901; "Ethel," words by Campau,
21 December 1901; "Pious Selinda," 19 October 1904; "Chloe," words by
William Congreve, 21 October 1904; "A Lenten Ditty," 31 October 1904;
"The Petition," 2 November 1904; "Sabina Wakes," 7 November 1904;
"Apelle's Song," 20 November 1904; "Pipe Song," words by Walter Leon
Gregory, 23 January 1905; "Love," words by Constance Johnson, 10
March 1905; "Valse Serenade," for violin and piano, dedicated to

Evelyn Allen Cooper with whom Van Vechten gave occasional public re-
citals in Chicago, 10 March 1905; "An Absinthe," for piano, 30 March
1905; "A Spanish Serenade," words by Gregory, dedicated to Mrs. Harriet Dement Packard, a member of the Chicago "Smart Set" whose society Van Vechten wrote about for the Chicago American, 9 May 1905;
"Au Claire de la Lune," setting for an unidentified French text, 20
August 1905; "Tone Picture," for violin and piano, dedicated to Nathalie Young, 31 August 1905; "Leave Us Remember the Love She Has
Gave," words by E. Richard Schayer, Thomas I. Hague, and George
Wheeler, newspaper acquaintances of the period, December 1905; "Ze-
nith," words by Anna Marble Pollock, 18 December 1906; "It is not
love I ask," undated fragment; "Candida: Valse Intermezzo -- with
gratitude to L.V.B. and apologies to G.B.S.," undated fragment; "Var-
sity we love the best of all," undated fragment.

A 2   Symphony Society Bulletin IV   1910-1911

SYMPHONY SOCIETY | BULLETIN [flanked on the left by] Vol IV | October 24
[and on the right by] No. 1 | 1910 [all of the foregoing in a decorative
border] | Issued Fortnightly by the Symphony Society of New York, 1 West
34th Street | PROGRAM NOTES BY CARL VAN VECHTEN | [double rule]

[Subsequent issues duplicate the foregoing title, altering the number and
date, as indicated under contents, below.]

32 pp. 27.3 X 23.9 cm.

[1, 5, 9, 17, 23, 25, 29] title and text in three columns; [remaining
pages] text in three columns.

Issued as single programs, but an unknown number of sets were later
bound together in rough black cloth without any lettering. As Scott
Cunningham contended in his 1924 bibliography, "Mr. Van Vechten's notes
occupy the entirety of each issue, and in the bibliographer's opinion,
this constitutes a first edition. . . ."

Contents: No. I, 24 October 1910: Brigg Fair [Delius], The Brahms Con-
certo [for violin], Villon [William Wallace], "Gerechter Gott" from "Ri-
enzi" [Wagner], The Rustic Wedding Symphony [Goldmark], "Che faro senza
Eurydice" from "Orfeo" [Gluck], Orient et Occident [Saint-Saëns]; No. II,
7 November 1910: Overture and Air "Diane Impitoyable" from "Iphigénie en
Aulide" [Gluck], Three Dances from "Iphigénie en Aulide," Overture and
Pagegeno's Air from "Die Zauberflöte" [Mozart], Overture to "Le Nozzi de
Figaro" and Air "Non Più Andrai" [Mozart], Schumann's First Symphony, Ex-
cerpts from "The Maid of Orleans" [Tschaikovsky], Overture, Spinning
Chorus, and Senta's Ballad from "Der Fliegende Holländer" [Wagner],
Rondes de Printemps [Debussy]; No. III, 21 November 1910: Hadley's Third
Symphony, Die Loreley [Liszt], The Obstinate Note [Moszowski], Stock's
Symphonic Waltz, Brahms' Fourth Symphony, Spanish Symphony [Lalo], Seid
Umschlungen Millionen [Johann Strauss]; No. IV, 5 December 1910: The Un-
finished Symphony [Schubert], Hugo Kaun's "Rondo" and "Joyous Wanderings,"
The Tempest [Tschaikovsky], Overture to "Reinzi" [Wagner, et seq], The
"Siegfried Idyl," Excerpts from "Die Meistersinger," The Tannhaüser Bac-
chanale, The Processional of the Knights of the Grail from "Parsifal,"
Entrance of the Gods into Walhalla, The Music of the Future [reprinted

from George Bernard Shaw, The Perfect Wagnerite, 1898]; No. V, 2 January
1911: Mendelssohn's Italian Symphony, Liszt's A Major Pianoforte Concerto,
Mazeppa [Liszt], Brahms' Fourth Symphony [reprinted from No. III], Bee-
thoven's Symphony in C Minor; Seid Umschlungen Millionen [reprinted from
No. III], Beethoven's Violin Concerto, "An die Hoffnung" [Beethoven], No.
VI, 30 January 1911: Music from France [Franck, d'Indy, Saint-Saëns],
Dukas' Symphony, César Franck's Variations Symphoniques, Chausson's Sym-
phony in B Flat, Chausson's Poème; No. VII, 14 February 1911: Enesco's
Symphony, César Franck's D Minor Symphony, L'après-midi d'un Faune [De-
bussy], The Children of Bethlehem [Pierné]; No. VIII, 8 March 1911:
Brahms' D Major Symphony, Victor Kolar's Hiawatha, Goldmark's A Minor
Violin Concerto, Tschaikowsky's Sixth Symphony, Wagner's Symphony, Ru-
binstein's D Minor Concerto for the Pianoforte, Beethoven's First Symphony

A 3   Why and What   1914

[cover title, in red] WHY | [double rule] | AND | [double rule] | WHAT
[all of the foregoing enclosed in a border of six parallel wavering
lines]

8 pp. 17.5 X 12.5 cm.

[1-2] blank; [3-6] text; [7-8] blank. A single rule, red border encloses
the text of each page, and the first initial of the text is printed in
red.

Gray deckle-edge stiff wrapper, tied with a red cord, lettered in red on
front, as above. There is no title page, and date, copyright notice,
address, publisher, and author are not indicated.

   About a thousand copies were printed as a publicity brochure for
   Trend, the magazine Van Vechten edited for three months -- October,
   November, and December 1914 -- shortly before its demise. The text
   of Why and What, titled "The Publisher's Workbench," appeared in the
   November issue of the magazine, signed "Atlas." [D28]

A 4   Music After The Great War   1915

a. First edition

Music | After the Great War | AND OTHER STUDIES | [rule] | BY | CARL VAN
VECHTEN | [rule] | NEW YORK | G. Schirmer | MCMXV [the foregoing in a
two line border]

viii, 168 pp., blank leaf. 19 X 12.6 cm.

[i] half-title; [ii] blank; [iii] title; [iv] copyright, 1915, by G.
Schirmer | 26311; [v, dedication] FOR FANIA; [vi] blank; [vii] contents;
[viii] blank; [1]-168, text, including divisional titles.

Lavender cloth boards with white paper label printed in black on upper
front, listing contents between a double rule above and below, and with
white paper label printed in black on spine: [double rule] | MUSIC |
AFTER | THE | GREAT | WAR | [rule] | Van | Vechten | [double rule].
Cream dust jacket printed in lavender.

Published 22 December 1915, $1.50.

Contents:
Music After the Great War [D36]
Music for Museums? [D34]
The Secret of the Russian Ballet [A25; D153. Quoted in Aileen St. John
    Brennon, "Fokine, Creator of Ballets, Coming Here in Aphrodite," New
    York Morning Telegraph, 26 October 1919]
Igor Strawinsky: A New Composer [A25. Quoted in Chicago Symphony Orches-
    tra 34th Season Fifth Program, 7-8 November 1924, p. 19, and Seventh
    Program, 16-17 April 1925, pp. 17, 19; Pierre Monteux, "Onze Monteux,"
    Knickerbocher Weekly, 13 September 1943, p. 15; Richard Williams,
    "Stravinsky: from enfant terrible to old master," House Beautiful,
    September 1954, pp. 162, 203; Emile H. Serposs and Ira C. Singleton,
    Music in Our Heritage, 1962, p. 220; Paul Horgan, Encounters With
    Stravinsky, 1972, pp. 11-19.]
Massenet and Women [D17]
Stage Decoration as a Fine Art [A25; D25; EIII52]
Adolphe Appia and Gordon Craig [D38]

b. Second edition

Identical with A4a, with these exceptions: p. [iii] SECOND EDITION
[printed above the title, outside the border]; a lighter weight text
stock made the volume slightly thinner; white dust jacket printed in
lavender.

Published circa 1920, $1.50.

A5   Music and Bad Manners   1916

a. First edition

Music | and Bad Manners | [rule] | Carl Van Vechten | [borzoi] | [rule] |
New York Alfred A. Knopf | MCMXVI [the foregoing enclosed in a three-
line border]

246 pp., blank leaf. 18.6 X 12.6 cm.

[1] half-title; [2] previous book listed; [3] title; [4] Copyright, 1916,
by Alfred A. Knopf; [5, dedication] To my father; [6] blank; [7] contents;
[8] blank; [9]-246, text, including divisional titles and, at back, publisher's advertisements.

Light aqua paper boards with white paper label printed in blue on upper
front, listing title and contents enclosed in a decorative border, and
with white paper label printed in blue on spine: [decorative rule] |
MUSIC | AND BAD | MANNERS | [decorative rule] | VAN | VECHTEN | [decor-

tive rule]; publisher's monogram printed in blue in center of back. Blue
or green top edges. Light blue or salmon dust jacket printed in green,
with an advertising blurb by Van Vechten [F3].

Published 14 November 1916, $1.50.

Contents:
Music and Bad Manners [Quoted in The World of Opera, Ed. Wallace Brock-
    way and Herbert Weinstock, 1942, pp. 22, 452.]
Music and the Movies [A15]
Spain and Music [A8]
Shall We Realize Wagner's Ideals? [D41]
The Bridge Burners
A New Principle in Music [D40]
Leo Ornstein

b. Second binding

Black paper boards with yellow paper label on front: [rule] | MUSIC AND
| BAD MANNERS | by | CARL | VAN VECHTEN | [rule], and on spine: [rule] |
MUSIC | AND | BAD | MANNERS | by | Carl | Van Vechten | MCMXVI | [rule].
Blue top edges. Orange dust jacket printed in black, with a revised advertising blurb by Van Vechten [F8].

Issued 16 June 1919, $1.75; later increased to $2.00.

A6   Interpreters and Interpretations   1917

a. First edition

Interpreters and | Interpretations | [rule] | Carl Van Vechten | [borzoi]
| [rule] | New York Alfred A. Knopf | MCMVII [the foregoing enclosed in
a three-line border]

374 pp., blank leaf. 19.5 X 13.2 cm.

[1] half-title and publisher's monogram; [2] previous books listed; [3]
title; [4] Copyright, 1917, by Alfred A. Knopf | Published October, 1917;
[5, dedication] To the unforgetable [sic] interpreter of Ariel . . Zelima
. . . Louka . . . . Wendla . . . . . My Wife; [6] blank; [7] contents;
[8] reprint acknowledgments; [9]-374, text, including divisional titles,
quotations, and, at the back, publisher's advertisements and quotations
from reviews of Music and Bad Manners.

Black cloth boards lettered on front: Interpreters | and | Interpreta-
tions | by | Carl Van Vechten, the lettering in black on a yellow rec-
tangle enclosed in a green ornamental design; lettered on spine: Inter-
preters | and | Interpretations | Carl | Van Vechten, the lettering in
black on a yellow square with green ornamental designs above and below
it, running down the spine to: ALFRED A KNOPF, lettered in yellow.
Borzoi and publisher's monogram in blind on back. Lower edges untrimmed;
fore edges untrimmed and partially unopened; green or yellow top edges.
Claude Bragdon designed the binding, which Knopf later used for Lords of
the Housetops [B3]. Yellow dust jacket printed in green, with an advertising blurb by Van Vechten [F4].

Published 8 October 1917, $2.00.

Contents:
Olive Fremstad [A10; D42. Quoted in Irving Kolodin, "Great Artists of
    Our Time: Birgit Nilsson," Saturday Review, 26 February 1966, p. 49.]
Geraldine Farrar [A10; D43]
Mary Garden [A10; D50. Quoted in Baird Leonard, "Mary Garden's 'Thais'
    Excellent," New York Morning Telegraph, 26 January 1918; John Freder-
    ick Cone, Oscar Hammerstein's Manhattan Opera House, 1964, pp. 76-78.]
Feodor Chaliapine [A10; D45; EV6]
Mariette Mazarin [A10; D49]
Yvette Guilbert [A10; D56. Quoted in A. Giviley, "Music and Musicians,"
    Indianapolis Star, 6 January 1918.
Waslav Nijinsky [A10; A25; D47. Quoted in Lincoln Kirstein, Nijinsky
    Dancing, 1975, p. 148; George Balanchine, Complete Stories of the Great
    Ballets, 1977, pp. 428, 644]
The Problem of Style in the Production of Opera
Notes on the Armide of Gluck [D54; EII534]
Erik Satie [A17; D61]
The Great American Composer [A15; D44]
The Importance of Electrical Picture Concerts [A15; D46]
Modern Musical Fiction
Why Music is Unpopular [A15; D48; D160]

b. Limited edition

At the suggestion of E. Byrne Hackett of the Yale University Press, Alfred A. Knopf simultaneously issued ten tall paper copies. Although nei-
ther numbered nor signed, these were left entirely unopened, and the top
edges unstained. The books measured 19.9 X 13.6 cm.

Ten copies published 8 October 1917, $10.00.

The manuscript for Interpreters and Interpretations, of 243 leaves,
is filed with two other groups of papers in the Carl Van Vechten Col-
lection of the New York Public Library: "Miscellaneous Manuscripts,
Early Draughts, 1911-1922" and "Musical Papers, Manuscripts and Early
Draughts, 1918-1922." There are no extant manuscripts for Music and
Bad Manners, Music After the Great War, or The Music of Spain, but
versions of some of the papers are in these collections. The first,
"1911-1922," of 312 leaves, contains manuscripts for the following:
A20, B1, B4, B5, C3, D51, D52, D78, D80, D82, D83, D87, D90, D91,
D95, D96, D99, D100, D117, EV19, EV21, F21; it also contains manu-
scripts for two papers for Van Vechten's projected second book, "Pastiches et Pistaches" (see note following D85): "The Rape of the Madonna Stella" and "After Death What?" and an unpublished review of
Cosas de España by Charles Alfred Turrell. The second collection,
"1918-1922," of 177 leaves, contains manuscripts for the following:
A5, A6, A8 (selections), A10, B6, D66, D78, D79, D89, D93, D172,
EIV49, EIV50, EV2; it also contains "Enter Iberia!" which was written
for but never published in The Chronicle and fugitive drafts for other
essays. A working table of contents for Interpreters and Interpretations indicates that several other papers were initially intended for
inclusion:
Margaret Anglin in As You Like It [A7; EIII142 and 147]
Johnston Forbes-Robertson in The Merchant of Venice [EIII71 and 77]

Josef Hofmann's Recital [EIV22]
Music and Cooking [A7; D68]
Three Unfamiliar Operas: The Golden Cockerel, Ariane et Barbeleu, and
    Habañera [never written]
Notes on Comic Opera, later titled Old Days and New [A7; D58]
The Song of the Lark by Willa Cather [intended as a section of Modern
    Musical Fiction]
Enter Iberia! [written for The Chronicle but never published]

A 7   The Merry-Go-Round   1918

The | Merry-Go-Round | [rule] | Carl Van Vechten | "Tournez, tournez,
bons chevaux de bois, | Tournez, cent tours, tournez mille tours, |
Tournez souvent et tournez toujours, | Tournez au sons de hautbois." |
PAUL VERLAINE | [borzoi] | [rule] | New York Alfred A. Knopf | MCMXVIII
[the foregoing enclosed in a three-line border]

344 pp. 19 X 13 cm.

[1] half-title and publisher's monogram; [2] list of previous books; [3]
title; [4] Copyright, 1918, by Alfred A. Knopf, Inc.; [5, dedication] For
Mary Garden; [6] blank; [7] contents; [8] reprint acknowledgments; [9]-
343, text, including divisional titles and quotations, and an index.

Black paper boards with orange paper label on front: [rule] | THE |
MERRY-GO-ROUND | by | CARL | VAN VECHTEN | [rule], and orange paper label
on spine: [rule] | THE | MERRY- | GO-ROUND | by | Carl | Van Vechten |
MCMXVIII | [rule]. Lower and fore edges rough trimmed, orange top edges.
Yellow dust jacket printed in green, with an advertising blurb by Van
Vechten [F5] and on the back for The Music of Spain [F6] by Van Vechten.

Published 30 September 1918, $2.00.

Contents:
In Defence of Bad Taste [D67]
Music and Supermusic
Edgar Saltus [A17. Quoted in Current Opinion, September 1918, as "The
    Stylist Who Created a Mythology of Manhattan."]
The New Art of the Singer [A17; EIV49. Quoted in John Frederick Cone,
    Oscar Hammerstein's Manhattan Opera House, 1964, pp. 116-17.]
Music and Cooking [D68]
Au Bal Musette [A22]
An Interrupted Conversation [A22; D35]
The Authoritative Work on American Music [A15]
Old Days and New [D58]
Two Young American Playwrights [D60]
De Senectute Cantorum [D70]
Impressions of the Theatre:
    I   The Land of Joy [A8; A25; D59; EIV47]
    II   A Note on Mimi Aguglia [D55]
    III The New Isadora [A25, C33; D72; D135. Quoted in "Isadora Duncan,"
             dans Kroniek, 6e Joargang 12, October 1952, p. 139]
    IV   Margaret Anglin Produces As You Like It [EIII142 and 147]
The Modern Composers at a Glance [C56; D57; H319]

The manuscript for The Merry-Go-Round consists of 165 leaves plus an
index of 13 leaves; there are 287 leaves of early drafts. Van Vech-
initially intended to title the collection "Music and Supermusic,"
and to include the following additional essays:
Josef Hofmann's Recital [EIV22]
Prince Igor at the Metropolitan [EIV24]
Gertrude Stein [D24]

A 8   The Music of Spain   1918

a. First edition

The | Music of Spain | [rule] | Carl Van Vechten | [borzoi] | [rule] |
New York Alfred A. Knopf | MCMXVIII [the foregoing enclosed in a single
line border which is, in turn, enclosed in a two-line border]

224 pp. Illustrations tipped-in. 19 X 13 cm.

[1] half-title and publisher's monogram; [2] list of previous books; [3]
title; [4] Copyright, 1918, by Alfred A. Knopf, Inc.; [5, dedication]
Pour Blanchette [Blanche Knopf]; [6] blank; [7]-223, text, including
preface, contents and illustrations, divisional titles and quotations,
index, and quotations from reviews of previous books.

Orange paper boards lettered in red on front: THE | MUSIC OF SPAIN |
Carl Van Vechten; and on spine: THE | MUSIC | OF | SPAIN | Carl | Van |
Vechten | ALFRED A. | KNOPF; publisher's monogram in center of back.
Lower and fore edges rough trimmed, red top edges. Yellow dust jacket
printed in red, with advertising blurbs on the front for The Music of
Spain [F6] and on the back for The Merry-Go-Round [F5] by Van Vechten.

Published 15 November 1918, $1.50.

Contents:
Spain and Music [A5; A25. Quoted in Gervaise Hughes, Composers of Oper-
    etta, London, 1962, pp. 171-72]
The Land of Joy [A7; A25; D59; EIV47]
From George Borrow to Mary Garden
Notes on the Text [Quoted in Philip Hale's notes on Manuel deFalla in
    the program for the Boston Symphony Orchestra, Carnegie Hall, 5 Janu-
    ary 1922.]

b. Second binding

Identical to A8a with the following exceptions: publisher's borzoi de-
vice in lower right corner of back in place of publisher's monogram in
center; dark red top edges.

Issued circa December 1919, $1.50.

c. English edition

THE | MUSIC OF SPAIN | BY | CARL VAN VECHTEN | WITH A PREFACE AND NOTES |
BY | PEDRO G. MORALES | LONDON: | KEGAN PAUL, TRENCH, TRUBNER & CO., LTD |
BROADWAY HOUSE, 68-74 CARTER LANE, E.C. | 1920

blank leaf tipped-in, xxix, 167 pp., blank leaf. Illustrations tipped-
in. 18 X 11.8 cm.

[i] Library of Music and Musicians edited by A. Eagelfield Hull, and
half-title; [ii] list of titles in series; [iii] title; [iv] quotation
from Nietzsche used in the first edition as divisional title for "Spain
and Music"; [5, dedication] For Blanche Knopf; [vi] blank; [vii] contents; [viii] blank; ix-xxiii, preface and notes by Morales; verso of
xxiii -- which is the conjugate leaf to page 7 (the first six pages are
unaccounted for) -- blank; 7-172, text, including divisional titles and
index as in the first edition, but lacking Van Vechten's extensive "Notes
on the Text." These were incorporated directly into "Spain and Music."
Every page of the text carries the head title of the first essay, "Spain
and Music."

Published 17 May 1920.

Red cloth boards, quarter bound in vertically rippled maroon leatherette,
stamped in gold: [quadruple rule] | THE | MUSIC | OF | SPAIN | [rule] |
VAN VECHTEN | [blind stamp: LIBRARY OF | MUSIC | & | MUSICIANS, in a
circle] | KEGAN PAUL | [quadruple rule]. Gray top edges. Machine fin-
ish dust jacket printed in black.

d. Underline: English edition, variant binding

In at least one copy, the blind stamp is missing, the leatherette ripples
run horizontally, the red cloth is replaced by dark red paper on boards,
and the publisher's name is enlarged on the spine. For both bindings,
Scott Cunningham's observation, in his 1924 bibliography, is apt: "a
format chiefly notable for its inspired ugliness."

In his preface to the manuscript of "Spain and Music," Van Vechten
acknowledged John Garrett Underhill who "suggested many valuable
changes and additions." These are listed in a note with the manuscript for "Spain and Music," which first appeared in Music and Bad
Manners, and with Van Vechten's injunction; "Prior to the issuing
of the English edition at my request." Some of these alterations
Van Vechten included in his own "Notes on the Text" for The Music
of Spain. In "Spain and Music," printed from the plates for Music
and Bad Manners, he made the following changes: "Señor" to "Don,"
p. 28; "Spain's leading dramatist, Echegaray" to "Miguel Echegaray,
brother of José Echegaray," p. 65; accent corrections, pp. 29, 31,
32, 33, 34, 45, 49, 51, 57, 62, 67, 69, 71, 74, 75, 76, 77, 78, 80,
81, 82, 83, 84, 85, 87.

A 9   In the Garret   1919

a. First edition

In the Garret | [rule] | Carl Van Vechten | "Memory is the mother of the
Muses." | GEORGE MOORE | [borzoi] | New York . Alfred . A . Knopf |
MCMXX [the foregoing enclosed in a three-line border]

348 pp., blank leaf. 18.8 X 13 cm.

[1] half-title; [2] list of previous books; [3] title; [4] Copyright,
1920, by Alfred A. Knopf, Inc.; [5, dedication] To Dorothy and Joseph
Hergesheimer, | with warm affection, I send this book. | Tout est rein
pour l'indifference; | Un rien est tour pour l'amitié.; [6] blank; [7]
contents; [8] blank; [9]-347, text, including divisional titles and quotations.

Black paper boards with blue paper labels printed in black, on front:
[rule] | IN THE | GARRET | by | CARL | VAN VECHTEN | [rule], and on
spine: [rule] | IN | THE | GARRET | by | Carl | Van Vechten | MCMXX |
[rule]. Lower and fore edges untrimmed, blue-green top edges. Yellow
dust jacket printed in red, with an advertising blurb by Van Vechten
[F10]

1500 copies published 15 December 1919, $2.50.

Contents:
Variations on a Theme by Havelock Ellis [A15; D75]
A Note on Philip Thicknesse [A17]
Isaac Albéniz [A17]
The Folksongs of Iowa [A22. Quoted in the Des Moines (Iowa) Register,
    August 1921.]
The Holy Jumpers [A22; A28]
On the Relative Difficulties of Depicting Heaven and Hell in Music [A15;
    D74]
Sir Arthur Sullivan [A17]
On the Rewriting of Masterpieces [A15]
Oscar Hammerstein: An Epitaph [A17; EV8. Quoted in Vincent Sheean, Oscar
    Hammerstein, 1956, pp. 345-46.]
La Tigresse [A22; C18]
In the Theatres of the Purlieus:
    I   Mimi Aguglia as Salome [D73; EIII91]
    II   Farfariello [D71]
    III The Negro Theatre [A28; D19; EIII83, 153, and 155]
    IV   The Yiddish Theatre
    V   The Spanish Theatre

b. Second binding

Identical to A9a, with the following exceptions: Black cloth boards.
Lower and fore edges rough trimmed, unstained top edges.

500 copies issued 16 February 1921, $2.50.

The manuscript for In the Garret has 356 leaves, including those of
early drafts. The third draft of "La Tigresse" -- an essay originally entitled "Louise Goes Back to the Old Life" -- contains the
first appearance of Peter Whiffle; in the early drafts, he is an un-
named companion. Initially, In the Garret was to include an essay
about religious groups in Chicago at the turn of the century, but
Van Vechten never completed it, and its drafts are only fragmentary.
In the Garret is the first of Van Vechten's books for which records
of printing and publication are still available. (Records of earlier
volumes are either incomplete or missing.) Apparently, all presswork
was completed at the same time, but 500 copies were remaindered for
later binding.

a. First edition

Interpreters | [rule] | Carl Van Vechten | A new edition, revised, with
sixteen | illustrations and an epilogue | [borzoi] | New York Alfred .
A . Knopf | MCMXX [the foregoing in a three-line border]

206 pp., blank leaf. Illustrations tipped-in. 19 X 13.4 cm.

[1] half-title; [2] list of previous books; [3] title; [4] Copyright,
1917, 1920, by Alfred A. Knopf, Inc.; [5, dedication] To the unforget-
table interpreter of Ariel, Zelima, Louka, Wendla, and Columbine, Fania
Marinoff, my wife; [6] blank; [7] contents; [8] list of illustrations;
[9]-206, text, including divisional titles and quotations, and, at the
back, review quotations for previous books.

Black paper boards with yellow paper labels printed in black, on front:
[rule] | INTERPRETERS | by | CARL | VAN VECHTEN | [rule], and on spine:
[rule] | INTER- | PRETERS | by | Carl | Van Vechten | MCMXX | [rule].
Lower and fore edges untrimmed, yellow top edges. Yellow dust jacket
printed in black, with advertising blurbs for Interpreters on the front
[F11] and The Tiger in the House on the back [F12], both by Van Vechten.

Published Autumn 1920, $2.00.

Contents: [A6, Olive Fremstad through Waslav Nijinsky, plus an epilogue]

b. Reprint edition

Interpreters | Carl Van Vechten | [publisher's logo] | ARNO PRESS | A New
York Times Company | New York/1977

iv, 204 pp., blank leaf.

[i] Opera Biographies; [ii] series information, listing Advisory Editor
Andrew Farkas and Associate Editor W.R. Moran; [iii] title; [iv] copyright and publication information; [1-202] pagination as in A10a, with
one exception: [2] frontispiece replaces list of previous books, and all
other illustrations are printed on conjugate leaves of text; [203-04]
list of Arno Press Collection of Opera Biographies.

Rust cloth boards, the title lettered in gold on a black rectangle on the
front; printed in black, running across the front, spine, and back, a
music staff with drawings of operatic characters (from left to right:
Boris Godunov, Werther, Canio, Doña Ana, Butterfly, Don Giovanni, Rhada-
mes, and Aida); down spine, in gold: Van Vechten INTERPRETERS [treble
clef symbol on music staff] ARNO. Issued without a dust jacket.

Published 1977, $15.00.

    Although Van Vechten's dust jacket blurb indicates the essays in In-
    terpreters "have been revised to some extent," they were printed from
    the plates of Interpreters and Interpretations. There is no manu-
    script, except for the Epilogue, nor are there any apparent revisions
    to the original essays in A6.

A 11   The Tiger in the House   1920

a. First edition

The | Tiger in the House | [rule] | Carl Van Vechten | "Dieu a fait le
chat pour donne à | l'homme le plaisir de caresser le tigre." | MÉRY |
[four hieroglyphics] | New York . Alfred . A . Knopf | MCMXX [the fore-
going enclosed in a three-line border]

xiv, 368 pp., blank leaf. Illustrations tipped-in. 24 X 16 cm.

[i] half-title; [ii] THE FIRST EDITION OF THIS BOOK | PRINTED ON ARTCRAFT
INDIA TINT | LAID PAPER IS LIMITED TO TWO | THOUSAND COPIES OF WHICH THIS
| IS NUMBER _____ [number stamped in red]; [iii] blank; [iv] list of pre-
vious books; [v] title; [vi] Copyright, 1920, by Alfred A. Knopf, Inc.;
[vii, dedication] FOR EDNA KENTON | . . . AND FEATHERS | "How lucky to be
a cat | Free to accept or -- refuse | what is offered!"; [viii] blank;
[ix] contents; [x] blank; [xi-xii] list of illustrations; [xiii] half-
title; [xiv] blank; 1-367, text, including acknowledgments, bibliography,
and index.

Blue paper boards flecked with gold or plain blue paper boards; coarse
natural linen quarter cloth spine lettered in blue. Alfred A. Knopf
described this as "half-canvas with purple Japanese Toyogami sides
stamped in gold" in his "Postscript" to The Borzoi 1920 [C3]. On the
front in gold: two circular parallel lines to form a medallion, enclosing THE TIGER IN THE HOUSE across the top half of the circle and CARL VAN
VECHTEN along the bottom half, the title separated from the author at
each end by a small ornament duplicated on the title page in place of the
customary dot between New York and Alfred A. Knopf. The circle encloses
a reproduction of a cat's head from a medal struck in 1725. On the spine
in blue: The | Tiger | in the | House | Carl | Van | Vechten | Alfred A.
Knopf. On the back in gold: two circular parallel lines enclosing
LIBERTAS SINE LABORE across the top half and AMICA NON SERVA along the
bottom half, the halves again separated by small ornaments. Lower and
fore edges untrimmed, blue top edges. Glassine dust wrapper. Issued in
a white cardboard box with a green paper label on the lid carrying an advertising blurb by Van Vechten with an illustration, "Minette Washes,"
from a drawing by Gottfried Mind [F12a]. According to Scott Cunningham's
1924 bibliography, "Upon the ridiculous objection of a Philadelphia book-
seller this illustration was later changed to the picture facing page
142," "Cat with Muff," from a drawing by Grandville [F12b].

2,000 copies printed; 1,550 copies bound; published 21 September 1920,
$5.00. The remaining 450 copies were sent to William Heinemann in London
for an English edition.

Contents:
By Way of Correcting a Popular Prejudice [Quoted in Cats and Dogs, Ed.
    Claire Necker, 1969, pp. 164-65, 191, 197.]
Treating of Traits [C48]
Ailurophobes and Other Cat Haters [C48]
The Cat and the Occult [D151]
The Cat in Folklore
The Cat and the Law

The Cat in the Theatre
The Cat in Music [C19; D77]
The Cat in Art
The Cat in Fiction
The Cat and the Poet
Literary Men Who Have Loved Cats
Apotheosis [C47. Quoted in John R. Gilbert, <u>Cats</u>, London, 1961, p. 6;
   Val Gielgud, <u>Cats: A Personal Anthology</u>, London, 1966, pp. 151-54.]

b. First English edition

Imported sheets uniform with collation and contents of the American issue, except for substituted publisher's name on the title page, an al-
teration made by Knopf prior to shipping: London . William . Heinemann
| MCMXXI

Gray-blue or teal-blue paper boards and beige linen quarter bound spine
lettered in gray, designed to resemble the American binding; "Heinemann"
is substituted for "Alfred A. Knopf" on the spine. Light blue dust jacket
printed in blue with an illustration from the book of the tomb of Madame
de Lesdiguiere's cat.

450 copies published 1921, 18 shillings.

c. Second edition

Identical to Alla, with the following exceptions: [iii] blank; [iv]
Published, September, 1920 | Second Printing, August, 1924; 22 X 14.7 cm.

Blue cloth boards printed in blind on front with cat medal from the first
edition; lettered in gold on spine: <u>The</u> | <u>Tiger</u> | <u>in the</u> | <u>House</u> | <u>Carl</u>
| <u>Van Vechten</u> | <u>Alfred.A.Knopf</u>; borzoi in blind on back. Lower and fore
edges rough trimmed, yellow top edges. Gray dust jacket printed in blue
with box illustration from the first edition, and with Van Vechten's advertising blurb [F12d].

2,000 copies printed; 1,500 bound; published August 1924, $4.00. In May
1927, 250 copies were bound and offered at 16 shillings through Knopf's
London publishing house. In April 1929, the balance was bound.

   Van Vechten made a number of minor revisions to the first edition for
   this second printing. Although most of them were typographical or
   clerical errors in spelling and punctuation, a few are worth noting:
   pp. [vi], 152, Mamaro/Utamaro; 2, regard/view, less/disdain; 76,
   has/made; 129, mention...their/mentions...his; 144, signel/signal,
   nor/or; 150, story/fable; 199, in hearing/on hearing; 240, females/
   felines; 287, 301, "La vie de deux chats"/"Vies de deux chats"; 308,
   and perhaps most of all, my friend, Alfred E. Goldsmith, who has
   scoured Europe, Asia, and Hoboken for some books which were very
   difficult to find [deleted]; 352, two etchings/three etchings; 355,
   latter/later; 357, 1845/Paris 1845. Corrected errors in punctuation
   and capitalization, and in spelling occur on pp. 4, 10, 15, 65, 97,
   100, 108, 115, 122, 129, 135, 138, 141, 148, 156, 161, 180, 182,
   184, 188, 201, 233, 244, 257, 261, 262, 263, 269, 275, 292, 312,
   318, 330, 337, 339, 343, 351, 360, 361, and in the illustrations
   facing pp. 152 and 264.

d. Third edition

Identical to Allc, with the following exceptions: [on title page, fol-
lowing author's name] WITH A NEW INTRODUCTION | BY THE AUTHOR; [title
page date altered to] MCMXXXVI; [verso] Third Printing, October 1936.
Prefatory pages renumbered to accommodate the introduction, pp. vii-[x].

blank leaf, xvi, 368 pp. 21.9 X 14.7 cm.

Dark blue cloth boards lettered in gold and printed in blind to duplicate
binding of Allc. Lower and fore edges rough trimmed, yellow top edges.
Yellow, blue, white, and red dust jacket.

2,000 copies printed; 500 copies bound; published October 1936, $4.00.
500 copies were sent to Jonathan Cape Ltd for a second English edition,
December 1937. 250 copies were bound, October 1938; 254 copies, March
1943; 269 copies, May 1944.

e. Second English edition

THE TIGER | IN THE HOUSE | by | CARL VAN VECHTEN | [Méry quotation] |
[publisher's logo] | LONDON | JONATHAN CAPE

Imported sheets uniform with collation and contents of Allc, with the
following exceptions: [ii] blank; [iii] title, as above; [iv] First
published 1920 | New edition | first published in Great Britain 1938;
first illustration tipped-in as a frontispiece.

Blue cloth boards lettered on spine in gold: THE TIGER | IN | THE HOUSE
| [decorative rule] | CARL | VAN VECHTEN | [publisher's logo]. Lower
edges rough trimmed, blue top edges. Gray dust jacket printed in black
and red.

500 copies published February 1938, 12/6.

> Although called a "new edition" and advertised on the dust jacket as
> "enlarged" with "a new introduction by the author," this second Eng-
> lish issue does not contain "An Introduction to the Third Edition,"
> published two years earlier. Blanche Knopf offered her opinion in
> a letter to Van Vechten, dated 17 November 1938, suggesting that the
> folded title signature, including the introduction was sent to Eng-
> land without any cancellation. Knopf had printed a four-page cancel
> for Jonathan Cape which did not include the introduction; it was
> possible, according to Mrs. Knopf, that Cape removed the entire sig-
> nature, including the introduction which had been shipped along with
> the sheets. She believed Van Vechten had received a single imperfect
> copy. Her conjecture about Jonathan Cape's actions may have been
> correct, but her final guess was not.

f. Fourth edition

Identical to Alld, with the following exceptions: [iii, date altered to]
MCML; [iv] Fourth Printing, February 1950; the illustrations are gathered
in signatures of eight, printed recto and verso, and bound into the book.
22 X 14.5 cm.

Blue cloth boards lettered in gold to duplicate the third edition. Lower and fore edges rough trimmed, yellow top edges. Chartreuse, black, and white dust jacket, with a halftone illustration of a cat lithograph by Steinlen.

725 copies (and the remaindered 227 copies from the third edition) published February 1950, $4.00.

g. Fifth edition

Identical to Allf, with the following exceptions: [iii, date altered to] MCMLX; [iv] Fifth Printing. 23.5 X 16 cm.

Light blue paper boards; coarse natural linen quarter cloth spine lettered in light blue, to imitate binding of the first edition. Orange end papers. Lower and fore edges rough trimmed, purple top edges. Blue, black, white, and orange dust jacket, with a photograph of Van Vechten by Alfred A. Knopf and a biographical note on the back.

1,000 copies published October 1960, $6.75.

h. Sixth edition

Identical to Alld, with the following exceptions: [iii, in substitution for publisher and date] BONANZA BOOKS . NEW YORK; [iv, publication history deleted] This edition published by Bonanza Books, | a division of Crown Publishers, Inc., | by arrangement with Alfred A. Knopf, Inc.; the illustrations are printed in the text rather than in separate signatures. 22.3 X 15 cm.

Rust cloth boards lettered on spine in black: THE | TIGER | in the | HOUSE | [rule] | Carl | Van Vechten | BONANZA. Orange, black, and white dust jacket, plastic coated.

Published 1974, $2.98.

> The manuscript for The Tiger in the House consists of 310 leaves and and an index of 13 leaves. The first draft consists of 439 leaves. The original dedication, intended for Fania Marinoff as well as for Edna Kenton, read: "Deux femmes qui ament les chats; Deux femmes que j'aime!" The manuscript of 10 leaves of the "Introduction to the third edition" -- one of the few Van Vechten manuscripts not in the collections in the New York Public Library and the Beinecke Library at Yale University -- is in the Clifton Waller Barrett Library at the University of Virginia.

A 12   Peter Whiffle: His Life and Works   1922

a. First edition

Peter Whiffle | His Life and Works [in green] | [rule] | Carl Van Vechten | [borzoi in green oval] | New York Alfred . A . Knopf | MCMXXII [the foregoing enclosed in a two-line green border which is, in turn, enclosed in a one-line border] viii, 248 pp.   19.1 X 13 cm.

[i] half-title; [2] list of previous books; [3] title; [iv] Copyright,
1922, by Alfred A. Knopf, Inc.; [5, dedication] TO THE MEMORY OF | MY
MOTHER, | ADA AMANDA FITCH VAN VECHTEN; [vi] blank; [vii] introductory
quotations; [viii] blank; 1-247, text; [248] blank.

Java Kunst batik paper boards: Scott Cunningham's 1924 bibliography
claims "ninety-seven colour variations"; Alfred A. Knopf, in an interview in the Chicago News, 10 May 1922, said the book was bound in "half
a dozen different designs and colors"; Van Vechten once referred to
"about seventy"; more than six exist in libraries and private collections. Natural coarse linen quarter cloth spine with a paper label
ruled by seven horizontal and two vertical lines, lettered in black:
PETER | WHIFFLE | HIS LIFE | AND WORKS | [publisher's monogram] | CARL |
VAN VECHTEN. Lower and fore edges rough trimmed, gray top edges. Light
blue dust jacket printed in dark blue, with an advertising blurb by Van
Vechten [F14].

2,000 copies printed; 1,950 bound, as above; published April 1922, $2.50.

Contents: Preface and eleven chapters, no titles [C17; C25. Quoted as
"Tingling is the Test" in The Daily News of Business: A Bulletin for
Buyers, VIII.18, 3 July 1922. Condensed in Masterplots in Story Form
from the World's Fine Literature, Ed. Frank McGill, 1949, pp. 749-51;
Masterplots Cyclopedia of Literary Characters, Ed. Frank McGill, 1963,
p. 867.]

b. Private edition

Fifty of the 2,000 copies of the first edition were withheld for this
special edition. It is identical to A12a, with the following exceptions:
Limitation page tipped-in between [ii] and [iii]: recto blank; verso,
THIS IS ONE OF AN EDITION | OF FIFTY COPIES | MADE FOR BOOKSELLER FRIENDS
| OF BORZOI BOOKS. 18.7 X 12.6 cm.

Orange paper boards -- the same stock as the binding of The Music of
Spain [A8] -- with paper label on spine. All edges were trimmed, making
a volume smaller than the first edition; green top edges.

50 copies issued April 1922, none for sale.

c. Second printing

Identical to A12a, with the following exceptions: [iv] Published, April,
1922 | Second Printing, April, 1922. All edges trimmed, gray top edges.

1,000 copies.

   Revisions to the first edition for the second printing: pp. 92, began on/began with; 147, Gorevan/Bergamo; 241, brocade/damask. Errors
   in spelling, capitalization, and punctuation corrected pp. 6, 15, 25,
   34, 44, 56, 102, 123, 150, 198, 240, 243.

d. Third through fifth printings

Identical to A12c, with the following exceptions: [iv] Third Printing,

May, 1922; Fourth Printing, June, 1922; Fifth Printing, July, 1922. Van Vechten's dust jacket blurb was replaced with quotations from reviews by H.L. Mencken, Carl Van Doren, and Fanny Butcher, varying from one printing to another, the number of each printing indicated on the spine.

3rd and 4th printings, 1,000 copies each; 5th printing, 2,000 copies.

e. Sixth and seventh printings

Identical to A12d, with the following exceptions: [iv] Sixth printing, August, 1922; Seventh Printing, October, 1922.

6th and 7th printings, 1,000 copies each.

An additional error was corrected, beginning with the sixth printing: pp. 45, 93, rockwood/rookwood.

f. Eighth through twelfth printings; second binding

Identical to A12e, with the following exceptions: [iv] Eighth Printing, March, 1923; Ninth Printing, July, 1923; Tenth Printing, October, 1923; Eleventh Printing, February, 1924; Twelfth Printing, September, 1925.

Beige cloth boards with duplicate paper label on spine. Pink dust jacket printed in dark blue, of which the ninth carries an advertising blurb for The Blind Bow-Boy by Van Vechten [F21c]; quotations from reviews by Hugh Walpole and Ernest Boyd, varying from one printing to another, the number of each printing again indicated on the spine.

8th, 9th, and 10th printings, 1,000 copies each; 11th printing, 2,000 copies; 12th printing, 1,000 copies.

g. English edition

Peter Whiffle | His Life and Works | [rule] | A Novel by | Carl Van Vechten | [decoration] | London: Grant Richards Ltd. | mdccccxxiii [the foregoing in a two-line border]

254 pp., blank leaf. 18.6 X 12.5 cm.

[1] half-title; [2] blank; [3] title; [4] Copyright 1922 in the United States of America by Alfred A. Knopf, Inc., Printed in Great Britain by the Riverside Press Limited Edinburgh; [5] dedication; [6] blank; [7] introductory quotations; [8] blank; 9-254, text.

Beige cloth boards, printed in black on front and on spine to duplicate -- minus Alfred A. Knopf's monogram -- the paper label of the American edition; Grant Richards's name at foot of spine similarly divided by horizontal and vertical lines. Lower and fore edges rough trimmed, gray top edges. Light and medium blue striped dust jacket printed in dark blue.

Published 1923, 7/6.

On the flyleaf of his copy of this edition, Van Vechten noted several typesetter's errors: pp. 21, 38, 55, 64, 145, 165, 190, 198, 212, 246, 247, 250.

h. Second English binding

Identical to A12g, with the exception of the binding: red cloth boards
lettered in gold; Alfred A. Knopf's name at the foot of the spine.

> This may be an edition issued by Alfred A. Knopf, circa 1927, when
> he first opened his London office, made up of remaindered copies of
> Grant Richards's initial issue. The records for Knopf's English
> transactions -- involving his own English editions of The Tattooed
> Countess [A14f], Firecrackers [A16f, A16g], Nigger Heaven [A18f,
> A18g, A18h, A18i], Spider Boy [A19e, A19f], and Parties [A21e] --
> are missing. Only one copy of this binding -- in the collection of
> Paul Padgette -- is available for collation. The dust jacket for
> the English edition of Parties lists Peter Whiffle at two prices:
> 7/6, presumably this is the Grant Richards version; 18 shillings,
> presumably for Knopf's 1927 illustrated edition [A12i].

i. Illustrated edition

[CVV rule] | PETER [in green] | WHIFFLE [in green] | HIS LIFE AND WORKS
| [CVV rule] | Carl Van Vechten | MCM [borzoi in green oval] XXVII | NEW
YORK . ALFRED A. KNOPF . LONDON | [CVV rule]

xii, 246 pp., blank leaf. Illustrations tipped-in. 20 X 16 cm.

[i] half-title; [ii] list of previous books; [iii] title; [iv] Copyright
1922, 1927, by Alfred A. Knopf, Inc., | acknowledgement of Ralph Barton's
"celebrated map of Paris" on the binding; [v] dedication; [vi] blank;
[vii] introductory quotations; [viii] blank; [ix-x] list of illustrations; [xi] half-title; [xii] blank; 1-244, text; [245] colophon. Illustrations include the Café d'Harcourt, photograph by Van Vechten, facing
p. 16

Illustrated paper boards, printed in gray, black, turquoise, and white,
identified in upper left on back as "Plan de PARIS Monumental," buildings
in gray, shrubbery in black, the Seine and other bodies of water in tur-
quoise; turquoise quarter cloth lettered in gold on spine: [CVV rule] |
Carl | Van Vechten | PETER | WHIFFLE | [CVV rule] | ALFRED A. KNOPF. End
papers printed in turquoise from the map illustration of bodies of water.
Lower and fore edges rough trimmed, yellow top edges. Glassine dust
wrapper. Issued in a cream paper slipcase printed in pink, blue, and
black, on front: PETER WHIFFLE | HIS LIFE AND WORKS | [drawing by "FM"
(Francis MacIntosh) of a boy standing with hands on hips] | CARL VAN
VECHTEN; on spine: PETER | WHIFFLE | HIS | LIFE | AND WORKS [star] |
CARL | VAN | VECHTEN | [scattered stars] | [borzoi in pink square] | AL-
FRED A. KNOPF; back duplicates front, with a new advertising blurb by Van
Vechten [F58] in place of the drawing.

2,000 copies printed; 1,500 bound, as above; published September 1927,
$7.50.

> For this edition, Van Vechten made substantial revisions, noting them
> in a copy of the twelfth printing. Where paging differs from the
> earlier editions to the illustrated edition, both are given, divided
> by slant lines: pp. 18, and [deleted]; 24, further/farther; 27, our
> presidents, our mayors, our politicians/our senators, our mayors, our

our scientists; 33, brushes/brush; 51/50, Every/Each; 53/52, finally/
eventually; 73/72, had/lacked; 81/79, as/as much; 93/91, O/Oh; 104/
101, check/cheque; 110/108, will/shall; 119/116, baskets/basket; 126/
124, garment-workers/garment-makers; 148/146, Yes, you/Yes. You; 163/
161, brief few/few brief; 166/163, grew/increased; 169/166, brocaded/
damasked, distant/faraway; 182/180, C.V.V. [deleted]; 190/188, Yet, I
suppose/Yet I presume; 211/209, monsters/creatures; 213/211, research
/researches; 222/220, shall/will, will/shall; 236/234, it/him, it/he,
its/his; 245/242, further/farther. Alterations or corrections in
spelling, punctuation, and capitalization occur on pp. 11, 15, 28,
36, 38, 40, 43, 44, 45, 49, 55, 57/56, 58/57, 59/58, 65/64, 67/66,
74/73, 80/79, 82/80, 89/87, 96/94, 98/96, 99/97, 101/99, 107/105,
111/109, 121/119, 123/121, 124/122, 125/123, 129/127, 132/130, 134/
132, 136/134, 138/136, 150/148, 182/180, 192/190, 194/192, 199/197,
202/200, 210/208, 220/218.

j. Limited illustration edition

Identical to A12i, with the following exceptions: Limitation page tipped
in between [ii] and tipped-in frontispiece, recto blank; verso: OF THIS
EDITION OF | PETER WHIFFLE | TWENTY COPIES HAVE | BEEN BOUND, UNCUT, |
IN SILK AND SIGNED | BY THE AUTHOR | [signature in ink] | THIS IS NUMBER
[number in ink]

Illustrated silk boards, printed in two shades of gray, black, chartreuse,
and turquoise, of an enlargement of a section of Ralph Barton's map;
light green silk quarter bound spine, lettered in gold to match the trade
illustrated edition. Edges untrimmed and unopened, top edges painted
gold. Glassine dust wrapper.

20 copies bound, as above; published September 1927, $20.00.

k. Modern Library edition

PETER WHIFFLE | [rule] | BY | CARL VAN VECHTEN | [rule | publisher's logo
| rule] | THE MODERN LIBRARY | PUBLISHERS : NEW YORK [the foregoing in a
two line border]

Paging identical with A12a and subsequent trade editions, with the following exceptions: [ii] publisher's advertisement in place of list of
previous books; [iii] title, as above; [iv] Copyright, 1922, by Alfred A.
Knopf, Inc., | First Modern Library Edition 1929. 16.5 X 10.5 cm.

Flexible cloth boards lettered in gold on front with publisher's logo,
and on spine: PETER | WHIFFLE | [rule] | VAN VECHTEN | [decoration] |
MODERN | LIBRARY. At this period, the Modern Library used a variety of
colors of cloth. Peter Whiffle was issued in blue, red, green, and brown
with decorated end-papers to match the various colors. Light blue dust
jacket printed in black and dark blue, or yellow printed in red and black.
This edition contains all of the corrections made for the limited illustrated edition, but it was prepared from a set of galleys for A12a.

1,000 copies published 1930, $.95.

l. The AMS Press has announced a reprint edition of Peter Whiffle: His
Life and Works, to be published at $21.00.

Peter Whiffle: His Life and Works had its genesis in 1917 in an incomplete short story entitled "Undecided Sasha." In his notebook for
The Music of Spain, written at about the same time, Van Vechten jot-
ted down, "The Life and Works of Peter Whiffle," as a title, although
Peter Whiffle as a character did not emerge until "La Tigresse,"
dated 1919, and published in In the Garret [A9]. The first draft of
the novel included a play, "What Do You Think It Is?" as an additional chapter, pp. 27-41. Seven leaves of "Undecided Sasha" were incorporated, pp. 81-85, 87, 88. A letter to Van Vechten from Mabel Dodge
Luhan was incorporated, following p. 91. An earlier two-page essay
on dummies was inserted, pp. 105-06. "War Is Not Hell" [D29] and
"Once Aboard the Lugger San Guglielmo"[D26] were originally included
as additional chapters, pp. 149-66, and 167-76, respectively. Pages
118-48 are unaccounted for. The first draft -- too fragmented to
reckon an accurate leaf count -- is dated February 1921. The second
draft deleted "What Do You Think It Is?" and added "How the Twelve
Best Sellers Ended" [C56; D11]. The draft, of 181 leaves, is dated
29 April 1921. The third draft, from which type was set, deleted
"Once Aboard the Lugger San Guglielmo," "War Is Not Hell," and "How
the Twelve Best Sellers Ended." The draft, of 171 leaves, is dated
August 1921. In several copies of the book, Van Vechten's inscrip-
tion read: "A modern pilgrim's progress & allegory of a period quest
of disillusion."

A 13   The Blind-Bow Boy   1923

a. First edition

THE BLIND | BOW-BOY | [green rule] | Carl Van Vechten | With a decoration
by | Robert E. Locher | [borzoi in green oval] | New York Alfred . A .
Knopf | MCMXXIII [the foregoing enclosed in a two-line green border which
is, in turn, enclosed in a one-line black border]

viii, 262 pp., blank leaf. 19.2 X 13 cm.

[i] half-title; [ii] list of previous books; [iii] title; [iv] Copyright,
1923, by Alfred A. Knopf, Inc. | Published August, 1923 | colophon; [v,
dedication] To | ALFRED A. KNOPF | My publisher and my friend; [vi] blank;
[vii] introductory quotation; [viii] blank; 1-261, text. Illustration
and tissue tipped-in facing [iii].

Decorated paper-covered boards. In his 1924 bibliography, Scott Cunningham refers to "four colour variations"; there were at least five, three
of which were employed for the first printing: red, green, and white;
orange, green, and white; green and natural. Natural coarse linen quarter cloth spine with paper label duplicating design of the Peter Whiffle
label. Lower and fore edges rough trimmed, green top edges. White dust
jacket printed in blue, with Locher's illustration on the front and an
advertising blurb by Van Vechten on the back [F21a].

3,500 copies printed; published 15 August 1923; $2.50.

Contents: Fourteen chapters, no titles [Quoted in A Dictionary of Modern
Quotations, Ed. Edward Cohen, 1929, p. 193; Arthur Mizener, "Fitzgerald
in the Twenties," Partisan Review, January 1950, p. 13]

b. Tall paper edition

Identical to A13a with the following exceptions: [ii] limitation note in
place of list of previous books: This first edition of THE BLIND BOW-BOY
consists | of thirty-six hundred and fifteen copies as follows: | fifteen
on Borzoi all rag paper signed by the au- | thor and numbered A to O; one
hundred copies on | Borzoi all rag paper signed by the author and num- |
bered 1 to 100; and thirty-five hundred copies on | English featherweight
paper. | This is Number ⌊number in ink | signature⌋; ⌊iv⌋ colophon dele-
ted. 23.5 X 15 cm.

Green paper boards; orange coarse linen quarter cloth, with green paper
label, on spine: ⌊decorative rule | dotted line⌋ | The | Blind | Bow-
Boy | Carl | Van Vechten | ⌊dotted line | decorative rule⌋. Edges un-
trimmed and unopened. Extra spine label tipped-in on back paste-down
end paper. Glassine wrapper. Issued in a blue slipcase with duplicate
spine label, white rather than green.

130 copies printed; 115 copies numbered and signed; published 15 August
1923; $10.00.

c. Second printing

Identical to A13a, with the following exceptions: [iv] First and second
printings before publication.

Decorated paper boards in either green and natural (as in the first printing) or green and blue; gray top edges.

3,500 copies.

    Of the second printing, 262 copies were prepared for Macmillan Pub-
    lishers in Canada. Knopf prepared a cancel title page for these
    copies; otherwise, according to publication records, they were iden-
    tical to A13c. No copy of this issue has surfaced.

d. Third printing

Identical to A13c with the following exceptions: [iv] Third printing,
August, 1923

Decorated paper boards in blue and magenta.

2,000 copies.

    This printing included a correction in punctuation, p. 260.

e. Fourth through seventh printings, second binding

Identical with A13d with the following exceptions: [iv] Fourth Printing,
August, 1923; Fifth Printing, October, 1923; Sixth Printing, August,
1924; Seventh Printing, February, 1927.

Green cloth boards printed on front and spine in gold to duplicate the
paper label of the first binding; at foot of spine: ALFRED A KNOPF;
borzoi in blind on back. The dust jacket substitutes reviewer's squibs

for Van Vechten's blurb, by Nunnally Johnson, Laurence Stallings, Ernest
Boyd, Burton Rascoe on Nigger Heaven, and Alfred Knopf on The Tattooed
Countess, varying from printing to printing; the number of each printing
was indicated on the spine.

4th printing, 5,000 copies; 5th printing, 2,000 copies; 6th and 7th
printings, 1,000 copies each; of the seventh, 750 copies were issued in
1933 for $1.00 each.

 These printings include a revision: blue stars/gold stars, p. 124.

f. English edition

The Blind | Bow-Boy | [rule] | A Novel by | Carl Van Vechten | [publish-
er's logo] | London: Grant Richards Ltd. | mdcccxxiii [the foregoing en-
closed in a two-line border]

268 pp. 18.8 X 12.8 cm.

[1] half-title; [2] review quotations for the English edition of Peter
Whiffle; [3] title; [4] Copyright 1923 in the United States of America by
Alfred A. Knopf, Inc. | colophon; [5] dedication; [6] blank; [7] intro-
ductory quotation; [8] blank; 9-267, text. Tissue tipped-in between pp.
[2-3].

Beige cloth boards, printed in black, on front: The Blind Bow-Boy |
[drawing of a boy looking toward a cityscape, with clouds and a cupid,
by Wyndham Payne] | By | Carl Van Vechten [enclosed in a border]; spine
lettered to duplicate the paper label of the American edition but with
publisher's monogram deleted and, at foot of spine, Grant Richards's name
similarly divided by lines. Lower and fore edges rough trimmed. Gray-
blue and white dust jacket with Payne's drawing and Van Vechten's advertising blurb [F21f].

Published October 1923, 7/6.

 Grant Richards set type from a printing preceding the fourth, since
 the revision on page 124 is not included. Richards disapproved of
 several passages, and with Van Vechten's permission -- Van Vechten
 avowed it was "a matter of complex indifference" to him -- they were
 altered as follows: A thing of beauty is a boy forever, p. 117 [de-
 leted. This motto, which graces the stationery of Ronald, Duke of
 Middlebottom, was the invention of Allen Norton, the American poet.]
 One of his young ladies wished to whip me, sir/One of his young ladies wished to kiss me, sir, p. 55; A little later, Basil, alone with
 her, became confidential. . . . Then you don't have to, pp. 257-58
 [deleted].

g. First pocketbook edition

THE BLIND- | BOW-BOY | by | Carl Van Vechten | [borzoi in oval] | NEW
YORK | ALFRED . A . KNOPF [the foregoing in a wide decorative border]

Paging identical with A13a and subsequent trade editions, with the following exceptions: [ii] publisher's advertisement; [iii] title, as above.
17.2 X 11 cm.

Blue ribbed cloth boards, printed in light green and black, on front:
blue borzoi in green oval enclosed in a two-line black border; on spine:
THE | BLIND | BOW-BOY | [decoration] | VAN VECHTEN | ALFRED . A . KNOPF
[in green]; borzoi in blind on back. Yellow top edges. Cream, chartreuse, and blue end-papers. Pink and lavender dust jacket with a drawing of a boy dancing with a bird.

3,000 copies printed; 2,000 copies bound, as above; published February
1925; $1.00.

h. Second pocketbook printing, second binding

Identical to A13g with the following exceptions: [iv] printing history
from sixth printing | Pocketbook Edition, Published, February, 1925 |
Second Printing, October, 1926

Green cloth boards printed in silver, on front: decoration; on spine:
[decoration] | The Blind | Bow-Boy | [rule] | VAN | VECHTEN | [decora-
tion] | Knopf; borzoi in blind on back. Gray top edges. Green and tur-
quoise end-papers. Green, black, and white dust jacket.

1,976 copies printed; 1,954 copies bound, as above; published October
1926; $1.00.

i. English pocketbook edition

The Borzoi Pocket Books | .XXVI. | Carl Van Vechten | The Blind Bow-Boy |
[small drawing of Wyndham Payne's illustration for the first English edi-
tion] | Alfred A. Knopf [borzoi] Publisher, London

Paging identical with A13f with the following exceptions: [1] publisher's
title and half-title; [2] blank; [3] title, as above; [4] colophon. 17.1
X 11.1 cm.

Brown cloth boards, lettered in gold, on front in a box: THE BORZOI POC-
KET BOOKS | [rule | two dots | borzoi | two dots | rule] | THE BLIND |
BOW-BOY | Carl Van Vechten | [rule] | [borzoi] KNOPF [borzoi]; on spine:
THE BLIND | BOW-BOY | VAN | VECHTEN | [borzoi] | ALFRED A. | KNOPF.
Orange top edges. Lavender, purple, and brown dust jacket with drawing
from the title page.

Published circa 1928; 3/6

> Although issued by Alfred A. Knopf during the brief period of his
> London publishing firm, this edition of The Blind Bow-Boy is Grant
> Richards's expurgated version. It is not, however, composed of re-
> maindered signatures of Richards's edition which were trimmed down;
> both the pages and the typeface are reduced.

j. The AMS Press has announced a reprint edition of The Blind Bow-Boy,
$24.50.

> The first draft of The Blind Bow-Boy is titled "Daniel Matthews' Tu-
> tor." It consists of 147 leaves, dated 8 June 1922. The second
> draft, of 195 leaves, is dated 6 August 1922. The third draft, from
> which type was set, of 224 leaves, is dated 28 October 1922.

A 14   The Tattooed Countess   1924

a. First edition

The Tattooed | Countess | [red rule] | A romantic novel with a happy end-
ing | [red rule] | Carl Van Vechten | [borzoi in red-lined oval] | New
York Alfred . A . Knopf | MCMXXIV [the foregoing in a two-line red bor-
der within a one-line black border]

x, 286 pp. 19 X 13 cm.

[i] half-title; [ii] list of previous books [iii] title; [iv] Copyright,
1924, by Alfred A. Knopf, Inc. | colophon and note on number of copies
printed | First printing, July, 1924; [v, dedication] FOR HUGH WALPOLE;
[vi] blank; [vii] introductory quotation; [viii] blank; [ix] half-title;
[x] blank; 1-286, text.

Wine cloth boards; front and spine lettered in gold to duplicate paper
labels of earlier novels, with publisher's name at foot of spine; borzoi
in blind on back. Lower and fore edges rough trimmed, green top edges.
Green, white, black, and orange dust jacket with an illustration by Ralph
Barton; advertising blurb on back by Alfred A. Knopf.

7,500 copies printed; published 15 August 1924; $2.50.

Contents: Eighteen chapters, no titles. Quoted in the Cedar Rapids
[Iowa] Gazette, 11 August 1946, pp. 131-35

b. Tall paper edition

Identical to A14a with the following exceptions: [ii] list of books re-
placed by note from [iv] THE FIRST EDITION OF THE TATTOOED | COUNTESS
CONSISTS OF SEVENTY-SIX | HUNDRED AND SIXTY COPIES AS FOL- | LOWS: TEN
ON BORZOI ALL RAG PAPER | SIGNED BY THE AUTHOR AND NUM- | BERED A TO J;
ONE HUNDRED AND FIFTY COPIES ON BORZOI ALL RAG | PAPER SIGNED BY THE AU-
THOR AND | NUMBERED I TO 150; AND SEVENTY- | FIVE HUNDRED COPIES ON ENG-
LISH | FEATHERWEIGHT PAPER. | THIS IS NUMBER [number in ink | signature
in ink]; [iv] note and printing date deleted.

Black paper boards with flower design in pink, white, and green; pink
linen quarter cloth spine, with black paper label printed in pink: [flor-
al rule] | Carl | Van | Vechten | [floral rule]. Edges untrimmed and un-
opened. Extra spine label tipped-in on back pastedown end-paper. Glassine dust wrapper. Lettered copies issued in black cloth slipcase; numbered copies issued in black paper slipcase, with duplicate spine labels.

160 copies printed; published 15 August 1924; $10.00.

c. Second through fifth printings

Identical to A14a with the following additions: [iv] First, second and
third printings before publication; Fourth printing, August, 1924; Fifth
printing, August, 1924

2nd printing, 2,500 copies; 3rd printing, 2,000 copies; 4th printing,
3,000 copies; fifth printing, 3,000 copies.

d. Sixth and seventh printings

Identical to A14c with the following exceptions: [iv] Sixth printing,
September, 1924; Seventh Printing, December, 1924. The sixth printing
included three revisions: bobbing/docking, p. 31; basketball/baseball,
p. 115; has/had, p. 281; spelling and punctuation corrections, pp. 5, 41,
55, 70, 78, 103, 127, 156, 170, 216, 220, 224, 228, 242.

6th printing, 2,000 copies; seventh printing, 2,000 copies, of which
1,000 were shipped to London for the English edition.

e. English edition

Identical to A14d, with the following exceptions: [iii] London [substi-
tuted for New York, and the date altered to] MCMXXVI.

Blue cloth boards with a four-line border in blind on front and borzoi in
blind on back; spine lettered in gold: [CVV rule] | THE TATTOOED | COUNT-
ESS | [decoration] | VAN VECHTEN | [CVV rule] | ALFRED . A . KNOPF | [CVV
rule]. Lower edges untrimmed and unopened, fore edges rough trimmed.
Blue, black, and white dust jacket with an illustration by K. Romney
Towndrow; advertising blurbs for Excavations and The Tiger in the House
on back and flyleaf by Van Vechten [F12f, F43c], and for The Tattooed
Countess by W. Somerset Maugham and Peter Whiffle by Hugh Walpole.

1,000 copies published 1926, 7/6.

f. Reprint edition

THE TATTOOED | COUNTESS | [heavy and light rules] | A Romantic Novel with
a Happy Ending | [rule] | By CARL VAN VECHTEN | [publisher's logo | heavy
and light rules] | A. L. BURT COMPANY | Publishers New York | Published
by arrangement with Alfred A. Knopf | Printed in U.S.A. [the foregoing in
a two-line border]

xii, 292 pp. 18.8 X 12.8 cm.

Identical to A14d with the following exceptions: [i-ii] blank; [iii]
half-title; [iv] blank; [v] title, as above; [vi] colophon and printing
history deleted; [vii] dedication; [viii] blank; [ix] quotation; [x]
blank; [xi] half-title; [xii] blank; [287-92] catalog of fiction published by A.L. Burt.

Red cloth boards printed in gold, on front: THE | TATTOOED COUNTESS |
COUNTESS | CARL VAN VECHTEN | on spine: THE | TATTOOED | COUNTESS |
[rule] | CARL VAN | VECHTEN | A . L . BURT | COMPANY. Blue, white, and
red dust jacket with Barton's illustration.

g. French edition

VAN VETCHEN [sic] | [rule] | La Comtesse tatouée | (The Tattooed Countess
| Roman traduit de l'anglais par Maurice REMON | [drawing of the acropo-
lis] | ÉDITIONS DE LA MADELEINE | 11 rue Tronchet, 11 | PARIS

340 pp. 19.4 X 13.6 cm.

[1-2] blank; [3] half-title; [4] list of other novels translated; [5]

title; [6] Copyright, 1932, by Editions de la Madeleine; [7]-339, text,
including a note on the number of copies printed.

Mottled gray and orange paper boards; spine lettered in brown: [wide,
rule, narrow rule] | VAN VETCHEN [sic] | [rule] | LA | COMTESSE TATOUEE
| [wide rule, narrow rule]. Edges untrimmed and unopened. Red, black,
and cream dust jacket with a skull, a butterfly, and the Countess's tat-
too on a banner beneath it; in addition to the title and author, spelled
correctly, it reads: DANS L'AMERIQUE DE 1900, UNE COMTESSE ET SON CHER-
UBIN GIGOLO.

3,015 copies printed; published 1932.

> Despite Van Vechten's resolute preservation of everything connected
> with his career — all editions of all books — this is the only ver-
> sion of the French edition in his collections, and the only version
> available, for collation. According to the limitation note, five
> copies were printed on Madagascar vélum and numbered, ten on Lafuma
> vélum and numbered, and 3,000 unnumbered copies on Alfa.

h. Paperback edition

The Tattooed | Countess | CARL VAN VECHTEN | POPULAR LIBRARY | NEW YORK

176 pp.   17.5 X 10.5 cm.

[1] plot squib, review quotations, Knopf acknowledgment; [2] biographical
note; [3] title; [4] Copyright, 1924, by Alfred A. Knopf, Inc.; renewed
1952, by Carl Van Vechten; [5] dedication and quotation; [6] blank; 7-
176, text.

Stiff paper wrappers, printed on front: a woman as scandalous as | LADY
CHATTERLY | ...as fascinating as | SCARLETT O'HARA -- The Tattooed |
countess [title in red] | [illustration of a hand holding a champagne
glass, diamond bracelet and tattoo on wrist, in full color] | by Carl Van
Vechten [in red] | Originally published by | Alfred A. Knopf, Inc.; on
spine: SP217 | 50c | THE TATTOOED COUNTESS [down spine in red] Carl Van
Vechten [down spine in black] | [rule] | POPULAR | LIBRARY; on back:
plot squib, illustration repeated, advertising squib. Green edges.

Published April 1963, $.50.

> Although the copyright and acknowledgments page accounts for only
> three printings by Knopf, this paperback version contains the revi-
> sions and corrections made for the sixth printing.

i. The AMS Press has announced a reprint edition of The Tattooed Countess, $23.50.

> The first draft of The Tattooed Countess, preceded by 23 unnumbered
> leaves, consists of 174 leaves and is dated 26 March 1923. The sec-
> ond draft consists of 231 leaves and is dated 20 June 1923. The
> third draft, from which type was set, consists of 286 leaves and is
> dated 20 October 1923. A film version, entitled A Woman of the World
> and starring Pola Negri, was made in 1925. It featured Charles Emmett
> Mack as Gareth Johns, and Holmes Herbert, Blanche Mchaffey, Lucille

Ward, Guy Oliver, Dot Farley, May Foster, Dorothea Wolbert, and —
in a comedy role invented for the film — Chester Conklin. Pierre
Collings wrote the screenplay, which bore little resemblance to the
novel, and Malcolm St. Clair directed the film. A print on A Woman
of the World is in the collection of the Museum of Modern Art. A
musical version of the novel, entitled The Tattooed Countess, with
score, lyrics, and book by Coleman Dowell, opened at the Barbizon
Plaza Theatre in New York City on 3 May 1961 and closed after five
performances. Irene Manning played the Countess, John Stewart played
Gareth Johns, and Robert K. Adams directed.

A 15   Red   1925

a. First edition

Carl Van Vechten | RED [in red] | PAPERS ON MUSICAL SUBJECTS | [decora-
tion, in red | borzoi in red lined oval] | New York . 1925 | ALFRED . A .
KNOPF [the foregoing in a decorative border]

xxii, 206 pp. 19 X 13 cm.

[i] half-title; [ii] list of previous books, including the first refer-
ence to The Blind Bow-Boy as "a cartoon for a stained glass window";
[iii] title; [iv] Copyright, 1925, by Alfred A. Knopf, Inc.; colophon;
[v, dedication] For Ralph Barton, | with my admiration, | this superflu-
ous pigment for his | immarcescible palette; [vi] blank; [vii] introduc-
tory quotation; [viii] blank; ix-xvii, introduction; [xviii] blank; [ixx]
contents; [xx] blank; [xxi] half-title; [xxii] blank; 1-205, text; [206]
blank.

Red cloth boards, front and spine lettered in gold to duplicate binding
of The Tattooed Countess. Lower and fore edges rough trimmed, yellow top
edges. Yellow dust jacket printed in red and black, with an advertising
blurb by Van Vechten [F32a].

2,500 copies printed; 2,465 published 9 January 1925, $2.00.

Contents:
A Valedictory
Why Music is Unpopular [A6, D48, D160]
The Great American Composer [A6, D44]
The Authoritative Work on American Music [A7]
Music for the Movies [A5]
The Importance of Electrical Picture Concerts [A6, D46]
Movies for Program Notes [D84]
The New Art of the Singer [A7, EIV49]
Variations on a Theme by Havelock Ellis [A9, D75]
On the Relative Difficulties of Depicting Heaven and Hell in Music [A9,
    D74]
On the Rewriting of Masterpieces [A9]
On Hearing What You Want When You Want It [D79]
Cordite for Concerts [D81]

b. Tall paper edition

Thirty-five of the copies printed for A15a were signed on the title page
by Van Vechten. They were left entirely unopened, and the top edges
were unstained. There was no limitation indicated, nor do they seem to
have been offered for sale. 20.1 X 13.1 cm.

c. Second binding

Identical to A15a, with the following exception of the binding: beige
cloth boards lettered identically but printed in red.

500 copies issued 10 October 1928, $1.00.

Although composed entirely of essays previously printed, Red had a
complete retyping. Van Vechten revised all of the essays, some of
them extensively, but retained the original dates. "A Valedictory,"
written as an introduction to the collection, is dated 11 March 1924.
The manuscript consists of 176 leaves, including preliminary material.

A 16   Firecrackers   1925

a. First edition

[medium floral decoration, in red] | FIRECRACKERS | [large floral decora-
tion, in red] | a realistic novel | BY CARL VAN VECHTEN | [small floral
decoration, in red] | 1925 . ALFRED . A . KNOPF . New York [the foregoing
in a wide decorative border]

x, 246 pp. 19 X 13 cm.

[i] half-title; [ii] list of previous books; [iii] title; [iv] Copyright,
1925, by Alfred A. Knopf, Inc. | colophon; [v, dedication] FOR JAMES
BRANCH CABELL; [vi] blank; [vii] introductory quotations; [viii] blank;
[ix] half-title; [x] blank; 1-246, text.

Yellow cloth boards, lettered in red, on front: CVV dentelle; on spine:
[CVV rule] | FIRE- | CRACKERS | [floral decoration] | VAN VECHTEN | [CVV
rule] | ALFRED . A . KNOPF | [CVV rule]; borzoi in blind on back. Lower
and fore edges rough trimmed, green top edges. Yellow, green, and red
dust jacket, with an advertising blurb by Van Vechten on the front.[F38a]
and blurbs about The Tattooed Countess by Sinclair Lewis, Gertrude Atherton, and others, on the flyleaves.

10,000 copies printed; published August 1925; $2.50.

Contents: sixteen chapters, no titles.

b. Tall paper edition

Identical to A16a, with the following exceptions: [i] blank; [ii] OF THE
FIRST EDITION OF FIRECRACKERS | TWO HUNDRED FIVE LARGE PAPER COPIES |
HAVE BEEN PRINTED AS FOLLOWS: TEN | ON BORZOI RAG PAPER SIGNED BY THE |
AUTHOR AND NUMBERED A TO J; | ONE HUNDRED NINETY FIVE COPIES ON | BORZOI

RAG PAPER SIGNED BY THE AUTHOR AND NUMBERED FROM 1-195 | THIS IS NUMBER
| [number in black ink | signature in purple ink]; [iii] half-title; [iv]
list of previous books; [v] title; [vi] colophon from p. iv deleted; [vii]
dedication; [viii] blank; [ix] introductory quotations; [x] blank; [xi]
half-title; [xii] blank; [247] colophon; [248] blank. 23 X 15 cm.

Pink, yellow, and white decorated paper boards, with black quarter cloth
spine lettered in gold as in A15a. Edges untrimmed and unopened. Glassine dust wrapper over a plain wrapper of text stock, folded around boards
and printed on spine to duplicate the book's spine. Black paper slipcase
with black label printed in white to duplicate book's spine.

205 copies printed; published August 1925; $10.00.

c. Second printing

Identical to A16a with the following exceptions: [iv] Published, August,
1925 | Second Printing, August 1925. Edges trimmed but unstained.

2,500 copies

d. Third printing

Identical to A16c with the following exceptions: [iv] Third Printing,
August, 1925. Gray top edges. Dust jacket blurbs by Carl Van Doren and
Scott Cunningham.

2,500 copies

e. Fourth printing

Identical to A16d with the following exceptions: [iv] Fourth Printing,
October, 1925. Green top edges. This printing included one revision:
You are/I am, p. 8.

2,000 copies

f. English edition

[decoration in red] | FIRECRACKERS | a realistic | novel | [decoration in
red] | by | CARL VAN VECHTEN | [decoration in red] | [double red rule] |
LONDON: ALFRED A. KNOPF : 1927 [the foregoing in a one-line red border
against a ground of vertical red dots connecting the red decorations]

x, 246 pp. 18.3 X 12.3 cm.

Paging identical to A16e with the following exceptions: [ii] expanded
list of previous books; [iii] title, as above; [iv] colophon.

Yellow cloth boards with two-line blind border on front and borzoi in
blind on back, lettered in gold on spine: [CVV rule] | FIRECRACKERS |
[decoration] | VAN VECHTEN | [CVV rule] | ALFRED . A . KNOPF | [CVV rule]
Red top edges. Yellow dust jacket printed in blue and red, with the ad-
vertising blurb of the first edition on the back [F38c], and blurbs for
Peter Whiffle by Hugh Walpole and W. Somerset Maugham, and for Nigger
Heaven by Beverley Nichols on the fly leaves.

Published January 1927, 7/6.

> Although the colophon indicates that this edition was printed "by the Edinburgh Press," it is made up of the American sheets with a new title signature. The complete publishing records for Firecrackers are unavailable, but it would appear that additional copies were printed for the English edition following the fourth printing of the American edition, to which an English cancel was added.

g. Second English binding

Identical to A16f with the following exception: Black cloth boards lettered in red; blind border and borzoi printed in red.

h. Reprint edition

FIRECRACKERS | a realistic novel | By CARL VAN VECHTEN | [drawing by Nelson White of couples dancing in white silhouette against blue decorative background] | GROSSET & DUNLAP | PUBLISHERS | By arrangement with Alfred A. Knopf

x, 246 pp. 19.6 X 13.4 cm.

Paging identical to A16e with the following exceptions: [ii] blank; [iii] title, as above; [iv] printing history and colophon deleted.

Black cloth boards; author and title printed in yellow on front within a blue cloud with three blue stars; on spine: [yellow rule | blue CVV rule] | FIRE- | CRACKERS | BY | CARL | VAN | VECHTEN | [blue CVV rule | yellow rule | blue rule] | GROSSET | & DUNLAP [all lettering in yellow] | [blue rule]; publisher's logo in blind on lower front corner. Lower and fore edges rough trimmed, yellow top edges. Yellow and black dust jacket with a biographical note, plot blurb, and caricature by Miguel Covarrubias on the back.

Published circa January 1929, $1.50.

> Although the only date listed is Knopf's 1925 copyright, the dust jacket lists Nigger Heaven as one of Grosset & Dunlap's "Novels of Distinction." Knopf issued the fourteenth printing of Nigger Heaven in January 1928. The plates for Firecrackers went to Grosset & Dunlap in December 1928. Grosset & Dunlap's binding for Firecrackers imitated Knopf's binding for Nigger Heaven. The plates for Nigger Heaven had gone to Grosset & Dunlap in June. See A18k.

> The first draft of Firecrackers, preceded by seven unnumbered leaves of notes, consists of 168 leaves and is dated 7 June 1924 — 23 July 1924, to which Van Vechten appended a note: "Such as it is!" The second draft consists of 205 leaves and is dated 2 August 1924 — 10 September 1924. The third draft, from which type was set, consists of 224 leaves and is dated 16 October 1924. Van Vechten did not often discuss his writing with others, but he wrote to James Branch Cabell, on 29 September 1924: "I am finishing the third & final changes of a book called Firecrackers which I have decided to send into the world as 'a realistic novel'. . . . Firecrackers has afforded me so many difficulties, so many tiresome days, so much real perplexity, that,

on the eve of setting down finis, I am inclined to regard it with
reasonable scorn." In several inscribed copies of the book, Van
Vechten referred to Firecrackers as "Sentimental impressions of contemporary behaviour" or as a "modern version of Parsifal."

A 17   Excavations   1926

a. First edition

EXCAVATIONS [in blue] | a book of advocacies | BY | CARL VAN VECHTEN |
[borzoi in blue lined oval] | 1926 . ALFRED . A . KNOPF . New York [the
foregoing in a CVV border enclosed in a decorative border]

blank leaf, xiv, 287 pp., blank leaf. 19.3 X 13 cm.

[i] half-title; [ii] list of previous books; [iii] title; [iv] Copyright,
1926, by Alfred A. Knopf, Inc.; [v, dedication] FOR MY BROTHER | RALPH
VAN VECHTEN; [vi] blank; [vii] introductory quotations; [viii] blank;
[ix]-287, text, including "Proem," contents, and colophon.

Blue cloth boards, lettered in gold; on front: CVV dentelle in blind;
on spine: [CVV rule] | EXCAVATIONS | [decoration] | VAN VECHTEN | [CVV
rule] | ALFRED . A . KNOPF | [CVV rule]; borzoi in blind on back. Lower
and fore edges rough trimmed, orange top edges. Red, blue, green, orange,
or lavender dust jacket, with an advertising blurb by Van Vechten [F43a]
on the front, and blurbs for Peter Whiffle by H.L. Mencken, Fanny Butcher,
and Percy Hammond, and for Firecrackers by Carl Van Doren and Louis Bromfield on the flyleaves.

2,500 copies printed; 2,480 copies published January; $2.50.

Contents:
Proem
On Visiting Fashionable Places Out of Season [A25, A28, D95]
A Note on Philip Thicknesse [A9]
Ouida [B5]
The Later Work of Herman Melville [C61, D83]
Edgar Saltus [A7]
Henry Blake Fuller [D91]
Matthew Phipps Shiel [B9]
Ronald Firbank [B7, C58, D87, EV27]
Sophie Arnould [B1]
Oscar Hammerstein: An Epitaph [A9, EV8]
Léo Delibes [A25, D93]
Isaac Albéniz [A9]
Sir Arthur Sullivan [A9]
Erik Satie [A6, D61]
A Note on Dedications [C10, D99]

b. Tall paper edition

Twenty of the copies printed for A17a were left entirely unopened, and
the top edges were unstained. Van Vechten did not sign them, nor was
any limitation indicated. 19.7 X 13.2 cm. Blue cloth boards without

blind borders or printing, but with a white paper label on the spine:
[rule | three decorations | rule] | Excavations | [decoration] | Van
Vechten | [rule | three decorations | rule]. Glassine dust wrapper.
These copies do not seem to have been offered for sale.

c. Second printing, second binding

Identical to A17a with the following exceptions: [iv] Published January,
1926 | Second printing, March, 1926. Blue cloth boards printed in orange
on spine: borzoi in orange rectangle on back; no blind border on front.
Top edges unstained. Blue, red, or orange dust jacket.

1,000 copies printed; 500 copies issued March 1926.

> The following revisions were made to the first edition for the second
> printing: pp. 152, romance/realism; 153, House of Commons/House of
> Lords; 160, quickly/quietly, tenderness/gentleness; 272, the names of
> which he/whose names he had; accent added, p. 110.

d. Reprint edition

Identical to A17a with the following exceptions: [iii] Essay Index Re-
print Series [within border] | [publisher's logo] | BOOKS FOR LIBRARIES
PRESS | FREEPORT, NEW YORK [below border]; [iv] reprinted 1971 by ar-
rangement; [286] blank; two blank leaves. Blue cloth boards; publisher's
logo in blind on front; down spine: [gold band] EXCAVATIONS. Van Vech-
ten [gold band | publisher's monogram in silver]. 21 X 13.5 cm.

Published 1971, $16.00.

> The manuscript for Excavations consists of 303 leaves, some of it com-
> piled from the typescripts of uncollected articles and some older
> pieces retyped, or — as in the Firbank essay — stitched together
> from several sources. The introductory "Proem" is dated 10 March
> 1925. There are three published references to an English edition of
> Excavations: in the bibliography in Spider Boy; on the rear flyleaf
> of the dust jacket of the English edition of Sacred and Profane Mem-
> ories; on the dust jacket of the English edition of Parties where it
> is listed with all of the Van Vechten titles published in England,
> for 7/6. No copy has surfaced. According to the records of Alfred
> A. Knopf, Inc., the balance of copies of the second printing was dis-
> posed of as a "cleared lot to Syndicate Trading Co." in October 1928.
> Presumably, they were not remaindered, but bound, in March 1926.

A 18   Nigger Heaven   1926

a. First edition

Nigger Heaven [surrounded by three stars, a half-moon, and curved lines
representing clouds, all in light blue] | BY | CARL VAN VECHTEN | 1926 |
[borzoi in lined oval] | NEW YORK. ALFRED . A . KNOPF . LONDON [the fore-
going in a CVV border within a two-line border]

viii, 288 pp. 19.8 X 13 cm.

[i] half-title; [ii] list of previous books; [iii] title; [iv] Copyright, 1926, by Alfred A. Knopf, Inc.; [v, dedication] FOR FANIA MARINOFF; [vi] blank; [vii] introductory quotation; [viii] blank; [1]-286, text, including divisional titles and glossary; [287] colophon; [288] blank.

Tan ribbed cloth boards, printed in blue: CVV dentelle on front; on spine: [rule | CVV rule] | NIGGER | HEAVEN | BY | CARL | VAN VECHTEN | [CVV rule | double rule] | ALFRED . A . KNOPF | [rule]; borzoi in blind on back. Fore edges rough trimmed, blue top edges. Light blue dust jacket printed in white, with an advertising blurb by Van Vechten [F50a] and review squibs for earlier books by W. Somerset Maugham, Elinor Wylie, Ernest Boyd, and others.

16,000 copies printed, of which 1,000 unbound sheets were sent to England; 15,000 copies published August 1926; $2.50.

Contents:
Prologue [A28]
Book One — Mary, nine chapters, no titles
Book Two — Byron, nine chapters, no titles

b. Tall paper edition

Identical to A18a with the following exceptions: Limitation leaf tipped-in between [ii-iii], recto blank; verso: OF THE FIRST EDITION OF NIGGER | HEAVEN TWO HUNDRED AND FIVE | COPIES HAVE BEEN PRINTED AS FOL- | LOWS: TEN ON BORZOI RAG PAPER | SIGNED BY THE AUTHOR AND NUM- | BERED FROM A TO J; ONE HUNDRED | AND NINETY FIVE COPIES ON BORZOI | RAG PAPER SIGNED BY THE AUTHOR AND NUMBERED FROM I-195 | THIS IS NUMBER | [number in black ink | signature in purple ink]. 23.5 X 15 cm.

Yellow cloth with red and black floral pattern boards; black paper label printed in white on spine: [floral decoration] | Nigger | Heaven | [floral decoration] | Carl | Van Vechten | [floral decoration]. Edges untrimmed and unopened. Glassine dust wrapper. Issued in black and tan or green and tan batik paper slipcase.

210 copies printed; 205 copies published August 1926; $10.00.

c. Second through fifth printings

Identical to A18a with the following exceptions: [iv] Published, August, 1926; Second printing, September, 1926; Third printing, September, 1926; Fourth printing, October, 1926; Fifth printing, October, 1926. Beginning with the fourth printing, the dust jacket carried reviewer's squibs for Nigger Heaven by Ellen Glasgow and Franklin P. Adams.

2nd printing, 5,000 copies; 3rd printing, 2,450 copies; 4th printing, 5,000 copies; 5th printing, 5,000 copies.

d. Sixth printing

Identical to A18c with the following exceptions: [iv] Sixth printing, October, 1926.

3,000 copies printed, of which 1,000 unbound sheets were sent to England.

Van Vechten had quoted the lyrics to several published songs, among
them, "Somebody Else is Sneakin' In," pp. 246-47; "Shake That Thing,"
pp. 248-49; "Ef You Hadn't Gone Away," pp. 277-78. Almost immediately
ASCAP threatened legal action over the second of these. Van Vechten
settled out of court for $2,250. Simultaneously, he asked Langston
Hughes, the career he had fostered, to supply some lyrics to fit the
pages — line for line — on which the published songs had been
quoted. Hughes's substitute lyrics are "You ain't gonna ride no char-
iot tonight 'less you take your sweet mama along!" pp. 246-47; "Harlem
to duh bone," pp. 248-49; "Baby, lovin' baby, won't you come home today?" pp. 277-78. These changes were made after the sixth printing
had been run and added through a cancel.

e. Seventh through fourteenth printings

Identical to A18d with the following exceptions: [iv] Seventh printing,
November, 1926; Eighth printing, December, 1926; Ninth printing, January,
1927; Tenth printing, February, 1927; Eleventh printing, February, 1927;
Twelfth printing, May, 1927; Thirteenth printing, September, 1927; Four-
teenth printing, January, 1928; [287, in place of the deleted colophon]
The songs and snatches of Blues sung by characters | on pages 34, 35, 52,
137, 139, 142, 144, 145, 146, | 207, 246, 247, 248, 249, 277, 278 and 281
were | written especially for Nigger Heaven by Mr. Langston | Hughes.
The dust jacket, beginning with the seventh printing, carried additional
squibs by Paul Robeson, James Weldon Johnson, George Gershwin, Walter
White, Anita Loos, and the ninth printing carried additional squibs by
William Rose Benét and Burton Rascoe. The fourteenth printing, on a light
stock resulting in a volume one cm. narrower than previous ones, printed
Van Vechten's name in blue on p. [ii] to match the title on p. [iii].

7th printing, 5,000 copies; 8th printing, 3,000 copies of which 1,000
were sent to England; 9th printing, 2,000 copies; 10th printing, 2,000
copies; 11th printing, 2,000 copies; 12th printing, 1,500 copies; 13th
printing, 1,000 copies; 14th printing, 1,250 copies.

Langston Hughes supplied additional lyrics for all of the songs Van
Vechten had quoted, against the possibility of later difficulties:
"Oh, how I'm aching for love!" for "Yes sir, that's my baby," p. 34;
"What does it matter that I want you?" for "I had some one else before
I had you," p. 35; "Ah wants to hop a train" for "Nobody knows duh way
Ah feel dis mornin'," p. 52; "Takes a better man than you to make
sweet mama shout!" for "Not on the first night, baby, an' mebbe not
atall!" p. 137; "Ah wants mah man to be mine alone," for "Ah want all
you gals to leave mah man alone," p. 139; "Roses used to was so sweet,
so sweet, dear," for "Seems lak to me I jes' can't help but sigh," p.
142; "A sweetie like you" for "Everybody loves mah baby," p. 144;
"Till summer leaves the jungle" for "As long as the Congo flows to the
sea," pp. 145-46; "She did me dirty, she did me wrong" for "I'll take
her back if she wants to come back," p. 207; "Ah'll tell duh world
dat Ah can stir et roun'" for "Nobody in town can bake a sweet jelly-
roll so fine," p. 281.

f. First English edition

Identical to A18a with the following exceptions: [ii] blank; [iii] New
York deleted and date moved below borzoi to make a new line: LONDON .
ALFRED . A . KNOPF . 1926; [iv] copyright deleted; [287] colophon deleted.

Brown cloth boards, with two-line border on front and borzoi on back, in
blind; on spine, lettered in gold: [CVV rule] | NIGGER | HEAVEN | [decor-
ation] | VAN VECHTEN | [CVV rule] | ALFRED . A . KNOPF | [CVV rule]. La-
vender top edges. Black dust jacket printed in silver.

1,000 copies (from sheets of the first American printing) published circa
September 1926, 7/6.

g. Second through sixth printings of English edition

Identical to A18f with the following additions: [iv] First published in
England..October 1926; Second impression....November 1926; Third impression....December 1926; Fourth impression....January 1927; Fifth impression....February 1927; Sixth impression....April 1927

   It is impossible to determine in what sizes these "impressions" were
   issued, on the basis of the records of Alfred A. Knopf, Inc. In October 1926, 500 sheets of the 6th American printing were sent to England; the 8th American printing, in December 1926, is listed as "London," but only 1,000 of the 3,000 copies seem to have been exported;
   there is no indication of further copies having been shipped.

h. Seventh printing and second binding of English edition

nigger heaven [in green] | by | Carl Van Vechten | [star and crescent] |
London | ALFRED A. KNOPF | Publisher | [green borzoi]

[i-viii] identical to A18g, with the following exceptions: [iii] title,
as above; [iv] Seventh (cheap) impression...August 1927; [1]-286, [287]
identical to A18e, that is, including the Langston Hughes lyrics. 18.3
X 12.3 cm.

Tan cloth boards with blind border and printing on spine from A18f-g in
black. Orange, cream, blue, black, and white dust jacket, with an illustration of silhouettes in a balcony and a dancer on stage, by Ellen Edwards.

Remaindered copies (from sheets of the eighth American edition) published
August 1927, 3/6.

i. English pocketbook edition

The Borzoi Pocket Books | .XXI. | Carl Van Vechten [in brown] | Nigger
Heaven | [drawing of a black dancer, on stage, in brown] | Alfred A.
Knopf [borzoi] Publisher, London

252 pp. 17.1 X 11.1 cm.

[1] half-title; [2] blank; [3] title; [4] list of printing dates as in
A18h, minus "cheap" as a descriptive epithet for the seventh impression |
Eighth impression....July 1928 | colophon; [5] dedication; [6] introduc-
tory quotation; 7-251, text, including divisional titles, glossary, and
acknowledgment to Langston Hughes, but without specifying pages on which
his lyrics appear.

Brown cloth boards lettered in gold, on front: THE BORZOI | POCKET BOOKS
| [rule] | .XXI. | [rule] | NIGGER | HEAVEN | Carl Van Vechten | [rule] |

⌊borzoi⌋ KNOPF ⌊borzoi⌋ ⌊the foregoing in a one-line box⌋; on spine:
⌊rule⌋ | NIGGER | HEAVEN | VAN | VECHTEN | ⌊borzoi⌋ | ALFRED A. | KNOPF
| ⌊rule⌋. Orange top edges. Lavender dust jacket printed in brown, dup-
licating title page drawing.

Published July 1928, 3/6.

j. Tauchnitz edition

NIGGER HEAVEN | BY | CARL VAN VECHTEN | COPYRIGHT EDITION | LEIPIZ |
GERNHARD TAUCHNITZ | 1928

270 pp. 16.1 X 11.1 cm.

⌊1⌋ COLLECTION | OF | BRITISH AUTHORS | TAUCHNITZ EDITION | VOL. 4857 |
NIGGER HEAVEN. By CARL VAN VECHTEN | IN ONE VOLUME; ⌊2⌋ TAUCHNITZ EDITION
| By the same Author | SPIDER BOY. I VOL.....Vol. 4858; ⌊3⌋ title; ⌊4⌋
blank; ⌊5⌋ dedication; ⌊6⌋ blank; ⌊7⌋ introductory quotation; ⌊8⌋ blank;
9-270, text, type set from the sixth American printing.

Stiff white wrappers, printed with the standard Tauchnitz cover in black.

Published circa October 1928.

k. First reprint edition

Identical to A18e with the following exceptions: ⌊ii⌋ blank; ⌊iii⌋ title
page reverses blue and black print and substitutes GROSSET & DUNLAP | PUB-
LISHERS | By arrangement with Alfred A. Knopf for date, borzoi, and pub-
lisher. 19.3 X 13.1 cm.

Black cloth boards, author and title printed in yellow on front within
a blue cloud with three blue stars; on spine: ⌊yellow rule | blue CVV
rule⌋ | NIGGER | HEAVEN | BY | CARL | VAN VECHTEN ⌊the foregoing in yel-
low⌋ | ⌊blue CVV rule | yellow rule | blue rule⌋ | GROSSET & DUNLAP ⌊in
yellow⌋ | ⌊blue rule⌋; publisher's logo in blind on lower front. Lower
and fore edges rough trimmed, yellow top edges. Yellow, red, orange,
black, and white dust jacket with a drawing of a black couple.

Printed from Knopf's plates and backbone dies; published after June 1928;
$1.50.

l. First paperback edition

NIGGER | HEAVEN | By | CARL VAN VECHTEN | With a Note by the Author — |
and a Critical Commentary by | GEORGE S. SCHUYLER | of the "Pittsburgh
Courier" | Avon Publishing Co., Inc. | NEW YORK | Published by arrange-
ment with Alfred A. Knopf, Inc. ⌊the foregoing enclosed in a decorative
border⌋

194 pp. 16.4 X 10.9 cm.

⌊1⌋ decorative wrapper reckoned as first page; ⌊2⌋ quotation from Schuy-
ler's essay, and a plot squib; ⌊3⌋ title; ⌊4⌋ introductory quotation |
drawing of Shakespeare | acknowledgment of Langston Hughes's lyrics |
Copyright, 1926, by Alfred A. Knopf, Inc. Avon Re- | print Edition, copy-

right, 1951, by Avon Publishing | Co. Inc. Printed in U.S.A.; [5] table
of contents; [6-7] glossary; [8] cast of characters; 9-186, text; [187-
90] A Note by the Author; 191-94, essay by Schuyler.

Full-color illustration of many blacks of various professions walking
forward, on heavy wrapper, with a review squib by Harry Hansen on front;
down spine: CARL VAN VECHTEN [black on yellow] NIGGER HEAVEN [yellow on
black] 314 | AVON [in circle]; inside back cover: list of Avon publica-
tions; blurbs for Nigger Heaven on back. All edges stained red. Lami-
nated clear plastic coating.

10,000 copies published September 1951, $.25.

Contents:
Text, as in A18e
A Note by the Author [A28]

m. Second paperback edition

NIGGER HEAVEN | BY | CARL VAN VECHTEN | [publisher's logo] | HARPER COLO-
PHON BOOKS | Harper & Row, Publishers | New York, Evanston, San Francisco,
London

xviii, 286 pp. 18 X 10.5 cm.

[i] half-title; [ii] blank; [iii] title; [iv] acknowledgment of Langston
Hughes's lyrics, critical commentaries, original copyright, reprint re-
strictions | First Harper Colophon edition published 1971; v-vi, Pub-
lisher's Note; vii-x, review of Nigger Heaven by W.E.B. DuBois; xi-xii,
excerpt from A Long Way Home by Claude McKay; xiii-xv, excerpt from Along
This Way by James Weldon Johnson; xvi-xviii, excerpt from The Big Sea by
Langston Hughes; [1] introductory quotation; [2] blank; 3-284, text,
printed by photo-offset from the seventh Knopf printing; 285-86, glossary
similarly printed.

Stiff paper wrappers printed in coral, yellow, red, purple, orange, olive,
and black, in an art-deco design, on front: title in red, author in black
against yellow; on spine: title in red, author in black against coral;
on both front and spine: HARPER COLOPHON BOOKS | CN 1001; quotations from
critical commentary on back.

Published autumn 1971, $2.45.

n. Second reprint edition

Identical to A18e with the following additions: [iii, publisher's logo] |
OCTAGON BOOKS | [rule] | A Division of Farrar Straus and Giroux. | New
York 1973 [the foregoing printed below title page information. 19.8 X
12.8 cm. Printed by photo-offset from the seventh Knopf printing.

Wine cloth boards printed in gold: publisher's logo on front; on spine,
NIGGER | HEAVEN | CARL | VAN VECHTEN | OCTAGON. All edges trimmed. Is-
sued without dust jacket.

Published 1973, $13.00.

o. French edition

CARL VAN VECHTEN | [rule] | LE PARADIS DES NÈGRES | traduction de J. SA-
BOURAND | Préface de Paul MORAND | Éditions originale | [publisher's logo]
| "LES DOCUMENTAIRES" | SIMON KRA, 6 RUE BLANCHE, PARIS

blank leaf, 280 pp. 18.6 X 12.3 cm.

[1-2] blank; [3] half-title; [4] blank; [5] title; [6] publication notice;
7-[12] "Sous Pavillon Noir" by Paul Morand; 13-275, text; [276] blank;
[277] contents; [278] blank; [279] colophon; [280] blank.

White paper wrappers printed in orange. Edges rough trimmed.

Published November 1927, 20 fr.

p. French tall paper edition

Identical to A18o with the following exceptions: 21 to 20 X 18.7 to 13
cm., signatures of varying dimensions. A limitation note, p. [4] indicates ten numbered copies on Lafuma and 200 copies, numbered 11 through
210 on vellum.

> In an inscription, Van Vechten referred to this translation as "this
> lynching of Nigger Heaven." Over forty pages, including all of chap-
> ters 4 and 7 from Book One and nearly all of chapters 1 and 3 from
> Book Two, as well as Hughes's lyrics, were deleted. [C8. Quoted as
> "Bonne Feuilles Les Paradis des Nègres" in Le Peuple, 26 April 1928.]

q. German translation

Nigger-himmel | [triple rule] | UNSER NEUER ROMAN | [triple rule] | von |
Carl Van Vechten | beginnt in diesen Tagen. Er spielt in Harlem, | der
Negerstadt von New York

> This translation appeared in daily installments in Frankfurter Zeit-
> ung, beginning 30 December 1926 and concluding 27 February 1927. The
> only copies available for collation, in Van Vechten's collection in
> the New York Public Library, conclude on page 281 of the novel, de-
> leting therefore the final six hundred words. Alfred Knopf wrote to
> Van Vechten, 29 May 1927, that Nigger Heaven would appear in Berlin
> in October or earlier, but it was never published in book form in
> Germany and has, therefore, no German "edition." (Similarly, Ull-
> stein Publishers planned a German translation of Spider Boy, in 1930,
> but, in Knopf's words, "outwent its contract.") [EV38]

r. Swedish edition

CARL VAN VECHTEN | NEGRERNAS HIMMELRIKE | BEMYNDIGAD ÖVERSÄTTNING | AV |
BERTEL GRIPENBERG | HELSINGFORS | HOLGER SCHILDTS FÖRLAG

254 pp. 19.5 X 13 cm.

[1] half-title; [2] blank; [3] title; [4] HELSINGFORS | 1927 | A.-B.F.
TILGMANNS TRYCKERI; [5]-253, text, including divisional titles; [254]
blank.

Stiff white paper wrappers printed in red on front: NEGRERNAS | HIMMEL-
RIKE | AV | CARL VAN VECHTEN | HOLDER SCHILDT | [illustration of blacks
in a restaurant]; in blue on spine: author and title between red lines;
publisher's blurb on back. Langston Hughes's lyrics are not included.

Published 1927, 40 mk.

s. Czech edition

CARL VAN VECHTEN: | CĚRNOŠSKÉ NEBE | ROMÀN | V PRAZE | [rule] | 1930

228 pp. 18.8 X 13 cm.

[1] half-title; [2] blank; [3] title; [4] blank; [5] introductory quota-
tion; [6] blank; 7-[226] text; [227] a note on the translation | colophon
[228] blank

Green cloth boards printed in black, on front: _CARL_VAN_VEÇHTEN | [gold
star | large gold cross | gold and black flower] | CERNOSSKE NEBE [the
foregoing in a black border]; on spine: [rule] | [star] | Carl Van |
Vechten | CĚR- | NOŠSKĚ | NEBE | [three stars | rule]; on back: UDKN [in
black box within a black border]. Yellow end-papers. The translation
includes Langston Hughes's lyrics.

Published 1930.

t. Czech tall paper edition

Identical to A18s with the following exceptions: 20 X 13.5 cm. Stiff
gray paper wrappers, printed in red on front: KNIHOVNA MODERNÍ BELETRIE
„KRIZOVATKY" | CARL VAN VECHTEN: CĚRNOŠSKÉ | NEBE | ROMÀN | UDKN | [cream
star | cross | large cross] [all the foregoing in a red border]; on spine:
author and title | Kc20. Edges untrimmed and unopened.

Published 1930.

u. First Italian edition

CARL VAN VECHTEN | IL PARADISO | DEI | NEGRI [in red] | Prefazione e tra-
duzione dall'inglese di | GIAN DÀULI | [boxed drawing of a hand, a book,
and a streak of lightning, in tan] | SOC. AN. "MODERNISSIMA„ | MILANO

xx, 316 pp. 19 X 12.4 cm.

[i] blank; [ii] advertisement; [iii] half-title; [iv] drawing of Van Vechten by Francesco Chiappilli; [v] title; [vi] Proprietà Letteraria Riser-
vata | Printed in Italy | (1930 Anno VIII); vii|xix, [preface] I NEGRI
NELLA VITA E NELL' ARTE; [xx] blank; 1-[313] text; [314] blank; [315]
1000 DI LUSSO È 4000 COMUNI È STATE FINITA DI STAMPARE COI TIPI

Stiff cream paper wrappers, printed in brown and black, on front: CARL
VAN VECHTEN | IL PARADISO DEI NEGRI | [banjo, sun and cacti] | „MODERNIS-
SIMA" | MILANO; on spine: SCRITTORI DI TUTTO IL MONDO 7. Red, green, and
white dust jacket of black girl dancing with musical instruments. Green
advertising band: NON È DURO ESSERE | NEGRO, NEGRO, NEGRO? | Vecchia
canzone del Sud. The translation includes Langston Hughes's lyrics.

4,000 copies published August 1930, 15 lire.

Although the limitation note indicates a deluxe edition of a thousand copies, none is available for collation. The illustration by Francesco Chiappilli is based on a photograph of Van Vechten taken by the poet, Witter Bynner.

v. Second Italian edition

IL PARADISO | DEI NEGRI | Romanzo | di | CARL VAN VECHTEN [introductory quotation by Countée Cullen translated into Italian] | MILANO | DALL' OGLIO, EDITORE

264 pp.   18 X 11 cm.

[1] I CORVI | COLLANA UNIVERSALE MODERNA | NUMERO 123 | 36° DELLA „SEZIONE SCARLATTA" | [publisher's logo] | half-title; [2] blank; [3] title; [4] Proprietà artistico-letteraria dell'editore dall'Oglio; 5-259, text; [260] colophon; [261-63] list of publisher's other books; [264] subscription blank and advertisement.

Stiff red paper wrappers printed in black and white, on front: CARL VAN VECHTEN | IL PARADISO | DEI NEGRI | ROMANZO | [publisher's logo] | DALL' OGLIO [the foregoing in black, within a white border which is in turn in a black border, banded in white reading, in continuous sequence] I CORVI | UNIVERSALE | MODERNA | COLLANA |; up spine, printed in white on black: Il Paradiso dei negri di Carl Van Vechten [banded, with number at top in white and publisher's logo in black at bottom.

Published August 1964, 400 lire.

Although no translator is indicated, this appears to be a reprint of Gian Dàuli's 1930 version in A18u.

w. Estonian edition

ILMUB TARTUS 12 KORDA AASTAS | LLLDUSE KROONINE ROMAAN | Nr. 32 TELLIM-ISHIND AASTAS 10 KROONI | [rule] | ÜKSIKHUMBRI HIND 1 KROON | AUGUST 1931 | [double rule] | CARL VAN VECHTEN | [rule] | Neegrite taevas | Autori loal inglise keelest | M. Luht. | K. | U. „KOODUS", TARTUS, 1931

224 pp.   18.2 X 12 cm.

[1] title; [2] K. Mattieseni trükikoda O. | U., Tartus, 1931; 3, biography; [4] blank; [5] dedication; [6] blank; 7-224, text.

Stiff cream paper wrappers printed in brown, on front: a guitar player against a cityscape | neegrite | taevas [in cream on brown] | No. 32 CARL | van Vechten 1 | KROOM | [rule] | LOODUSE KROONINE ROMAAN; up spine: author and title. Edges untrimmed and unopened. The translation does not include the Langston Hughes lyrics.

Published 1931.

x. Polish edition

CARL VAN VECHTEN | RAJ MURZYNÔW | (NIGGER HEAVEN) | AUTORYZOWANY PRZEKLAD
| STEFANJI HEYMANOWEJ | WARSZWA - 1931 | [rule] | TOWARZYSTWO WYDAWNICZE
„RÓJ"

256 pp. 19.2 X 12.3 cm.

[1] publisher's logo; [2] blank; [3] title; [4] CZCIONKAMI DRUNKARNI
MARODOWEJ W KRAKOWIE; [5] explanatory note; [6] blank; 7-[250] text;
[251-56] advertisements

Stiff white paper wrappers with a drawing of a black man and a white woman dancing, in gray, orange, and black. The translation includes the
Langston Hughes lyrics.

Published 1931.

y. First Danish edition

CARL VAN VECHTEN | NIGGERLIMLEN | PAA DANSK VED | KELVIN LINDEMANN |
[double rule] | WILHELM HANSEN - KØBENHAVN | MCMXXXIII

236 pp. 20.3 X 15.1 cm.

[1] half-title; [2] blank; [3] title; [4] TRYKT I | WILHELM HANSENS ETABL.
| KØBENHAVN; [5] translator's note; [6] blank; [7] introductory quotation;
[8] blank; 9-235, text; [236] blank.

Stiff black paper wrappers, printed on front: NIGGER | HIMLEN | AF | CARL
VAN VECHTEN [in red, depth-shaded in cream] | [line drawing of New York
skyline] | WILHELM HANSEN [in matching lettering] [the foregoing enclosed
in cream and red border]; author and title down spine in cream against
red and black, and editor's initials. Lower and fore edges untrimmed, red
top edges.

Published 1933, 8.50 kr.

    The translator wrote Van Vechten that the Tauchnitz edition contained
    fewer "blues lyrics" than the Knopf edition. Despite his own acknow-
    ledgment of Langston Hughes's verses, in his translator's note, Linde-
    mann did not use them. "Yes Sir, That's My Baby," for which Hughes
    substituted "Oh, how I'm aching for love," appears in English, page
    136; the offending "Shake That Thing," over which ASCAP threatened
    suit, appears — in part, at least — as "Vil du ryste," page 205.
    Some other lyrics were simply omitted and still others seem to have
    been invented for this translation. Lindemann acknowledged the as-
    sistance of Roy de Coverley and Bruce Nugent — both Harlem residents
    — in the translating.

z. Second Danish edition

CARL VAN VECHTEN | NIGGERLIMLEN | OVERSAT AF | KELVIN LINDEMANN | [pub-
lisher's logo] | ASCHEHOUG DANSK FORLAG | INDEHAVER: G. M. STEFFENSEN |
1946

232 pp. 19.5 X 12.5 cm.

[1] LEVENDE LITTERATUR | author and half-title; [2] list of other foreign language novels; [3] title; [4] Oversat fra Amerikansk efter | „NIGGER-HEAVEN" | Trykt hos: | J. Jørgensen & Co | København 1946; [5-6] editor's note; [7] introductory quotation; [8] blank; 9-231, text; [232] translator's note from first Danish edition.

Stiff white paper wrappers; title and author on front and spine of dust jacket, printed in black on a cream rectangle on brown. Lower and fore edges untrimmed, top edges rough trimmed.

Published 1946. 18 kr.

aa. Norwegian edition

CARL VAN VECHTEN | NIGGERHIMLEN | OVERSATT AV | HELGE KROG | [publisher's logo] | OSLO 1933 | FORLAGT AV H. ASCHEHOUG & CO. (W. NYGAARD)

217 pp. 20.2 X 14 cm.

[1] half-title; [2] blank; [3] title; [4] Oversatt efter | Nigger Heaven | Printed in Norway | [rule] DETMALLINGJKE BOGTRYKKERI; [5] introductory quotation; [6] blank; [7] editor's note; [8] blank; [9]-217, text.

Stiff gray paper wrappers with illustration in black of blacks dancing, printed in red on front: CARL VAN VECHTEN | NIGGER = | HIMLEN [title printed over illustration] | 9H. ASCHEHOUG & CO 8W. NYGAARD; on spine: author, title, publisher's logo; explanation of title on back. Edges untrimmed. The translation does not include the Langston Hughes lyrics.

Published February 1933.

bb. Hungarian edition

VAN VECHTEN | NÉGER | MENNYORSZÁG | FORDÍTOTTA | PÁLÓCZI HORVÁTH GYÖRGY | [publisher's logo] | ATHENAEUM | IRODALMIÈS NYOMADI R.-T. KIADÁSA | BUDA-PEST

264 pp. 17.3 X 11.3 cm.

[1] half-title; [2] blank; [3] title; [4] 15935. -Athenaeum r.-t. nyomása, Budapest.; [5] editor's note; [6] blank; [7]-263, text; [264] blank.

Gray cloth boards printed in blue rectangles through which gray printing appears, on front: VAN VECHTEN | NÉGER MENNYORSZÁG; on spine: author, title, publisher. Cream dust jacket with orange and blue illustration by Sidos of one of the novel's characters, "The Scarlet Creeper," and publisher's logo printed in red. The translation does not include the Langston Hughes lyrics.

Published circa July 1934.

Twelve leaves of notes, filed separately from the manuscript, at Yale, precede the first draft of Nigger Heaven. Dated 3 November 1925 - 22 December 1925, the first draft consists of 184 leaves. The second draft consists of 237 leaves and is dated 15 January 1926 - 5 February 1926. The third draft, from which type was set, consists of 254

leaves, including the glossary, and is dated 1 March 1926. The galley proofs are heavily revised, making in effect an additional draft
of <u>Nigger Heaven</u>. The success of the novel led Alfred A. Knopf to
plan a deluxe edition. It was announced in the <u>Borzoi Broadside</u> in
the autumn of 1929, and advertised to contain illustrations by the
English artist, E. McKnight Kauffer. The project was never realized,
however, because of the stringencies of the depression. Van Vechten
donated the completed illustrations to the Museum of Modern Art in
1942.

A 19   <u>Spider Boy</u>   1928

a. <u>First edition, first and second printings, part of third printing</u>

SPIDER BOY [S and B in blue] | a scenario for a moving picture | by |
CARL VAN VECHTEN | 1928 | [borzoi in blue lined oval] | NEW YORK . ALFRED
. A . KNOPF . LONDON | [the foregoing in a CVV border and a one-line bor-
der enclosed in a blue one-line border]

x, 298 pp., 2 blank leaves. 19 X 13 cm.

[i-ii] blank; [iii] half-title; [iv] list of previous books; [v] title;
[vi] Copyright, 1928, by Alfred A. Knopf, Inc.; [vii] dedication] <u>For</u> |
<u>Blanche Knopf</u> | <u>with</u> | <u>Pansies and Kinkajous</u> | <u>and Love</u>; [viii] blank;
[ix] introductory quotations; [x] blank; [1] half-title; [2] blank; 3-
298, text, including bibliography.

Pink cloth boards, printed in gold, on front: CVV dentelle; on spine:
[rule | CVV rule] | SPIDER | BOY | BY | CARL | VAN VECHTEN | [CVV rule |
double rule[| ALFRED . A . KNOPF | [rule]; borzoi in blind on back. Lo-
wer and fore edges rough trimmed, blue top edges. Dust jacket illustration by Ronald McRae in full color; title and author in red on front and
spine, with an advertising blurb by Van Vechten on the back [F60a]. Review squibs for <u>Nigger Heaven</u> by James Weldon Johnson, for <u>The Tattooed</u>
<u>Countess</u> by Louis Bromfield, and for <u>The Blind Bow-Boy</u> by Burton Rascoe.

1st printing, 20,000 copies; 2nd printing, 5,000 copies, 3rd printing,
5,000 copies, of which 1,000 were prepared for a Canadian edition [A19g];
published August 1928; $2.50.

Contents: eighteen chapters, no titles.

b. <u>First tall paper edition</u>

Identical to A19a with the following exceptions: Limitation leaf tipped-
in between [ii] and [iii], recto blank; verso: <u>Of the first edition of</u> |
<u>SPIDER BOY</u> | <u>seventy-five copies</u> | <u>(of which seventy are for sale)</u> | <u>have</u>
<u>been printed on</u> | <u>INOMACHI JAPAN VELLUM,</u> | <u>numbered from 1 to 75.</u> | <u>Each</u>
<u>copy is signed by the author.</u> | <u>This is number</u> | [number in black ink |
signature in green ink]. 23 X 14.5 cm.

Red parchment boards, bevelled front and back edges, stamped in gold, on
front: [box, through which] CARL VAN VECHTEN | SPIDER BOY [appears in red,
enclosed in CVV border of red]; on spine: [CVV rule | rule | box, through
which title shows as on front | rule | CVV rule | rule | smaller box,

through which author shows as on front | rule | CVV rule] | ALFRED . A .
KNOPF; borzoi in blind on back. Edges untrimmed and unopened. Red satin
marking ribbon. Untrimmed sheet of text stock from second tall paper edition folded around boards and printed on spine to duplicate spine of A19a
with author and title. Orange paper slipcase with blue and orange label
lettered in gold: [rule] | SPIDER | BOY [in blue box] | [rule | CVV rule
| rule] | CARL | VAN | VECHTEN [in blue box] | [rule]

75 copies published August 1928; $25.00.

c. Second tall paper edition

Identical to A19a with the following exceptions: Limitation leaf tipped-
in between [ii] and [iii], recto blank; verso: Of this first edition of
| SPIDER BOY | two hundred and twenty copies | (of which two hundred are
for sale) | have been printed on | BORZOI RAG PAPER, | numbered from 1 to
220. | Each copy is signed by the author. | This is number | [number in
black ink | signature in green ink]. 23.5 X 15 cm.

Combed blue paper boards, pink quarter cloth spine, printed in gold on
front: CARL VAN VECHTEN [CVV rule] | SPIDER | BOY; on spine: [in vertical
blue rectangle] SPIDER | BOY | [in blue square] CARL | VAN | VECHTEN | [in
blue horizontal rectangle] ALFRED . A . KNOPF [These boxes are separated
from each other by a series of alternating wide blue and gold bands, gold
rules and CVV gold rules]. Edges untrimmed and unopened. Patterned glassine wrapper. Black paper slipcase with blue, gold, and orange label,
copying spine design for author and title.

220 copies published August 1928; $10.00.

d. Fourth printing

Identical to A19a with the following addition: [vi] First, second and
third printings | before publication | Published August, 1928 | Fourth
printing November, 1928

4th printing, 2,000 copies.

e. First English edition

Carl Van Vechten | [rule] | Spider Boy [in red] | a scenario for a moving
picture | Alfred A. Knopf : London ; 1928

240 pp. 18.4 X 12.1 cm.

[1] half-title; [2] list of previous books; [3] title; [4] Printed in
Great Britain; [5] dedication; [6] blank; [7] introductory quotations; [8]
blank; 9-239, text; [240] blank.

Red cloth boards; two-line border in blind on front and borzoi in blind on
back; on spine, lettered in gold: [CVV rule] | SPIDER | BOY | [decora-
tion] | VAN VECHTEN | [CVV rule] | ALFRED . A . KNOPF | [CVV rule]. Dust
jacket duplicates Ronald McRae design from A19a.

Published July 1928; 7/6.

Typeset in England, this edition precedes the American one by a month.

f. Second through fourth English printings

Identical to A19e with the following exceptions: [4] First edition...
July 1928 | Second impression...August 1928 | Third impression...November
1928 | Fourth impression...December 1928 | PRINTED IN GREAT BRITAIN | FOR
ALFRED A. KNOPF LTD. 18.4 X 12.3 cm.

Light red cloth boards; blind border and gold lettering from the first
English edition printed in black. Tag marker glued on spine of McRae
dust jacket indicating new price: 3/6.

g. Canadian edition

Identical to A19a with the following exceptions: [v] Longmans, Green &
Co. Toronto [in place of American publisher]; [vi] First, second and
third printings | before publication. At foot of binding spine, in place
of American publisher, Longmans | Green & Co. [rules deleted]. For part
of the third printing, Alfred A. Knopf prepared the cancel and change in
binding for this issue.

1,000 copies published August 1928.

h. Tauchnitz edition

SPIDER BOY | A SCENARIO | FOR A MOVING PICTURE | BY | CARL VAN VECHTEN |
COPYRIGHT EDITION | LEIPIZ | GERNHARD TAUCHNITZ | 1928

272 pp. 16.1 X 11.1 cm.

[1] Tauchnitz standard half-title, Vol. 4858; [2] Nigger Heaven, Vol.
4857; [3] title; 4] blank; [5] dedication; [6] blank; [7] introductory
quotations; [8] blank; 9-272, text.

Stiff white paper wrappers printed with the standard Tauchnitz cover.

Published circa October 1928.

i. Reprint edition

SPIDER | BOY | a scenario for a moving picture | by | CARL VAN VECHTEN |
GROSSET & DUNLAP | Publishers New York [the foregoing in a one-line
border enclosed in wavy-line and heavy-line borders]

x, 310 pp., blank leaf. 18.3 X 12.4 cm.

Identical to A19d with the following exceptions: [i] half-title; [ii]
blank; [iii] title; as above; [iv] publication history; [v] dedication;
[vi] blank; [vii] quotations; [viii] blank; [298] publisher's advertisement; [299-309] publisher's book list; [310] blank.

Blue cloth boards, lettered in orange on front and spine to imitate A19c,
minus bands and rules on spine. Orange top edges. Cream dust jacket
printed in red; title and author cuts from McRae's design and substituting a photograph of an unidentified starlet for the original illustration.

Published after August 1931.

j. Swedish edition

CARL VAN VECHTEN | EN FANGE I | HOLLYWOOD | Bemyndigar översättning | av | INGEGERD VON TELL | STOCKHOLM | [rule] | HOLGER SCHILDTS FORLAG

240 pp. 19.6 X 12.8 cm.

[1] half-title; [2] blank; [3] title; [4] Originalets titel: | SPIDERBOY | STOCKHOLM 1929 | SVENDKA TRYCKERIAK-TIEBOLGET; [5]-240, text.

Stiff white paper wrappers printed in wine, blue, and black, with a drawing of two girls chasing a boy and a man; on front: Carl Van Vechten | En fange i | Hollywood | [rule] HOLGERSCHILDTS FORLAG STOCKHOLM; on spine: preis 4:50 kr. Edges untrimmed and unopened.

Published 1929; 4.50 kr.

k. French edition

CARL VAN VECHTEN | [rule] | L'ARAIGNÉE MÂLE | Scènes de la vie à Hollywood | ROMAN | TRADUIT DE L'ANGLAIS | par | MAURICE RÉMON | [publisher's logo] | ALBIN MICHEL, ÉDITEUR | PARIS — 22, RUE HUYGHENS, 22, — PARIS

blank leaf, 316 pp. 18.8 X 11.4 cm.

[1] half-title; [2] list of novels translated by Rémon; [3] title; [4] blank; [5]-313, text, commencing with introductory quotations; [314] blank; [315] colophon; [316] blank.

Yellow paper wrappers lettered in black, with title page duplicated on front inside decorative border and, at top: NOUVELLE SÉRIE | COLLECTION DES MAITRES | DE LA LITTÉRATURE ÉTRANGÈRE; author, title, price label, and publisher on spine; list of other books in the series on back. Untrimmed and unopened. Glassine wrapper.

Published October 1930; 23.40 fr.

> This translation ran serially in La Revue Hebdomadaire, Paris, No. 4, in weekly installments between 25 January and 22 March 1930. [EV41] In Le Journal du Cairo (Egypt), 19 March 1932, a selection from this translation begins in the middle of a conversation on page 139 and ends in the middle of page 145 of the French edition (pp. 132-37 in the Knopf edition). No other issues of the paper are available; if Spider Boy did run serially in its entirety, it would have begun circa 26 February and concluded circa April 1932. [EV42]

l. Italian edition

CARL VAN VETCHEN [sic; thus spelled at top of every verso] | IL ROMANZO | D' HOLLYWOOD | (SPIDER BOY) | Unica traduzione autorizzata | de Giovanni Marcellini | [publisher's logo] | GIUSEPPE CARABBA | EDITORE LANCIANO

320 pp. 17.3 X 11 cm.

[1-4] blank; [5] half-title; [6] blank; [7] title; [8] PROPRIETA LETTERARIA | DELL'EDITORE GIUSEPPE CARABBA |TTip. R. Carabba. 1932; [9]-10,

translator's note; [11] quotations; [12] blank; [13]-317, text; [318]
blank; [319] chapter pages; [320] blank.

Orange cloth boards printed in black, border on front; on spine: IL RO-
MANZO | D'HOLLYWOOD | CARL VAN VETCHEN [sic] | GIUSEPPE CARABBA.   Red,
yellow, and blue dust jacket with a drawing of a Hollywood starlet by
Maru. Advertising band around the book, on which Van Vechten's name is
correctly spelled.

Published November 1932.

m. Danish edition

CARL VAN VECHTEN | FILM | (SPIDER-BOY) | ET FILMSMANUSKRIPT | 17 BILLEDER
| PAA DANSK VED | MODENS DAM | [publisher's logo] | STEEN HASSELBALCHS
FORLAG

240 pp.   20.5 X 14.5 cm.

[1] half-title and one of two introductory quotations; [2] blank; [3]
title; [4] DYVA & JEPPESEN A/S | GRAFISK ESTABLISSEMENT; [5]-240, text.

Stiff paper wrappers duplicating McRae's illustration from the American
dust jacket, but indicating the title as FILM; on spine: FILM | VAN VECH-
TEN. Edges untrimmed.

Published 1932.

n. Microfilm edition

Books on Demand, University Microfilms, Ann Arbor, Michigan, AT1-OP39339,
1978, $37.00.

> The first draft of Spider Boy consists of 191 leaves and is dated 16
> August 1927 — 20 October 1927. The second draft consists of 222
> leaves and is dated 21 October 1927 — 28 December 1927. The third
> draft, from which type was set, consists of 229 leaves, including pre-
> liminary leaves, is dated 27 January 1928. Eleven leaves of notes
> preceded the first draft.

A 20   Feathers   1930

Feathers | BY CARL VAN VECHTEN [drawing of a cat] | RANDOM HOUSE | New
York, 1930 [the foregoing in a decorative border]

2 blank leaves, 22 pp., 2 blank leaves. 21 X 13.4 cm.

[blank leaf conjugate with title leaf], recto paste-down endpaper, verso
blank; [blank leaf] recto and verso blank [conjugate with blank leaf]
recto, half-title and dedication: For | Anna Marble Pollock; verso blank;
[1] title; [2] 875 copies for Random House | PJ [between decorations] |
Printed in the U.S.A. by the Southworth Press | Copyright, 1930, by Carl
Van Vechten; 3-[23] text, beginning with another drawing of a cat; [24]
blank; [2 blank conjugate leaves; recto to conjugate leaf of [24] blank,
verso as paste-down endpaper.

Stiff gray deckle-edge paper wrappers, with white paper label on spine:
[decoration | down spine:] Feathers . VAN VECHTEN | [decoration]. Lower
and fore edges untrimmed. Boxed with five other pamphlets, similar in
design, with varying decorations, p. [2], and varying color wrappers.
Black cloth slipcase; chartreuse label the full length of the spine:
[decorative rule] | 1 [numbers between small decorations] | The Litter |
of Rose Leaves | BENÉT | 2 | Tabloid News | BROMFIELD | 3 | Gehenna |
AIKEN | 4 | Feathers | VAN VECHTEN | 5 | American County Fair | ANDERSON
| Fine Furniture | DREISER | [decoration] | RANDOM | HOUSE | 1930 | [de-
corative rule]

875 copies published 1930; $10.00.

[A22, C13, C19, C42, C45, C50. Paraphrased, with cullings from The Tiger
in the House, as a short story about Van Vechten and his cat, in Fairfax
Downey, Cats of Destiny, New York; Charles Scribner's Sons, 1950, titled
"Kitten on the Keys," pp. 124-27.]

A 21   Parties   1930

a. First edition

CARL VAN VECHTEN | [decoration in chartreuse]   PARTIES [decoration in
chartreuse] | Scenes from Contemporary | New York Life [drawing of cupid
crushing grapes in a bowl, in chartreuse] | [rule] | New . York . Alfred .
A . Knopf | [rule] | 1930 [the foregoing in a one-line border]

blank leaf, x, 260, xvi pp., blank leaf. 19 X 13 cm.

[i] half-title; [ii] blank; [iii] title; [iv] Copyright 1930 by Carl Van
Vechten; [v, dedication] This book is dedicated with deep affection | to |
Armina Marshall | and | Lawrence Langner | who have gone to many parties |
with me; [vi] blank; [vii] introductory quotation; [viii] blank; [ix]
half-title; [x] blank; 1-260, text; [xi] tail-piece; [xii-xiv] bibliography; [xv] colophon; [xvi] blank.

Yellow cloth boards printed in silver, on front: cupid crushing grapes
in a bowl — not a duplicate of the title page drawing — surrounded by
clusters of grapes; on spine: [silver cluster of grapes] | PARTIES [in
green] | [silver rule] | CARL VAN VECHTEN [in green] | [silver rule] |
[four descending clusters] | ALFRED . A . KNOPF; borzoi in blind on back.
Lower and fore edges rough trimmed, green or unstained top edges. Green
dust jacket printed in dark green with cupid from title page, surrounded
by clouds and clusters of grapes on spine, printed in silver. Advertising blurb by Van Vechten on the back [F74a]. Reviewer's squibs for other
books by Clemence Dane, Louis Bromfield, Carl Van Doren, Rebecca West.

10,000 copies published August 1930; $2.50

Contents: nineteen chapters, no titles [A25, A28, D135, chapter 14. Ex-
cerpted in Contemporary Trends in American Literature Since 1914, Ed.
John Herbert Nelson, New York: Macmillan Company, 1933; re-issued, 1936,
pp. 337-40]

b. Tall paper edition

Identical to A21a with the following exceptions: Limitation leaf tipped-
in between [ii] and [iii], recto blank, verso: Of the first edition of |
PARTIES | two-hundred fifty copies | (of which two hundred forty are for
sale) | have been printed on | CROXLEY HAND MADE PAPER. | Each copy is
signed by the author. | This is number | [number in red ink | signature
in green ink]; [v] title and date printed in dark green. 23.3 X 15.5 cm.

Yellow parchment boards printed to duplicate first edition, but all in
silver. Lower and fore edges untrimmed and unopened, top edges painted
silver. Text stock wrapper, untrimmed and folded around boards, printed
on spine to duplicate title and author from binding. Black paper slipcase with black label on spine printed in silver to duplicate title,
author, and two grape clusters from binding; number of copy written in
silver ink.

250 copies published August 1930; $15.00.

c. Second printing

Identical to A21a, with the following addition, [iv] First and Second
printings Before Publication | Published August, 1930.

3,500 copies

d. Third and fourth printings

Identical to A21c with the following additions: [iv] Third Printing, Aug-
ust, 1930 | Fourth Printing, August, 1930.

3rd printing, 4,000 copies; 4th printing, 1,500 copies of which 750 were
issued, and the balance issued in 1935.

e. English edition

CARL VAN VECHTEN | [decoration] PARTIES [decoration] | A Novel of Contem-
porary | New York Life | [decoration] | ALFRED A. KNOPF | London & [bor-
zoi] New York | 1930

286 pp., blank leaf. 18.9 X 12.3 cm.

[1-2] blank; [3] half-title; [4] blank; [5] title; [6] PRINTED IN THE
BRITISH ISLES | FOR ALFRED A. KNOPF LIMITED | BY THE STAR AND | GAZETTE
CO. LIMITED | GUERNSEY C.I.; [7] dedication; [8] blank; [9] introductory
quotation; [10] blank; 11-[285] text. [286] blank

Yellow cloth boards, printed in black and magenta, on front: drawing of
a cocktail glass and Pernod bottle; on spine: PARTIES [all but downstroke
of P in magenta] | [drawing of two lilies in a cocktail glass] | CARL |
VAN | VECHTEN [Van printed in outline only] KNOPF [printed in outline];
borzoi in black box on back. Magenta top edges. Cream dust jacket
printed in magenta, black, and turquoise, with an illustration of two
drunk — or hung-over — people, and a third person, passed-out, at their
feet. Advertising blurb on flyleaf by Van Vechten [F74d]

Published 1930; 7/6.

f. Reprint edition

Identical to A21a with the following exceptions: [iii] [decorations and
cupid printed in black] | [publisher's logo] BOOKS FOR LIBRARIES PRESS
| FREEPORT, NEW YORK [the foregoing printed below the border]; [iv] Re-
printed 1971 by arrangement with | Alfred A. Knopf, Inc.; [xi-xvi and
first blank leaf] deleted. 21.6 X 13.7 cm. Chartreuse cloth boards lettered down spine in gold: PARTIES . VAN VECHTEN [publisher's logo]

Published 1971; $11.00.

g. Paperback edition

PARTIES | SCENES FROM CONTEMPORARY | NEW YORK LIFE | CARL Van VECHTEN |
[publisher's logo] A BARD BOOK/PUBLISHED BY AVON BOOKS [the foregoing in
a one-line border]

224 pp. 17.8 X 10.5 cm.

[1] biographical note; [2] blank; [3] title; [4] Copyright history | First
Bard Printing, July, 1977; [5] dedication; [6] blank; [7] introductory
quotation; [8] blank; 9-221, text; [222] blank; [223-24] publisher's
catalog.

Stiff paper wrapper printed with full-color illustration of people in
evening dress watching fireworks; on front: A NOVEL ABOUT THE | DEATH OF
THE TWENTIES | PARTIES [in red] | Carl Van | Vechten [book number] 32631
[and price in upper right corner]; down spine: publisher, title [in red],
author, and identification numbers; on back: THE | SPLENDID | DRUNKEN |
TWENTIES | [advertising blurb | part of front illustration]

Published July 1977; $1.95

   The first draft of Parties consists of 176 leaves and is dated 13
   November 1929 — 15 March 1930. The second draft consists of 187
   leaves, titled "Theme and Variations," and is dated 13 February 1930
   — 25 March 1930. The third draft, from which type was set, consists
   of 218 leaves, including introductory material and bibliography, and
   is dated 22 April 1922. Ten leaves of notes preceded the first draft.
   Japanese and Russian translations of Parties are rumored to exist;
   correspondence regarding the former of these did occur, and Van Vechten approved of the venture. In his Columbia Oral History, Van Vechten averred that Truman Capote had told him, circa 1955, Parties was
   being read by "everyone" in Russia.

A 22   Sacred and Profane Memories   1932

a. First edition

SACRED AND PROFANE | MEMORIES | BY | CARL VAN VECHTEN | [drawing of a
sheaf of wheat] | NEW YORK | ALFRED . A . KNOPF | 1932 [the foregoing
in blue]

unreckoned leaf, xvi, 234, xxii pp., blank leaf, including divisional
titles; illustrations tipped-in. 19 X 13 cm.

⌊verso of unreckoned leaf⌋ THIS, THE FIRST EDITION | OF | <u>SACRED AND PRO-</u>
<u>FANE MEMORIES</u> | CONSISTS OF TWO THOUSAND COPIES | OF WHICH <u>THIS IS NUMBER</u>
⌈⌊number in ink⌋; ⌊i⌋ half-title; ⌊ii⌋ blank; ⌊iii⌋ title; ⌊iv⌋ Copyright
1918, 1920, 1921, 1925, 1930, 1932 by Carl Van Vechten | ⌊rights reserva-
tion⌋ | First Edition; ⌊v, dedication⌋ <u>For</u> | <u>Carrie and Florine Stetthei-</u>
<u>mer</u> | <u>and</u> | <u>Henrie Waste</u>; ⌊vi⌋ blank; vii-viii, Foreword; ⌊ix⌋ contents;
⌊x⌋ blank; ⌊xi⌋ illustrations; ⌊xii⌋ blank; ⌊xiii⌋ introductory quotation;
⌊xiv⌋ blank; ⌊xv⌋ divisional title; ⌊xvi⌋ blank; 1-230, text, including
divisional titles; ⌊231⌋ bibliography title; ⌊232⌋ blank; xvii-xx, bibliography; ⌊xxi⌋ blank; ⌊xxii⌋ colophon

Blue cloth boards with sheaf of wheat in blind on front; on spine, lettered
in silver: SACRED | and | PROFANE | MEMORIES | CARL | VAN VECHTEN | ALFRED
. A . KNOPF; borzoi in blind on back. Lower and fore edges rough trimmed,
blue top edges. Green, lavender, pink, and white dust jacket designed by
Prentiss Taylor, with an advertising blurb by Van Vechten on front flyleaf ⌊F80a⌋, and with squibs for <u>Nigger Heaven</u> by James Weldon Johnson
and <u>Spider Boy</u> by Gertrude Atherton on back flyleaf.

2,000 copies printed, of which 500 were reserved for an English edition;
1,500 published August 1932; $3.00.

Contents:
Foreword
The Tin Trunk ⌊D80, D82⌋
The Folksongs of Iowa ⌊A9⌋
Au Bal Musette ⌊A7⌋
How Mr. George Moore Rescued a Lady from Embarrassment ⌊D31⌋
An Interrupted Conversation ⌊A7, D35⌋
The Nightingale and the Peahen ⌊D33⌋
July — August 1914 ⌊D26⌋
The Holy Jumpers ⌊A9, A28⌋
La Tigresse ⌊A9, C18⌋
Feathers ⌊A20, C13, C19, C42, C45, C50⌋
A Note on Breakfasts ⌊D110⌋
Notes for an Autobiography ⌊C20, D129⌋
Bibliography

b. <u>English edition</u>

Identical to A22a with the following exceptions: ⌊iii⌋ title page printed
in black, and drawing of wheat sheaf deleted in favor of publisher's logo,
published and date deleted in favor of: CASSELL AND COMPANY LTD. | LONDON
. TORONTO . MELBOURNE . SIDNEY; ⌊iv⌋ copyright notice deleted; ⌊xxii⌋ colophon deleted. 18.9 X 12.8 cm.

Green cloth boards, with border in blind on front; printed in black on
spine: SACRED | AND | PROFANE | MEMORIES | CARL VAN | VECHTEN | CASSELL.
Yellow top edges. Gray dust jacket printed in red.

500 copies published 1932; 7/6.

c. <u>Reprint edition</u>

Identical to A22a with the following exceptions: ⌊iii⌋ title page printed
in black: <u>Essay Index Reprint Series</u> | ⌊publisher's logo⌋ BOOKS FOR LIBRAR-
IES PRESS ⌈ FREEPORT, NEW YORK ⌊in place of first publisher and date; ⌊iv⌋

publishing history and permission; [xxii] colophon deleted. 21.6 X 13.7
cm. Blue cloth boards; publisher's logo on front; title and author in
gold on red ground down spine with publisher's monogram in silver.

Published 1971; $15.00.

d. Second reprint edition

Identical to A22c with the following exceptions: [iii] [publisher's logo]
| GREENWOOD PRESS, PUBLISHERS | WESTPORT, CONNECTICUT [in place of first
reprint publisher]. 21.4 X 13.8 cm. Rust cloth boards lettered in black
down spine with author, title, and publisher's logo.

Published 1979; $18.75.

> The manuscript for Sacred and Profane Memories, retyped from published
> essays (save one), included "Once Aboard the Lugger San Guglielmo"
> [D26] as part of "July — August 1914." Van Vechten deleted most of
> it from the galley proofs. Early essays underwent extensive revision,
> too extensive, indeed, to account for them by page changes. "The Holy
> Jumpers" and "La Tigresse," in particular, are simply different essays
> in both form and content as well as in manner. The single draft, from
> which type was set, consists of 168 leaves and six preliminary leaves,
> and is dated 4 August 1931.

A23   Fragments From an Unwritten Autobiography   1955

Carl Van Vechten | FRAGMENTS | from an unwritten autobiography | VOLUME I
| New Haven: Yale University Library, 1955

xii, 66 pp., blank leaf. 16 X 10.8 cm.

[i-ii] blank; [iii] half-title; [iv] ". . .my autobiography, which Alfred
A. Knopf | will publish in two volumes in the fall of 1936." | PETER WHIF-
FLE (1922); [v] title; [vi] Copyright, 1955, by Carl Van Vechten; [vii]
reprint acknowledgment | They are here reprinted in honor of their author's
| seventy-fifth birthday, June 17, 1955; [viii] blank; [ix] contents, for
both volumes; [x] blank; [xi] illustrations, for both bolumes; 1-[65]
text, including divisional titles and illustrations. [Volume II is identical, with the following exceptions: II substituted for I on title page;
64 pp., deleting contents and list of illustrations.]

Red cloth boards lettered down spine in gold: VAN VECHTEN . VOLUME I [or
II]. Black cloth slipcase.

500 copies published June 1955; $5.00.

Contents:
How I Remember Joseph Hergesheimer [D142]
Mr. Cabell of Lichfield and Poictesme [D143]
Puss in Books [D144]
Random Notes on Mr. Mencken [D145]
Theodore Dreiser as I Knew Him [D146]
Some "Literary Ladies" I Have Known [D148]

A 24   With Formality and Elegance   1968

a. Regular edition

WITH FORMALITY | AND ELEGANCE | a selection | of inscriptions | to | Bruce
Kellner | from Carl Van Vechten | 1968

8 pp. 21.6 X 14 cm.

[1] title; [2] WITH FORMALITY AND ELEGANCE has been printed to celebrate
the pub- | lication of CARL VAN VECHTEN AND THE IRREVERENT DECADES by
Bruce | Kellner. | Set in sans serif Midcentury and Lydian Roman faces, by
The Village Printer, | Laurens, New York, during the summer of 1968, one
hundred twenty-six copies | have been made. | One hundred copies, printed
on Ticonderoga Text, are numbered 1 through | 100; twenty-six copies,
printed on Linweave Spectra and sewn into Japanese | woodcut wrappers,
are lettered A through Z. | This is copy ____ [number in red ink] | copy-
right 1968, Fania Marinoff Van Vechten; [3-8] text.

Handsewn into text stock wrapper and one of twelve Japanese block print
design papers or a gilt-flecked Chinese paper; on front, white label
printed in black: WITH FORMALITY | AND ELEGANCE | [rule] | CARL VAN VECH-
TEN [the foregoing in a one-line box]

100 copies issued July 1968, gratis.

b. Limited edition

Identical to A24a except as indicated on p. [2]. Handsewn into heavy
white deckle-edge wrapper and one of twenty-six Japanese woodcut papers,
all differing from those used for A24a; duplicate white label on front.

26 copies issued July 1968, gratis.

A 25   The Dance Writings of Carl Van Vechten   1975

The Dance Writings | of Carl Van Vechten | [rule] | Edited, and with an
Introduction by | PAUL PADGETTE | [publisher's logo] | DANCE HORIZONS .
NEW YORK

vi, 8 unnumbered leaves of photographs, xxii, 182 pp., 2 blank leaves.
20.2 X 12.8 cm.

[i] half-title; [ii] frontispiece; [iii] title; [iv] Copyright 1974 by
Paul Padgette; [v-vi] contents and list of illustrations; [16 photographs];
[vii-xxi] Acknowledgments and Introduction; [1]-182, text, including divisional titles and index.

Purple cloth boards; on front: Carl Van Vechten's bookplate, designed by
Prentiss Taylor, in blind; down spine, lettered in silver: The Dance
Writings of Carl Van Vechten [publisher's logo] PADGETTE. Blue endpapers.
Gray dust jacket printed in blue and purple, with Van Vechten's bookplate
on the front and a photograph of Paul Padgette by Van Vechten on the fly-
leaf.

2,000 copies published April 1975; $12.50.

Contents:
Terpsichorean Souvenirs [D158]
Interpretative Art [A10]
Ballet in New York [D135; EIV13]
Metropolitan Opera Ballet [D135; EII482]
Isadora Duncan [C33; EII373, 379, 591]
The New Isadora [A7; C33]
An Appreciation [C36]
Maud Allan [C36; EII406, 412]
Loie Fuller [C36; D135; EII386]
The Negro Theatre [A9; A28]
The Lindy Hop [A21; A28; D135]
Nassau Dancing [A17; A28; D95]
Eloquent Alvin Ailey [C51]
Choreography for Americans [EV46]
Belief in an Ideal [D149]
Terpsichore and the U.S. Army [D159]
Secrets of the Russian Ballet [A4; D153]
Waslav Nijinsky [A6; A10; C32]
Anna Pavlowa and Mikail Mordkin, 1910 [C34; D135; EII431, 432, 440, 526]
Anna Pavlowa [D102]
Swan Lake Ballet [D135; EII705]
Igor Strawinsky [A4]
Stage Decoration as a Fine Art [A4; D25; EIII52]
Queen of the Dance [D150]
Gardenias for Alicia [B33]
The Land of Joy [A7; D59; EIV47]
Spain and Music [A5; A8]
Léo Delibes [A17; D93]

   The bulk of this edition was destroyed in a Harrisburg, Pennsylvania,
   warehouse during a flood in the autumn of 1975. Only 370 copies had
   been distributed prior to the catastrophe.

A 26   [Photography]   1977

Carl Van Vechten [a facsimile signature] | Published by The Goodwin Gal-
lery in conjunction | with an exhibition of forty photographs by | Carl
Van Vechten. February 18, 1977 | First publication [the foregoing in
green]

2 leaves. 23.5 X 18.4 cm.

[1st leaf recto] title; [verso] blank; [2nd leaf recto] text, printed in
brown; [verso] Screen printed at the Goodwin Photographic, Westwood, |
New Jersey in an edition of one hundred from the | manuscript copy in the
collection of Bruce Kellner | and with the permission of Donald Gallup,
Literary | Trustee to Carl Van Vechten. [limitation note printed in green]

Cream Oilcrest laid paper fastened with a metal clip in upper left corner.

100 copies printed 18 February 1977, gratis.

[rule] | PORTRAITS | [rule] | THE PHOTOGRAPHY OF | [rule] | CARL VAN VECHTEN | [rule] | Compiled by | SAUL MAURIBER | The Bobbs-Merrill Company, Inc. | Indianapolis/New York

88 unnumbered leaves. 30.4 X 22.9 cm.

[1] half-title; [2] blank; [3] title; [4] Copyright 1978 by Saul Mauriber | rights reservations and publication data; [5] DEDICATION | To Carlo, | with | Cadenzas, | Calliopes, | Calico, | Canteloube, | Carnations, | Carnelians, | Casque d'Or, | Cassis, | Cashmere, | Caviar, | Cloisters, | Coins, | Cornucopias, | Cravats, | Crusades, | and Cuisine. | Con Amore | Saul; [6] blank; [7-8] Introduction by Natalie Hays Hammond; [9] half-title; [10] name of first subject; [11-72] portrait reproductions; [173-76] Subjects of Other Portraits by Carl Van Vechten.

Black cloth boards; half-title printed in blind on front; down spine in white: PORTRAITS THE PHOTOGRAPHY OF CARL VAN VECHTEN BOBBS- | MERRILL. Gray endpapers.   Glazed black dust jacket printed in white and gray on front and down spine; photograph of Van Vechten by Saul Mauriber, and an enlargement of impression stamp: PHOTOGRAPH BY | CARL VAN VECHTEN.

Published October 1978; $24.95 until 31 December, $29.95 thereafter.

Contents: Berenice Abbott, Alvin Ailey, Edward Albee, Judith Anderson, Marian Anderson, Sherwood Anderson, Henry Armstrong, Pearl Bailey, Josephine Baker, James Baldwin, Tallulah Bankhead, Jean-Louis Barrault and Madeleine Renaud, Ethel Barrymore, Cecil Beaton, Harry Belafonte, Thomas Hart Benton, Leonard Bernstein, Mary McLeod Bethune, the Baroness Karen Blixen [Isak Dinesen], Margaret Bourke-White, Marlon Brando, Dave Brubeck and Paul Desmond, Ralph Bunche, Alexander Calder, Cab Calloway, Truman Capote, Diahann Carroll, Henri Cartier-Bresson, Willa Cather, Marc Chagall, Carol Channing, Giorgio de Chirico, Jean Cocteau, George M. Cohan, Aaron Copland, Katharine Cornell, Salvador Dali, Alexandra Danilova, Jo Davidson, Ruby Dee, Agnes De Mille, Theodore Dreiser, W. E. B. Du Bois, Marcel Duchamp, Raoul Dufy, Katherine Dunham, Jacob Epstein, William Faulkner, Ella Fitzgerald, F. Scott Fitzgerald, Lynn Fontanne, Mary Garden, Ben Gazzara, George Gershwin, Althea Gibson, John Gielgud, Dizzy Gillespie, Lillian Gish, Martha Graham and Bertram Ross, Juanita Hall, Oscar Hammerstein II, Natalie Hays Hammond, William Christopher Handy, Julie Harris, Roland Hayes, Jascha Heifetz, Dame Myra Hess, Chester Himes, Al Hirschfeld, Geoffrey Holder, Billie Holiday, Lena Horne, Langston Hughes, Fannie Hurst, Burl Ives, Mahalia Jackson, Robinson Jeffers, Philip Johnson, James Earle Jones, Robert Earle Jones, Rockwell Kent, Lincoln Kirstein, Eartha Kitt, Alfred A. Knopf, Serge Koussevitsky, Charles Laughton, Canada Lee, Lotte Lenya, Leo Lerman, Sinclair Lewis, Joe Louis, Clare Boothe Luce, Mabel Dodge Luhan, Alfred Lunt, Aline MacMahon, Norman Mailer, Thomas Mann, Frederic March, Fania Marinoff, Alicia Markova, Mary Martin, Henri Matisse, W. Somerset Maugham, Saul Mauriber, Carson McCullers, Henry Louis Mencken, Mabel Mercer, Edna St. Vincent Millay, Henry Miller, Joan Miró, Grace Moore, Marianne Moore, Helen Morgan, Zero Mostel, Paul Muni, George Jean Nathan, Isamu Noguchi, Ramon Novarro, Clifford Odets, Georgia O'Keeffe, Laurence Olivier, Eugene O'Neill, Luigi Pirandello, Tyrone Power, Leontyne Price, Pearl Primus, Aileen Pringle, Luise Rainer, Ni Gusti Raka, May Ray, Diego Rivera, Jerome Robbins, Paul Robeson, Bill

Robinson, Artur Rubinstein, William Saroyan, Ravi Shankar, Beverly Sills,
Bessie Smith, Gertrude Stein, Frances Steloff, James Stewart, Alfred
Stieglitz, Laurette Taylor, Virgil Thomson, Alice B. Toklas, Gene Tunny,
Gloria Vanderbilt, Gore Vidal, Ethel Waters, Evelyn Waugh, Clifton Webb,
Orson Welles, Rebecca West, Walter White, Thornton Wilder, Roy Wilkins,
Tennessee Williams, Thomas Wolfe, Anna May Wong, Alexander Woollcott,
Richard Wright

A28   "Keep A-Inchin' Along"   1979

"KEEP A-INCHIN' ALONG | Selected Writings | of Carl Van Vechten | about
Black Art and Letters | Edited by | Bruce Kellner | Contributions in Af-
ro-American and African Studies, No. 45 | [publisher's logo] | Greenwood
Press, Westport, Connecticut . London, England

xiv, 304 pp., blank leaf. 23.5 X 15.3 cm.

[i] half-title; [ii] frontispiece; [iii] title; [iv] Copyright 1979 by
Bruce Kellner and the Estate of Carl Van Vechten, publication data and
reservation rights; [v, dedication] To the memory | of Fania Marinoff Van
Vechten | 1887-1971; [vi] blank; [vii] introductory quotations; [viii]
blank; [ix]-x, Contents; [xi]-xii, Illustrations; [xii]-xiv, Acknowledgments; [1] division title; [2] blank; [3]-15, Introduction; [16]-288,
text, including divisional titles and illustrations; [289]-300, index;
[301] note about the editor; [302] blank; [303] List of other titles in
series; [304] blank.

Rust cloth boards printed in black: title, sub-title, and editor on front
duplicating title page; on spine: Kellner | "Keep A-Inchin' | Along"
[title printed down rather than across] | [publisher's logo] | Greenwood.
Issued without dust jacket; see [F150]

Published May 1979; $16.95, later increased to $22.50.

Contents:
The Darktown Follies [EIII83]
The Negro Theatre [A9, D19, EIII83]
A Note on American Letters [EV19]
Prescription for the Negro Theatre [D115]
Folksongs of the American Negro [D109, D116, EV37]
The Black Blues [C49, D111, EV32, EV36]
"Moaning' Wid a Sword in Mah Han'" [D119]
Uncle Tom's Mansion [EV33]
The Negro in Art: How Shall He Be Portrayed? [D122]
A Belated Introduction to Nigger Heaven [A181]
Prologue to Nigger Heaven
My Friend: James Weldon Johnson [B14, B32, C21]
A James Weldon Johnson Memorial [D132, D133]
The James Weldon Johnson Memorial Collection of Negro Arts and Letters
   [C27, D134]
Walter White [EV34]
Countée Cullen [D108]
Langston Hughes [B13, D114, D121, EII856, EII857]
Zora Neale Hurston [D148]

W. C. Handy [EV47]
A'Lelia Walker
Paul Robeson and Lawrence Brown [D112]
Taylor Gordon [B15]
Bessie Smith [D120, D141]
Ethel Waters [D120, D131, EII854]
Clara Smith [D120]
Billie Holiday [D161]
Richmond Barthé [B19, B22]
Marian Anderson [C35]
Nora Holt
Josephine Baker
Henry Armstrong [D161]
Bricktop [D161]
Chester Himes
Alvin Ailey [C51]
George Walker [D158]
Bert Williams [D92, EIII88]
Nassau Out of Season [A17, A22]
The Lindy Hop [A21]
Twelve Endorsements [D137, EV53, F31, F62, F73, F88, F90, F91, F117, F118, F121, F146]
The Sabbath Glee Club of Richmond [D102]
An After-Dinner Speech for the James Weldon Johnson Literary Guild
Photographs of Celebrated Negroes [B21, B24]
Two Open Letters [D123, D126]
A Note for The Owl of Wadleigh High School [C26]
Inchin' Along [C11, D130]
Correspondence: letters to Walter White, James Weldon Johnson, Langston Hughes, Grace Nail Johnson, Claude McKay, Harold Jackman, Arna Bontemps, Chester Himes, Henry Van Dyke

Ex Libris: Carl Van Vechten's bookplate, design by Prentiss Taylor

THE TIGER IN THE HOUSE

By Carl Van Vechten

with 32 full page illustrations from photographs and drawings.
An Edition of 2000 numbered copies.

THE most complete book yet published relating to the domestic cat. It is not a breeder's manual or a cat fancier's guide. It is an urbane, informing, and amusing history of puss, his religion, his politics, his ethics, and his manners and habits. Incidentally the author makes no attempt to conceal his opinion that the feline race is superior to the human race. He discusses the cat's relation to folklore, law music, painting, the drama, poetry, and fiction and describes his occult powers in an informal and personal style. An elaborate, handsomely made volume, fully illustrated and includes the first bibliography yet published on the subject, carefully classified, and an index.

ALFRED A. KNOPF PUBLISHER, N. Y.

The Tiger in the House: "Minette Washes" by Gottfried Mind and blurb by Carl Van Vechten, suppressed box illustration [F12b]

The Blind Bow Boy: frontispiece and dust jacket illustration by Robert Locher [A13]

The Blind Bow Boy: drawing by Alastair [Hans Henning Voight] [B11]

The Tattooed Countess: dust jacket illustration by Ralph Barton [A14]

Nigger Heaven: advertising illustration by Aaron Douglas and blurb by Carl Van Vechten [50b]

Peter Whiffle: His Life and Works: illustrated edition binding map of Paris by Ralph Barton [A12i]

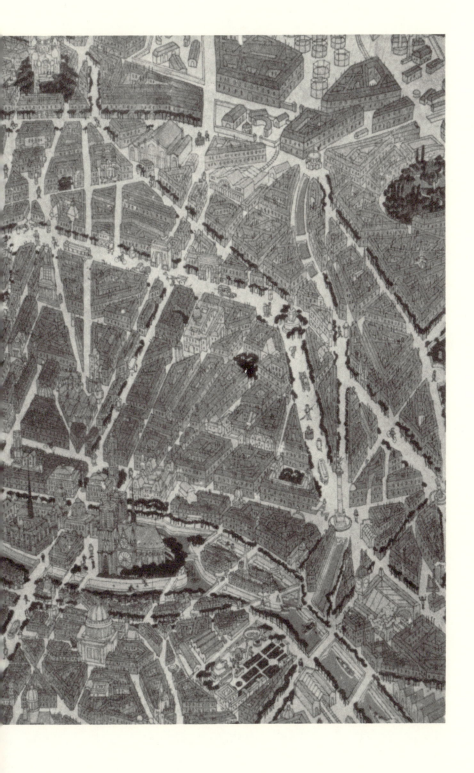

Spider Boy: dust jacket illustration by Ronald McRae [A19]

PARTIES

BY CARL VAN VECHTEN

PUBLICATION DATE · AUGUST 15

Exhausted by wars and peace conferences, worn out by prohibition and other dishonest devices of unscrupulous politicians, the younger generation, born and bred to respect nothing, make a valiant and heart-breaking attempt to enjoy themselves. $2.50

ALFRED·A·KNOPF

PUBLISHER · N·Y·

Parties: advertising illustration by Roese and blurb by Carl Van Vechten [F74]

Sacred and Profane Memories: dust jacket illustration by Prentiss Taylor [FA22]

SACRED
AND
PROFANE
MEMORIES

CARL
VAN VECHTEN

B.
BOOKS AND PAMPHLETS EDITED OR WITH INTRODUCTIONS

B 1   Sophie   1919

a. First edition

SOPHIE | A COMEDY | BY PHILIP MOELLER | WITH A PROLOGUE FOR THE READER BY
| CARL VAN VECHTEN | ". . . la seule courtisane de l'age | d'or des filles
Sophie Arnould." | De Goncourt. | ⌊borzoi in black oval⌋ | NEW YORK: AL-
FRED . A . KNOPF

[i-vi] vii-xx [1-2 unaccounted for] 3-246 pp. 19 X 13 cm.

Yellow paper boards with blue paper labels on front and on spine: SOPHIE
| by | Philip Moeller [in double-line borders]. Lower and fore edges
rough trimmed. Blue dust jacket printed in black.

Published 1919, $1.00.

Contains: A Prologue for the Reader, pp. vii-xx [A17]

b. Limited edition

Identical to Bla with the following exceptions: [ii, in place of a list
of plays by Moeller] OF THIS BOOK FIFTY COPIES HAVE BEEN PRINTED ON SAN
MARCO HAND-MADE PAPER AND AUTOGRAPHED BY THE AUTHOR. THIS IS NUMBER
[number in red ink | signature]

White paper boards with leaf and reindeer design silk-screened in light
blue; blue paper label only on spine. Edges untrimmed and unopened, top
edges painted gold. Glassine wrapper.

50 copies published 1919, $10.00.

> Moeller's dedication indicates that Van Vechten suggested Sophie Ar-
> nould as the subject for a play: "To Carl Van Vechten Who first gave
> me the key to Sophie's dressing room. . . ."

B 2   <u>A Letter Written in 1837 by Morgan Lewis Fitch</u>   1919

A LETTER | <u>Written in 1837 by</u> | MORGAN LEWIS FITCH | <u>With a Postscript by</u> | AMANDA ROBERTS FITCH | <u>Together with a Foreword</u> | by CHARLES LEWIS FITCH | <u>And an Introductory Note</u> | <u>By</u> CARL VAN VECHTEN | CHICAGO | PRIVATELY PRINTED | 1919

blank leaf [1-2] 3-10 [11] 12-13 [14-16] 17-27 [28] blank leaf.   19.1 X 13.5 cm.

Gray paper boards, with white paper label on front: A LETTER | <u>from</u> | MORGAN LEWIS FITCH [in a three-line box], and white paper label up spine: A LETTER [decoration] FITCH. Edges rough trimmed. Glassine wrapper.

200 copies printed November 1919, none for sale.

Contains: Introductory Note, pp. 11-13.

B 3   <u>Lords of the Housetops</u>   1921

a. <u>First edition</u>

LORDS | OF THE HOUSETOPS | THIRTEEN CAT TALES | [rule] | WITH A PREFACE BY | CARL VAN VECHTEN | <u>C'est l'esprit familier du lieu;</u> | <u>Il juge, il préside, il inspire</u> | <u>Toutes choses dans son empire;</u> | <u>Peut-être est-il fée, est-il dieu.</u> | CHARLES BAUDELAIRE | [borzoi in black oval] | NEW YORK   ALFRED . A . KNOPF   MCMXXI

[i-vi] vii-xiii [xiv-xviii] 1-238 pp.   19 X 13 cm.

Black cloth boards, printed in yellow and green to duplicate the binding of <u>Interpreters and Interpretations</u> [A6] by Claude Bragdon. Lower and fore edges rough trimmed, green top edges. Yellow dust jacket printed in brown, with Aubrey Beardsley's drawing for <u>The Black Cat</u> by Edgar Allan Poe and an advertising blurb by Van Vechten on the front [F13], and an advertising blurb for <u>The Tiger in the House</u> by Van Vechten on the back [F12e]

Published 28 July 1921, $2.50.

Contains: Preface, pp. ix-xiii, and a translation of "The Afflictions of an English Cat" by Honore de Balzac, pp. 103-23.

b. <u>Pocketbook edition</u>

LORDS OF | THE HOUSETOPS [in green] | THIRTEEN CAT TALES | WITH A PREFACE BY | CARL VAN VECHTEN | [Baudelaire quotation as in first edition | borzoi in black rectangle] | NEW YORK | ALFRED . A . KNOPF [in green] | 1930 [all the foregoing in a wide decorative border]

blank leaf [i-vi] vii-xiii [xiv-xviii] 1-238 [239-40] pp.   17.2 X 11 cm.

There are three bindings, identical in design, for this edition which was made from the plates for B3a: light green cloth boards printed in dark

green, with green decorative end-papers; tan cloth boards printed in brown
with tan decorative end-papers; blue cloth boards printed in silver, with
blue decorative end-papers. Decoration on front; on spine: [lower half of
front decoration] | Lords | of the | Housetops | [rule] | CARL | VAN VECH-
TEN | [upper half of front decoration, followed by quadruple rule] | Knopf;
borzoi in rectangle on back. Dust jackets in colors to match bindings.

Published 30 November 1930, $1.00.

    The pocketbook edition, printed from the plates of the first edition,
    carried four alterations: pp. xii, run/ran; 11, though/through; 111,
    Accompained/Accompanied; 116, congugal/conjugal. Other than the cus-
    tomary three drafts for the preface [D85 note], there is no manuscript
    for Lords of the Housetops. Van Vechten's translation for the Balzac
    story was no more than a revision to an unidentified, earlier English
    version, on the printed pages of which he made various stylistic al-
    terations.

B 4   Kittens   1922

Kittens: A Family Chronicle | Translated from the Danish of | Svend Fleu-
ron | by David Pritchard | Foreword by Carl Van Vechten | New York [borzoi
in black oval] Mcmxxii | Alfred . A . Knopf

[1-12] 13-19 [20] 21-248 pp. 18.7 X 12.6 cm.

Green cloth boards, printed in black on front and on spine; borzoi in
blind on back. Edges rough trimmed. Orange dust jacket printed in black
and white, with an advertising blurb on the back by Van Vecthen [F15].

Published January 1922, $2.00.

Contains: Foreword, pp. 13-19.

B 5   In a Winter City   1923

IN A | WINTER CITY | [rule] | BY "OUIDA" | [rule] | Introduction by | CARL
VAN VECHTEN | [rule| publisher's logo] | BONI AND LIVERIGHT | [rule] PUB-
LISHERS '. .' NEW YORK [the foregoing in a two-line border]

[i-iv] v-xxii [xxiii-iv] 1-253 [254-62] blank leaf. 16.5 X 10.5 cm.

Green, blue, or brown leatherette boards printed in gold, on front: pub-
lisher's logo; on spine: [double rule] | IN A | WINTER | CITY | [rule] |
OUIDA | MODERN | LIBRARY | [double rule]. Top edges stained to match bind-
ing. Pink and tan decorated end-papers.

Published 1923, $.95.

Contains: Introduction, pp. v-xxii. [Quoted in Hunter Stagg: "Novel of
Ouida is Republished," Richmond, Virginia, Times Dispatch, 14 October 1923;
Monica Stirling, The Fine and the Wicked, The Life and Times of Ouida,
1958, pp. 11, 118. A17.]

a. First edition

NIKOLAY ANDREYVICH RIMSKY-KORSAKOFF [in green] | MY MUSICAL LIFE | TRANS-
LATED FROM THE REVISED RUSSIAN EDITION BY | JUDAH A. JOFFEE | EDITED WITH
AN INTRODUCTION BY [in green] | CARL VAN VECHTEN [in green] | [green bor-
zoi] | New York ALFRED A. KNOPF Mcmvvix [all of the foregoing in a
three-line border]

[i-iv] v-xi [xii] xiii-xxiii [xxiv, 1-2] 3-389 [390] pp. blank leaf.
24 X 16 cm.

Black cloth boards, printed on front in red: RIMSKY-KORSAKOFF | MY MU-
SICAL LIFE [the beginning R in a blue box] | [small Viking ship and sail-
or printed in red, blue, orange, yellow, and gold on a sea of gold snow-
flakes and stars]; on spine: MY [three stars] | MUSICAL | LIFE [two
stars; lettering blue, stars gold] | RIMSKY- | KORSAKOFF [in red, sur-
rounded by gold stars] | ALFRED . A . KNOPF [in blue]; on back, gold
stars and snowflakes continue across center, borzoi in blind. Magenta
end-papers printed with black birds. Lower and fore edges rough trimmed,
blue top edges. Issued in a gray paper box with yellow paste-down title.

2,000 copies printed; 1,980 copies bound, as above, October 1923, $6.00.

Contains: Introduction, pp. xxi-xxiii, and notes.

b. Second printing

Identical to B6a, but yellow paste-down label on the box carried reviewer's squibs.

1,100 copies printed; 600 issued March 1924.

> Van Vechten made corrections to minor errors on pp. xv, xvi, xx, xxi,
> xxiii, 3, 5, 10, 12, 16, 22, 26, 27, 38, 40, 44, 50, 54, 55, 56, 57,
> 61, 67, 68, 69, 70, 71, 72, 78, 79, 80, 83, 86, 88, 93, 97, 101, 104,
> 112, 113, 115, 117, 124, 128, 133, 136, 141, 142, 143, 150, 158, 159,
> 163, 173, 175, 176, 177, 178, 185, 188, 189, 190, 199, 200, 203, 204,
> 207, 209, 210, 211, 214, 216, 123, 228, 230, 231, 232, 240, 241, 243,
> 246, 247, 248, 250, 253, 254, 258, 259, 262, 264, 265, 267, 269, 270,
> 271, 275, 276, 277, 278, 279, 280, 283, 289, 290, 291, 293, 295, 296,
> 297, 298, 306, 307, 308, 309, 310, 311, 315, 316, 319, 320, 221, 334,
> 335, 336, 341, 343, 344, 346, 352, 354, 359, 360, 365, 367, 375, 376,
> 377, 378, 379, 380, 381, 382, 383, 384, 385, 387, 388, 389.

c. English edition

N. A. RIMSKY-KORSAKOFF | [rule] | MY MUSICAL LIFE | TRANSLATED FROM THE |
RUSSIAN BY J. A. JOFFE | AND EDITED WITH AN INTRODUCTION BY | CARL VAN
VECHTEN | 1924 | [rule] LONDON: MARTIN SECKER

Black cloth boards, printed in white, on front to duplicate author and
title from title page, in a white border; on spine: [rule] MY | MUSICAL
| LIFE | [rule] | RIMSKY- | KORSAKOFF | SECKER | [rule]. Gray-blue dust
jacket. Lower and fore edges rough trimmed, blue top edges.

The English edition was made from imported American signatures. According to Knopf's printing records, cancels were placed in 600 copies, but only 520 were shipped to Martin Secker, of which 500 were
of the corrected second printing and of which the remaining 20 were
of the first edition. This created, in effect, two separate versions
within a single "edition."

d. Third and fourth printings

Identical to B6b. Third printing of 500 copies issued 1925. Fourth
printing of 500 copies issued 1928.

e. Reprint edition; first, second, and third printings

Identical to B6b with the following exceptions: [iii, in place of publisher's name] TUDOR PUB. Co.; title page printed entirely in black; [iv]
New Edition, 1935. 24.1 X 16.9 cm.

Blue cloth boards lettered in gold on front and spine. Lower and fore
edges rough trimmed, blue top edges. Dust jacket printed in red, blue,
green, and white, with a Russian-style illustration.

Published December 1935; second printing issued January 1936; third printing issued October 1936, $4.00.

> Although listed as a "new edition," this Tudor issue was printed from
> the plates, as corrected by Van Vechten, for the second Knopf print-
> ing.

f. Revised edition

Nikolay Andreyevich | RIMSKY- KORSAKOV | My musical | Life [title spread
across two pages, facing each other, decorative branches through M and
downstroke of f] | TRANSLATED FROM THE FIFTH REVISED | RUSSIAN EDITION BY
CARL VAN VECHTEN | [borzoi in oval] | NEW YORK . ALFRED . A . KNOPF .
MCMXLII

Blank leaf [i-iv] v [vi-xii] xiii-xxiii [xxiv] xxv-xliv [1-2] 3-480, i-
xxi [xxic] pp. 23.7 X 16 cm.

Dark blue cloth boards, designed in partial imitation of the first binding, on front: ship and sailor on sea of stars and snowflakes; on spine:
RIMSKY-KORSAKOV [in blue] | My | Musical | Life [in gold] | AlfredAKnopf
[in blue]; blue borzoi in circle and continuation of stars and snowflakes
on back. Lower and fore edges rough trimmed, gray top edges. Gray end-
papers printed with blue birds. Red, white, blue, gold, and aqua dust
jacket with "golden cockerel" design, also binding, by Boris Artzybasheff.

2,280 copies printed; 1,800 copies bound, as above; published January
1942, $6.00.

g. Revised edition, second binding

Identical to B6f, but bound in dark green cloth boards. 982 copies issued September 1944.

h. Revised edition, second printing

Identical to B6f, but bound in blue-green cloth boards, with blue top
edges. 1,500 copies published October 1947.

> At the time of the first printing of the revised edition, the London
> firm, Secker and Warburg, contracted for 500 copies of the next print-
> ing, for which Knopf planned to prepare a cancel. At the time of the
> second printing, however, Secker and Warburg took about 500 copies
> with Knopf's own imprint.

i. Revised reprint edition

Identical to B6f with the following exceptions: [iii, in place of publisher's name] Vienna House; blue cloth boards lettered in gold; red end-
papers; all edges trimmed; issued without dust jacket. Published 1972,
$30.00, later increased to $40.00.

j. English revised reprint edition

Identical to B6f, with the following exceptions: [iii, in place of publisher's name] Eulenberg Books London. Ernest Eulenberg Ltd; green cloth
boards lettered in black and gold; all edges trimmed; yellow dust jacket
printed in black. Published 1974.

> The manuscript for Van Vechten's introduction to My Musical Life, one
> of the few manuscripts he did not deposit with his collections in the
> New York Public Library and Yale, is in the Blanche and Alfred Knopf
> Collection in the Humanities Research Center of the University of
> Texas. Of ten leaves, it is dated 5 April 1922.

B 7   Prancing Nigger   1924

a. First edition

PRANCING NIGGER | BY | RONALD FIRBANK | WITH AN INTRODUCTION BY | CARL
VAN VECHTEN | [orange publisher's logo in blind frame] | NEW YORK | BREN-
TANO'S | PUBLISHERS

blank leaf [i-iv] v-xi [xii, 1-2] 3-126. Illustration tipped-in facing
[iii]. 18.8 X 12.4 cm.

Black cloth boards, lettered in gold, on front: PRANCING NIGGER; on spine:
PRANCING | NIGGER | RONALD | FIRBANK | BRENTANO'S. Lower and fore edges
rough trimmed, green top edges. White dust jacket printed in black and
orange, with a reproduction of the frontispiece, by Robert E. Locher, in
lavender half-tone.

300 copies published March 1924, $2.00.

Contains: An Icing for a Chocolate Éclair, pp. v-xi [A17, C58]

b. Second printing

Identical to B7a. Issued April 1924.

B8   A Bibliography of the Writings of Carl Van Vechten   1924

a. First edition

A Bibliography | of the Writings of | Carl Van Vechten [in green] | By |
Scott Cunningham | With an Overture in the form of a funeral march | by
Carl Van Vechten | [centaur logo in green] | PHILADELPHIA | THE CENTAUR
BOOK SHOP [in green] | 1924

3 leaves [1-5] 6-9 [10-11] 12 [13] 14-52 [53-62] 2 leaves. Photograph
tipped-in facing [13]. 19.4 X 12.2 cm.

[53] THIS IS NUMBER [number in ink] OF THREE HUN- | DRED NUMBERED COPIES
| THE FIFTH OF THE CENTAUR BIBLIO- | GRAPHIES DONE BY THE BOOKFELLOWS AT
| THE TORCH PRESS, CEDAR RAPIDS, IOWA, | PUBLISHED BY THE CENTAUR BOOK-
SHOP, | PHILADELPHIA | Uniform with this Volume | Joseph Hergesheimer |
Stephen Crane | James Branch Cabell | H.L. Mencken.

Green paper boards with silver labels, on front: A Bibliography of the |
Writings of | CARL VAN VECHTEN | By | SCOTT CUNNINGHAM [the foregoing in
a decorative border]; up spine: BIBLIOGRAPHY CARL VAN VECHTEN. Lower and
fore edges untrimmed. Glassine wrapper.

300 copies published Autumn 1924, $3.50.

Contains: An Overture in the Form of a Funeral March, pp. 5-7. [Quoted
in "Bibliography of Work of Van Vechten is Published," Galveston (Texas)
News, 25 January 1925.]

b. Limited edition

Identical to B8a with the following exceptions: [4] THIS IS NUMBER [num-
ber in ink] OF THE LARGE PAPER EDITION LIMITED TO EIGHTY-FIVE | COPIES,
SEVENTY-FIVE OF WHICH ARE FOR | SALE | [signature]; [53] limitation note
abbreviated to the statement regarding Centaur Bibliographies. 23.8 X
16 cm.

Silver marbled paper boards in either yellow, green, and brown, or pink,
chartreuse, and black, with silver labels. Spider-web patterned glassine
wrapper.

85 copies published Autumn 1924, $10.00.

c. First reprint edition

Identical to B8a with the following exceptions: [iii] Folcroft Library
Editions | 1972.

Cloth boards in various colors, six to eight each; all edges trimmed; no
wrapper.

100 copies published 1972, $15.00.

This library reprint edition was bound, a few volumes at a time, de-
pending on the demand, between 1972 and 1977, at which time its ex-
haustion led to B8d, also issued by Folcroft.

d. Second reprint edition

Identical to B8c with the following exceptions: [iii] Norwood Editions
| 1978

Light blue cloth boards lettered in gold.

100 copies printed 1978; 6 copies bound as above, $15.00.

B 9   The Lord of the Sea   1924

a. First edition

THE LORD OF THE SEA | BY M. P. SHIEL [in blue] | WITH AN INTRODUCTION BY
| CARL VAN VECHTEN | [blue borzoi] | NEW YORK ALFRED . A . KNOPF MCMXXIV
[all of the foregoing in a decorative border]

[i-iv] v-xvii [xviii-xx, 1-2] 3-299 [300]. 18.8 X 12.8 cm.

Mauve cloth boards printed in blue, on front: [decorative rule] | The
Lord of the Sea; on spine: [decorative rule] | The Lord | of the | Sea |
M. P. Shiel | Alfred A. Knopf; borzoi in blind on back. Lower and fore
edges rough trimmed, blue top edges. Red and black dust jacket, with a
quotation from Van Vechten's introduction [F30a]

Published September 1924, $2.50.

Contains: A Prolegomenon to be read, if ever, only after you have read
The Lord of the Sea. [A17; F30]

b. Limited edition

Twenty tall paper copies were issued simultaneously with the first edition, signed by Van Vechten, but without any limitation note. They were
identical to B9a with the following exceptions: edges untrimmed and unopened, top edges lightly stained. 19.4 X 13.

c. Pocket book edition

THE LORD | OF THE SEA [the foregoing in green] | M. P. SHIEL | With an
Introduction by | CARL VAN VECHTEN | [borzoi in black rectangle] | NEW
YORK | ALFRED . A . KNOPF [in green] | 1929 [all of the foregoing in the
customary Knopf Pocket Book decorative border]

With the following exceptions, this edition is identical to B9a: [ii]
the customary Borzoi Pocket Book advertisement, as in A13h; [iii] title
as above. 17.2 X 11.2 cm.

Blue cloth boards printed in either black or silver to duplicate the customary Knopf Pocket Book designs, as in A13h or B3b. Edges trimmed. Blue
and white dust jacket.

Published August 1929, $1.00.

d. Paperback edition

THE LORD | OF THE SEA | M. P. SHIEL | With an Introduction by | CARL VAN
VECHTEN | THE XANADU LIBRARY | CROWN PUBLISHERS, INC. | New York [the
foregoing printed in the Knopf decorative border of the pocketbook edition, identical except for publishers' names]

With the following exceptions, identical to B9c: [ii] blank; [iii] title
as above; [iv] publication history deleted. 18.4 X 12.3 cm.

Stiff white wrappers, printed in black, gray, and two shades of blue, on
front: [decorative rule] THE XANADU LIBRARY [decorative rule] | m. p.
shiel [in blue] | LORD OF THE SEA | [illustration filling remainder of
the cover]; on spine: THE | XANADU | LIBRARY [in blue] | shiel | [down
spine] LORD OF THE SEA [in white on black]; advertisements on back. All
edges trimmed.

Published circa 1960, $1.45.

B 10   Paul Robeson and Lawrence Brown   1925

PAUL ROBESON | and | LAWRENCE BROWN | IN A PROGRAM of NEGRO MUSIC | [dec-
oration] | GREENWICH VILLAGE THEATRE | Sunday Evening, May 3, 1925 | 8:40
P.M. | [decoration] | PROGRAM | [list of selections] | [rule] | [untitled
note]

1 cream leaf. 30.4 X 15.2 cm.

Issued 3 May 1925, gratis.

Contains: untitled note about Robeson and Brown [A28]

B 11   Fifty Drawings by Alastair   1925

FIFTY DRAWINGS | BY ALASTAIR | With an Introduction by | CARL VAN VECHTEN
| [borzoi in lined oval] | NEW YORK . ALFRED . A . KNOPF | MCMXXV [the
foregoing in a decorative scroll border]

54 leaves, tissues tipped-in to cover plates. 32 X 25.5 cm.

[2] Of this book 1,025 copies | of which 975 are for sale | have been
printed on Van Gelder paper | under the direction of | Harold Curwen at
the Curwen Press | London | The Collotype plates are by | Charles Whit-
tingham | & Griggs, Ltd | London

Gold dotted black paper boards; black quarter cloth printed in gold down
spine: FIFTY DRAWINGS by ALASTAIR. Lower and fore edges untrimmed, top
edges painted gold. Glassine wrapper. Purple and silver paper-covered
box with white label printed in purple.

1,025 copies published September 1925, $15.00.

Contains: Introduction, recto and verso of fourth leaf [F35]

B 12   <u>The Prince of Wales and Other Famous Americans</u>   1925

THE PRINCE OF WALES | AND OTHER FAMOUS AMERICANS | BY MIGUEL COVARRUBIAS | WITH A PREFACE BY | CARL VAN VECHTEN | [borzoi on double rule] | NEW YORK . ALFRED . A . KNOPF . MCMXXV

62 leaves. 23 X 17.5 cm.

Magenta, blue, yellow, and brown or red and green batik paper boards; yellow quarter cloth printed in green down spine: THE PRINCE OF WALES <u>and</u> <u>other famous Americans</u> [decoration] Covarrubias. Yellow dust jacket printed in red and black.

Published October 1925, $3.00.

Contains: Preface, recto and verso of 3rd and 4th leaves [H147]

B 13   <u>The Weary Blues</u>   1926

a. <u>First edition</u>

THE WEARY BLUES | by | LANGSTON HUGHES | <u>WITH AN INTRODUCTION BY</u> | <u>CARL</u> <u>VAN VECHTEN</u> | [borzoi in lined oval] | NEW YORK | ALFRED . A . KNOPF | 1926

[1-8] 9-13 [14] 15-17 [18-22] 23-109 [110]. 18.9 X 13 cm.

White and orange batik paper boards; blue quarter cloth lettered in gold down spine: T | H | E | W | E | A | R | Y | B | L | U | E | S | [decoration] | L | A | N | G | S | T | O | N | H | U | G | H | E | S. Lower and fore edges rough trimmed, blue-green top edges. Red, black, and yellow dust jacket with a Covarrubias illustration on the front and a quotation from Van Vechten's introduction on the back [F42].

Published January 1926, $2.00.

Contains: Introducting Langston Hughes to the Reader, pp. 9-13 [A28].

b. <u>Second through fourth printings</u>

Identical to B13a with the following exceptions: [4] Published January 1926 | Second Printing, February 1926 | Third Printing, October 1926 | Fourth Printing, April 1927

c. <u>Fifth printing, second binding</u>

Identical to B13b with the following exceptions: [4] Fifth Printing, January 1929; [2] reviewer's quotation.

Green cloth boards, lettered in gold down right front and down spine to duplicate spine lettering of the first binding. Borzoi in blind on back. Yellow top edges.

Published January 1929, $1.00.

d. Microfilm edition

Books on Demand, University Microfilms, Ann Arbor, Michigan, AT1-OP39290, 1978, $13.20.

B 14   The Autobiography of an Ex-Coloured Man   1927

a. First Knopf edition

THE | AUTOBIOGRAPHY | OF AN | EX-COLOURED MAN | JAMES WELDON JOHNSON | With an Introduction by | CARL VAN VECHTEN | [borzoi in decorative border] | NEW YORK AND LONDON | ALFRED . A . KNOPF | 1927 [the foregoing in a wide decorative border, the title in brown]

[i-v] vi-x [xi] xii [1-3] 4-211 [212] pp.   20.6 X 13.8 cm.

Orange cloth boards; black quarter cloth spine lettered in gold. On the front: BLUE JADE LIBRARY [in decorative border, in blind]; on spine: THE | AUTOBIOGRAPHY | of an | EX-COLOURED MAN | [rule | decoration] | KNOPF. Lower and fore edges rough trimmed, green top edges. Brown and white decorative end-papers. Orange, gray, black, and white dust jacket.

Published September 1927, $3.00.

Contains: Introduction to Mr. Knopf's New Edition, pp. v-x [A28].

b. Reprint edition

Identical to B14a with the following exceptions: [iii] title page entirely in black, minus "London" and substituting new date; [iv] publication history; [x] note by Alfred A. Knopf appended to Van Vechten's introduction.

Black cloth boards lettered in gold on spine: [decorative rule] | THE | AUTOBI- | OGRAPHY | OF AN EX- | COLOURED | MAN | JOHNSON | [decorative rule] | Knopf; borzoi in blind on back. Gray top edges. Red, white, and black dust jacket.

Published December 1970, $4.25.

> According to a dust jacket note, this is "a reprint of the third Borzoi edition." Apparently there were eight impressions of the Blue Jade Library edition. Knopf reprinted it as an Albabook in 1937, lacking Van Vechten's introduction. He explains in his note that the introduction was written for the "first reissue" of the 1912 edition.

B 15   Born to Be   1929

a. First edition

BORN TO BE | BY | TAYLOR GORDON | With an Introduction by Muriel Draper | a Foreword by Carl Van Vechten | and Illustrations by | Covarrubias [decoration] | NEW YORK | COVICI-FRIEDE . PUBLISHERS | 1929 [i-iv] v-vii [viii] ix-xvi [xvii-xviii, 1-2] 3-236, blank leaf.   20.6 X 14 cm.

Brown cloth boards lettered in orange, on front: BORN TO BE; on spine: BORN | TO | BE | TAYLOR | GORDON | [decoration] | COVICI | . | FRIEDE. Lower and fore edges rough trimmed, orange top edges. Cream dust jacket printed in black, rust, and brown, with a drawing by Covarrubias.

Published September 1929, $4.00.

Contains: Foreword, pp. v-vii [A28].

b. Second printing

Identical to B15a with the following addition: tipped-in leaf facing p. [iv] with a dedication to Van Vechten, verso blank.

c. Paperback edition

Identical to B15b with the following exceptions: [iii] New Introduction by Robert Hemenway | UNIVERSITY OF WASHINGTON PRESS | Seattle and London [replacing original publisher and date]; [iv] publication history; vii, list of photographs; INTRODUCTION TO THE 1975 EDITION, pp. ix-xliv; IN-TRODUCTION TO THE ORIGINAL EDITION, pp. xlv-xlvii. Color illustration facing p. [iii] deleted; tipped-in dedication deleted.

Stiff paper wrappers printed in black and white, with half-tone illustra-tion from p. 208 on the front: TAYLOR GORDON | BORN TO BE | With a New Introduction by Robert Hemenway | Illustrations by Covarrubias | [illus-tration] | Washington Paperbacks WP-78 $4.95; on spine: WP-78 | [down spine] GORDON BORN TO BE WASHINGTON; advertising blurb on back. Edges trimmed.

Published 1975, $4.95.

Contains: Introduction to the Original Edition, pp. xlv-xlvii [A28].

   One of Van Vechten's photographs of Taylor Gordon is included, facing
   p. 128. A photograph of Gordon, falsely attributed to Van Vechten,
   is included facing p. 5 of the photographic section.

B 16   Portraits by Robert Chanler   1929

[cover title] VALENTINE GALLERY | 43 East 57th Street | [double rule] | PORTRAITS BY | ROBERT CHANLER

4 leaves. 16.9 X 13.5 cm.

Two sheets, folded and stapled to make four leaves, issued in an envelope with the gallery's name as a return address.

Printed circa November 1929, gratis.

Contains: untitled essay about Robert Chanler, second leaf.

B17   Three Lives   1933

a. First Modern Library edition

THREE LIVES | [rule] | BY | GERTRUDE STEIN | [rule] | INTRODUCTION BY |
CARL VAN VECHTEN | [rule | publisher's logo | rule] | BENNETT A. CERF .
DONALD S. KLOPFER | THE MODERN LIBRARY | NEW YORK [the foregoing in a two
line border]

[i-iv] v-xi [xii, 1-4 missing, 5-10] 11-279 [280] pp. 16.7 X 10.6 cm.

Green, brown, or red flexible cloth boards printed in gold, on front:
publisher's logo within blind border; on spine: THREE | LIVES | [rule] |
STEIN | [decoration] | MODERN | LIBRARY. Top edges stained to match the
bindings. Orange decorative end-papers. White dust jacket printed in
two shades of blue.

5,000 copies published 11 March 1933, $.95.

Contains: Introduction, pp. v-xi.

b. New Classics edition

THREE LIVES | BY GERTRUDE STEIN | INTRODUCTION BY CARL VAN VECHTEN | THE
NEW CLASSICS | NEW DIRECTIONS | NORFOLK, CONNECTICUT

Paging identical to B17a. 17.7 X 12 cm.

Red cloth boards lettered in black on spine: THREE | LIVES. White dust
jacket printed in black and yellow.

2,500 copies published 1941, $1.00.

c. New Classics edition, second binding

Identical to B17b, with the following exceptions: blue cloth boards lettered in black down spine: THREE LIVES. White dust jacket printed in
green and black. Price increased to $1.50.

B 18   Four Saints in Three Acts   1934

Gertrude Stein | FOUR SAINTS | IN | THREE ACTS | AN OPERA TO BE SUNG |
INTRODUCTION BY CARL VAN VECHTEN | NEW YORK . RANDOM HOUSE | 1934

[1-4] 5-12 [13-14] 15-57 [58] pp., 3 blank leaves. 22.5 X 15 cm.

Black cloth boards lettered in gold down spine: GERTRUDE STEIN Four
Saints in Three Acts RANDOM HOUSE. Cream dust jacket printed in red and
black.

4,000 copies published 20 February 1934.

Contains: A Few Notes About Four Saints in Three Acts [C16]

B 19   Richmond Barthé [I]   1939

EXHIBITION OF | SCULPTURE | BY | RICHMOND BARTHÉ | March 8 through April
1 | ARDEN GALLERY | 460 PARK AVENUE. NEW YORK

six leaves. 23. 5 X 15.5 cm.

Rust paper wrapper, printed in black with name and address of the gallery,
stapled to folded sheets.

Printed circa March 1939, gratis.

Contains: Concerning Richmond Barthé, on versos of second and third
leaves [A28]

B20   Selected Writings of Gertrude Stein   1946

a. First edition

[publisher's logo on a blue rectangle] | SELECTED WRITINGS OF | Gertrude
Stein [in blue] | EDITED, WITH AN INTRODUCTION AND NOTES | by Carl Van
Vechten | RANDOM HOUSE . NEW YORK | [blue rectangle]

[i-iv] v-vii [viii] ix-xv [xvi, 1-2] 3-622 pp., blank leaf. 22 X 19.6 cm.

Tan cloth boards printed on spine: [blue publisher's logo | gold band |
in blue rectangle, lettered in gold] SELECTED | WRITINGS | OF | GERTRUDE
| STEIN | EDITED BY | CARL VAN | VECHTEN | [gold band | RANDOM HOUSE [in
blue]. Blue top edges. Cream dust jacket printed in blue and black with
a photograph of Gertrude Stein by Van Vechten on the back.

10,000 copies published 21 October 1946, $3.50.

Contains: A Stein Song, pp. ix-xv, and notes, pp. xvi, 2, 210, 228, 288,
298, 406, 464, 470, 480, 484, 488, 496, 504, 510, 542, 566.

b. First Modern Library edition

SELECTED WRITINGS | OF GERTRUDE STEIN | Edited, with an Introduction and
Notes, by | CARL VAN VECHTEN | and with an Essay on Gertrude Stein by |
F. W. DUPEE | [publisher's logo] | THE MODERN LIBRARY NEW YORK

[i-v] vi [vii-ix] x-xvii [xviii] ixx-xxv [xxvi, 1-3] 4-708, blank leaf.
18.5 X 12.7 cm.

Gray cloth boards lettered in gold on black rectangle, on front: SELECTED
| WRITINGS | OF | GERTRUDE | STEIN [in gold border with publisher's logo
in lower right corner]; on spine: [publisher's logo] | SELECTED | WRIT-
INGS | OF | GERTRUDE | STEIN | [decoration] | EDITED BY | Carl Van Vechten
| [decoration] | MODERN | LIBRARY. Blue top edges. Gray and white pat-
terned end-papers. White dust jacket printed in yellow and pink, with a
half-tone photograph of Gertrude Stein on the front.

7,500 copies published 1962, $1.95.

Contains: A Stein Song, pp. xviii-xxv, and notes, pp. 2, 240, 260, 328, 338, 460, 532, 542, 548, 554, 562, 570, 578-79, 640.

c. Paperback edition

Identical to B20b with the following exception: [iii] [publisher's logo] | VINTAGE BOOKS | A Division of Random House, New York. 18.4 X 10.8 cm.

Stiff white wrapper printed in black with Picasso's portrait of Stein on front; printed in black on front and down spine: SELECTED WRITINGS OF | GERTRUDE STEIN | Edited by Carl Van Vechten, with an Essay by F. W. Dupee

7,500 copies published 5 May 1972, $2.95.

B 21   American Negro Exhibit   1946

AMERICAN NEGRO EXHIBIT | Syracuse University Library | December 1946 | [3 dots] | Sponsored by | Syracuse University Library | Local Chapter N.A.A. C.P. | Sociological Department, Syracuse University | College of Fine Arts, Syracuse University

Five mimeographed leaves, stapled. 28 X 21.5 cm. Issued December 1946, gratis.

Contains: A Note by Carl Van Vechten, recto of first leaf [A28].

B 22   Richmond Barthé [II]   1947

BARTHÉ | February 17 - March 1, 1947 | GRAND CENTRAL GALLERIES, Inc. | Branch — 55 East 57th Street, New York

Yellow leaf, french-folded to make [1-4] pp., 16.5 X 11.5 cm., in matching envelope, both printed in brown, circa February 1947, gratis.

Contains: Foreword, p. [2] [A28].

B 23   A First List of Books   1948

A First List of books | printed and published | by The Banyan Press | [rule] | with a foreword by Carl Van Vechten

[1-8] pp. 16.5 X 11 cm.

Rose paper wrapper; title, as above, printed on front; on back: 2000 COPIES OF A First List WERE PRINTED AT | THE BANYAN PRESS ON ETRURIA IN JULY 1948. Folded leaves sewn in. Gratis.

Contains: Overture to a List of Books, pp. [1-2].

B 24   Jerome Bowers Peterson Memorial Collection   1949

Jerome Bowers Peterson | Memorial Collection | of Photographs of Celebrated Negroes | by | CARL VAN VECHTEN | [drawing] | MUSIC AND ART SALON FEBRU- ARY 1949 | Room 101 | Wadleigh High School | 114 Street, west of Seventh Avenue | New York City

2 leaves [1] 2-21 pp. 28 X 21.5 cm. Mimeographed yellow title leaf and mimeographed text by Dorothy Peterson, stapled. Issued February 1949, gratis.

Contains: Foreword, recto of second leaf [A28].

B 25   Last Operas and Plays   1949

a. First edition

LAST OPERAS AND PLAYS | [decorative rule] | BY GERTRUDE STEIN | EDITED AND WITH AN INTRODUCTION BY | CARL VAN VECHTEN | RINEHART & CO., INC. [decora- tion] NEW YORK, TORONTO

[i-vi] vii-xix [xx, 1-2] 3-480, blank leaf. Frontispiece photograph of Stein by Van Vechten tipped-in facing [iii]. 21.6 X 14 cm.

Orange paper boards printed on spine in gold and black: GERTRUDE | STEIN | LAST | [decorative rule] | OPERAS | [decorative rule] | AND | [decora- tive rule] | PLAYS [each word of the title in a separate black rectangle] | EDITED | BY | CARL | VAN | VECHTEN | RINEHART. White dust jacket print- ed in orange and black, with frontispiece photograph on back.

Published February 1949, $5.00.

Contains: "How Many Acts Are There In It?", pp. vii-xix.

b. Paperback edition

Identical to B25a with the following exceptions: [iii] VINTAGE BOOKS [and publisher's logo on title page]; no frontispiece. Stiff paper wrap- per with color illustration of Hommage à Gertrude by Picasso on front co- ver; title and author in black on spine. 20.1 X 13.4 cm.

Published 1975, $3.95.

B 26   Two   1951

a. First edition

TWO | Gertrude Stein | and Her Brother | AND OTHER EARLY PORTRAITS | (1908- 12) | BY GERTRUDE STEIN | with a foreword by Janet Flanner | NEW HAVEN : YALE UNIVERSITY PRESS | London . Geoffrey Cumberlege . Oxford University Press | 1951

Blank leaf "i-viii] ix-xvii [xviii] 1-355 [356] pp.   23.6 X 15.3 cm.

Black cloth boards printed front and back with blue dots and circles;
down spine in red: GERTRUDE STEIN TWO AND OTHER EARLY PORTRAITS YALE.
Gray, white, and chartreuse dust jacket.

2,000 copies published September 1951, $5.00.

Contains: Note, p. v.

b. Reprint edition

Identical to B26a, with the following exceptions: [iii] Select Biblio-
graphies Reprint Series | [publisher's logo] | BOOKS FOR LIBRARIES PRESS
| FREEPORT, NEW YORK [in place of corresponding information]; blank leaf
at end instead of beginning. 22.2 X 14.6 cm. Red cloth boards lettered
in black down spine: TWO STEIN.

400 copies published December 1969, $16.50.

B 27   Autobiographie von Alice B. Toklas   1955

GERTRUDE STEIN | AUTOBIOGRAPHIE VON | ALICE B. TOKLAS | ORIGO VERLAG
ZÜRICH

[1-6] 7-296, blank leaf. Illustrations tipped-in. 21.6 X 14 cm.

Orange cloth boards lettered in white, on front: GERTRUDE STEIN; up
spine: STEIN . AUTOBIOGRAPHIE TOKLAS. Orange and white dust jacket.

Published 1955, 17,80 Swiss francs.

Contains: Kurze Vorbemerkung, p. 5, and photographs of Stein and Toklas
by Van Vechten.

> Two cuts were made, presumably by the translator, Elisabeth Schnack,
> in Van Vechten's introduction: one referred to Stein's plane flight
> into Germany; the other listed several of her books. Van Vechten's
> typescript was titled "A Note About Gertrude Stein"; it has not been
> published in English. According to Robert Wilson's 1974 Stein biblio-
> graphy, Die Arche Verlag reissued this translation in 1959.

B 28   Yvette Guilbert   1955

GRAND PRIX DU DISQUE | Yvette Guilbert [in red] | [publisher's logo] |
ANGEL RECORDS [color drawing of Guilbert fills left half of record jacket,
below which is] d'apres Toulouse-Lautrec

Record jacket, 26.4 X 26.4 cm.; song sheet, 26 X 26 cm.

Contains: Yvette Guilbert, on back cover; synopses of songs paraphrased
in English on a single leaf, folded to make four pages, enclosed.

Published 1955, $2.50.

B 29   Cooking With the Chinese Flavor   1956

Cooking with | the Chinese Flavor | By Tsuifeng Lin and Hsianju Lin | Drawings by Siu Lan Loh | [drawing of Chinese couple at tea] | PRENTICE-HALL, INC. Englewood Cliffs, N. J.

[i-iv] v-vii [viii] ix-xix [xx-xxii] 1-196 pp., 3 blank leaves. 20.4 X 13.2 cm.

Gray and white patterned paper boards printed in orange, front and spine identically: Cooking | with | the | Chinese | Flavor | LIN | [decoration]. Orange top edges. White dust jacket printed in black, blue, and orange.

Published 1956, $3.95; in Canada: Ryerson Press, 1956, $4.95.

Contains: A Chat About Chinese Food and a Chinese Cook, pp. xv-xix.

> A subsequent edition of this book, entitled Secrets of Chinese Cooking, printed without revisions, deleted Van Vechten's introduction. It was quoted, in part, on the dust jacket [F140].

B 30   A Novel of Thank You   1958

a. First edition

A NOVEL | OF THANK YOU | BY GERTRUDE STEIN | with an Introduction by Carl Van Vechten | NEW HAVEN : YALE UNIVERSITY PRESS | 1958

Blank leaf [i-vi] vii-xiv [1-2] 3-262 pp., blank leaf. 23.6 X 15.3 cm.

Green cloth boards lettered in gold, on front: A NOVEL OF THANK YOU; down spine: GERTRUDE STEIN A NOVEL OF THANK YOU YALE. White, black, gray, and lavender dust jacket.

1,000 copies published November 1958, $5.00.

Contains: A Few Notes à propos of a "Little" Novel of Thank You, pp. xii-xiv.

b. Reprint edition

Identical to B30a, with the following exceptions: [iii] publisher listed as in B26b; both blank leaves reckoned at end. 22.2 X 14.6 cm. Red cloth boards lettered in black down spine: STEIN A NOVEL OF THANK YOU

400 copies published December 1969, $14.00.

> In addition to writing the introduction for this volume and the note for B26, Van Vechten served as general editor for all eight volumes of the Yale Edition of the Unpublished Writings of Gertrude Stein.

B 31   The Gershwin Years   1958

a. First edition

THE | GERSHWIN | YEARS | by EDWARD JABLONSKI and LAWRENCE D. STEWART |
with an Introduction by CARL VAN VECHTEN | Doubleday & Company, Inc.,
Garden City, New York 1958 [drawing by Al Hirschfeld as frontispiece]

[1-8] 9-11 [12] 13-26 [27-28] 29-313 pp. 26 X 18 cm.

Black cloth boards printed in gold, on front: G | I; title, authors, and
publisher down spine. Illustrated end-papers. Blue and white lettering
over color photograph on dust jacket, with a photograph of Jablonski by
Van Vechten on the back.

Published 1958, $6.95.

Contains: Introduction, pp. 21-26, and photographs of Eva Gauthier, p.
79; Marguerite d'Alvarez, p. 108; George Gershwin, p. 136; John W. Bubbles, p. 219.

b. Second printing, second binding

Identical to B31a with the following exceptions: wine cloth boards
printed in silver. Blue end-papers. New color photograph on dust jacket.

Published 1973, $6.95.

B 32   God's Trombones   1959

[All of the following printed over a photograph of a black preacher in
an open field] UAL 4039 | UNITED ARTISTS | UA | recorded for the talented
listener [in a white box] | Poems from | James Weldon | Johnson's [in
white] | GOD'S TROMBONES [in yellow] | interpreted by | HAROLD SCOTT |
The Montclair Gospel Chorale | Saffel Huggs, director | COMMEMORATIVE
EDITION [in yellow]

hinged record jacket, 31.2 X 31.2 cm.

Published spring 1959.

Contains: James Weldon Johnson, left inner lining of jacket, a memoir
based in part on "My Friend; James Weldon Johnson" [A28; C21]

B 33   Giselle and I   1960

a. First edition

ALICIA MARKOVA | Giselle and I | WITH A FOREWORD BY | CARL VAN VECHTEN |
LONDON | BARRIE AND ROCKLIFF

[1-11] 12-16 [17-19] 20-193 [194-200] pp. 22.9 X 16.3 cm.

Black cloth boards printed in gold, Markova's signature on front; on
spine: ALICIA | MARKOVA | [rose] | Giselle | and I | BARRIE | AND |
ROCKLIFF. Blue and white dust jacket with photographs front and back.

Published 1960, 25 shillings.

Contains: Gardenias for Alicia, pp. 11-16 [A25], and photographs of Markova between pp. 48-49, 64-65, 160-61.

b. American issue

Identical to B33a — sheets imported from the English edition — with
the following exceptions: Vanguard Press [in place of English publisher
on title page]. Two separate bindings: blue cloth boards printed on
spine: ALICIA MARKOVA [in gold] | [pink rose] | Giselle | and | I [in
silver] | [pink rose] | VANGUARD [in gold]; or orange plastic alligator-
patterned boards printed on spine in gold; pink, black, and white dust
jacket.

Published 1961, $5.50.

B 34   Between Friends   1962

BETWEEN FRIENDS | LETTERS OF | JAMES BRANCH CABELL | AND OTHERS | EDITED
BY | PADRAIC COLUM | AND MARGARET FREEMAN CABELL | WITH AN | INTRODUCTION
| BY | CARL VAN VECHTEN | [publisher's logo] | HARCOURT, BRACE & WORLD,
INC. NEW YORK

[i-v] vi [vii-viii] ix-xvi [1-2] 3-304 pp. 23.4 X 15.7 cm.

Mustard cloth boards printed on spine in blue: BETWEEN | FRIENDS |
[blind decoration] | LETTERS | OF | JAMES | BRANCH | CABELL | AND |
OTHERS | [blind decoration] | Edited by | PADRAIC | COLUM | and | MAR-
GARET | FREEMAN | CABELL | Harcourt, | Brace & World | [publisher's
logo]. Blue-green top edges. Gray end-papers. Blue, white, and mustard dust jacket.

Published 1962. $7.50.

Contains: An Introduction with Candor and Some Little Truth, pp. ix-
xvi; and letters, pp. 103-04, 114-15, 235-36, 278, 281.

B 35   Richard Banks   1962

a. First printing

richard banks richard banks richard banks richard banks richard banks |
richard banks [color plate pasted down]

[4] pp. 21.5 X 14 cm.

Stiff white card, folded once to make two leaves; color plate in yellow,
orange, black, and white. Issued in a mailing envelope.

Printed circa February 1962, gratis.

Contains: Richard Banks, p. 2 [F141]

B 36   More Mr. Cat   1962

a. First edition

GEORGE FREEDLEY | MORE MR. CAT | AND A BIT OF AMBER TOO | [drawing of a cat] | Drawings by VICTOR J. DOWLING | Foreword by CARL VAN VECHTEN | HOWARD FRISCH | New York

[1-9] 10-64 pp. 22.8 X 15 cm.

Tan cloth boards printed down spine in gold: GEORGE FREEDLEY MORE MR. CAT HOWARD FRISCH

Published 1962, $3.50.

Contains: A Letter of Credit to More. Mr. Cat, p. 7.

b. Boxed edition

Identical to B36a with the following exceptions: Blue cloth boards; issued as a matching, companion volume to the fourth printing of Mr. Cat by George Freedley, boxed together in a gray, black, and white slipcase.

Published 1962, $6.00.

c. Reprint edition

Identical to B36a with the following exceptions: [3] Grammercy Publishing Company [substituted for Howard Frisch]; orange paper boards printed in black.

Published 1963, $3.50.

d. Paperback edition

GEORGE FREEDLEY | MR. CAT | [drawing of a cat] | Drawings by VICTOR J. DOWLING | [publisher's logo] | NEW YORK, N.Y. [the foregoing on p. 3]; MORE MR. CAT | AND A BIT OF AMBER TOO | [drawing of a cat. The foregoing on p. 79]

[1-10] 11-77 [78-82] 83-84 [85-86] 87-160 pp. 17.7 X 10.7 cm.

Stiff white wrappers printed in black with title in red; on front and spine: CURTIS BOOKS | 502-09127-095; front and back, drawings of a cat. All edges red.

Published circa 1972, $.95.

Contains: A Letter of Credit to More Mr. Cat, pp. 83-84

B 37   Florine Stettheimer   1963

FLORINE STETTHEIMER | A Life in Art | BY PARKER TYLER | Farrar, Straus
and Company . New York

[i-xi] xii-xiv [1-3] 4-194; eleven 8-page signatures; ten color illustrations tipped-in. 28.5 X 20.2 cm.

White cloth boards printed in gold, on front: FLORINE | STETTHEIMER;
down spine: F [the following in red] LORINE S [the following in red]
TETTHEIMER PARKER TYLER | Farrar, Straus [in red]. Illustrated mustard
end-papers. White dust jacket printed in red, mustard, and blue.

Published 1963, $15.00.

Contains: Prelude in the Form of a Cellophane Squirrel Cage, pp. xi-xiv,
and extensive interview quotations; photographs of Henry McBride, between
pp. 66-67, Gertrude Stein, Alice B. Toklas, and self-portrait, 98-99,
theater marquees in 1934 and 1952 for Four Saints in Three Acts, 114-15.

B 38   Richard Hundley   1964

Musicale | Songs of | RICHARD HUNDLEY | Sung by | MEMBERS of the METRO-
POLITAN | OPERA COMPANY | Jeanette Scovotti | George Shirley | Ezio Fla-
gello | [decoration] | KARAMU HOUSE | Cleveland, | Ohio | Thursday, April
23, 1964 | 2:30 to 3:30

1 leaf, folded to make [1-4] pp. 13 X 10.5 cm.

Cream stock with deckle edge, printed in black.

Printed circa April 1964, gratis.

Contains: A Note on a Young Composer, p. 2.

B 39   Gertrude Stein   1964

GERTRUDE STEIN | CATALOG 1964 | GOTHAM BOOK MART [the foregoing printed
below a nearly full page photograph of Gertrude Stein and Alice B. Toklas
by Van Vechten]

[1-24] pp. 21.5 X 13.8 cm.

Twelve white leaves folded and stapled to make 24 pages, including cover.

Printed November 1963, gratis.

Contains: More Laurels for Our Gertrude, pp. 3-4 [D166]; [Gertrude Stein
rings bells....] p. 20 [B20; C22; C40; C64; D166, D167, D169] transcrip-
tion of a note from the back of cover photograph, p. 2.

C.
CONTRIBUTIONS TO
BOOKS AND PAMPHLETS

C 1   The Century Cyclopedia of Names   1911

THE CENTURY | CYCLOPEDIA OF NAMES | A PRONOUNCING AND ETYMOLOGICAL DIC-
TIONARY | OF NAMES IN GEOGRAPHY, BIOGRAPHY | MYTHOLOGY, HISTORY, | ETH-
NOLOGY, ART | ARCHAEOLOGY, FICTION, ETC., ETC., ETC. | [publisher's logo]
| EDITED BY | BENJAMIN E. SMITH, A.M., L.H.D. | MANAGING EDITOR OF THE
FIRST EDITION OF THE CENTURY | DICTIONARY, AND EDITOR OF THE CENTURY AT-
LAS | AND THE CENTURY DICTIONARY SUPPLEMENT | ASSISTED BY A NUMBER OF
SPECIALISTS | Revised and Enlarged | 1911 | The Century Co.

[i-viii, 1] 2-1085 [1086-1248] blank leaf. 29.9 X 22 cm.

Blue-green cloth boards; black quarter-cloth leatherette spine. Edges
marbled in orange and green. Title lettered in gold on spine.

Contains: Ninety-three unsigned biographies.

> Van Vechten was paid $47.50 for contributing these biographies, all
> of which appeared in the 1911 supplement. No list of subjects ex-
> ists; Van Vechten only recalled they were of "musicians"; he never
> saw a copy of the published volume. None of the biographies for
> which he was probably responsible bears the stamp of his later style.

C 2   Cincinnati Symphony Orchestra Program   1918

Cincinnati | Symphony | Orchestra | Edgar Varèse Guest Conductor | Ninth
Popular Concert | Music Hall | Sunday Afternoon | March 17th, 1918 [the
foregoing in a line and fringe border]

[1-12] pp. 22.9 X 15.3 cm., including ivory wrapper.

Contains: Trois Gymnopedies by Erik Satie, p. 9.

C 3   <u>The Borzoi 1920</u>   1920

a. <u>First edition</u>

THE BORZOI 1920 | <u>Being a sort of record</u> | <u>of five years' publishing</u> |
⌊borzoi in black oval⌋| New York | ALFRED . A . KNOPF | <u>1920</u>

⌊i-viii⌋ ix-xiv ⌊1-2⌋ 3-143 ⌊144⌋ blank leaf. Illustrations tipped-in.
18.5 X 12.8 cm.

Lavender paper boards printed in black and yellow, on front: tree pattern;
down spine, yellow on black: T | H | E | B | O | R | Z | O | I | 1 | 9 |
2 | 0; borzoi in black box on back. Blue top edges.

1,000 copies published 1920; $1.00.

Contains: On the Advantages of Being Born on the Seventeenth of June,
pp. 48-51.

b. <u>Tall paper edition</u>

Identical to C3a with the following exceptions: Limitation leaf tipped-
in preceding ⌊1⌋, recto: half-title; verso: OF THIS EDITION ONE HUNDRED
COPIES HAVE BEEN PRINTED ON SAN MARCO HANDMADE PAPER BY ALFRED A. KNOPF
FOR HIS FRIENDS. THIS, NUMBER ⌊number in ink⌋ IS FOR Carl Van Vechten |
Most amiable of authors. 19.5 X 14.5 cm.

Gold flecked lavender paper boards, white vellum quarter-cloth spine,
printed in gold as on first edition. Top edges unstained. Glassine
dust wrapper with a printed paper label on front carrying the name of each
recipient: CARL VAN VECHTEN

100 copies published 1920, none for sale.

    Issued some time after the first edition, this version contains six
    spelling and/or punctuation corrections in Van Vechten's essay, pp.
    49 and 51.

C 4   <u>When Winter Comes to Main Street</u>   1922

WHEN WINTER COMES | TO MAIN STREET | BY | GRANT OVERTON | AUTHOR OF "THE
WOMEN WHO MAKE OUR NOVELS" | NEW ⌊publisher's logo⌋ YORK | GEORGE H. DORAN
COMPANY

⌊1-4⌋ 15-384 pp. 19 X 12.8 cm.

Gray paper boards with green quarter-cloth spine, or tan paper boards with
tan quarter-cloth spine, printed in black, on front: WHEN WINTER COMES |
TO MAIN STREET | ⌊color illustration glued down⌋ | GRANT OVERTON; on spine:
WHEN | WINTER | COMES | TO | MAIN | STREET | ⌊rule⌋ | GRANT | OVERTON |
DORAN; publisher's logo on back. Dust jacket duplicates binding.

Contains: ⌊A Belated Biography⌋, review of <u>Herman Melville: Mariner and</u>
<u>Mystic</u> by Raymond Weaver, pp. 325-28 ⌊EV21⌋

C 5   Et Cetera   1924

ET CETERA [in red] | A Collector's | Scrap-Book | [publisher's logo] |
CHICAGO | PASCAL COVICI. Publisher | 1924 [the foregoing in a wide border
of mediaeval figures]

[i-xviii] 1-251 [252] 252 [254] pp.   23.4 X 15.8 cm.

Limitation note on verso of title page: This Edition is Limited to Six
Hundred and Twenty-Five Copies of Which This is [number in ink]

Gray paper boards and natural linen quarter-cloth spine with gray paper
label: Et Cetera | A Collector's Scrapbook [decorative rules above and
below]; publisher's logo in gold at foot of spine. Edges untrimmed, red
top edges painted gold. Gray end-papers. Gray dust jacket.

Contains: Edgar Saltus: A Postscript, pp. 229-35, reprinted without Van
Vechten's permission. [D78]

C 6   The Borzoi 1925   1925

a. First edition

THE | BORZOI | 1925 | [borzoi in lined oval] | Being a sort of record |
of ten years of | publishing | ALFRED . A . KNOPF | NEW YORK [the fore-
ing in a decorative border of borzois]

2 blank leaves [i-iv] v-xii [xiii-xiv] 1-351 [352-54] blank leaf. 19.3
X 13 cm.

Magenta and beige batik boards; black quarter-cloth spine with a gold box
through which black lettering shows: THE | BORZOI | 1925. Lower and fore
edges rough trimmed, blue top edges. Blue, gray, and white endpapers
printed with a continuous pattern of borzois. Cream dust jacket printed
in blue to duplicate title page, front and back.

5,000 copies published December 1925; $2.50.

Contains: Ernest Newman, pp. 212-16.

b. Tall paper edition

Identical to C6a with the following exceptions: [353] limitation note.
23.5 X 15.2 cm. Blue batik boards; natural linen quarter-cloth spine with
a blue box through which natural lettering shows. Gray paper slipcase.

500 copies published December 1925; $10.00.

C 7   Ellen Glasgow   1927

a. First edition

ELLEN GLASGOW | by | DOROTHEA LAWRENCE MANN | with | critical essays and
| a bibliography | [publisher's logo] | 1927 | DOUBLEDAY, PAGE & COMPANY
| GARDEN CITY NEW YORK

2 blank leaves, 1-42 pp., 3 blank leaves. 18.7 X 12.6 cm.

Yellow paper wrapper with small lavender gummed square printed in black
on front: ELLEN GLASGOW | [publisher's logo] | DOROTHEA LAWRENCE MANN.

Contains: A Virginia Lady Dissects a Virginia Gentleman, pp. 43-52 [EV35]

b. Reprint edition
Identical to C7a with the following exceptions: THE FOLCROFT PRESS, INC
| FOLCROFT, PA [at foot of title page; verso indicates reprinting]. 19.6
X 13 cm. Blue cloth boards printed down spine in gold: [decoration]
ELLEN GLASGOW [decoration] MANN [decoration].

100 copies published 1969; $10.00. The first edition cost ten cents.

C 8   Almanach Littéraire 1928   1929

Almanach | LITTÉRAIRE | 1929 [in red] | offert par | SIMON KRA [in red] |
6, Rue Blanche | PARIS (ixe) | Tel.: Trudaine 41-85 Chèques P.; 437-86 |
qui serait heures d'être VOTRE LIBRARIE [the foregoing in a triple line
red border within a black fringe border, all as a cover title on stiff
tan paper wrapper]

[1-5] 6-76 [77-80] pp. 15.2 X 11.5 cm.

Contains: Un Bal nègre à Harlem (U.S.A.), pp. 77-80 [A180]

C 9   Henry Blake Fuller   1929

Tributes to | Henry B. | from friends in whose minds | and hearts he will
live always | compiled and edited by | Anna Morgan | Ralph Fletcher Sey-
mour | Publisher

[1-10] 11-143 [144] blank leaf. 21.5 X 11.6 cm.

Black cloth boards; white vellum quarter-cloth spine printed in black on
spine and in white on front: henry | b. | fuller. Edges rough trimmed.
Tan endpapers. Glassine dust wrapper.

Contains: [Henry Blake Fuller], p. 107.

C 10   Once and For All   1929

Once and For All | Selected by | David McCord [two squiggle lines on each
side of the foregoing] | [double rule] | PUBLISHED IN NEW YORK BY | Coward-
McCann, Inc. | IN THE YEAR 1929

[i-iv] v-ix [x] 1-293 [294] pp. 20.6 X 14 cm. or 20.3 X 13.7 cm.

Blue cloth boards printed with title, editor, and publisher in orange on
spine, lower and fore edges untrimmed; or red cloth boards printed in
black, trimmed. (It is impossible to determine which issue came first.)
Yellow top edges. Light blue end-papers. Rust, yellow, and black jacket.

Contains: A Note on Dedications, pp. 225-38 [A17, D99]

C 11   NAACP Benefit Concert   1929

[drawing by Aaron Douglas] | Forest Theatre Night of Dec 8, 1929 | All-
Star Benefit Concert | for the | National Association for the | Advance-
ment of Colored People | Mall off 69 5th Avenue New York [cover title]

[1-2] 3-11 [12] pp. 28 X 21.8 cm.

Contains: Keep A-Inchin' Along, p. 6 [A28]

C 12   Innocence Abroad   1931

Innocence | Abroad | EMILY [divided from] CLARK [by a stylized green tree,
its top a line beneath the title and its base a long line above the fol-
lowing:] | 19 [borzoi] 31 | NEW YORK . ALFRED . A . KNOPF . LONDON

blank leaf [i-xii] 1-270 [271-72] blank leaf. 20.7 X 14 cm.

Lime or turquoise cloth boards printed in dark green: design on front; on
spine: [decoration] | Innocence | Abroad | EMILY CLARK | [title page pat-
tern] | ALFRED . A . KNOPF; borzoi in blind on lime cloth and in dark
green rectangle on turquoise cloth. Lower and fore edges rough trimmed,
blue or green top edges. Green and white dust jacket.

Contains: excerpts from thirteen letters, pp. 99, 129, 133-37; Ernest
Boyd, pp. 158-59 [D90]

C 13   Puss in Books   1932

a. English edition

[rule] | PUSS IN BOOKS | A Collection of Stories about Cats | [rule] |
Edited by | ELIZABETH DREW | AND | MICHAEL JOSEPH | [rule] | GEOFFREY
BLES | 22 SUFFOLK STREET PALL MALL | LONDON S.W. I

[1-4] 5 [6] 7-269 [270] blank leaf. 20.4 X 15.3 cm.

Light blue cloth boards printed in black, or rust cloth boards printed in
gold: title on front; title, author, publisher's logo and name on spine.
Cream or orange dust jacket printed in red and black.

Contains: Feathers, pp. 244-58 [A20, A22, C19, C42, C45, C50]

b. American edition

[drawing of a cat] | [rule] | PUSS IN BOOKS | A Collection of Stories
about Cats | EDITED BY | ELIZABETH DREW | AND | MICHAEL JOSEPH | ILLUS-
TRATED BY | A. R. WHEELAN | [rule] | DODD, MEAN & COMPANY | NEW YORK

[i-iv] v-xi [xii] xiii [xiv] xv [xvi] 1-275 [276] pp. 20.3 X 14.2 cm.

Blue cloth boards printed on front and spine in gold as on English edition. Blue endpapers. Edges rough trimmed. Light blue dust jacket
printed in red and black with an illustration of a cat.

Contains: Feathers, pp. 248-64 [A20, A22, C19, C42, C45, C50]

C 14   Collected Prose of Elinor Wylie   1933

[rule] | Collected Prose | OF | ELINOR WYLIE | [double rule] | 1933 |
[borzoi] | ALFRED A. KNOPF | NEW YORK

10 leaves [1-2] 3-879 [880] 2 blank leaves. 22.3 X 14.6 cm.

Turquoise cloth boards printed in gold on spine: decorations, title, and
publisher; borzoi in blind on back. Lower and fore edges rough trimmed,
blue top edges. Red, white, and black dust jacket.

Contains: Preface to Jennifer Lorn [The Lady Stuffed with Pistachio
Nuts], pp. 3-8 [D103]

C 15   Four Saints in Three Acts   1934

FOUR | SAINTS | IN | THREE | ACTS | 1934 [the foregoing in gold, enclosed
in a wide black lace border, as a cover title]

[24] pp. 30.4 X 22.2 cm.

Stiff white wrappers printed with title as above on front; on back: Edited by Nathan Zatkin, Aronson & Cooper, 276 West 43rd Street., New York
City. Glassine dust wrapper.

Contains: How I Listen to Four Saints in Three Acts, pp. 2-3 [EII853]]

C 16   Four Saints in Three Acts   1934

Monday Night Music Series | Auditorium Theatre [Chicago, Illinois]

[1-2] 2-22 [23-24] pp. 25.7 X 17.5 cm.

No cover; white leaves folded and stapled as a program for performances,
November 7 through 10, of the opera.

Contains: A Few Notes About Four Saints in Three Acts, pp. 13, 16 [B18]

C 17   _Modern American Prose_   1934

a. First edition

MODERN | AMERICAN | PROSE | Edited by | CARL VAN DOREN | HARCOURT, BRACE
AND COMPANY | NEW YORK [the foregoing in a double line border with decora-
tive corners]

blank leaf [i-iv] v-vii [viii] ix-xiii [xiv, 1-2] 3-939 [940] 2 blank
leaves. 21.6 X 14.5 cm.

Rose cloth boards, on front: blind rule | title | blind rule; on spine:
title, editor, and publisher printed in gold. Yellow top edges. Cream
dust jacket printed in black and red.

Contains: First Day in Paris, pp. 228-35 [Chapter One from Peter Whiffle: His Life and Works, pp. 9-22, A12k]

b. Literary Guild edition

Identical to C17a with the following exceptions: publisher's name substituted on title page; wine cloth boards with blind border and publisher's logo on front; cream dust jacket printed in orange and three shades
of red.

C 18   The Borzoi Reader   1936

a. First edition

THE BORZOI [in vermillion, flowers in downstrokes] | READER | EDITED WITH
AN INTRODUCTION AND NOTES BY | CARL VAN DOREN [two vermillion rules] |
1936 | NEW YORK | ALIFRED A KNOPF | [vermillion sunburst with borzoi in
center]

3 blank leaves [i-ii] iii-v [vi-vii] viii-xi [xii, 1] 2-1033 [1034] 2
blank leaves. 21 X 14.2 cm.

Red cloth boards with borzoi in blind on front; printed in gold on spine:
[decorative banner through which lettering appears] THE [double rule]
BORZOI [double rule] | READER | [borzoi in decorative oval] | Knopf.
Blue top edges. Cream dust jacket printed in blue and chartreuse.

Contains: La Tigresse, pp. 616-26 [A9, A22]

b. Reprint edition

THE | BORZOI | READER | [rule] | EDITED WITH AN INTRODUCTION AND NOTES
BY | CARL VAN DOREN | [rule] | [publisher's logo] | Deluxe Edition |
GARDEN CITY PUBLISHING CO., INC. | GARDEN CITY NEW YORK

Identical to C18a with the following exceptions: title page, as above;
verso adds date, 1938. Red cloth boards printed in black and gold without borzois, front and spine. Unstained top edges. Black paper slipcase.

C 19   Cats and Cats   1937

CATS — and [this word descending at an angle to] | CATS | [rule] | GREAT
CAT STORIES | OF OUR DAY | [rule] | Compiled by | FRANCES E. CLARKE | New
York | THE MACMILLAN COMPANY | 1937

[i-vi] vii-ix [x] xi-xii [xiii-xiv] 1-342 pp.   21.2 X 14.2 cm.

Wine cloth boards printed in gold, front and spine. Yellow top edges.
Cream dust jacket printed in black, with photographs.

Contains: The Cat in Music, pp. 265-82 [Chapter VIII from The Tiger in
the House, pp. 187-210; A11, D77]

C 20   Breaking into Print   1937

Breaking into print | BEING A COMPILATION OF PAPERS | WHEREIN | EACH OF
A SELECT GROUP OF AUTHORS | TELLS | OF THE DIFFICULTIES OF AUTHORSHIP |
& | HOW SUCH TRIALS ARE MET | TOGETHER WITH | BIOGRAPHICAL NOTES AND COM-
MENT | BY AN EDITOR OF THE COLOPHON | ELMER ADLER | NOW | PUT IN A BOOK
BY SIMON AND SCHUSTER | PUBLISHERS OF NEW YORK IN MCMXXXCII [the forego-
ing in a wide rust border containing names of authors included in white]

[i-vi] vii-x [1-2] 3-196 [197-98] pp.   23.4 X 15.5 cm.

Black cloth boards lettered in gold, on front: Breaking | into print |
[duplicate title in blind] | Breaking | into print | [duplicate title in
blind, all four titles in a wide border in blind]; on spine: Breaking |
into | print | [blind decoration] | [names of authors in alphabetical
order] | [blind decoration] | SIMON AND | SCHUSTER. Orange, green, and
white dust jacket.

Contains: [a letter to Elmer Adler], pp. 171-72; Notes for an Autobiography, pp. 173-77 [from Sacred and Profane Memories, pp. 225-30; A22,
D129]

C 21   James Weldon Johnson   1938

JAMES WELDON JOHNSON | [decoration] | A BIOGRAPHICAL SKETCH | AN APPRE-
CIATION OF JAMES WELDON JOHNSON | By Arthur D. Spingarn | MY FRIEND:
JAMES WELDON JOHNSON | By Carl Van Vechten | THE NEGRO IN AMERICAN LITER-
ATURE | By Sterling A. Brown | [decoration] | Published by | THE DEPART-
MENT OF PUBLICITY | FISK UNIVERSITY | Luanna J. Bowles, Director

[1-36] pp.   24 X 16 cm.

Heavy white deckle edge wrappers with facsimile signature on front in
gold. Fore edges untrimmed. Issued in a white paper envelope.

Published 29 September 1939, gratis.

Contains: My Friend: James Weldon Johnson, pp. 22-24 [A28, B32]

C 22   <u>We Moderns</u>   1939

a. <u>First edition, deluxe issue</u>

[cover title, in white panels on full page photograph] WE MODERNS | GOTHAM
BOOK MARK | 1920 - 1940 | The Life of the Party at FINNEGAN'S WAKE in our
Garden | on Publication Day | <u>Painting by Ruth Bower</u> <u>Photograph by Carl</u>
<u>Van Vechten</u>

[1-2] 3-88 [89-92] pp. 19.9 X 13.5 cm.

Stiff glazed paper wrappers printed in black and white over halftone
photograph. Spiral bound.

3,500 copies published December 1939, $.50.

Contains: Gertrude Stein, p. 63 [quoted in W.G. Rogers: <u>Wise Men Fish</u>
<u>Here</u>, 1965, p. 207; B20, B39; C40, C64; D166, D167, D169]

b. <u>First edition, trade issue</u>

Identical to C22a; printed on lighter stock, pages stapled, cover glued.

3,500 copies published December 1939, gratis.

C 23   <u>Greece 1821 - 1941</u>   1941

GREECE | 1821 - 1941 | THE AMERICAN FRIENDS OF GREECE | Affiliated with
the | GREEK WAR RELIEF ASSOCIATION | 730 Fifth Avenue | New York

[1-15] 16-17 [18] 19-61 [62] 63 [64] 27.4 X 21 cm.

Stiff wrappers printed in blue and black with title lettered in Greek
symbols and a Greek head, stapled

Contains: [The timely heroism of the Greeks], p. 39.

C 24   <u>Concert Life in New York 1902 - 1923</u>   1942

<u>Concert Life</u> | <u>in New York</u> | <u>1902-1923</u> | <u>By</u> | RICHARD ALDRICH | [publish-
er's logo, in red] | G. P. PUTNAM'S SONS | NEW YORK

[i-x] 1-490 pp. 23.5 X 15.8 cm.

Pale green cloth boards lettered in gold on spine, title, author, and
publisher. Gray top edges. Gray dust jacket printed in blue.

Contains: Kitty Cheatham, Englebert Humperdinck, pp. 310-11 [erroneously
attributed to Richard Aldrich; EII567]

C 25   The Paris We Remember   1942

The Paris We Remember | [rule] | Edited and Translated by | ELISABETH
FINLEY THOMAS | With an Introduction by | ELLIOT PAUL | [publisher's mono-
gram] | D. APPLETON-CENTURY COMPANY | INCORPORATED | NEW YORK LONDON |
1942

[i-vi] vii-xviii [xix-xx, 1-2] 3-475 [476] 477-78, blank leaf. 21 X 15.5
cm.

Blue cloth boards printed on spine in white, title and publisher. Lower
and fore edges rough trimmed. Blue dust jacket printed in brown and white.

Contains: Terrace Café, pp. 228-32 [from Peter Whiffle: His Life and
Works, pp. 11-18; A12k]

C 26   The Owl   1944

Wadleigh High School | The Owl | Pan-American Issue | June 1944 | Margaret
C. Byrne, Principal

[1-4] 5-30 [31-32] 33-64 [65-66] pp.   21.5 X 18 cm.

Stiff cream paper wrappers printed in red with blue quarter cloth spine;
a few copies, for presentation, were bound in blue cloth and lettered in
gold on the front, and issued in a brown paper wrapper.

Contains: For the Girls of Wadleigh High School, p. 32 [The yearbook was
dedicated to Van Vechten.]

C 27   The Theatre Annual   1944

THE | THEATRE ANNUAL | 1943 | [decoration] | A PUBLICATION | of | INFORMA-
TION AND RESEARCH | in | THE ARTS AND HISTORY | of | THE THEATRE

blank leaf [1-5] 6-62 pp., 13 plates. 22.9 X 15.2 cm.

Stiff tan paper wrappers printed in green and wine

Contains: How the Theatre is Represented in the Negro Collection at Yale,
pp. 32-38 [A28]

C 28   Isadora Duncan in Her Dances   1945

Isadora Duncan in Her | Dances | By Abraham Walkowitz | [decoration] |
With Introductions by Maria-Theresa, Carl Van Vechten, Mary | Fanton Rob-
erts, Sheamus O'Sheel and Arnold Genthe | Included are Dance Sequence
Drawings of Ballet, Agna Enters, | Martha Graham, a Group of Pupils of
Isadora, and Drawings | Against War and Fascism by Walkowitz, with an

Introduction by | Konrad Bercovici | [decoration] | "Walkowitz, you have written my biography in lines without words. I can pass on." — Isadora Duncan. | PRINTED IN U.S.A. HALDEMAN-JULIUS PUBLICATIONS | GIRARD, KANSAS

[1-3] 4-8 [9] 10 [11] 12 [13-32] pp.   28 X 21.5 cm.

Green paper wrapper, printed in black on front to duplicate title and author from title page, stapled.

Contains: An Appreciation, p. 8 [quoted, translated, in Jennie Schulman, "Isadora Duncan getekend door Abraham Wolkowitz," dans knoniek, Amsterdam, Oktober, 1952, p. 139]

C 29   Words and Music   1945

WORDS | AND | MUSIC | Comment by Famous Authors | about the World's Greatest Artists

[1] 2-75 [76] pp.   19.5 X 12.6 cm.

Black paper wrapper with white musical note and RCA Victor dog printed in white, lettered in gold, stapled.

Contains: Pierre Monteux, p. 45 [F127]

C 30   Florine Stettheimer   1946

a. First edition

HENRY MC BRIDE | florine stettheimer | THE MUSEUM OF MODERN ART

[1-8] 9-55 [56] pp.   25.5 X 19 cm.

Stiff pink and white stippled wrappers, printed in black, on front: florine stettheimer; down spine: FLORINE STETTHEIMER THE MUSEUM OF MODERN ART. Blue-gray and light gray lace-patterned endpapers.

10,000 copies published September 1946, $1.00.

Contains: [Florine Stettheimer], p. 53 [D85]

b. Reprint edition

Three Romantic Painters | Charles Burchfield | with an introduction by Alfred H. Barr, Jr. | Florine Stettheimer | by Henry McBride | Franklin C. Watkins | by Andrew Carnduff Reteke | THE MUSEUM OF MODERN ART | Reprint Edition 1969 | Published for the Museum of Modern Art by Arno Press

Paging identical to C30a, following and preceding the other two monographs which follow their own original paging.

Beige cloth boards printed down spine in wine.

C 31   <u>Stieglitz Memorial Portfolio</u>   1946

STIEGLITZ | MEMORIAL PORTFOLIO | 1864 - 1946 | 18 Reproductions of PHOTO-
GRAPHS | by ALFRED STIEGLITZ | TRIBUTES — In Memoriam | TWICE A YEAR
PRESS. NEW YORK

[1-7] 8-64 pp, 6 plates. 40.6 X 30.5 cm.

Black paper wrap-around folder with black quarter cloth spine, paper
label on front reproducing Stieglitz's signature in facsimile. Pages
sewn with cloth strip, preceding loose plates of photographs.

1,500 copies published 1946, $20.00.

Contains: [Alfred Stieglitz], p. 37

C 32   <u>Nijinsky</u>   1946

a. First edition

NIJINSKY [in parallel to the following four lines] | AN ILLUSTRATED |
MONOGRAPH | EDITED BY | PAUL MAGRIEL | HENRY HOLT AND COMPANY . NEW YORK

blank leaf [i-x] 1-81 [82] blank leaf. 23.4 X 18.3 cm.

Red cloth boards printed in black down spine: NIJINSKY | HOLT. Pink,
black, and white dust jacket with photographs and illustrations.

Published November 1946, reprinted March 1947, $3.00.

Contains: The Russian Ballet and Nijinsky, pp. 1-14 [from <u>Interpreters
and Interpretations</u>, 1916, and <u>Interpreters</u>, 1920; A6, A10, A25; D47]

b. Reprint edition

[rule] NIJINSKY, | PAVLOVA, | DUNCAN | [rule] | Three Lives in Dance |
Edited by Paul Magriel | A DA CAPO PAPERBACK

[i-xii] 1-81 [82, iii-iv] v-vi [vii-xii] 1-78 [iii-iv] v-vii [i-ii] 1-85
[86] 2 blank leaves. 23.5 X 17.7 cm.

Stiff white wrapper printed in blue, red, and purple, with halftone photographs on front; or rose cloth boards lettered in silver.

Published 1977, $6.95, paper; $22.50, cloth.

C 33   <u>Isadora Duncan</u>   1947

a. First edition

<u>Isadora</u> | <u>Duncan</u> | EDITED BY PAUL MAGRIEL | [rule] | HENRY HOLT AND COM-
PANY . NEW YORK

[i-iv] v-vii [viii-x] 1-85 [86] pp.   23.4 X 18.3 cm.

Rust cloth boards printed down spine in black: <u>Isadora Duncan</u> HOLT. Subsequent printings were bound in gray linen paper boards printed down spine
in lavender. Cream, black, gray, and white dust jacket.

Published April 1947, reprinted October 1947, June 1948, $3.00.

Contains: Duncan Concerts in New York, pp. 19-25 [EII373, 379, 591, 594]
and The New Isadora, pp. 27-33 [from <u>The Merry-Go Round</u>, pp. 307-17; A7]

b. Reprint edition, C32b

C 34   Pavlova   1947

a. First edition

PAVLOVA | AN ILLUSTRATED MONOGRAPH | EDITED BY PAUL MAGRIEL | HENRY HOLT
AND COMPANY . NEW YORK

blank leaf [i-iv] v-vi [vii-xii] 1-78 [79-80] blank leaf.   23.4 X 18.3 cm.

Black cloth boards printed in gold down spine: PAVLOVA | HOLT. Blue,
black, and white dust jacket.

Published 1947, $3.50.

Contains: Pavlova at the Metropolitan Opera House, pp. 17-25 [A25;
EII431, 432, 440, 526]

b. Reprint edition, C32b

C 35   Marian Anderson   1947

[1-20] pp.   30.1 X 22.5 cm.

[cover title on light green paper wrapper, color photograph] | <u>Marian</u>
<u>Anderson</u> [in white]

Printed as a souvenir program, 1947, $.25.

Contains: Marian Anderson, pp. 7-8, and a photograph of Marian Anderson
by Van Vechten, p. 6. [A28]

C 36   Chronicles of the American Dance   1948

CHRONICLES OF | THE AMERICAN DANCE | EDITED BY PAUL MAGRIEL | HENRY HOLT
AND COMPANY . NEW YORK

[i-iv] v-vii [viii] ix [x] xi-xii [1-2] 3-268 [269-70] blank leaf.   23.4
X 18.3 cm.

Black cloth boards, printed down spine in gold: CHRONICLES OF THE AMERI-
CAN DANCE | HOLT. Blue, white, and black dust jacket.

Published 1948, $3.50.

Contains: Maud Allan, pp. 221-23 [A25; EII406, 412]

C 37   Improvisations of New York   1948

IMPROVISATIONS OF | NEW YORK | A SYMPHONY IN LINES | By A. WALKOWITZ |
[drawing] | HALDEMAN-JULIUS PUBLICATIONS | GIRARD, KANSAS

[1-32] pp. 27.8 X 21.3 cm.

Manila paper wrapper, printed on front to duplicate author and title from
title page. Stapled leaves.

Contains: Comments, p. 2.

C 38   Catalogue of the Alfred Stieglitz Collection   1948

CATALOGUE | OF THE | ALFRED STIEGLITZ | COLLECTION FOR | FISK UNIVERSITY
| [Fisk University seal] | THE CARL VAN VECHTEN | GALLERY OF FINE ARTS

[1] 2-48 pp. 23.5 X 18.4 cm.

Blue paper wrapper, printed in black to duplicate title page. Stapled
leaves.

Contains: Foreword, p. 3.

C 39   Art From Life to Life   1949

a. First edition

ART | FROM LIFE TO LIFE | BY | A. WALKOWITZ | With Introductions By | Li-
onello Venturi, A. L. Chanlin, Amedee J. Ozenfant, Bernard | Myers, Kath-
erine S. Dreier, David Diamondstein (Dobson) | David Ignatoff, Carl Van
Vechten | With Appreciations By | Walter Pach, Benjamin Copman, Jerome
Melquist, | Clifford Williams, Jennings Toffel | Haldeman-Julius Publica-
tions | Girard, Kansas | PRINTED IN THE U.S.A.

[1-48] pp. 27.2 X 20 cm.

Cream wrappers printed to duplicate title page title and author, with an
illustration. Stapled leaves.

Contains: A General View, p. 5.

b. Second edition

Identical to C39a, but containing only [24] pp., that is, minus one-half
the plates. 24.8 X 17.7 cm. Issued 1951.

C 40   Doctor Faustus Lights the Lights   1951

THE LIVING THEATRE | [drawing of a sunburst] | DOCTOR FAUSTUS | LIGHTS
THE LIGHTS | GERTRUDE STEIN

1-16 pp. 23.6 X 15.8 cm.

title cover on Inomachi Japan vellum wrapper, printed in black, stapled
to folded leaves of the program.

Printed December 1951, gratis.

Contains: Notes Written on Stone, pp. 5, 7 [concluding with "Gertrude
Stein rings bells. . ., B20, B39; C22, C64; D166, D167, D169]

C 41   Alfred A. Knopf at Sixty   1952

ALFRED A | KNOPF | PRIVATELY PRINTED [first half of a two-page title];
AT | 60 [number in rust] | SEPTEMBER 12, 1952 [second half of the two-
page title]; borzois in a line against a stylized landscape across the
tops of the pages]

blank leaf [1-2] 3-59 [60] blank leaf. 19.3 X 13.2 cm.

Rust paper boards printed with a gold borzoi in a gold sunburst; wine
quarter cloth spine printed in gold, with the title. Turquoise top edges.
Acetate dust wrapper. Light blue paper slipcase.

250 copies printed for presentation only.

Contains: Introducing Mr. Knopf or Alfred in a Nutshell, pp. 3-14 [C52]

C 42   Best Cat Stories   1952

BEST CAT STORIES | [star] | Edited with an Introduction by | MICHAEL
JOSEPH | Illustrated by | EILEEN MAYO | FABER AND FABER | 24 Russell
Square | London

[1-6] 7 [8] 9-13 [14] 15-270 [271-72] pp. 20.1 X 13.3 cm.

Light orange cloth boards printed on spine in blue: Best | CAT | STORIES
| [star] | edited by | MICHAEL | JOSEPH | [outline drawing of a cat] |
Faber & Faber. Green dust jacket printed in black and white with drawings of cats

Contains: Feathers, pp. 209-23 [A20, A22, C13, C45, C50]

C 43   The Flowers of Friendship   1953

THE | FLOWERS of FRIENDSHIP | Letters written to | GERTRUDE STEIN | Edited
by DONALD GALLUP | Before the Flowers of Friendship Faded Friendship Faded
| (TITLE OF A BOOK BY GERTRUDE STEIN) | ⌊borzoi⌋ 1953 | ALFRED A. KNOPF
NEW YORK

blank leaf [i-vii] viii [ix] x-xxvi [xxvii-xxviii, 1-3] 4-403 [404, i]
ii-xiii [xiv] pp. 21.2 X 14.5 cm.

Turquoise cloth boards printed in gold: non-objective design on front;
title, editor, publisher, and decorations on spine; borzoi in blind on
back. Lower and fore edges rough trimmed, light blue top edges. Black,
white, and lavender dust jacket with a photograph of Stein front and back.

Contains: Twenty-five letters, pp. 97, 105-6, 108, 116-17, 151, 153-54,
156-58, 160, 171-72, 179, 228, 262-63, 266-67, 272-73, 275, 292-93, 324,
332, 335-36, 349-50, 372, 374, 381, 393; photograph of Stein by Van Vechten facing p. 282. [A selection of letters from this book, issued as an
advertising brochure, contains Van Vechten's letters, pp. 116 and 324.
[F132]

C44   The Alice B. Toklas Cook Book   1954

a. First edition

THE | ALICE B. | TOKLAS | COOK BOOK | ILLUSTRATIONS BY | SIR FRANCIS ROSE
| [publisher's logo] | Harper & Brothers NEW YORK

Blank leaf [i-vi, errata leaf tipped-in, vii-viii, 1-2] 3-288 pp. 20.2
X 13.8 cm.

Orange paper boards with green quartercloth spine printed in gold and
orange. Illustrated end papers. White and mustard dust jacket printed
in green, black, and orange.

Contains: Two recipes: Garlic Ice Cream, p. 251, and Viennese Cheese
Pancakes, p. 256.

b. English edition

THE | ALICE B. | TOKLAS | COOK BOOK | ILLUSTRATIONS BY | SIR FRANCIS ROSE
| [publisher's logo] | London | MICHAEL JOSEPH

[i-viii] ix-xi [xii, 1-2] 3-288 pp., blank leaf. 23.5 X 15.9 cm.

Tan cloth boards printed on spine in gold and green. Illustrated end
papers as in C44a. Full color dust jacket printed in black.

c. Paperback edition

THE | ALICE B. TOKLAS | COOK BOOK | [decoration] | ANCHOR BOOKS | DOUBLE-
DAY & COMPANY, INC. | GARDEN CITY, NEW YORK | 1960

4 leaves [1-3] 4-305 [306] pp. 3 leaves.   18.4 X 10.5 cm.

Stiff white wrappers printed in yellow, gray, black, and blue. Van Vechten's recipes are on pp. 265 and 271.

C 45   Favorite Cat Stories   1956

FAVORITE CAT | STORIES | OF PAMELA AND JAMES MASON | [drawing of a cat] |
Illustrated by GLADYS EMERSON COOK | JULIAN MESSNER, INC., NEW YORK

[1-6] 7-8 [9-10] 11-158 [159-60] pp.   25.4 X 18.4 cm.

Off-white shot-paper boards with maroon quarter cloth spine printed in
gold. Gray dust jacket printed in yellow with a color illustration on
front and photograph of the editors on back.

Contains: Feathers, pp. 123-34 [typographical errors, pp. 127, 121.
A20, A22; C13; C42; C50]

C 46   New York City Ballet [George Platt Lynes]   1957

NEW YORK CITY BALLET | Photographs from 1935 through 1955 | taken by |
GEORGE PLATT LYNES 1907-1956 | [list of ballet company titles and inclu-
sive dates | list of directors] | THE NEW YORK CITY CENTER OF MUSIC AND
DRAMA . 1957

[1-32] pp.   30 X 22.5 cm.

Stiff photographic wrapper, printed in yellow on front over a photograph
from Symphony in C: NEW YORK CITY BALLET

Contains: [George Platt Lynes], p. 4.

C 47   Of Cats and Men   1957

[black cat] | OF CATS | AND MEN | compiled by FRANCES E. CLARK | New York
1957 | THE MACMILLAN COMPANY

[i-iv] v-vi [vii-viii] ix-xii [xiii] xiv, 1-250 pp.   22.2 X 15.2 cm.

Turquoise cloth boards; black quarter cloth spine printed in gold, with
editor, title, drawing of an Egyptian cat, and publisher. Gray dust jacket printed in black and turquoise.

Contains: Apotheosis, pp. 243-50 [from The Tiger in the House, pp. 302-6.
All]

C 48   Plain and Fancy Cats   1958

PLAIN | & | FANCY | CATS | A Collection | EDITED BY | John Beecroft |
RINEHART & COMPANY, INC. | NEW YORK . TORONTO

[i-xii] 1-436 pp.   22.7 X 15.2 cm.

Black cloth boards printed on spine in blue, white, and yellow. Yellow-
orange and blue dust jacket printed in black and white.

Contains: Treating of Traits, pp. 189-212, and Aurilophobes and Other
Cat Haters, pp. 213-18 [from The Tiger in the House, pp. 22-80. All]

C 49   Vanity Fair   1960

[drawing of a peacock] | VANITY FAIR | SELECTIONS FROM AMERICA'S MOST
MEMORABLE MAGAZINE | A CAVALCADE | of the | 1920s AND 1930s | [decorative
rule] | Edited by | CLEVELAND AMORY | and FREDERICK BRADLEE | Picture
Editor: KATHARINE TWEED | THE VIKING PRESS . PUBLISHERS . NEW YORK

[1-4] 5-327 [328] pp.   30.2 X 22.7 cm.

Gray and cream paper boards stamped with a gold peacock in center of
front; red quarter cloth spine, lettered with title and publisher in
gold. Black dust jacket printed in red, blue, lavender, white, and cream
with illustration by Benito on front and photographs on back.

Contains: The Ten Dullest Authors: A Symposium, p. 77 [D100], and The
Black Blues, pp. 95-96 [D111].

C 50   All Cats Go to Heaven   1960

All Cats | Go to Heaven | an anthology of stories about cats | SELECTED
BY BETH BROWN | ILLUSTRATED BY PEGGY BACON | PUBLISHERS Grosset & Dunlap
NEW YORK

[i-vi] v-vi [vii-viii] ix-xi [xii] xiii-xiv [xv-xvi] 1-494 pp.   22.9 X
15 cm.

Yellow paper boards with drawings of cats in blind, front and back; black
quarter cloth spine printed in gold, with title, editor and illustrator,
drawing of a cat, gravestone, and flowers, and publisher. Yellow top
edges. Full-color dust jacket with drawings of cats on front and contents
on back.

Contains: Feathers, pp. 386-96 [A20, A22; C13, C42, C45]

C 51   Dance 62   1963

DANCE 62 [verso: a bonus offering for subscribers to Dance Perspectives
and is not offered for sale.]

[1-3] 4-52 pp.   22.8 X 19 cm.

Stiff photographic wrapper, printed on front in white: DANCE 62; stapled.

Contains: Alvin Ailey, pp. 26-28. [A28]

C52   Portrait of a Publisher   1965

Portrait | of a Publisher | 1915/1965 | II | [rule] | ALFRED A. KNOPF |
AND THE | BORZOI IMPRINT: | RECOLLECTIONS AND | APPRECIATIONS [This the
second of two volumes, the first one — written by Knopf — indicates
date and publisher on the title page as follows: New York THE Typo-
philes 1965.]

[i-v] vi-ix [x] xi-xiii [xiv, 1-2] 3-301 [302] blank leaf.

Gray cloth boards; green quarter-cloth spine printed in gold, on front:
1915 | [rule] | AAK | [rule] | 1965; on spine: [decorative rules] |
[in a black square: rule] | Portrait | of a | Publisher | [rule] | [tri-
ple rule] | [in a black square:] Volume II | [triple rule]. Gray paper
slipcase to hold both volumes; Volume I identical in binding except for
red quarter cloth spine.

2000 copies published for The Typophile Society "subscribers, the contributors, and friends of Alfred A. Knopf." Typophile Chapbook 42.

Contains: Introducing Mr. Knopf or Alfred in a Nutshell, pp. 113-21 [C41]
four photographs of Alfred Knopf and three of Blanche Knopf by Van Vechten.

C53   Isak Dinesen   1965

a. American edition

ISAK DINESEN | [decoration] | A MEMORIAL | Edited by Clara Svensen |
[publisher's logo] | RANDOM HOUSE NEW YORK

1 leaf [i-iv] v-vii [1-2] 3-209 [210] 2 blank leaves. 20.8 X 13.2 cm.

Black cloth boards; blind decorations on front; printed in gold on spine
with decorations, title, editor, publisher's logo and name. Orange top
edges. Green endpapers.

Contains: [What a unique personality was Tania Blixen!], p. 30.

b. Danish edition

KAREN BLIXEN | Redigeret af | Clara Svendsen og Ole Wivel | Gyldendal |
1962

229 pp. 24.2 X 16.5 cm.

Stiff gray paper wrappers printed on front: KAREN BLIXEN | GYLDENDAL.
Photographic dust jacket, covered with acetate wrapper, by Jesper Høm

This is, of course, the original edition from which the American version was prepared three years later. It is entirely in Danish; it contains 27 contributions by Danes omitted from the American edition; Van Vechten's contribution, also in Danish, is on page 109.

C 54   Carl Van Vechten   1965

a. First edition

CARL VAN VECHTEN | [rule] | by EDWARD LUEDERS | Hanover College | [publisher's logo] | Twayne Publishers, Inc. [dot square] New York

[1-14] 15-16 [17-18] 19-158, blank leaf. 20.3 X 13.7 cm.

Gray paper boards printed on front and spine in gold and blue gray. Gray top edges. Gray end papers. Orange, black, and white dust jacket with a Van Vechten self-portrait photograph on the back.

Contains: Passages from Columbia University Oral History [1960], pp. 29-30, 76-77, 97-98; a letter to Arthur Davison Ficke, p. 41; a letter to Edward Lueders, p. 108; a passage from the Manuscript Inventory for the James Weldon Johnson Memorial Collection of Negro Arts and Letters, pp. 144-45; unpublished notes for Nigger Heaven, pp. 97-98.

b. Paperback edition

Identical to C54a, but bound in stiff black, gray, and white paper wrappers and issued without jacket of course.

C 55   Cats   1966

CATS | A Personal Anthology | by | VAL GIELGUD | NEWNES : LONDON

[1-10] 11-155 [156] 157 [158] blank leaf. 24.6 X 15.4 cm.

Turquoise paper boards printed in gold down spine. Photographic end papers. Photographic dust jacket printed in black and white in turquoise.

Contains: [the conclusion of Apotheosis from Tiger in the House, pp. 151-54 [All]

C 56   The Smart Set   1966

The | Smart Set | [drawing of a masked devil trailing streamers to connect the following, in a two-line decorative box] | A HISTORY | AND ANTHOLOGY BY | Carl R. Dolmetsch | WITH AN INTRODUCTORY REMINISCENCE BY | S. N. Behrman | [the following below box] THE DIAL PRESS | [publisher's logo] | NEW YORK 1966

[i-vi] vii-xvii [xviii] xix-xxv [xxvi, 1-2] 3-262 pp. 30.3 X 22.7 cm.

White cloth boards printed in gold, on front: another drawing of a devil trailing streamers; on spine: title, editor, publisher, and logo. Peacock blue end papers. White dust jacket printed in black, blue, orange, and magenta, duplicated front and back.

Contains: How the Twelve Best Sellers Ended, pp. 160-61. [D11]

C 57   Wallace Stevens   1966

WALLACE STEVENS | Art of Uncertainty | [rule] | by | Herbert F. Stern | Ann Arbor | The University of Michigan Press

2 blank leaves [i-vi] vii-xiii, 1-206, 2 blank leaves. 20.4 X 14 cm.

Taupe cloth boards printed with author and title down spine in cream.

Contains: [a letter to Stern about Wallace Stevens], p. 173.

C 58   Carl Van Vechten and the Irreverent Decades   1968

CARL VAN VECHTEN | and the | IRREVERENT DECADES | [Leda and the Swan intaglio drawing] | By Bruce Kellner | UNIVERSITY OF OKLAHOMA PRESS | NORMAN [the foregoing in a single line border]

[i-vi] vii-xi [xii] xiii-xvii [xviii] xix-xxii [1-2] 3-354 pp. 22.8 X 15.3 cm.

Dark red cloth boards with Leda and the Swan in blind on front; lettered on spine, in red on white. Pink top edges. Tan end papers, with Van Vechten's bookplate, designed by Prentiss Taylor, reproduced on front paste-down. Cream dust jacket printed in black and two shades of red, with an uncredited photograph of Van Vechten by Mark Lutz on front and photograph of Kellner by Van Vechten on back flap.

3700 copies published November 1968, $7.95, later increased to $16.95.

Contains: excerpts from letters, most of them to Kellner, pp. viii, ix, xi, 3, 9, 12-13, 20, 37, 38, 65, 70, 73, 78, 82, 86-87, 95, 96, 104, 109 [C43], 115-16, 120, 128-29, 132, 133, 134, 136, 143, 147, 163-64, 166-67, 181-82, 188, 189, 190, 195, 208, 211, 214, 218, 224, 232, 233, 238 [C43], 252, 258, 262 [C43], 267 [C43], 269, 276, 277, 280, 282, 287, 292-304; unpublished verse, p. 26; unpublished manuscript passage from The Blind Bow-Boy, p. 145; "The Modern Composers at a Glance," pp. 113-14 [A7, D57], passages from Columbia University Oral History [1960], pp. 30, 58, 191, 261, 289, 305, 306, 311-12; thirty-three photographs by Van Vechten.

C 59   Ronald Firbank   1969

RONALD FIRBANK | [decoration] | A Biography | [rule] | MIRIAM J. BENKOVITZ | [rule] | [borzoi] | ALFRED . A . KNOPF | New York | 1969 [the foregoing in a single line border]

blank leaf [i-vii] viii-xi [xiii] xiv-xv [xvi-xvii] xviii [1-3] 4-300 [i]
ii-x, 3 leaves. 21.1 X 14.3 cm.

Black cloth boards; title in blind on front; author, title, and publisher
down spine in gold. Lower and fore edges rough trimmed; blue top edges.
Blue, black, white, and manilla dust jacket.

Contains: [three letters to Ronald Firbank], pp. 218, 235, 247-48; photograph of Hunter Stagg by Van Vechten.

C 60   Moby-Dick as Doubloon   1970

MOBY-DICK | AS DOUBLOON | ESSAYS AND EXTRACTS | (1951-1970) | "I look,
you look, he looks; we look, ye look, they look." Ch. 99, "The Doubloon."
| Edited by | HERSHEL PARKER | UNIVERSITY OF SOUTHERN CALIFORNIA | HAR-
RISON HAYFORD | NORTHWESTERN UNIVERSITY | [publisher's logo] | W.W. NOR-
TON & COMPANY . INC . New York

[i-iv] v-xix [xx] xxi [xxii-xxiv] 1-388 pp. 21.2 X 13 cm.

Stiff paper wrapper with standard design for the Norton Critical Editions.

Contains: [The Greatest American Book], pp. 148-49. [A17; D83]

C 61   The Confidence Man   1971

A NORTON CRITICAL EDITION [flanked by decorations] | HERMAN MELVILLE |
THE CONFIDENCE-MAN: | His Masquerade | AN AUTHORITATIVE TEXT | BACKGROUNDS
AND SOURCES | REVIEWS . CRITICISM | AN ANNOTATED BIBLIOGRAPHY | Edited by
| HERSHEL PARKER | UNIVERSITY OF SOUTHERN CALIFORNIA | [publisher's logo]
| W.W. NORTON & COMPANY . INC. New York

blank leaf [i-iv] v-vii [viii] ix-xi [xii-xiv] xv-xvii [xviii] 1-376 pp., 2
blank leaves. 21.2 X 13 cm.

Stiff paper wrapper with standard design for the Norton Critical Editions.

Contains: [The Great Transcendental Satire], p. 283. [A17; D83]

C 62   In His Own Time   1971

F. SCOTT | FITZGERALD | [rule] | IN HIS | OWN TIME: | A MISCELLANY | Edit-
ed by Matthew J. Bruccoli and Jackson R. Bryer | POPULAR LIBRARY . NEW
YORK

[i-viii] ix [x] xi-xxvi [xxvii-xxviii, 1-2] 3-481 [482-84]. 17.5 X 10.5
cm.

Stiff paper wrappers printed on front and spine in black and orange with
illustration and blurb. No. 445-08274. All edges green.

Contains: Fitzgerald on the March, pp. 355-56. [D106]

C 63   Gertrude Stein: A Composite Portrait   1974

GERTRUDE STEIN | A COMPOSITE PORTRAIT | Edited by | LINDA SIMON | [pub-
lisher's logo] DISCUS BOOKS | PUBLISHED BY AVON [the foregoing in a one
line border]

[1-10] 11-192 pp. 17.8 X 10.7 cm.

Stiff paper wrappers printed in brown with a multi-color collage of portraits and paintings of Gertrude Stein, including Van Vechten's profile
photograph of her, cut-up. No. 20115.

Contains: How To Read Gertrude Stein, pp. 50-58 [D24]; photograph of
Stein by Van Vechten.

C 64   A Centennial Celebration for Gertrude Stein   1974

a. Regular issue

A CENTENNIAL CELEBRATION FOR GERTRUDE STEIN 1874 — February Third —
1974 [photograph by Van Vechten of Gertrude Stein; all of the foregoing
on front] | Millersville State College, Millersville, Pa. [painting by
Picasso of Gertrude Stein; all of the foregoing on back]

1 leaf, 43 X 27.8 cm., french-folded to 21.7 X 14 cm.

Ticonderoga text, printed recto and verso. Limitation note: One thousand twenty-six copies of this brochure have been printed at Millersville
State College, of which twenty-six are lettered A through Z.

Contains: Gertrude Stein [C22]; four photographs by Van Vechten.

b. Limited issue

Identical to C64a with the following exceptions: The limitation note
adds: This is copy ___ [number in red ink]; printed on heavy white (as
opposed to light-weight tan) paper and enclosed in decorative envelopes
in one of five color variations: gold and either blue, red, brown, tan,
black.

C 65   Ronald Firbank Memoirs and Critiques   1977

RONALD FIRBANK | MEMOIRS AND CRITIQUES | edited with an introduction by |
MERVYN HORDER | [publisher's logo] | DUCKWORTH

[i-v] vi [vii] viii-xii [1-3] 4-226, 1 leaf. 21.5 X 13.8 cm.

Black cloth boards printed down spine in gold. No free front end paper.
Purple, white, and half-tone dust jacket.

Contains: Ronald Firbank, pp. 161-65. [A17; D87]

C66   Selections from the Gutter   1977

[triple rule] | Selections | from the | Gutter | [double rule] | Jazz
Portraits from 'The Jazz Record' | Edited by | Art Hodes and Chadwick
Hansen | [rule] | UNIVERSITY OF CALIFORNIA PRESS | Berkeley . Los An-
geles . London

[i-viii] xi [xii] xiii-xiv [1-2] 3-233 [234] pp.   25.2 X 17.3 cm.

Blue cloth boards; title printed down spine in silver. Issued simultaneously in paperback with illustrated cover.

Contains: Memories of Bessie Smith, pp. 60,62-63 [D141]; photograph of
Bessie Smith by Van Vechten.

C67   Alastair   1979

VICTOR ARWAS | ALASTAIR | Illustrator of Decadence | With 96 illustra-
tions, 4 in colour | [publisher's logo] | THAMES AND HUDSON

[1-4] 5-100 pp.   28 X 20.3 cm.

stiff white paper wrappers printed, front and back, in black and teal
blue, with illustrations.

Contains: [Alastair, reprinted with a brief cut from B11], pp. 15-16;
three illustrations for The Blind Bow-Boy, each with a brief quotation
from the novel, pp. [4] 62-63.

D.
CONTRIBUTIONS TO
PERIODICALS

1901

D1 Letter From Chicago, Pulse [Cedar Rapids, Iowa], 2:17-18 (18 October).

1902

D2 Love Me, Love My Dog, University of Chicago Weekly, 10:331-32 (9 January).

D3 The Change in Harlowe, University of Chicago Weekly, 10:332-33 (9 January).

D4 The Power of Circumstance, University of Chicago Weekly, 10:372-73 (23 January).

D5 Snell Hall Stories: "Dick," University of Chicago Weekly, 10:392 (30 January).

D6 Coming Events Cast Their Shadows, University of Chicago Weekly, 10:411-12 (6 February).

D7 A Relief, University of Chicago Weekly, 10:942-43 (31 July).

1904

D8 Letter From Chicago, Pulse, 4:88 (January).

1907

D9 Salomé — The Most Sensational Opera of the Age, Broadway Magazine, 17:381-91 (January).

D10 The Coming Opera Season, Bookman, 26:256-65 (November).

1908

D11 How the Twelve Best Sellers Ended, Smart Set, 24:160 (March). [C56]

D12 Story of My Operatic Career, by Luisa Tetrazzini [ghostwritten by
     Van Vechten], Cosmopolitan Magazine, 45:49-51 (June).

1909

D13 The Coming New York Season, New Music Review, 9:17-26 (December).

     According to Klaus Jonas's 1955 bibliography, Van Vechten contri-
     buted "Foreign Notes" and "Facts, Rumors, and Remarks" to the New
     Music Review "from 1910 to 1911." Van Vechten's collection in the
     New York Public Library contains no issues of the periodical during
     this period, nor did he sign the "Facts, Rumors, and Remarks" column
     in this issue. Some of the entries read as if they were Van Vech-
     ten's work, however.

1910

D14 Can the American Girl Succeed in Opera?, Pictorial Review, 11:16
     (January).

D15 The Shoes of Clyde Fitch, by Walter Tempest [pseudonym], Green Book
     Album [Chicago], 3:569-72 (March).

     In his copy, Van Vechten wrote, "Channing [Pollock] got me the order
     for this, and, naturally, furnished most of the material. Even at
     the time I was ashamed to sign my own name."

1912

D16 Typhoons and Troubadours: A Review of the Month's Drama, Trend, 3:
     57-60 (April).

1913

D17 Massenet and Women, New Music Review, 12:69-72 (February). [A4]

1914

D18 Drama: The Dying Audience, Trend, 7:109-13 (April).

D19 A Cockney Flower Girl and Some Negroes [Pygmalion and Granny Maumee],
     Trend, 7:231-38 (April). [A9, A28]

D20 George Moore Gossips Again, Trend, 7:291-95 (June).

D21 The Last Look Back, Trend, 7:373-81 (June).

D22 Plays About Letters and Liars, Trend, 8:476-84 (July).

D23 Bernard Shaw Liberates the Children [Misalliance], Trend, 8:449-52 (July).

D24 How To Read Gertrude Stein, Trend, 8:553-57 (August). [C63]

D25 Stage Decoration as a Fine Art, Trend, 8:621-30 (August). [A4, A25; EIII52]

D26 Once Aboard the Lugger, San Guglielmo; an Account of a Flight from Italy in War Time, Trend, 8:13-24 (October).

D27 Some Glimpses at the European Stage, Trend, 8:69-73 (October).

D28 The Editor's Workbench, signed "Atlas" [pseudonym], Trend, 8:100-1 (October). [A3]

     Van Vechten edited the October, November, and December issues of Trend.

D29 War Is Not Hell, Trend, 8:146-52 (November).

D30 Away Go the Critics — and On Come the Plays, Trend, 8:233-39 (November.

D31 How Mr. George Moore Rescued a Lady From Embarrassment, Trend, 8:320-32 (December). [A22]

                              1915

D32 How Donald Dedicated His Poem, Rogue, 1:8-10 (1 April).

D33 The Nightingale and the Peahen, Rogue, 1:7-9 (1 May). [A22]

D34 Music For Museums?, Rogue, 1:10-15 (15 May). [A4]

D35 An Interrupted Conversation, Rogue, 1:7-9 (1 August). [A22]

D36 Music After the Great War, Forum, 54:356-67 (September). [A4]

D37 Three Lives, Rogue, 2:8-9 (1 October).

D38 Adolphe Appia and Gordon Craig, Forum, 54:483-87 (October). [A4]

D39 The Fifth Alternative, Snappy Stories, 15:27-30 (18 December).

                              1916

D40 A New Principle in Music: Strawinsky and His Work, Russian Review, 1:160-63 (April). [A5]

D41 Shall We Realize Wagner's Ideals?, Musical Quarterly, 2:387-401 (July). [A5]

1917

D42 Olive Fremstad, <u>Bellman</u>, 22:238-43 (3 March). [A6, A10]

D43 Geraldine Farrar, <u>Bellman</u>, 22:322-26 (24 March). [A6, A10]

D44 The Great American Composer, <u>Vanity Fair</u>, 8:75,140 (April).
     [A6, A10]

D45 Feodor Chaliapine, <u>Bellman</u>, 22:431-34 (21 April). [A6, A10; EV6]

D46 Music and the Electrical Theater, <u>Seven Arts</u>, 2:97-102 (May). [A6,
     A15]

D47 Waslav Nijinsky, <u>Bellman</u>, 22:628-33 (9 June). [A6, A10, A25; C32]

D48 The Bane of the Musical Critics. The Reason Why Music Is Unpopular,
     <u>Vanity Fair</u>, 8:71 (June). [A6, A15; D160]

D49 Mariette Mazarin, <u>Bellman</u>, 23:16-18 (7 July). [A6, A10]

D50 Mary Garden, <u>Bellman</u>, 23:207-12 (25 August). [A6, A10]

D51 Rondes de Printemps [in French], <u>Rongwrong</u>, third issue of <u>Blind Man</u>,
     September.

D52 Pour Amuser Rich, <u>Rongwrong</u>, third issue of <u>Blind Man</u>, September.

D53 Communications: Letter to the Editor, <u>Seven Arts</u>, 2:669-79 (September).

D54 Notes on Gluck's <u>Armide</u>, <u>Musical Quarterly</u>, 3:539-47 (October).
     [A6; EII534]

D55 In Defense of the Art of Acting, and a Demand for a Truce to Actor-
     Baiting, <u>Vanity Fair</u>, 9:142-44 (November). [A7]

D56 Yvette Guilbert, <u>Bellman</u>, 23:495-96 (3 November). [A6, A10]

D57 The Critic Crystallizes, <u>Chronicle</u>, 2:13 (November). [A7; C54, C58]

D58 Old Days and New, <u>Theatre Magazine</u>, 26:292 (November). [A7]

D59 Valverde and "The Land of Joy," <u>Bellman</u>, 23:628-31 (8 December).
     [A7, A8; EIV47]

1918

D60 Two Young American Playwrights [Philip Moeller and Avery Hopwood],
     <u>Reedy's Mirror</u> [St. Louis], 27:104-6 (22 February). [A7]

D61 Erik Satie: Master of the Rigolo. A Frenchman Extremist in Modernist
     Music, <u>Vanity Fair</u>, 10:57,92 (March). [A6, A17]

D62 Memoirs, by Fania Marinoff [ghost-written by Van Vechten], <u>American
     Weekly Jewish News</u>, 1:7 (15 March).

D63 Memoirs, by Fania Marinoff, Second Installment [ghost-written by Van
Vechten], American Weekly Jewish News, 1:8 (22 March).

D64 Memoirs, by Fania Marinoff, Third Installment [ghost-written by Van
Vechten], American Weekly Jewish News, 1:10 (29 March).

D65 New York's Operatic Greatness, Musical Courier, 28 March.

D66 Russian Opera — An Unexplored Field, Chronicle, 3:15-17 (April).

D67 In Defense of Bad Taste, Bellman, 25:131-32 (3 August). [A7]

D68 Music and Cooking, Smart Set, 66:71-76 (September). [A7]

D69 The New Art of the Singer, Bellman, 25:319-24 (21 September). [A7,
A15]

D70 De Senectute Cantorum, Musical Quarterly, 4:604-17 (October). [A7]

1919

D71 A Night With Farfariello. Popular Bowery Entertainer Who Impersonates
Italian Types, Theatre Magazine, 28:32-34 (January). [A9]

D72 The New Isadora, Bellman, 26:270-71 (8 March). [A7, A25; C33]

D73 Mimi Aguglia as Salome, Bellman, 26:322-26 (22 March). [A9; EIII91]

D74 On the Relative Difficulties of Depicting Heaven and Hell in Music,
Musical Quarterly, 5:553-60 (October). [A9, A15]

1920

D75 Variations on a Theme by Havelock Ellis, Smart Set, 61:101-7 (January). [A9, A17]

D76 Marguerite d'Alvarez. A Remarkable Tribute to a Remarkable Artist,
Musical Courier, 22 April. [F10]

D77 The Cat in Music, Musical Quarterly, 6:573-85 (October). [A11]

D78 Edgar Saltus: A Postscript, Double-Dealer, 2:162-64 (October). [C5]

1921

D79 On Hearing What You Want When You Want It, Musical Quarterly, 7:559-
64 (October). [A15]

D80 The Tin Trunk, The Reviewer, 2:81-86 (November). [A22]

D81 Cordite For Concerts, Smart Set, 66:127-30 (October). [A15]

D82 An Old Daguerreotype, The Reviewer, 2:129-35 (December). [A22]

1922

D83 The Later Work of Herman Melville, Double-Dealer, 3:9-20 (January).
     [A7; C61]

D84 Movies For Program Notes, Wave [Chicago], February. [A15]

D85 Pastiches et Pistaches: Concerning the Simplicity of the Great; The
     Intelligence of Cats; Charles Demuth and Florine Stettheimer [C30];
     The King of the Jews; Atmosphere in Music; Romance versus Realism;
     Mr. George Jean Nathan; Marguerite d'Alvarez, The Reviewer, 2:268-73
     (February).

     This is the first installment of a projected book which was never
     published. Under the same title, Van Vechten had sent out a group
     of thirteen "sketches, half-story, half-essay, in the semi-fictional
     vein that has been worked by George Moore." Thirteen publishers re-
     jected Pastiches et Pistaches. Eleven of the pieces were published
     separately: "Au Bal Musette" [A7, A22]; "An Interrupted Conversa-
     tion" [A7, A22; D35]; "The Holy Jumpers" [A9, A22, A28]; "The Night-
     ingale and the Peahen" [A22; D33]; "Once Aboard the Lugger San Gug-
     lielmo" [D26]; "How Donald Dedicated His Poem" [D32]; "How Mr. George
     Moore Rescued a Lady From Embarrassment" [A22; D28]; "The Fifth Al-
     ternative" [D39]; "Why Not Do It Yourself?" [A7; D67, published as
     "In Defense of Bad Taste"]; "Three Lives" [D37]; "How the Twelve Best
     Sellers Ended" [C56; D11]. "The Rape of the Madonna Stella" and
     "What Do You Think It Is?" were never published; see notes following
     A6 and A12. Van Vechten continued to add and deleted materials under
     the title, Pastiches et Pistaches, until 1922 when it served to cover
     six installments in The Reviewer. The manuscript includes title and
     dedication pages, suggesting that Van Vechten continued to think of
     the contents for a book. Other manuscripts are laid in [B and C].

D86 Pastiches et Pistaches: Modern Music in the Far East; Artists and
     Business Men; Eva Tanguay; Music and the Stomach; Law and Custom;
     The Signatures of Things; A Suggestion for Parents; The New Art of
     Stage Decoration; Uses for a Million Dollars, The Reviewer, 2:306-11
     (March).

D87 Ronald Firbank, Double-Dealer, 3:185-86 (April). [[A17; C 59]

D88 The Great White Borzoi [Alfred A. Knopf], Bookman [Toronto], April.

D89 Marie Jeritza, The Reviewer, 3:377-82 (April). [Quoted in Literary
     Digest, 6 May 1922.]

D90 Pastiches et Pistaches: A Note Addressed, Sensa Rancore, to Certain
     Ultra-Virile Adolescents; Ernest Boyd [C12]; The Power of Weakness;
     Rosinante to the Road Again; Paul Thévenaz; The Secret Glory; Satir-
     ist or Decadent?; The Chocolate Czarina, The Reviewer, 3:455-59 (May).

D91 Henry Blake Fuller, Double-Dealer, 3:289-99 (June). [A17]

D92 Pastiches et Pistaches: Our Country, 'Tis Of Thee!; First Editions;
     Very Destructive Criticism; Another Note on Jeritza; A Note by Mr.
     Machen; Perhaps; Bert Williams [A28]; Louis Bouché; A New Definition;

Something to Think About; True Politeness; Norman Bel Geddes Triumphs, The Reviewer, 3:588-93 (July).

D93   Back to Delibes, Musical Quarterly, 8:605-10 (October). [A17, A25]

D94   Pastiches et Pistaches: Notes for Collectors; Louis Wilkinson; Humor: Literary and Musical; Thought for the Bath-Tub; The Revenge of Time; The Grand Street Follies; Art and Prostitution; A Note on French Dress; Eternal Naïveté; Monsieur Croce, Anti-Dilettante; An Artist Cook; Sermon on the Mount; Fermé; The Best Orchestra in America, The Reviewer, 3:632-38 (October).

1923

D95   On Visiting Fashionable Places Out of Season, The Reviewer, 3:758-77 (January). [A28]

D96   An Unrealized Art, Fashions for the Home [Chicago], p. 8, January.

D97   Arthur Machen: Dreamer and Mystic, International Book Review, 1:36-37 (February). [A17]

D98   A Lady Who Defies Time [Gertrude Atherton, Black Oxen], Nation, 116:194-94 (14 February).

D99   A Note on Dedications, Bookman, 57:502-8 (July). [C10]

D100 The Ten Dullest Authors: A Symposium, Vanity Fair, 20:58 (August). [C49]

D101 Choosing the New Century's Best Books, International Book Review, 6:7 (May).

1924

D102 Pastiches et Pistaches: The Sabbath Glee Club of Richmond; Ornaments in Jade by Arthur Machen; A Prophet in 1873; Quand Même; A Sweetly Solemn Thought; Anna Pavlowa [A25; D135]; Miguel Covarrubias; A Message for Women's Clubs; The Circus, The Reviewer, 4:98-103 (January).

D103 The Lady Stuffed With Pistachio Nuts [Elinor Wylie, Jennifer Lorn], Dial, 126:283-86 (March). [C14]

D104 A Note on Tights, American Mercury, 2:428-32 (August).

1925

D105 George Gershwin: An American Composer Who is Writing Notable Music in the Jazz Idiom, Vanity Fair, 24:40,78,84 (March).

D106 Fitzgerald on the March [F. Scott Fitzgerald, The Great Gatsby], Nation, 120:575-76 (20 May). [C62]

D107   Credo of a Musical Critic [Ernest Newman, A Musical Critic's Holi-
       day], Saturday Review of Literature, 1:772-73 (23 May).

D108   Countée Cullen, a Note About the Young Negro Poet, Author of The
       Shroud of Color, Vanity Fair, 24:62 (June). [A28]

D109   The Folksongs of the American Negro, Vanity Fair, 24:52,92 (July).
       [A28]

D110   A Note on Breakfasts, American Mercury, 5:485-88 (August). [A22]

D111   The Black Blues. Negro Songs of Disappointment in Love: Their Pathos
       Hardened With Laughter, Vanity Fair, 24:57,86,92 (August). [A28;
       C49. Translated and printed, without permission, as "Die Schwarze
       Welle. Waschechte Chocolate Kiddies als ,Blues' Sängermen von Carl
       Van Vechten, New York," in Die Bühne, Vienna, 1926. The transla-
       tion seems to include some passages from D120 as well.]

D112   All God's Chillun Got Songs, Theatre Magazine, 42:24,63 (August).
       [A28]

D113   A Whisper Spun in Murano [Elinor Wylie, The Venetian Glass Nephew],
       Saturday Review of Literature, 2:171 (3 October).

D114   Langston Hughes: A Biographical Note, Vanity Fair, 25:62 (September).
       [A28]

D115   Prescription for the Negro Theatre, Vanity Fair, 25:46,92,98 (Octo-
       ber). [A28]

D116   Religious Folk Songs of the American Negro [The Book of American
       Negro Spirituals, Ed. James Weldon Johnson], Opportunity, 3:330-31
       (November). [A28]

D117   Mutations Among Americans, American Mercury, 6:487-89 (December).

                              1926

D118   Fast and Loos [Anita Loos, Gentlemen Prefer Blondes], Book Review,
       1:20 (January).

D119   Moanin' Wid a Sword in Ma Han', Vanity Fair, 25:61,100,102 (Febru-
       ary). [A28]

D120   Negro "Blues" Singers, Vanity Fair, 26:67,106,108 (March). [A28;
       see note, D111. Quoted in Time, 22 November 1937.]

D121   Langston Hughes, Vanity Fair, 26:70 (May). [A28]

D122   The Negro in Art: How Shall He Be Portrayed?, Crisis, 31:129 (March).

       Van Vechten prepared the anonymous questionnaire for this symposium.
       His own reply appeared in the March issue; the questionnaire was re-
       printed in each subsequent issue through September 1926. It had been
       sent out to "the artists of the world" under the signature of the
       black novelist, Jessie Fauset.

1927

D123 A Letter of Invitation, Opportunity, 5:1 (January). [A28]

D124 Fabulous Hollywood, Vanity Fair, 28:54,108 (May).

D125 Hollywood Parties, Vanity Fair, 28:47,86,90 (June).

D126 A Letter to Benjamin Brawley, Opportunity, 5:1 (July). [A28]

D127 Hollywood Royalty, Vanity Fair, 28:38,86 (July).

D128 Understanding Hollywood, Vanity Fair, 28:45,78 (August).

1930

D129 Notes For An Autobiography, Colophon, A Book Collectors' Quarterly,
      Part Three, unpaged signatures, 4 pp. (June). [A22; C20]

1934

D130 Carl Van Vechten Comments, Challenge [Boston], 1:28 (September).
      [A28]

1939

D131 "Mamba's Daughters," Opportunity, 17:46-47 (February). [A28]

1940

D132 The James Weldon Johnson Memorial Project, Crisis, 47:41,50 (Feb-
      ruary). [A28]

D133 The Proposed James Weldon Johnson Memorial, Opportunity, 18:38-40
      (February). [A28; F108]

1942

D134 The James Weldon Johnson Collection at Yale, Crisis, 49:19-18 (July).
      [A28; F111]

D135 The Dance Criticism of Carl Van Vechten, Dance Index, 1:144-89
      (September, October, November). [A4, A6, A7, A8, A10, A17, A21, A25;
      C32, C33, C34, C36; D102; EII373, 379, 386, 406, 412, 431, 432, 440,
      482, 526, 591, 594, 705; EIV13]

1943

D136 An Ode to the Stage Door Canteen, Theatre Arts, 27:229-31 (April).

1944

D137 Unsung Americans Sung [W.C. Handy, Unsung Americans Sung], Respon-
      sibility [Brooklyn], 2:ii (Fall). [A28]

1945

D138 First Night in Paris, Encore, 7:354-61 (March). [A12]

D139 Lens-Pictures [John LaTouche, Congo; Clark Kinnard, This Must Not
      Happen Again], View, 5:18-19 (November).

1946

D140 The World of Florine Stettheimer, Harper's Bazaar, 80:238,353-56
      (October). [Quoted in Ettie Stettheimer, "Foreword" to Florine
      Stettheimer, Crystal Flowers, 1949.]

D141 Memories of Bessie Smith, Jazz Record, 58:6-7,29 (September).
      [A28; C66; D120]

1948

D142 How I Remember Joseph Hergesheimer, Yale University Library Gazette,
      22:87-92 (January). [A23]

D143 Mr. Cabell of Lichfield and Poictesme, Yale University Library Ga-
      zette, 23:1-7 (July). [A23]

1949

D144 Puss in Books, Yale University Library Gazette, 23:175-80 (April).
      [A23]

1950

D145 Random Notes on Mr. Mencken of Baltimore, Yale University Library
      Gazette, 24:165-71 (April). [A23]

1951

D146 Theodore Dreiser as I Knew Him, Yale University Library Gazette,
      23:87-92 (January). [A23]

D147 Prima Donna of Yesteryear [Mary Garden and Louis Biancolli, Mary
      Garden's Story], Saturday Review of Literature, 34:19-20 (26 May).

1952

D148   Some "Literary Ladies" I Have Known, Yale University Library Gazette, 26:97-116 (January). [A23, A28]

D149   Belief in an Ideal [Agnes DeMille, Dance to the Piper], Saturday
Review, 35:17-18 (26 January). [A25]

1953

D150   Queen of the Dance [Anton Dolin, Alicia Markova], Saturday Review,
36:34 (25 April). [A25]

D151   Cats, Magic, and Occultism, Fate Magazine [Evanston, Illinois], 6:
55-70 (November). [A11]

1954

D152   A Good Little Devil [Fritzi Scheff], Saturday Review, 37:33,35-36
(29 May).

D153   The Secret of the Russian Ballet, Dance Magazine, 28:30-31,57,60-
61 (September). [A4, A25]

D154   Blustery Madame Fremstad [Mary Watkins Cushing, The Rainbow Bridge],
Saturday Review, 37:45-46 (13 November).

1955

D155   The Voice and the Temperament [Marguerite d'Alvarez, Forgotten Al-
tars], Saturday Review, 38:9,43 (26 February).

Originally commissioned by Rupert Hart-Davis as a preface for d'Alvarez's autobiography, Van Vechten's essay was titled "A Camellia
for Marguerite." At page-proof stage, it was suppressed on the au-
thority of representatives of the d'Alvarez Estate because of various unflattering references. The book review is a revised version
of the preface.

1956

D157   Soft Voice of Feeling [Marian Anderson, My Lord, What a Morning!],
Saturday Review, 39:22 (3 November). [A28]

1957

D158   Terpsichorean Souvenirs, Dance Magazine, 1:16-18,92 (January).
[A25. Quoted in Cedar Rapids Gazette, 27 January 1957].

1958

D159 Terpsichore in the U. S. Army [Agnes DeMille, And Promenade Home],
      Saturday Review, 41:16-17 (18 October). [A25]

1960

D160 Why Music Is Unpopular, American Record Guide, 26:778-81 (June).
      [A6, A15]

1962

D161 Portraits of the Artists, Esquire, 18:170-74,256-58 (December).

1963

D162 Ma-Draper [Muriel Draper], Yale University Library Gazette, 37:125-
      29 (April).

D163 Rogue Elephant in Porcelain [Wallace Stevens], Yale University Li-
      brary Gazette, 38:41-50 (October).

1965

D164 On Words and Music: How I Listen to "Four Saints in Three Acts,"
      American Record Guide, 31:521-22 (February). [C15; EII853]

1967

D165 The Origin of the Sonnets From the Patagonian, Hartwick Review, 3:
      50-56 (Spring).

1974

D166 More Laurels for Our Gertrude [B39] and [Gertrude Stein rings bells]
      [C22], Confrontation, 8:12, 18-19 (Spring).

1975

D167 [Gertrude Stein rings bells], Journal of Modern Literature, 4:814
      (April). [C22]

D168 [a letter to Emma Gray Trigg, 8 April 1924], The Glasgow Newsletter,
      3:9 (October).

1977

D169 Gertrude Stein: An Epilogue [EV50], [Gertrude Stein rings bells],
      [C22], [journal entries], Books at Iowa, 26:6-9,13,14-16 (April).

E.
CONTRIBUTIONS TO
NEWSPAPERS

I   Articles from The Chicago American and Inter-Ocean

Van Vechten wrote regularly for the Chicago American from May 1904
to September 1905. All of his work was anonymous, although a series
of regular articles, most of them titled "Gossip of the Chicago
Smart Set," were signed "The Chaperone." The scrapbook containing
his work "has been lost," according to Van Vechten's note in his
collection in the New York Public Library. The extant examples he
later discovered among his step-mother's effects. Toward the end of
his tenure with the Chicago American, he wrote occasional colums for
the Chicago Inter-Ocean. Three examples, all titled "The Whirl of
Society," signed "Willie Dearborn," were similarly preserved. Van
Vechten believed there was "more than a faint resemblance" to his
later writing in the pieces for the Chicago Inter-Ocean.

                              1904

EI1 Only Woman Banker "Tells How," 26 May.

EI2 $100,000 Cost of Entertainment for G.O.P. Leaders, 21 June.

EI3 Ideal Motherhood Rebukes Its Opposite, 17 December.

EI4 Xmas Toys Boy's Death Messenger, Little Louis Simpson Dies of Joy
     at Sight of Pretty Things Brought Him by Santa Claus, 26 December.

                              1905

EI5 Mexican Project, 9 March.

EI6 First Picture Ever Published of a Beautiful Chicago Girl, 19 March.

EI7 Find Hanish an Imposter; Two of Faithful Desert, 21 March.

EI8   "High Priest" Forced to Flee from New York in Order to Avoid Arrest, <u>circa</u> March.

EI9   The Second Bertha Honoré, Mrs. Potter Palmer's Successor, 9 April.

EI10 Society's Latest Fad, <u>circa</u> April.

EI11 A New Type of Chorus Girl, <u>circa</u> May.

EI12 Charming Chicago Girls, 14 May.

EI13 Little Daughters of Chicago Society and Dear Mothers, <u>circa</u> June.

EI14 Gossip of the Chicago Smart Set, 18 July.

EI15 The Catch of the Season, Who Is She?, 10 September.

EI16 Sues Suitor, Cooled by Glass Eye, <u>circa</u> September.

EI17 Why Café Chantant Gayety Drew Crowds, <u>circa</u> September.

EI18 The Whirl of Society, 26 September.

EI19 The Whirl of Society, 27 September.

EI20 The Whirl of Society, 1 October.

<u>II   Contributions to The New York Times</u>

During his six and a half years with the <u>New York Times</u>, Van Vechten had no by-line. This record of his contributions, therefore, is based almost exclusively on his own scrapbooks. He did not date his work for some time, so more specific dating than that given is difficult though not impossible. He began contributing minor fillers in October 1906; in November he was hired as a staff reporter; in January 1907 he began to serve as assistant music critic. Hundreds of brief and inconsequential paragraphs have been deleted in the following compilation. After a selection of those written prior to Van Vechten's first feature article in January 1907, only those fillers of historical significance are included.

1906

EII1 Nordica May Sing in Opera [Lillian Nordica], <u>circa</u> October, <u>et seq.</u>

EII2 We May Hear "Pagliacci"

EII3 "Lakme" at Metropolitan

EII4 Hammerstein Still Smiles [Oscar Hammerstein I]

EII5 Couldn't Get Enough Bonci [Alessandro Bonci]

EII6 Concert Master Franko [Sam Franko]

EII7   Opera Singers Arrive [Nellie Melba]

EII8   More Opera Singers Arrive

EII9   New Baritone in Opera [Charles Gunther]

EII10   Revival of "Lakme"

EII11   Caruso's Moustache Off [Enrico Caruso], circa November, et seq.

EII12   Fuse Ablaze at New Opera

EII13   Hammerstein is Satisfied

EII14   Conreid Takes a Rest [Heinrich Conreid]

EII15   Mr. Hammerstein Concert

EII16   Leoncavallo at the Opera [Ruggerio Leoncavallo, at the American
        premiere of Pagliacci]

EII17   Renaud Still Hoarse [Maurice Renaud]

EII18   Opera at Manhattan Begins Tonight [opening performance of the Man-
        hattan Opera House], 3 December.

EII19   Sleuth with Opera Singers [Lina Cavallieri], circa December, et
        seq.

EII20   Saint-Saëns at the Opera [Camille Saint-Saëns]

EII21   Makes Hammerstein Laugh

EII22   Cast for Melba's Premiere

EII23   Signor Campanari Quits [Leandro Campanari]

EII24   Manhattan Stars in Demand

EII25   De Reszke Can't Come [Jean De Reszke]

EII26   Conreid's Illness Serious?

EII27   Renaud in Fine Voice Again

EII28   To Repeat "Carmen"

EII29   "Aida" Tomorrow Night

EII30   Mme. Fremstad Returns [Olive Fremstad]

EII31   Melba Here Jan. 2

EII32   Aida's Face Bruised

EII32   Mme. Kirkby Lunn Ill [Louisa Kirkby Lunn]

1907

EII34   Two Lohengrins Sing at the Metropolitan [Carl Burrian and Andreas Dippel], circa January, et seq.

EII35   Hammerstein Wins in "La Boheme" Suit

EII36   A'Choo! Cry Singers at Both Opera Houses

EII37   Puccini Wants a Book for an American Opera

EII38   Take Off "Salome," Say Opera House Directors

EII39   No Decision on "Salome"; Seats Still on Sale

EII40   Saint-Saëns Conducts [first American performance]

EII41   Fight to Keep "Salome" From Another Theatre

EII42   "Salome" Withdrawn; Conreid Fully Yields

EII43   Combined Calvé-Hading Fools Walter Damrosch

EII44   Conreid Plans Opera Road Tour; "Salome" to be Given

EII45   "La Boheme" Heard at the Manhattan

EII46   Baby Checked at Opera, circa February, et seq.

EII47   Conreid Company Pays for "Salome"

EII48   Tenor War Excites Two Opera Worlds [Bonci and Giovanni Zenatello]

EII49   Bonci Must Stay, Says Hammerstein

EII50   "Salome" Next Year, Says Herr Conreid, circa March, et seq.

EII51   Cohan to Write for New Combine [George M. Cohan]

EII52   Fritzi Scheel Dies; Pneumonia Victim

EII53   "La Boheme" Presented at Manhattan

EII54   Stars of the Opera in Charity Frolic

EII55   Melba's Farewell at the Manhattan

EII56   Opera Comique Plans

EII57   "Das Rheingold" Presented

EII58   Mme. Eames Sues to Divorce Story [Emma Eames and Julian Story]

EII59   Bonci's Reply to Suit

EII60   Melba Sails

EII61   Big House for "Rigoletto"

EII62   Sings Songs of Childhood [Kitty Cheatham]

EII63   Calvé Reappears in "Navarisse"

EII64   Herr Conreid Says He is Not to Resign, circa April, et seq.

EII65   Conducts Oratorio in a Monk's Garb

EII66   Herbert Opera for Hammerstein [Natoma by Victor Herbert]

EII67   Miss Abbot to Quit Conreid [Bessie Abbot]

EII68   Singer Beseiged in Hotel Rooms [Bessie Abbot]

EII69   Lhévinne's Recital [Josef Lhévinne]

EII70   "Aida" Closed at the Manhattan

EII71   Miss Abbot Dodging Summons

EII72   Hammerstein Tells of His Opera Fight

EII73   Actors Deny Lack of Ability Here, circa September, et seq.

EII74   Declares Nothing Ever Happened to Him [Denman Thompson]

EII75   Wall Street and the Drama

EII76   Conreid Opera Co to be Reorganized

EII77   Nordica to Sing for Hammerstein

EII78   Some Experiences and Some Opinions by Marie Lloyd, Connie Ediss, and Hetty King, circa October, et seq.

EII79   Madame Hanako — Tragedy Queen in Miniature, the Japanese Duse

EII80   Mary Garden Likes American Nerve

EII81   Gala Re-Opening of Opera Season

EII82   Fremstad in Danger as Wave Hit Liner

EII83   Miss Farrar Denies Criticizing America [Geraldine Farrar]

EII84   New Basso to Sing in "Mephistofele" [Feodor Chaliapin], circa November, et seq.

EII85   Why France Gives Singers Small Pay [Mary Garden]

EII86   Three Singers Ill; Changes in Opera

EII87   Mme. Tetrazzini May Sing Here This Year [Luisa Tetrazzini]

EII88   Mme. Eames Studies Real Japanese Ways

EII89   Wagner Revival at Metropolitan [The Flying Dutchman]

EII90   Love of Dante and Beatrice in Music, circa December, et seq.

EII91   Conductor Mahler Here for the Opera [Gustav Mahler]

EII92   Hammerstein and Mme. Nordica Part

EII93   Mary Garden Ill; "Louise" Postponed

EII94   Fremstad to Give Us a New Isolde

1908

EII95   Geraldine Farrar to Sing New Roles, circa January, et seq.

EII96   The Versatile Chaliapine, Enemy of Tradition

EII97   Tetrazzini Here for New York Debut

EII98   Opera Stars Clash Over Judgment

EII99   Professor MacDowell Dies at Forty-Six [Edward MacDowell]

EII100 Schumann-Heink Tells a Secret [Ernestine Schumann-Heink]

EII101 M. Renaud Hopes to Sing Wagner Here

EII102 Conreid Resigns as Opera Director

EII103 Children of Opera Singers, circa February, et seq.

EII104 "A Dream Waltz" Wins Applause [by Oscar Strauss and Joseph Her-
        bert]

EII105 Opera Directors at Odds Over Lease

EII106 New Manager for Opera Named [Giulio Gatti-Casazza], 20 February.

EII107 Herr Knote Again Fills Opera Gap [Heinrich Knote]

EII108 Bone for Critics in Next Opera [Pelléas et Mélisande]

EII109 Our Faults As Seen by Mr. Chaliapine

EII110 Dalmorès is Back with Hammerstein [Charles Dalmorès]

EII111 Fremstad Sings Role of Brunhilde

EII112 Conreid's Successor as Seen by Critic

EII113 Dippel Doubles Up to Finish "Siegfried"

EII114 Best in Opera Here, Says Bessie Abbot

EII115 Sunday Night Opera at the Manhattan

EII116 Opera Benefit Nets $7,000 for Charity, _circa_ March, _et seq._

EII117 Right Note Soprano on Her Opera Chance [Ellen Beach Yaw]

EII118 Miss Yaw Pleases at the Metropolitan

EII119 How Miss Fornia Won Her Chance in Opera [Rita Fornia]

EII120 "Waltz Dream" Tenor May Sing Real Opera [Edward Johnson]

EII121 Black Hand Threat at Metropolitan

EII122 Glad Closing Night at the Manhattan

EII123 Record of Successful New Opera This Season at the Manhattan

EII124 DePachmann Gives Last N.Y. Recital [Vladimir dePachmann]

EII125 Farewell Talk from Miss Garden

EII126 Metropolitan Now Under New Officers

EII127 "Rigoletto" Sung at the Academy

EII128 Mme. DeLussan Likes Vaudeville [Zélie deLussan]

EII129 Singers, Not Operas, Attract Most Here

EII130 Tetrazzini to Sing Here for Five Years, _circa_ April, _et seq._

EII131 Like Dippel, Sings Oft on Hurry Calls [Mathilda Bauermeister]

EII132 The Pleasing Art in Miss Kitty Cheatham's Singing of Children's Songs Will be Enjoyed Again Tomorrow

EII133 Festival Concerts by Mahler in 1909

EII134 Review of the Season at the Metropolitan, 5 April.

EII135 Gatti-Casazza Here, Visits Opera House

EII136 Loss on Concert for Jewish Charity

EII137 William Jennings Bryan Speaks Today

EII138 Spurious Paintings Sold and Exhibited

EII139 400 Boys Drill Like Veterans

EII140 Dynamiters Wreck a Railroad Light

EII141 Bogus Art Charge Repeated by Evans

EII142 Spurious Paintings Bring Legal Fights

EII143 Melba to Sing Here with Tetrazzini

EII144 Clausen Arrested in Picture Suits

EII145 Artists Drop Work to Boom Roosevelt

EII146 Berkman Put Out of Labor Meeting [Alexander Berkman]

EII147 Episcopal Split Over Pulpit

EII148 The Organization of the Metropolitan Opera, 26 April.

EII149 Hotel for Women Suddenly Closes, _circa_ May, _et seq._

EII150 Trinity Thronged at Dr. Dix's Funeral

EII151 Clausen Out on Bail, Hints at Conspiracy

EII152 Episcopal Monk Would be a Catholic

EII153 Gatti-Casazza Has Great Opera Plans

EII154 Hammerstein Home, Tells of His Jaunt

EII155 Hammerstein to Set a New Place in Opera

        At the end of May, Van Vechten was appointed Paris Correspondent
        for the _New York Times_. He assumed duties at the end of June.
        His work, dated by wireless when relayed, probably appeared a
        few days after the dates indicated.

EII156 "Gotterdammerung" in Paris to be Given at the Opera for the First
        time in September, 30 June.

EII157 One-Price Tickets at Paris Theatre, 4 July.

EII158 Opera Trust Plans Fight on New York, 11 July.

EII159 Would Make Opera of "Three Weeks" [by Elinor Glyn], 11 July.

EII160 France Will Adopt Life Imprisonment, 16 July.

EII161 Butler Talks Peace to the Parisians [Nicholas Murray Butler] 18
        July.

EII162 G. W. Sands Killed in Motor Accident, 29 July.

EII163 Paris Multitude Cheers Thomas Carr, 31 July.

EII164 Plan Plaza Hotels in London and Paris, 3 August.

EII165 An Opera War of Two Worlds, 8 August.

EII166 Isadora Duncan Raps Maud Allan, 8 August.

EII167 Tetrazzini in Paris, Speaks American, 8 August.

EII168 Will Make Author Their Leading Man, 15 August.

EII169 Americans Do Not Buy French Silks, 15 August.

EII170 To Avoid Giving Us Warmed Over Plays, 22 August.

EII171 Caruso is Unknown in Paris Crowds, 22 August.

EII172 New York to Have Notable Orchestra, 22 August.

EII173 Has Face Slapped in the Rue Scribe [Baron Sacco], 29 August.

EII174 Moving Pictures for Wagner Opera, 12 September.

EII175 Swindle Based on Plot of a Play, 12 September.

EII176 Not a Musician, Writes an Opera [The Old Eagle, by Raule Gun-bourg], 19 September.

EII177 Mary Garden May Wed Russian Prince, 22 September.

EII178 Living in Paris on 94 Cents a Day [Mary Mortimer Maxwell], 23 September.

EII179 Spurious Turned Long in the Louvre, 26 September.

EII180 Insanity From Love Known to Alienists, 26 September.

EII181 Rostand to Delay His Barnyard Drama [Chanticleer by Edmond Ros-tand], 3 October.

EII182 Annual Fall Salon Exhibit of Freaks [Henri Matisse], 3 October.

EII183 Only One Woman in Bernstein Play [Henri Bernstein]

EII184 Naval Disasters Stir French Public, 9 October.

EII185 Bernstein's "Israel" Produced in Paris, 13 October.

EII186 Farrar to be "Girl of the Golden West," 17 October.

EII187 Paris Plans Tax on Foreign Visitors, 17 October.

EII188 New Tuberculosis Serum Discovered, 17 October.

EII189 Paris Absorbed in Two New Plays, 17 October.

EII190 Playwright Upsets Comedie Francais, 17 October.

EII191 "Gotterdammerung" at the Paris Opera, 20 October.

EII192 Mary Garden Makes a Thrilling Salome, 24 October.

EII193 Brings Rich Cargo of Opera Singers, 24 October.

EII194 Child Actors Seen in German Sex Play [Spring's Awakening by Frank Wedekind], 28 October.

EII195 Painted De Musset; Dead at Eighty-One, 30 October.

EII196 Few American Plays Interest Paris, 31 October.

EII197 Rodin Makes Bust of Thomas F. Ryan, 7 November.

EII198 Paris Angry at New Skyscrapers, 14 November.

EII199 Paris Suspects Man With Bare Feet, 14 November.

EII200 Shonts Overjoyed at Birth of Duke, 17 November.

EII201 Six Vacant Chairs in French Academy, 21 November.

EII202 Paris Grand Prix Later Next Year, 21 November.

EII203 Paris Stage Has a New Thriller, 22 November.

EII204 Paris Newspapers Handled Severely on the Stage, 22 November.

EII205 Paris Women Now Wear Small Hats, 28 November.

EII206 French President Opens Paris Show, 28 November.

EII207 To Rake Up Scandal Against Castellane, 28 November.

EII208 Sues J. G. Bennett For Girl's Support, 28 November.

EII209 Original "Salome" is to be Destroyed, 4 December.

EII210 Princess De Sagan Checks Scandals, 4 December.

EII211 Maeterlinck Sues Paris Opera [Monna Vanna], 5 December.

EII212 De Lara's "Sangä" New Opera in Paris [by Isidore Cohen], 9 December.

EII213 Two Storms in Paris Theatrical World, 12 December.

EII214 Paris Has No Topic [the Steinheil Case], 12 December.

EII215 Pistol Was Taken From Mme Steinheil, 19 December.

EII216 Bennet Defense Closes in Paris, 19 December.

EII217 Riots of Students to Bring Reforms, 26 December.

EII218 Big Crowds Attend Area Show in Paris, 26 December.

EII219 Money and Dancer Cause Prince Suit, 26 December.

1909

EII220 Princess De Sagan Is Not Very Happy, 2 January.

EII221 France is Active in Relief of Italy, 9 January.

EII222 Experts Deceived by Forged Scarabs, 9 January.

EII223 Thirst for Blood Among the French [public executions], 16 January.

EII224 "Monna Vanna" Makes Success as Opera, 16 January.

EII225 Abruzzi May Resign His Rank to Marry, 19 January.

EII226 Kills Wife to End Her Long Suffering, 6 February.

EII227 Chanticler Sought for Rostand Play, 6 February.

EII228 Paris Again Turns to Beauty Patches, 13 February.

EII229 Loie Fuller to Aid New Boston Opera, 13 February.

EII230 Stepson Not Suing Pianist Paderewski, 22 February.

EII231 Paderewski Blamed by Stephson's Wife, 27 February.

EII232 Two Holidays for Americans in Paris, 27 February.

EII233 Statue is Married and Painted Red, 6 March.

EII234 Can't Sing "Salome" at Paris Opera, 6 March.

EII235 Finds Love for France in Kaiser [Stephane Luazanne], 7 March.

EII236 Calais Fights Move on Lace-Making Here, 9 March.

EII237 Miss Muriel White to be a Countess, 9 March.

EII238 Calais's Lace Boycott, 13 March.

EII239 Van Dyke to Lecture in French Provinces, 13 March.

EII240 Paris in Darkness If One Man So Wills [Pataud Electrician's Union], 13 March.

EII241 Faust Anniversary at the Paris Opera, 20 March

EII242 Strike Cripples Paris [telegraphers' strike], 21 March.

EII243 Rodin's Latest Work [Victor Hugo], 27 March.

EII244 John Bigelow Finds Paris Much Changed, 3 April.

Van Vechten was relieved of his duties as Paris Correspondent in April. His scrapbook articles are then undated until he began to date them himself in January 1910.

EII245 100,000 Cheer Police in Annual Parade, circa April, et seq.

EII246 Slips of "Der Gi'nts" Bothers Suffragist

EII247 $150,000 to Opera Co. by Conreid's Death, circa May, et seq.

EII248 Mme. Eames Sued by Gogorza's Wife, 14 May.

EII249 Hebrew Charities May Renew Pensions

EII250 Hebrew Charities Drop Old Pensioners

EII251 Aid Pours in for Widowed Mothers

EII252 $250,000 Raised by a Sick Boy's Smile

EII253 Mind Reader Fails in Blindfold Test

EII254 The New Music Cult in France and Its Leader [Claude Debussy], 16 May.

EII255 Saengerbund Opens Its Music Festival

EII256 Children Swamp Saengerbund Stage

EII257 "The Midnight Sons" Has Two Good Parts [by Glen MacDonough and Raymond Hubble, with Blanche Ring and Vernon Castle]

EII258 $10,000 Art Robbery at T. S. Clark's Home

EII259 Fun for Patients on Ward's Island

EII260 Pack Academy for "Romeo and Juliet" [with Julia Marlowe and Edward Southern]

EII261 4,500 White Wings March in Review

EII262 Children Orate for M'Manus's Gold

EII263 Thousands Honor Gordin's Memory [Jacob Gordin]

EII264 Helen Hale a Bride; Weds William Hodge

EII265 Cheer "Bwano Tumbo" in Y.M.C.A. Jungle

EII266 On the Stage in Australia [Margaret Anglin]

EII267 Societies to Sing for Kaiser's Prize

EII268 Small Blaze Fanned Into $150,000 Fire [Peck Piano Company]

EII269 Seize $1,000 Jewels and Fine Fur Coat

EII270 Julia Marlowe to Play "Hamlet"

EII271 Thief in College, Girls Searched [Adelphi College]

EII272 2,000 Happy Orphans Let Loose at Coney, circa June, et seq.

EII273 Miss Adams Trains Her Stage Mount [Maud Adams]

EII274 Urges Suffragists to Become Militant [Anna Shaw]

EII275 Miss Adams Thrills Throng in Stadium [in Joan of Arc]

EII276   Dancing Masters Fight License Law

EII277   Metropolitan Opera Gets Marie Delna

EII278   Mme. Nordica Weds G. W. Young in London

EII279   Robert Pitcairn Dies in Pittsburgh, 25 June.

EII280   Hammerstein Opera for Chicagoans, circa July, et seq.

EII281   Citizen's Union After Alien Vote

EII282   East Side Flocks to New Playground

EII283   Robillard Held for Flora Cooke's Death [Norbert Robillard]

EII284   East Side Revels in Street Sprays

EII285   Revolution's Son Celebrates at 87 [Dr. C. L. Morehouse]

EII286   R. Stuyvesant Dies Suddenly in Paris [Rutherford Stuyvesant]

EII287   "I Do Care!" Cries Eva Tanguay, Shrieks of Actress When Arrested
         Scares Rockaway Audience

EII288   Slain Man's Widow Avenges Husband

EII289   Gordin Benefit Nets $4,000 for Widow

EII290   Hammerstein Wants Dazie

EII291   Hammerstein Tells of His Opera Plans

EII292   Got $60,000 Fortune by Picking Rags

EII293   To Teach the Poor How to Keep Well [Dr. Rosalie Morton]

EII294   Clermont Once More Floats in the Bay

EII295   Sufferers Crowd to Novena of St. Anne

EII296   Emma Goldman Unmuzzled, Not a Policeman Present to Stop Her Talk-
         ing, 23 July.

EII297   Modjeska Mourned Among Her Own Folk [Helena Mojeska]

EII298   Hammerstein Back; Tells Plans Today

EII299   Veteran Horses End Police Days

EII300   Hammerstein Plans Opera for Chicago

EII301   Opera Stars Here on the Lorraine

EII302   Marguerite Sylva a New Carmen Here

EII303   Hattie Williams in "Detective Sparkes" [by Michael Morton]

EII304 New Belasco Play Full of Fun and Vim [Is Marriage a Failure?]

EII305 Strike May Tie Up 4 Yiddish Theatres

EII306 Adler Gives Up Fight With Unions

EII307 Yiddish Theatres Yield to Unions

EII308 Get Merry Party in Stolen Auto

EII309 Chorus of Roosters in Play at Circle [MacIntyre and Heath in Hayti]

EII310 Gowns Play Part in "Sins of Society" [by Cecil Raleigh and Henry Hamilton]

EII311 Flower Theft Trial Bungled, Smith Says [Park Commissioner Report]

EII312 Operates on Cobra in Bronx Zoo, 7 August.

EII313 Chicago Will Have Full Month of Opera, 7 August.

EII314 Opera Notes from Abroad, circa August, et seq.

EII315 Emma Goldman Defiant

EII316 Musical Ghosts Pad City Payroll [silent band members]

EII317 Suffragist Harmony at Mrs. Belmonth's

EII318 Many New Plays for the Shuberts [Bertha Kalich and Alla Nazimova]

EII319 Khan Collection to be Shown Here [Maurice Khan]

EII320 Educational Opera Hard to Prepare

EII321 Music News Here and Abroad

EII322 Loie Fuller's Thirty Dancers

EII323 Italian Company Opens with "Aida"

EII324 Gorgeous Pageant at the Hippodorome [A Trip to Japan by Manuel Klein]

EII325 "Rigoletto" Pleases at the Manhattan, circa September, et seq.

EII326 "Dollar Princess" Mild Musical Show [by Leo Fall]

EII327 Manhattan Opera Surprises in Store

EII328 Italian Singers Give Two Operas [Cavalleria Rusticana, Pagliacci]

EII329 Lillian Russell in a Dull Comedy [The Widow's Mite by Edward Day]

EII330 Eva Grippon Sings "Tosca," Sylva Ill

EII331 Sylva and Caruso Win Opera Plaudits

EII332 Metropolitan Plans Great Opera Season

EII333 "The Jewess" at the Manhattan

EII334 Woman to Manage Italian Opera [Mrs. Alanson S. Appleton]

EII335 Sing "Travatore" Without Zerola

EII336 "Rigoletto" Sung by the Italians

EII337 The New Theatre

EII338 Many New American Singers Engaged to Appear with the Metropolitan
        Opera Company

EII339 The Tragic History of Sir John Franklin

EII340 Marguerite Sylva Charming in "Faust"

EII341 "Barber of Seville" Sung by Italians

EII342 "Tosca" Gala Night for Italian Singers

EII343 Directors Oust Mrs. A. S. Appleton

EII344 "Louise" Applauded at the Manhattan

EII345 "Noble Spaniard" an Amusing Farce [by W. Somerset Maugham]

EII346 Strike in Chorus of Italian Company

EII347 Alice Nielsen Tells of Opera Triumphs

EII348 Hammerstein Opera Opening Advanced

EII349 Moors Come to See with Their Slaves [the Sultan of Morocco]

EII350 Rehearsals to Begin Tomorrow at the Metropolitan Opera House

EII351 Hotels Now Have Notable Guests [Hudson-Fulton celebration]

EII352 Collapse Comes to Italian Opera

EII353 Dippel Promises Fine Opera Season

EII354 Early Preparations for the Season at the Metropolitan

EII355 More than a Million Now at the Hotels

EII356 "Tales of Hoffman" at the Manhattan

EII357 Lieblers in Opera with Bessie Abbot

EII358 Mme. Noria Arrives in Striking Costume [Jane Noria], circa Octo-
        ber, et seq.

EII359 Paris Invasion by Metropolitan

EII360 "The Bohemian Girl" Manhattan Revival

EII361 Metropolitan Will Give Atlanta Opera

EII362 St. Louis to Have Metropolitan Opera

EII363 Japanese Businessmen See New York

EII364 Commerce Chamber Welcomes Japanese

EII365 Japanese Editor Defends the Press

EII366 Hammerstein Lost $50,000 Early Season

EII367 Massenet Favored at the Manhattan

EII368 Calls Tetrazzini Fairy Godmother [John McCormack]

EII369 New Theatre Has Bad Opera Acoustics

EII370 Dippel Takes the Chicago Auditorium

EII371 Mary Garden Cried All the Way Over

EII372 How Kreisler Finds Musical Novelties [Fritz Kreisler]

EII373 Isadora Duncan Reappears, Gives Her Dances Assisted by Damrosch
        and Symphony Orchestra, 10 November [A25, C33, D135]

EII374 Young Irish Tenor at the Manhattan [John McCormack]

EII375 Children's Society Curbs Ballet School

EII376 Miss Garden Again Heard as Thais

EII377 Light Opera at the Manhattan

EII378 Slezak as Otello at Metropolitan [Leo Slezak]

EII379 Miss Duncan's Vivid Dances, 17 November [A25, C33, D135]

EII380 Rachmaninoff's Recital, Russian Pianist Plays His Own Compositions
        With Much Charm [Sergei Rachmaninoff's first American performance]

EII381 News of the Musical World Here and Abroad

EII382 Revive "Mascotte" at the Manhattan

EII383 Must Educate Folk to Light Opera

EII384 Cavalieri Gay in Role of Carmen

EII385 German Light Opera at the New Theatre

EII386 Loie Fuller Shows Her Dancing Girls, 1 December [A25, D135]

EII387 Far From Bankrupt, Says Hammerstein, circa December, et seq.

EII388 Hammerstein Stars to Sing in Pittsburgh

EII389 Geraldine Farrar Again Sings "Manon"

EII390 Melis Leaves "Thais" to Miss Garden [Carmen Melis]

EII391 Mary Garden a Poetic Marguerite [in Faust]

EII392 [Opera Finances]

EII393 "Madame Angot" Sung at the New Theatre

EII394 "Siegfried" Sung at Metropolitan

EII395 To Give Children a Christmas Party [Kitty Cheatham]

EII396 Mme. Cavalieri in Hoffman "Tales," 25 December.

EII397 "Die Walkure" Sung at Metropolitan

1910

EII398 Merger of Opera Under Negotiation [Metropolitan and Manhattan],
        1 January.

EII399 Directors to Pass on Opera Merger, 2 January.

EII400 Deny Negotiations With Hammerstein, 4 January.

EII401 Dealt With Kahn to Unite Operas [Otto Kahn], circa January, et seq.

EII402 Mme. Homer Ill, Opera Plans Upset [Louise Homer]

EII403 Old "Fra Diavlo" at New Theatre .

EII404 Changes May Come to the Metropolitan

EII405 Maud Allan in Greek Dances

EII406 Miss Allan Dances, 21 January [A25, C36, D135]

EII407 "Elektra" by Richard Strauss, 24 January.

EII408 Hector Defranne to Metropolitan, 24 January.

EII409 Delna, Pet of Paris, to Sing Saturday, 25 January.

EII410 Rachmaninoff as Conductor, 29 January.

EII411 Hammerstein May Quit Philadelphia, 30 January.

EII412 Maud Allan as Salome, 30 January. [A25, C36, D135]

EII413 The Proper Mood to Enjoy "Elektra," 1 February.

EII414 Mazarin Faints at "Elektra" [Mariette Mazarin], 2 February.

EII415 Flonzaley Quartet in Pleasing Concert, 2 February.

EII416 Mary Garden Makes $200,000 a Year, 3 February.

EII417 Gogny Saves Opera at the Manhattan, 6 February.

EII418 Strauss Saddens Milka Ternina, 8 February.

EII419 Dalmorès Loses Suit for $20,000, 9 February.

EII420 Mary Garden Gets $10,000 for Paris, 9 February.

EII421 Greeks Condemn Opera of "Elektra," 9 February.

EII422 Hammerstein Offer to Metropolitan, 11 February.

EII423 Mme. Mazarin's Great Opera Feat, 14 February.

EII424 "Elektra" Studied in Lunatic Asylum, 15 February.

EII425 Anna Pavlowa's Debut, Russian Dancer to Appear at Metropolitan,
        20 February.

EII426 Hammerstein Gives an Ultimatum Here, 21 February.

EII427 $6,000 From Opera for Italian Charity, 24 February.

EII428 Two Donizetti Operas Are Sung, 27 February.

EII429 G. Lowes Dickinson, "Modern Composers," 23 February.

EII430 Pavlowa to Help Revive Ballet, 1 March.

EII431 Anna Pavlowa a Wonderful Dancer, 1 March. [A25, C34, D135]

EII432 Russian Dancers in Amazing Feats, 2 March. [A25, C34, D135]

EII433 Bessie Abbot in Mascagni Opera, "Ysobel," 4 March.

EII434 Crisis in Affairs at Metropolitan, 5 March.

EII435 Pavlowa at New Theatre, 6 March.

EII436 "Salome" Heard Again at the Manhattan, 7 March.

EII437 New Dances by Pavlowa, 8 March.

EII438 Boston Opera as Metropolitan Ally, 13 March.

EII439 Mme. Delna Raps Metropolitan Opera, 14 March.

EII440 Pavlowa in New Dances, 18 March. [A25, C34, D135]

EII441 Opera Songsters Revel at a Benefit, 20 March.

EII442   Clément to Quit the Metropolitan [Edmund Clément], 20 March.

EII443   Metropolitan Drops Rates to Agents, 22 March.

EII444   No National Favored at Metropolitan, 23 March.

EII445   Confusion in Dances at Metropolitan, 26 March.

EII446   Hammerstein Tells of Losses in Opera, 27 March.

EII447   Gustav Mahler to Rest Abroad, 31 March.

EII448   Hammerstein Goes Abroad April 13, 1 April.

EII449   Dippel Resigns From Metropolitan, 2 April.

EII450   Gatti-Casazza Gets Marriage License, 3 April.

EII451   Frances Alda Now Mme. Gatti-Casazza, 4 April.

EII452   Russian Dancers to Return in Fall, 7 April.

EII453   Dancers to Bring Ballet [Anna Pavlova]

EII454   Opera Stars Leaving Our Shores, 8 April.

EII455   Mary Garden Sails, Raps Hammerstein, 10 April.

EII456   Mrs. Fiske Acts the Child, "Hanelle" [Minnie Maddern Fiske in The
         Green Cockatoo by Arthur Schnitzler and Hanelle by Gerhard Haupt-
         mann], 12 April.

EII457   Garden Will Return, Says Hammerstein, 15 April.

EII458   Wilma Neruda's 71st Birthday, 17 April.

EII459   Gatti-Casazza Tells Next Season's Plans, 25 April.

EII460   "Buffalo Bill" Opera Farewell Season, 26 April.

EII461   Hammerstein Quits Opera, 28 April.

EII462   Shuberts May Lease Vacant Opera House, 29 April.

EII463   News of the Music World, 2 May.

EII464   Four Days of Song by Swedish Singers, 8 May.

EII465   Singers Took Away Almost a Million, 12 May.

EII466   Hammerstein Plans a Concert Tour, 20 May.

EII467   Dalmorès Gets $50,000 a Year, 24 May,

EII468   Swedes Hail King With Cries of "Bra!" 24 May.

EII469   Music News and Notes [Josephine Jacoby], 29 May.

EII470 Swedish Singers Give Last Concert, 30 May.

EII471 Opera Salaries Will Be Lowered, 4 June.

EII472 Music Notes, 12 June.

EII473 Through Hell Gate Standing on a Log, Main Log Jammer Rides, 13 June.

EII474 Dancing Masters Fix Waltz Time, 14 June.

EII475 Mme. Nordica Sings for the Suffragists, 17 June.

EII476 First Park Concert, "Salome" Next Week, 20 June.

EII477 Metropolitan and Hammerstein Clash," 21 June.

EII478 No Hitch in Deal With Hammerstein, 22 June.

EII479 Dippel Announces Opera Repertoire, 25 June.

EII480 Dippel Gets Melba For Next Season, 26 June.

EII481 "Salome" Given In Park, 27 June.

EII482 American Dancers Show Their Skill, 29 June.

EII483 Opera Ball Team Trounces Boston, 30 June.

EII484 "I Want to Play the Part of a Good Woman"—Polaire, 3 July.

EII485 Music Notes, 3 July.

EII486 Artistic Thieves Rob the Vedders [Enoch R. Vedder], 6 July.

EII487 Mary Garden Wants $90,000 Contract, circa July.

EII488 Music Notes, 10 July.

EII489 Hammerstein Plan Pleases Singers, 11 July.

EII490 Herr Dippel's Fiat Angered Tetrazzini, 16 July.

EII491 Hammerstein Ill, But Has Opera Plans, 16 July.

EII492 Tetrazzini Still Hammerstein Star, 16 July.

EII493 Rain of Bills Answers Plea [Salvation Army], 20 July.

EII494 American Setting for Puccini Opera, 20 July.

EII495 London Alliance for Metropolitan, 22 July.

EII496 Music Notes, 24 July.

EII497 Music Notes, 31 July.

EII498   Wins Scholarship in Academy at Rome, 6 August.

EII499   Barrymore to Wed, But Not Just Yet [John Barrymore], 7 August.

EII500   Barrymore Gets License to Wed, 12 August.

EII501   Carryington Exposes Tricks of Mediums, 13 August.

EII502   Mme. Melba Back to Sing in Halifax, 21 August.

EII503   Sophie Brandt's Idol is Marie Tempest, 22 August.

EII504   Opera Singers Here on Way to Mexico [Jane Noria and Rita Fornia],
         24 August.

EII505   Vienna Students Give a Concert, 24 August.

EII506   A Plea for the Development of National Opera [signed "Jane Noria"
         but ghost-written by Van Vechten], 28 August.

EII507   Polka Dominates "Madame Sherry" [by Otto Hauerbach and Karl
         Hoschna], 31 August.

EII508   Hammerstein Buys London Site, 9 September.

EII509   Music Notes, 11 September.

EII510   Hammerstein's Son Weds Mrs. Hoagland, 15 September.

EII511   "Hans, Flute Player" Is Full of Melody [by Louis Ganne, Maurice
         Vaucaire, and Georges Mitchell], 20 September.

EII512   Music Notes, 25 September.

EII513   Trentini Is Ready to Try Comic Opera [Emma Trentini in The Lit-
         tle Devil], 26 September.

EII514   Many New Operas for Metropolitan, 28 September.

EII515   Russian Dancers Arrive in Furs, 28 September.

EII516   Symphony Concerts for Young People [Walter Damrosch], 2 October.

EII517   Sings in English, Yet Speaks It Not [Georges Chadell], 3 October.

EII518   "Girl in the Train" is Rather Daring [by Harry B. Smith and Leo
         Fall], 5 October.

EII519   Gatti-Casazza Back From Europe, 5 October.

EII520   Successful Opera Season Predicted, 6 October.

EII521   Hammerstein Has London Plans Fixed, 9 October.

EII522   Mme. Fremstad Can Cook, Spent Time in Her Villa Singing "Armide"
         and Preparing Dinner, 9 October.

EII523 Victor Herbert's First Serious Opera [Natoma], 9 October.

EII524 Charles Gilbert, French Singer, Dead, 13 October.

EII525 Hammerstein Ready to Build in London, 15 October.

EII526 Russian Dancers Again Triumph Here [Pavlova in Giselle], 16 October. [A25, C34, D135]

EII527 Mme. Homer Downed the Paris Claque, 17 October.

EII528 Says New Operas Will Be Popular [Alfred Hertz], 24 October.

EII529 Mary Garden Back, Says She's Married, 26 October.

EII530 London's New Opera House Underway, 30 October.

EII531 Mary Garden Has New Trousers Fad, 31 October.

EII532 "The Gamblers" an Intense Play [by Charles Klein], 1 November.

EII533 Maybe Mary Garden is Bride of a Bey, 5 November.

EII534 [Armide], 6 November. [A6, D54]

EII535 Mascagni Tells Story of "Ysobel," 6 November.

EII536 "Naughty Marietta" and Trentini a Hit [by Victor Herbert], 8 November.

EII537 New Operas, 13 November.

EII538 Bonci to Sing Some Songs in English, 14 November.

EII539 Big Receipts at Metropolitan, 16 November.

EII540 Rachmaninoff Again, 18 November.

EII541 Puccini Here: His Opera Views, 18 November.

EII542 Why Has Mascagni Forgiven America?, 20 November.

EII543 "Ysobel" Finished for New Year Debut, 21 November.

EII544 Tetrazzini Here, Meets Injunction, 25 November.

E EII545 Two Operas Sung in Fine Spirit [Emmy Destinn and Enrico Caruso in Cavalleria Rusticana and Pagliacci], 26 November.

EII546 Mme. Edith Walker on Variety Stage, 27 November.

EII547 Hadley Conductor for Third Symphony [Henry Hadley], 28 November.

EII548 Gluck's Music Wins Olive Fremstad, 28 November.

EII549 Russian Balaliaka Orchestra Charms, 29 November.

EII550 Melba Appears in "La Traviata," 30 November.

EII551 Tetrazzini in Court Smiles at Hammerstein Who is Suing to Keep Her Services, 3 December.

EII552 Teaching the West to Singers of It [David Belasco and The Girl of the Golden West with Caruso and Destinn], 5 December.

EII553 Tetrazzini Wins Over Hammerstein, 6 December.

EII554 Nethersole Not a Simple Magdalene [Olga Nethersole], 6 December.

EII555 Humperdinck Arrives, Falls Into Arms of Caruso, 8 December.

EII556 Emmy Destinn Sang Under a Handicap, 12 December.

EII557 Pierne's Cantata as a Mystery Play [Children of Bethlehem], 18 December.

EII558 Unfamiliar Music by Kneisel Quartet, 14 December.

EII559 Celebrities Honor Sarah Bernhardt, 19 December.

EII560 Singers Have Cold; Opera is Changed, 23 December.

EII561 Wagon Thief Gets Opera Scores Here, 25 December.

EII562 Two Opera Scores Lost From Wagon, 26 December.

EII563 Miss Parlow Brilliant [Kathleen Parlow], 26 December.

EII564 Miss Farrar Talks of Her Newest Role [Koenigskinder], 26 December.

EII565 "The Spring Maid" Has Pretty Music [by Heinrich Reinhart and Christie MacDonald], 27 December. [F1]

EII566 Humperdinck's Newest Opera Tonight [Koenigskinder], 28 December.

EII567 Kitty Cheatham's Recital, 28 December. [C24]

EII568 Bundle He Carried Was Stolen Operas, Vigilant Policeman Finds Scores, 30 December.

1911

EII569 Music Notes, 1 January.

EII570 Canadian Violinist Trained in Russia [Kathleen Parlow], 2 January.

EII571 Menu Marriage a Hit [Marriage à la Carte by C.M.S. McClellan and and Ivan Caryl], 3 January.

EII572 Mme. Novello's Recollections, a Famous Singer Who Died Only Two Years Ago at Ninety [Clara Anastasia Novello], 7 January.

EII573 Blame Mascagni for "Ysobel" Fiasco, 9 January.

EII574 Opera Singer Tells of Stage Jealousies, 9 January.

EII575 Demand Royalty for French Music, 12 January.

EII576 Has Mme. Nordica a Senate Candidate? [G.W. Young], 12 January.

EII577 More Russian Music New York Might Like, 16 January.

EII578 "Die Meistersinger" at Metropolitan, 21 January.

EII579 Story of Strauss's New Viennese Opera [Der Rosenkavalier], 22 January.

EII580 A Violinist Who Need Not Practice [Mischa Elman], 23 January.

EII581 Backstage at the Opera, 29 January.

EII582 Hammerstein Sued; Wife Wants Divorce, 29 January.

EII583 Mary Garden Is To Write a Book, 30 January.

EII584 Greet New York's First Marguerite [Clara Louise Kellog], 5 February.

EII585 Richard Strauss Enters the Field of Comic Opera, 5 February.

EII586 Mme. Alda Favors Opera in English [Frances Alda], 6 February.

EII587 "Tosca" Revived with Miss Farrar, 9 February.

EII588 Isadora Duncan Returns, Says She Will Found Temple of Dance Here or in Paris, 11 February.

EII589 "The Twelve Pound Look" with Ethel Barrymore [by James M. Barrie], 14 February.

EII590 "Tales of Hoffman" Welcomed Again, 15 February.

EII591 Miss Duncan Dances to Wagner Music, 16 February. [A25, C33, D135]

EII592 Music Notes, 19 February.

EII593 Dalmorès Sings in Three Tongues, 20 February.

EII594 Isadora Duncan, 21 February. [A25, C33, D135]

EII595 Mme. Gadski Talks of Concert Singing [Johanna Gadski], 27 February.

EII596 New Theatre Lost $400,000 in 2 Years, 3 March.

EII597 Tetrazzini Tells of Experiences on Tour, 6 March.

EII598 Leo Ornstein's Recital: New Prodigy Makes His Appearance at the New Amsterdam, 6 March. [A5]

EII599 Big Opera Losses in Philadelphia, 8 March.

EII600   Emma Calvé Here, Perhaps a Wife, 9 March.

EII601   Founders Abandon New Theatre, 10 March.

EII602   New Theatre Has Box Holder Problem, 11 March.

EII603   Plans for New Theatre, 11 March.

EII604   Noted Tenor Longs to Give Up Opera [Ricardo Martin], 13 March.

EII605   Tetrazzini and Musical Taste, 14 March.

EII606   "The Pink Lady" Gay and Amusing [by C.M.S. McLellan and Ivan
         Caryl], 14 March.

EII607   Kaiser May Have Urged Twilight, 15 March.

EII608   Anna Pavlowa Reappears, 17 March.

EII609   Ticket Speculators Begin Test of Law, 18 March.

EII610   Speculators Renew Their Announcements, 22 March.

EII611   Pavlowa in a New Dress, 24 March.

EII612   Music Notes, 26 March.

EII613   How "Ariane" Came to Metropolitan, 22 March.

EII614   Hammerstein Got $1,200,000 to Quit, 30 March.

EII615   Tetrazzini Stirs 5,500 to Mad Cheers, 3 April.

EII616   "Little Miss Fix-It" is Thin [with Nora Bayes, by William Hurl-
         burt], 4 April.

EII617   Pavlowa Dances Farewell, 4 April.

EII618   Coronation Music for King George's Ceremony, 9 April.

EII619   Opera Season Ends; a Prosperous Year, 16 April.

EII620   Opera Singers Off for Brief Tour, 17 April.

EII621   Kitty Cheatham's Recital [with H.T. Burleigh], 18 April. [A28]

EII622   Caruso's Voice, 21 April.

EII623   "Saltimbanchi" Gay and Tuneful [by Louis Ganne and Maurice Or-
         donneau], 25 April.

EII624   340 Lb. Prima Donna Rouses a Tempest [Teresa Lina Paccielfantica],
         27 April.

EII625   Metropolitan Opera Profit is $32,000, 29 April.

EII626   Opera Jury May Be Deadlocked [over American opera], 2 May.

EII627   Hammerstein Gives $100,000 Mortgage, 3 May.

EII628 $10,000 Opera Prize Won by Yale Man [Mona by Horatio Parker], 3 May.

EII629   Dr. Schechter Back From Long Vacation, 4 May.

EII630   Music Notes [Russian ballet], 7 May.

EII631   Famous Old Singer Indigent in Hospital [F. Varrington Foote], 12 May.

EII632   Music Notes [French opera], 13 May.

EII633   Knife Even May Not Save Caruso's Voice, 14 May.

EII634   Music Notes [Salome, Mary Garden, The Girl of the Golden West, George Bernard Shaw], 21 May.

EII635   Italian Opera on Bowery [Sarnella Company], 22 May.

EII636   Two Great Musicians, Fuller Maitland's Life of Brahms and Judith Gautierl's Reminiscences of Wagner [J.A. Fuller Maitland, Brahms; Effie Dunreith, from the French of Judith Gautierl, Wagner at Home], 28 May.

EII637   Sir William S. Gilbert, 30 May.

EII638   Old Pinafore as Merry as Ever [H.M.S. Pinafore by Gilbert and Sullivan], 30 May.

EII639   Music and Musicians [W.J. Henderson, Some Forerunners of the Italian Opera; J. Cuthbert Haddon, Master Musicians; Edward Dickinson, The Education of a Music Lover], 4 June.

EII640   Miss Clyde Bride of Opera Singer [to William Hinshaw], 5 June.

EII641   D'Annunzio's Works Under Papal Ban, 5 June.

EII642   Russian Ballets in Winter Garden, 9 June.

EII643   "Mme. Sans Gene" for Metropolitan, 10 June.

EII644   Opera Conductor Needs No Scores [Giuseppe Canepa], 12 June.

EII645   "Aida" Opera Season at Daly's, 13 June.

EII646   Mary Garden Back, Adores the West, 13 June.

EII647   Russian Ballets at Winter Garden, 15 June.

EII648   Music of Russia at Popular Concert, 26 June.

EII649   Zelda Seguin Talks of Old Opera Days, 26 June.

EII650   Dinner Show and Taxicab in Job Lot [Terrace Garden], 27 June.

EII651   Cavalazzi Pupils Give Entire Ballet, 30 June.

EII652   Concerts on Top of Century Theatre, 4 July.

EII653   Australia Shies at American Plays, 10 July.

EII654   Opera Novelties for Metropolitan, 26 July.

EII655   Liszt the Misunderstood [Arthur Hervey, Liszt], 5 August.

EII656   Our Opera Best, Says Otto Kahn, 8 August.

EII657   Plans for Russian Dancers, 17 August.

EII658   Round the World Racer Here on Time [André Jaeger Schmidt], 19 August.

EII659   Music Notes [Franz Liszt], 3 September.

EII660   American Singers Winning Abroad [Kitty Cheatham], 11 September.

EII661   New Contralto for Metropclitan [Theodora Orridge], 14 September.

EII662   "Sweet Sixteen" at Daly's [by Victor Herbert], 15 September.

EII663   Songbirds Sailing for Opera Season, 16 September.

EII664   Gaby Delys Here in Startling Gown, 17 September.

EII665   Mme. Eames Knows She's Legally Wed, 17 September.

EII666   "The Kiss Waltz" Musical Cocktail [by C.M. Ziehrer and J.C. Huffman], 19 September.

EII667   Russian Dancers Quit Miss Hoffman [Gertrude Hoffman], 20 September.

EII668   Mordkin Dancers Arrive, 20 September.

EII669   Banker Young Sued, New Law Discloses [G.W. Young], 22 September.

EII670   Symphony Society Plans, Walter Damrosch's Concert All Liszt, 21 September.

EII671   Beecham to Give Opera in New York [Der Rosenkavalier conducted by Sir Thomas Beecham], 23 September.

EII672   Hichens to Stage "Garden of Allah" [Robert Hichens], 24 September.

EII673   Music Notes, 24 September.

EII674   Dippel Back; Tells of Opera Novelties, 27 September.

EII675   Metropolitan Tells of Season's Plans, 2 October.

EII676   Mordkin Seriously Ill, 5 October.

EII677   "Forty Years of Song" [by Emma Albani and Mills Boon], 8 October.

EII678   Kubelik Talks of His Native Music [Jan Kubelik], 9 October.

EII679   Mary Garden and Other Stars Arrive, 10 October.

EII680   Olive Fremstad Gets a Divorce, 18 October.

EII681   "Gypsy Love" Given With Star Ill [by Franz Lehar], 18 October.

EII682   Efrem Zimbalist, Violinist, Here, 23 October.

EII683   Godowsky Master, Says De Pachmann [Leopold Godowsky], 30 October.

EII684   Jean Christophe Comes to Paris! [Romain Rolland, Jean Christophe in Paris], 5 November.

EII685   We Like Musicians Only When Tagged [Harold Bauer], 6 November.

EII686   The Opera Claquer, 6 November.

EII687   There's a Claque to Check Applause; Mme. Cantatance Pays for Sh, 7 November.

EII688   "The Red Widow" is Entertaining [by Channing Pollock and Rennold Wolfe], 7 November.

EII689   Caruso Returns in Splendid Voice, 9 November.

EII690   DeKoven Maintains Opera is Influenced, 11 November.

EII691   "Lobetanz" by Ludwig Thuille, 11 November.

EII692   Mary Garden, 12 November.

EII693   Tiniest Prima Donna Tells of Her Start [Maggie Teyte], 13 November.

EII694   Opera Season Opens; Throngs Hear "Aida," 14 November.

EII695   Puccini's "Girl" Is Sung Again, 18 November.

EII696   "Tristan Und Isolde" at Metropolitan, 19 November.

EII697   Newest Contralto Has Soprano Aims [Marguerite Matzenauer] 20 November.

EII698   Ibsen No Puzzle to Hedwig Reicher, 27 November.

EII699   "Little Boy Blue" [by Rudolph Schanzer and Carl Lindau], 28 November.

EII700   Berlin Hostile to American Singers, 4 December.

EII701   "Haensel Und Gretel" at Metropolitan, 5 December.

EII702   Caruso's Discoverer Dies at His Dinner, 6 December.

EII703   Cavalieri's $80,000 Raised by Chanler [Robert Chanler], 18 December.

EII704 Moscow's Ballerina to Dance Dual Role [Ekaterina Gelzer, ie., Katherina Geltzer], 18 December.

EII705 Fantastic Ballet of Russian Dancers, 20 December. [A25, D135]

EII706 Founders Abandon the New Theatre, 21 December.

EII707 Music Notes [La Donna Curiose], 24 December.

EII708 The Philharmonic, 30 December.

1912

EII709 Maeterlinck's Work as His Wife Sees It [Georgette LeBlanc], 1 January.

EII710 Emma Eames Sings in Sunday Concert, 1 January.

EII711 Russians Dance "Coppelia," 3 January.

EII712 Wolf-Ferrari Here to Hear His Operas, 6 January.

EII713 Hammerstein Back; London Opera Pays, 6 January.

EII714 Wolf-Ferrari Cries for Joy at His Opera [Jewels of the Madonna], 7 January.

EII715 Music Notes [Wolf-Ferrari], 7 January.

EII716 Bonci Whispers of an Opera Invasion [Tito Huffo], 8 January.

EII717 Foy in "Over the River" [Eddie Foy with Elsie Janis], 9 January.

EII718 Visitor From Vienna Fooled Opera Folk, 13 January.

EII719 Leo Blech's "Versiegelt," 14 January.

EII720 Opera Has No Lures for Elena Gerhardt, 15 January.

EII721 Leo Slezak in Song Recital, 16 January.

EII722 Sees Little Good in Modern Music [Josef Hofmann], 22 January.

EII723 Georgette LeBlanc on "The Bluebird," 25 January.

EII724 Renaud Ambitious to Sing New Roles, 29 January.

EII725 Miss Barrymore's Surprise "A Slice of Life" [by James M. Barrie], 30 January.

EII726 Wolf-Ferrari Sails, 2 February.

EII727 Hammerstein's New Idea, 5 February.

EII728 American Operas Praised by Martin [Ricardo Martin], 5 February.

EII729 Broadway Blocked by Opera Crowd [Tetrazzini and Caruso in <u>Rigo-letto</u>], 7 February.

EII730 Boston's Operatic Muddle, 11 February.

EII731 Miss Destinn Paints Roses and Toads, 12 February.

EII732 Can't Resign From Society of Authors [Blair Fairchaild], 13 February.

EII733 Smirnoff Angry, Quits Metropolitan [Dimitri Smirnoff], 14 February.

EII734 Opera Stories New and Old [Sir Charles Stanford, <u>Treasury of Musical Composition</u>; <u>The Family Letters of Richard Wagner</u>, Ed. William Ashton Ellis; Robert Haven Schauffler, <u>The Musical Amateur</u>; William H. Grattan Flood, <u>The Story of the Bagpipe</u>; Arthur A. Clappé, <u>The Wind Band and Its Instruments</u>; Charles L. Graves, <u>Post-Victorian Music</u>], 18 February.

EII735 "Centrillon" by Jules Massenet, 18 February.

EII736 Fremstad in Tights Sang Our Ragtime, 19 February.

EII737 "The Jewels of the Madonna" by Wolf-Ferrari, 25 February.

EII738 Composed "Sumurun" Racing Against Time [by Victor Hollander], 26 February.

EII739 Mrs. Fiske Acts "Lady Patricia" [by Rudolph Besler], 27 February.

EII740 Double Opera Bill at Metropolitan [<u>Le Jongleur de Notre Dame</u> and <u>The Secret of Suzanne</u>], 28 February.

EII741 Violinists Shackled, Cries Miss Powell [Maud Powell], 4 March.

EII742 "Mona" by Horatio Parker, 10 March.

EII743 Gadski Would Be Heard as Carmen, 11 March.

EII744 "The Typhoon" an Absorbing Play [by Meynhert Lengyel], 12 March.

EII745 "Oriental Fantasy" at Winter Garden [<u>The Captive</u> by William Wilson], 15 March.

EII746 A Youth the Wizard of New Stagecraft [Loomis H. Taylor], 24 March.

EII747 Negro Put Mannes on Road to Fame [David Mannes], 20 March.

EII748 Holt Critizes the Philharmonic [Henry Holt], 24 March.

EII749 Clara Schumann [Florence May, <u>The Girlhood of Clara Schumann</u>], 24 March.

EII750 New York Holding a Brahms Festival, 25 March.

EII751 Frances Alda's Domestic Affairs, 26 March.

EII752   Volpe Symphony Gives Last Concert, 27 March.

EII753   Caruso Composer, 27 March.

EII754   Massenet's "Manon" at Metropolitan, 31 March.

EII755   Ragtime's Rage a Regular Riot, 1 April.

EII756   National Opera Damrosch's Theme, 7 April.

EII757   Mrs. Cahier Puts Acting Above Tone [Sarah Walker], 8 April.

EII758   Mme. De Cisheros Likes Australia [Eleanora deCisheros], 15 April.

EII759   "Wall Street Girl" is Rather Tame [by Edgar Selwyn], 16 April.

EII760   Mr. Gatti-Casazza, 18 April.

EII761   "Cyrano de Bergerac" an Opera Novelty, 18 April.

EII762   Mary Garden Again With Chicago Opera, 19 April.

EII763   American Singers the Best Linguists, 22 April.

EII764   New Tivoli Opera Rises From Ashes, 29 April.

EII765   "Robin Hood" Returns To Win Our Hearts [by Harry Smith and Reginald DeKoven], 7 May.

EII766   Music Notes, 28 May.

EII767   "Robin Hood" for London, 30 May.

EII768   Carl Pohlig Got $12,000, 12 June.

EII769   Hammerstein May Return, 16 June.

EII770   Miss Hammerstein to Wed, 22 June.

EII771   Music Teachers' Meeting, 23 June.

EII772   Maud Powell Better, 24 June.

EII773   Say No to Musicians' Union, 25 June.

EII774   Music Notes, 25 June.

EII775   Walter Damrosch Explains, 26 June.

EII776   500 Music Teachers Here, 26 June.

EII777   Charlton Engages Maggie Teyte, 27 June.

EII778   Find Cremona Violin With Date of 1720, 27 June.

EII779   Ballet Pupils Show Skill, 28 June.

EII780 The Musicians' Strike, 7 July.

EII781 Thrown Overboard Manacled in a Box [Harry Houdini], 8 July.

EII782 Return of Jean De Reszke, 19 July.

EII783 Theatre Employees Smoke Peace Pipe, 4 August.

EII784 Hammerstein Back: Gay Over His Losses, 6 August.

EII785 Opera Novelties For Metropolitan, 7 August.

EII786 Bessie Abbot Wins Favor in "Robin Hood," 13 August.

EII787 Hammerstein on the Dead Massenet [signed "Oscar Hammerstein" but
        ghostwritten by Van Vechten], 14 August.

EII788 Hammerstein Line of 20 Opera Houses, 18 August.

EII789 Hammerstein Gives Up Opera in London, 20 August.

EII790 Show Girls Annoyed at the Vanderbilts, 28 August.

EII791 Interesting New Works Promised at the Metropolitan, 8 September.

EII792 Hammerstein Plan for Theatrical Chair, 8 September.

EII793 "Within the Law" a Vivid Melodrama [by Bayard Veiller], 12 Sep-
        tember.

EII794 Hammerstein Asks $100,000 in Libel Suit, 24 September.

EII795 Bessie Abbot Wed to T. Waldo Story, 27 September.

EII796 Hammerstein is Author Now, 29 September.

EII797 Sembrich Laments End of Pure Singing [Marcella Sembrich] 30 Sep-
        tember.

EII798 The Opera Season Longer This Year, 30 September.

EII799 "Oh, Oh, Delphine" Gay and Tuneful [by C.M.S. McLelland and Ivan
        Caryl], 1 October.

EII800 Mme Calvé Plans an Opera School, 1 October.

EII801 "The Charity Girl" is Disappointing [by Edward Peple and Victor
        Hollander], 3 October.

EII802 Alma Gluck Likes Carpenter's Songs, 7 October.

EII803 Hammerstein Won't Support Daughters, 9 October.

EII804 Zimbalist Believes in Violin Novelties, 14 October.

EII805 Giorgio Polacco Arrives, 18 October.

EII806 This is No Land for Vocal Duets [Giuseppe Campanari], 21 October.

EII807 New York News and AeolianMusic Hall, 27 October.

EII808 H. Hamilton Fyfe Reverses the Usual Process, 27 October.

EII809 Gagliardi Sings Isolde in Convent, 28 October.

EII810 Titta Ruffo Here for American Debut, 29 October.

EII811 Play for Children at Little Theatre [Snow White by Jessie White], 2 November.

EII812 Limits Great Piano Composers to Five [Gottfried Galston], 4 November.

EII813 "The Dove of Peace" Has Some Novelties [by Walter Damrosch] 4 November.

EII814 Simina Opera Co. to Tour Here in 1914, 6 November.

EII815 "La Gioconda" Sung at Matropolitan, 15 November.

EII817 Adeline Genee Again Charms, 4 December.

EII818 "Secret of Suzanne" Abounds in Melody, 14 December.

EII819 Music Notes, 15 December.

EII820 Metropolitan Says No to Hammerstein, 19 December.

EII821 "Miss Princess" is Dull Musical Play [by Will B. and Alex Johnstone], 24 December.

EII822 Geraldine Farrar on American Styles, 29 December.

EII823 "Eva" Has One Charm [by Franz Lehar and Glen MacDonough] 31 December.

1913

EII824 Music Notes: Lovers of Literature; The MacDowell Colony, 5 January.

EII825 Hammerstein Lets Lawyers Fight, 7 January.

EII826 Hammerstein Tells of Stotesburg Gift, 8 January.

EII827 Hammerstein Finds Art Wholly Selfish, 9 January.

EII828 Leo Rains Gives Recital, 12 January.

EII829 Independent Woman is Nordica's Ideal, 15 January.

EII830 "Siegfried" Sung with Dramatic Vim, 18 January.

EII831 Felix Weingartner Takes Opera Bride, 30 January.

EII832 Fine Cast to Sing "Cyrano" on Feb. 27, 16 February.

EII833 "The Miracle" a Splendid Pageant [by Max Reinhardt], 18 February.

EII834 Rostand Indignant at "Cyrano" Here, 20 February.

EII835 New York to be Given Its Premiere by the Metropolitan Company
Next Thursday Night [Cyrano de Bergerac by Walter Damrosch], 22

EII836 Cubist of Letters Writes a New Book [Gertrude Stein, Portrait of
Mabel Dodge at the Villa Curonia], 24 February.

EII837 Caruso Tells How He Didn't Pay $15,000, 8 March.

EII838 "A Lover's Quarrel" Produced in English [by Victor Herbert], 10
March.

EII839 Hammerstein Out With an Opera Plan, 26 March.

EII840 Metropolitan Says Hammerstein Can't, 28 March.

EII841 Hammerstein Has a New Cigar Machine, 29 March.

EII842 Rival Russians in Battle of Discords, 10 April.

EII843 Threat Put an End to Italian Concert, 11 April.

EII844 Predict Success of Popular Opera, 11 April.

EII845 Oratorio Society Honors Carnegie, 11 April.

EII846 Caruso and Farrar Speak at Opera, 14 April.

EII847 Zimbalist Plays for Big Audience, 24 April.

EII848 Six Novelties for Opera Next Year, 29 April.

EII849 Italian Company Gives "La Cigale," 30 April.

EII850 Hammerstein Rails at City Club Opera, 5 May.

EII851 "Iolanthe" Brings More Joy to Casino, 13 May.

1915

EII852 Schönberg and Leschetizky, 21 November.

1934

EII853 On Words and Music: A Letter About Gertrude Stein's Four Saints
[in Three Acts], 18 February. [C15, D164]

1939

EII854   An Open Letter on Behalf of Ethel Waters [in Mamba's Daughters],
          6 March. [A28]

1949

EII855   An Actor, an Actress—and Many Cats [Pamela and James Mason, The
          Cats in Our Lives], 10 April.

1950

EII856   Simple Speaks His Mind [Langston Hughes, Simple Speaks His Mind],
          7 May. [A28]

1953

EII857   In the Heart of Harlem [Langston Hughes, Simple Takes a Wife],
          31 May. [A28]

1960

EII858   Serious Loss [a letter to Bosley Crowther about dubbing foreign
          films], 11 September.

1962

EII859   [a letter to Brooks Atkinson in "Critic at Large" about New York],
          23 November.

Contributions to the New York Press

Van Vechten resigned from the New York Times to serve as drama
critic for the New York Press, reviewing individual plays and
writing weekly articles for the Sunday editions. He developed
several of these into papers which he included in later volumes
of essays. In his scrapbooks, Van Vechten did not preserve the
titles of his weekly editorials, with three exceptions; the others
may be the inventions of the editor.

1913

EIII1   "When Dreams Come True" Full of Tune [by Philip Bartholomae], 19
          August.

EIII2   New Play Mixture of Many Elements [Believe Me, Xantippe, by Lucien
          Ballard], 20 August.

EIII3   Chorus Girl in "Family Cupboard" [by Owen Davis], 22 August.

EIII4   Success of "Damaged Goods" Has Let Down Bars to Plays on "Forbid-
den" Subjects [by Susan Glaspell], 24 August.

EIII5   "Doll House" Opens in Globe Theatre [by Leo Fall], 26 August.

EIII6   "Kiss Me Quick" is "Movies" in Farce [by Helen Lowell], 27 August.

EIII7   "Adele" is a Real Musical Comedy [by Paul Hervé and Jean Briquet],
28 August.

EIII8   Poison Cups and Daggers of Ancient Playwrights Supplied "Punch"
We Crave Now, 31 August.

EIII9   Another Triumph for Hippodrome [America by Arthur Voegtlin], 31
August.

EIII10   John Drew Plays in Shakespeare [Much Ado About Nothing], 2 September.

EIII11   "Her Own Money" Comes as Relief [by Mark E. Swan], 2 September.

EIII12   "The Fight" More Exciting Than "Within the Law" [by Bayard Veil-
ler], 3 September.

EIII13   This "Triangle" Has Only Two Sides [Where Ignorance is Bliss, by
Ferenc Molhár], 4 September.

EIII14   Dietrichstein Here in French Comedy [The Temperamental Journey
by André Rivoire and Yves Mirandel], 5 September.

EIII15   "Nearly Married" Proves a Success [by Edward Selwyn], 6 September.

EIII16   Modern Actors' Inability to Change "Technique" Largely Cause Good
Plays' Failures, 7 September.

EIII17   "Lieber Augustin" Casino Success [by Leo Fall], 7 September.

EIII18   Herbert Operetta Scores Success [Sweethearts by Victor Herbert],
9 September.

EIII19   "Who's Who" is Mildly Amusing [by Richard Harding Davis], 12 September.

EIII20   Old World Applauds Some Plays We Reject, 14 September.

EIII21   "Madam President" Opens at Garrick [by Maurice Hennequin and Pierre
Veber], 16 September.

EIII22   "Rob Roy" by Reginald De Koven, 21 September.

EIII23   Big Idea Shown in "The Escape" [by Paul Armstrong], 21 September.

EIII24   Mystery Farce Pleases in Astor [Seven Keys to Baldpate by George
M. Cohan], 23 September.

EIII25   Newcomers Brighten Winter Garden Show [The Passing Show of 1913],
24 September.

EIII26 "Smouldering Flame" Opens [by William LeGrand Howland], 24 September.

EIII27 "Shadowland" Opens in Fulton [by Dion Clayton Calthorp and Cosmo Gordon Lennox], 25 September.

EIII28 "Half an Hour" Seen in Lyceum [by James M. Barrie, with The Younger Generation by Stanley Houghton], 26 September.

EIII29 George Moore, British Playwright, Tells How He Will Finish New Play, "The Apostle," 28 September.

EIII30 John Drew Seen in Pleasing Roles [The Tyranny of Tears by Haddon Cambens and The Will by James M. Barrie], 30 September.

EIII31 Warfield Back in "The Auctioneer" [by Auburn Lee and Charles Klein], 1 October.

EIII32 New Shubert Theatre Opens [Hamlet with Johnston Forbes-Robertson], 3 October.

EIII33 Gertrude Eliot Charms in Comedy [Mice and Men by Madelaine Lucette], 4 October.

EIII34 "Evangeline" Lacks Right Anniversary [by Thomas W. Broadhurst], 5 October.

EIII35 "Half and Hour" and "The Will" Are Proof of a New and More Powerful Barrie, 5 October.

EIII36 Olga Nethersole Plays in One Act of "Sapho" [by Clyde Fitch], 7 October.

EIII37 "Today" Opens in 48th Street Theatre [by George Broadhurst and Abraham S. Schomer], 7 October.

EIII38 "At Bay" Another Play of Thrills [by George Scarborough], 8 October.

EIII39 Thrills Curbed in Princess Theatre [five one-act Grand Guignol plays], 10 October.

EIII40 Forbes-Robertson in Kipling Play [The Light That Failed by George Fleming], 10 October.

EIII41 Sordid Sex Plays Please the Public, 12 October.

EIII42 "Musical Play" Pleases Hearers [Her Little Highness by Channing Pollock, Rennold Wolfe, and Reginald DeKoven], 14 October.

EIII43 Marie Lloyd Greeted in Palace Theatre, 14 October.

EIII44 New Barrie Skit is Tamer Than Usual ["The Censor and the Dramatist" in Doll Girl], 15 October.

EIII45 Southern and Marlowe Seen in "Twelfth Night," 16 October.

EIII46 Booth Theatre Has Its Opening [The Great Adventurer by Donald
Bennet], 17 October.

EIII47 New Plays Read Like Shakespeare, 19 October.

EIII48 New Comedy Opens in Harris Theatre [The Love Leash by Anna Steese
Richardson and Edmund Breese], 21 October.

EIII49 Shaw's Play Gets Hearty Welcome [Caesar and Cleopatra by George
Bernard Shaw], 22 October.

EIII50 Wilkie Bard Scoring Hit in Hammerstein's, 24 October.

EIII51 Matty Scores in Playwright Role [The Girl and the Pennant by Rida
Johnson Young and Christy Matthewson], 24 October.

EIII52 Plays Suffering for Lack of a New Type of Scenery, 26 October.
[A4, A25, D25]

EIII53 Ames Produces Poetic Fantasy [Prunella, or Love in a Garden by
Lawrence Housman, Harley Granville Barker, and Joseph Moorat],
27 October.

EIII54 44th Street Theatre Becomes Music Hall [Lew Fields Vaudeville],
28 October.

EIII55 "Indian Summer" Seen in Criterion [by Augustus Thomas], 28 October.

EIII56 Artistic Temper Shown in "Tante" "by C. Haddon Chambers, with Ethel
Barrymore], 29 October.

EIII57 "Marriage Game" is Well Played [by Anne Crawford Flexner], 30 October.

EIII58 "Oh, I Say!" Has Opening in Casino [by Jerome Kern, Sidney Blow,
and Douglas Hoare], 31 October.

EIII59 New Plays Based on Artistic Temperament, 2 November.

EIII60 Cyril Maude Seen in Quaint Comedy [The Second in Command by Robert
Marshall], 4 November.

EIII61 Polaire is Back; As Lively as Ever, 8 November.

EIII62 Critic Must Decide Whether Writer Has Hit Mark, 9 November.

EIII63 Polaire Isn't Ugly—She's a Beauty, For She Says So Herself and
Grieves for a Serious Role, 9 November.

EIII64 "General John Regan" is Amusing Play [by George A. Birmingham],
11 November.

EIII65 Striking One Act Plays Presented [By-Products by Joseph Mendill
Patterson and Countess Mizzi by Schmid], 12 November.

EIII66 "The Man Inside" Has Opening [by Roland Burnham Molineux], 12
November.

EIII67   Cyril Maud Seen in a Double Bill [The Ghost of Jerry Bundler by
          W.W. Jacobs and Charles Rock, and Beauty and the Barge by W.W.
          Jacobs and Louis B. Patterson], 14 November.

EIII68   "Ourselves" Keen Play by Woman [by Rachel Crothers], 15 November.

EIII69   Irish Theatre Movement and Russian Ballet Have Had a Beneficial
          Influence on Drama, 16 November.

EIII70   "Strange Woman" Pleasant Comedy [by W.J. Hurlburt], 18 November.

EIII71   Forbes-Robertson Scores as Shylock [in The Merchant of Venice],
          19 November.

EIII72   Henrietta Crosman, with Her Acting, and Belasco, with His Stag-
          ing, are Saviors for Playwrights, 23 November.

EIII73   Maude Welcomed in Creaky Comedy [Grumpy by Horace Hodges and
          Wigney Percyvale, with Cyril Maude], 25 November.

EIII74   McCutcheon and Maxwell a Hit at Hammerstein's, 25 November.

EIII75   "Midleading Lady" Funniest Farce [by Charles Goddard and Paul
          Dickey], 26 November.

EIII76   "Hop O'My Thumb" a Pretty Comedy [by George R. Sims, Frank Dix,
          Arthur Collins, and Manuel Klein], 27 November.

EIII77   Forbes-Robertson Evolves a New Shylock That Impresses No Two
          Critics Alike, 30 November.

EIII78   Mme. Kalich Seen in Role of "Rachel" [by Carina Jordan], 2 Decem-
          ber.

EIII79   Shaw Has a New Recipe for Play Writing, and None Has Yet Success-
          fully Imitated Cohan, 7 December.

EIII80   "Children of Today" Opens in Harris [by Clara Lipman and Samuel
          Shipman], 9 December.

EIII81   "Things That Count" a Christmas Play [by Lawrence Eyre], 9 Decem-
          ber.

EIII82   "High Jinks" Well Received in Lyric [by Leo Dietrichson and Otto
          Harbach], 11 December.

EIII83   New York's "Darktown" Would Do Well on Broadway ["My Friend From
          Kentucky" at The Darktown Follies by J. Leubrie Hill], 14 Decem-
          ber. [A9, A25, A28]

EIII84   Stage Society Gives Benefit [The Cassilis Engagement by St. John
          Handkin], 16 December.

EIII85   Forbes-Robertson Plays in "Othello," 16 December.

EIII86   Chesterton Misses Mark in "Magic," First Dramatic Essay [by G.K.
          Chesterton], 21 December.

EIII87 "New Henrietta" Better Than Old [by Winchell Smith and Victor Mapes, based on The Henrietta by Bronson Howard], 23 December.

EIII88 Bert Williams Is Back, 23 December [A28]

EIII89 French Drama Society Begins Public Career [La Vierge Folle by Henri Bataille and Le Passot by Françoise Coupée], 23 December.

EIII90 Bernstein Play Shows "A Punch" [The Secret by Henri Bernstein], 24 December.

EIII91 "Salome" Given in Realistic Manner [Mimi Aguglia in the play by Oscar Wilde], 24 December. [A9, D73]

EIII92 New Gates Play a Whimsical Hit [We Are Seven by Eleanor Gates], 25 December.

EIII93 Hans Andersen Tale in Princess Theatre [Ib and Little Christina by Basil Hood], 26 December.

EIII94 Billie Burke in Serious Play [The Land of Promises by W. Somerset Maugham], 26 December.

EIII95 Princess Theatre Has Demonstrated Public Has a Taste for Big Things in Capsule Form, 28 December.

EIII96 Shaw Play Shows in Little Theatre [The Philanderer], 29 December.

EIII97 "Girl on the Film" [by James Tanner, Walter Kollo, and Willy Bredschender], 30 December.

EIII98 Aguglia in "Elektra" [by Hugo von Hofmannsthal], 31 December.

EIII99 "Iole" Presented in the Longacre [by William Frederick Peters and R.C. Benteal], 31 December.

1914

EIII100 "Girl on the Film" is Proof Musical Comedy Succeeds Mostly Because of Its Cast, 4 January.

EIII101 Maude Adams Back in Barrie's Play [The Legend of Leonora], 6 January.

EIII102 Roshanara Proves Art [Hindu dance recital], 6 January.

EIII103 Oriental Romance a Big Theatre Hit [Thousand Years Ago by Percy MacKaye, with Fania Marinoff], 7 January.

EIII104 "A Little Water on the Side" [by William Collier], 8 January.

EIII105 Esmond's "Eliza" Proves Amusing [Eliza Comes to Stay by H.V. Esmond], 8 January.

EIII106 Why MacKaye Has Italians in Chinese Play, 11 January.

EIII107   Novel Effects in "Whirl of World" [by Harold Aldridge and Sigmund Romberg], 11 January.

EIII108   "Queen of the Movies" Song-and-Girl Hit [by Julius Freund, Glen
Y. MacDonald, and Jean Gilbert], 13 January.

EIII109   "Sari" is Gay with Poiret Costumes [by Julius Wilhelm, Fritz
Greenbaum, and Emmerich Kallman], 14 January.

EIII110   "Don't Weaken" a Well Acted Farce [by Walter Hackett], 15 January.

EIII111   Cooperative Plays by British Schoolboys, Perse Scholars for Boys
Who Have Written, 18 January.

EIII112   White Slave Play Seen at Longacre [The House of Bondage by Joseph Byron Totten], 20 January.

EIII113   "Yellow Ticket" a Stirring Play [by Michael Morton], 21 January.

EIII114   Play Barred in Vienna Opens Here [Professor Bernhardi by Arthur
Schnitzler], 22 January.

EIII115   This is Come-Back Year for Many Players Now Appearing in Broadway Theatres, 25 January.

EIII116   "Dear Fool" Has Charm and Humor [by H.V. Esmond], 27 January.

EIII117   Stage Society Gives New American Play [Heap Game Watch by Elizabeth Read], 27 January.

EIII118   "Change" a Welsh Play in the Booth [by J.O. Francis], 28 January.

EIII119   Impressions Called Forth by Dramatic Events of the Week, 1 February.

EIII120   Princess Offers Five Short Plays [Neglected Lady, Hard Man, Kiss
in the Dark, The Fountain, It Can Be Done, with Holbrook Blinn],
1 February.

EIII121   French Drama Society Gives "La Gioconda" [by Gabriel D'Annun-
zio], 2 February.

EIII122   "Laughing Husband" a Tuneful Comedy [by Arthur Wimperis and Edmund Eysler], 3 February.

EIII123   Europe is Only Play Field Open to Stage Society, 8 February.

EIII124   Faversham Gives Colorful "Othello" [William Faversham], 10 February.

EIII125   Blanche Bates Seen in "Half an Hour" [by James B. Barrie], 10
February.

EIII126   Stenographer as Red Riding Hood [Help Wanted by Jack Lait], 12
February.

EIII127 Repertory Playhouse to Solve Theatrical Problem, 15 February.

EIII128 Fun With Divorce in "Rule For Three" [by Guy Bolton], 17 February.

EIII129 College Boys Hit in Musical Show [The Misleading Lady, Dartmouth College], 17 February.

EIII130 Old Fashioned "Comedy-Drama" Back in Broadway's Favor, 22 February.

EIII131 William Faversham in "Julius Caesar," 20 February.

EIII132 "Along Came Ruth" Pleasing Comedy [by Holman Day], 24 February.

EIII133 "Midnight Girl" Pleasing to Eye [by Paul Hervé, Jean Briquet, and Adolphe Phelipe], 24 February.

EIII134 "Too Many Crooks" a Clever Comedy [by Frank Craven], 26 February. [F2]

EIII135 Stage Stars Who Leave New York's White Way Are Soon Forgotten by Broadway, 1 March.

EIII136 New Scarborough Play in Longacre [The Last Resort by George Scarborough], 3 March.

EIII137 "What Would You Do?" Has Opening [by Augustin McHugh], 4 March.

EIII138 Laurette Taylor in One Act Plays [Just as Well, Happiness, and The Day of Dupes by J. Hartley Manners], 7 March.

EIII139 Two New Plays Prove It Isn't Necessary to be Realistic in Writing Melodrama, 8 March.

EIII140 Faversham Draws in Vaudeville Act [scenes from The Squaw Man, on a bill with Fannie Brice], 10 March.

EIII141 Six Headliners in Vaudeville to Compete with the Movies, 15 March.

EIII142 Anglin's Rosalind Hailed by Throng [Margaret Anglin in As You Like It], 17 March.

EIII143 Eltinge is Clever in "Crinoline Girl" [by Otto Mauerbach, J. Ely, and Percy Wenrich, with Julian Eltinge], 18 March.

EIII144 "Marrying Money" Opens in the Princess [by Washington Pezet and Bertram Marburgh], 19 March.

EIII145 "Maid of Athens" Found Diverting [by Franz Lehar, Victor Leon, and Caroline Wells], 20 March.

EIII146 "A Pair of Sixes" Opens at Longacre [by Edward Peple], 21 March.

EIII147 Margaret Anglin's Interpretation of "As You Like It" Smacks of "Man and Superman," 22 March. [A7]

EIII148   Miss Anglin in "Twelfth Night," 24 March.

EIII149   Shaw Introduces His Flower Girl to German Audience First [Pyg-
          malion by George Bernard Shaw], 23 March.

EIII150   "Pygmalion" in German, 25 March.

EIII151   Billie Burke Seen in a New Comedy [Jerry by Catherine Chisolm
          Cushing], 30 March.

EIII152   Margaret Anglin Adds to Laurels [Lady Windemere's Fan by Oscar
          Wilde], 31 March.

EIII153   Real Thrills in "Granny Maumee" [by Ridgely Torrence], 31 March.
          [A9, A28; D19. Quoted in Literary Digest, 9 May 1914.]

EIII154   Stars Play in "Belle of Bond Street" [with Gaby Delys], 1 April.

EIII155   Ridgely Torrence's New Play Furnishes Basis for Fresh Field in
          American Drama, 5 April. [A9, A28; D19]

EIII156   "Pinafore" a Hit at Hippodrome [by Gilbert and Sullivan], 10
          April.

EIII157   Soliloquies, Dubbed Old Fashioned in the Theatre, Coming in
          Again, 12 April.

EIII158   "The Truth" Given in Little Theatre [by Clyde Fitch], 13 April.

EIII159   "The Beauty Shop" Makes Many Laugh [by Channing Pollock and J.
          Charles Gebest], 14 April.

EIII160   New Musical Play by Orlob Given [The Red Canary by Harold Orlob
          and Willard Johnstone], 15 April.

EIII161   The Plain Truth About "The Truth," 19 April.

EIII162   Plays That Bloom in Spring; Late Productions in Broadway Houses,
          26 April.

EIII163   "Koenig Oedipus" at Metropolitan [by Sophocles, translated into
          German], 28 April.

EIII164   "Vik" a Drama Spoiled in the Making [by Myra Wilson], 30 April.

EIII165   Many Conspicuous Dramatic Successes Stand Out, 3 May.

EIII166   "The Shepherd King" Finds Audience Loyal [the United Catholic
          Works], 5 May.

EIII167   "Charm of Isabel" Mildly Amusing [by Sidney Rosenfeld], 6 May.

EIII168   Marc Antony Visits Cleopatra in Movies [Antony and Cleopatra by
          George Kleine], 8 May.

EIII169   Revival of Sardou's "Scrap of Paper" Suggests Other Parisian
          Features We Have Taken Up, 10 May.

EIII170 "Scrap of Paper" Still Brilliant [by Eugene Sardou], 12 May.

EIII171 "Headliners" Fill Vaudeville Bills [Marie Lloyd], 13 May.

EIII172 Student Comedy Broadway Musical [The Royal Arms by the Mask and
         Wig of the University of Pennsylvania], 17 May.

EIII173 New Plays in Old Plays, 17 May.

EIII174 Lamblets Caper Down Broadway [Fourth Annual Lamb's Day Parade],
         23 May.

EIII175 Bowery Theatrical Season at its Height, Marionette Sicilian
         Players, and Two Vaudeville Houses Provide Some Unusual Forms
         of Entertainment, 24 May.

EIII176 "Madame Moselle" in Need of "Punch" [by J. Ludwig Englander and
         Edward A. Paulton], 24 May.

EIII177 Two New Summer Shows [Ziegfeld Follies of 1914, with scenes from
         "My Friend From Kentucky" (EIII83), and The Passing Show of
         1914], 31 May.

                   Contributions to The New York Globe

         Van Vechten wrote occasional articles for his friends, John Pitts
         Sanborn and Louis Sherwin — sometimes signing them with pseudonyms
         — in this newspaper. It was variously known as The Globe and Com-
         mercial Advertiser and The Evening Globe. In his 1924 bibliography,
         Scott Cunningham indicates that Van Vechten was "editorial writer
         on the New York Globe, writing two or three editorials a day for
         about three months." No record of such industry exists in Van Vech-
         ten's scrapbooks; however, between 25 January and 12 February 1916,
         he did contribute several short editorials, all anonymous.

                                1909

EIV1 The Symphony Society, circa November.

EIV2 Russian Symphony, circa November.

EIV3 The Musical Art Society, circa December.

EIV4 The Tollefsen Trio, circa December.

EIV5 The Margulies Trio, circa December.

                                1910

EIV6 "Reingold" Sung Again, 24 February.

EIV7 Music [Anna Pavlova], 1 March.

EIV8   The Russian Dancers Again, 3 March.

EIV9   "La Navarisse," _circa_ March.

EIV10   "Orfeo," 20 December.

1911

EIV11   Tetrazzini's Farewell, 3 April.

EIV12   Pavlowa's Farewell, 4 April.

EIV13   Dancing Critics, 28 June [A25; D135]

EIV14   The Original Aeroplane, 12 August.

EIV15   Miss Parlow Again, 13 November.

EIV16   At the Opera [Cavalleria Rusticana and Il Pagliacci], 5 December.

1912

EIV17   Gaby and Jolson in a Riotous Music Play [The Honey Moon Express, signed "Louis Sherwin," ghostwritten by Van Vechten], 8 February.

EIV18   Stransky's Programming [Josef Stransky], 15 March.

EIV19   "Stop Thief!" [by Carlyle Moore], 28 December.

1913

EIV20   "The Unwritten Law" [by Edwin Milton Royle], 9 February.

1914

EIV21   At the Opera: Romeo and Juliet in English, 15 September.

1915

EIV22   Josef Hofmann Recital, 1 February.

EIV23   [a letter to the editor about Algernon St. John Brennon], 20 December. [EV1]

EIV24   "Prince Igor," 31 December.

1916

EIV25   Opera Without Artists [signed "Evelyn Burt," pseudonym] 3 January.

EIV26   The Need For New Operas [signed "William G. Allen," pseudonym] 5 January.

EIV27 His Debt to Plattesburg [Percy Heighton], 24 January.

EIV28 A Shakespearean Partnership [Margaret Anglin]; Thieves Among Dis-
honor [Anna T.L. Field]; The Return of Dr. Cook, 25 January.

EIV29 Russian Ballet Revisited; Scotti's Fiftieth Birthday, 26 January.

EIV30 Art and Dollars; Tobacco for Soldiers; The Knish War; "Sheherazade"
Again, 27 January.

EIV31 Health and the Cigar Butter; The Weather; Le Pavillon d'Armide; Our
Friend the Cat, 28 January.

EIV32 Russian Ballet, 29 January.

EIV33 Harvard Lampoon; War and Religion, 31 January.

EIV34 Making Bookshops Comfortable; Oscar Hammerstein, 1 February.

EIV35 Metropolitan New Gifts; Colonna Madonna; Better Side of New York;
Hoentschel College, 3 February.

EIV36 A Fine Policy; Male Chauvinism; An Expurgated Ballet, 4 February.

EIV37 The New Ways of Repentance; Alex Wildon Drake, 5 February.

EIV38 William Winter's Testimonial; General Booth's Memorial, 7 February.

EIV39 Sleeping Outdoors, 8 February.

EIV40 Women's Dress and Propriety; A Model Rookie, 9 February.

EIV41 A String of Pearls, 10 February.

EIV42 Mrs. Pankhurst's War Babies; Mr. Mellsas' Plan; La Argentina, 11
February.

EIV43 Dress for Men, 12 February.

EIV44 Mr. Stravinsky's Pedigree, 24 February.

EIV45 The French Theatre, 19 December.

1917

EIV46 Symphony Society, 26 February.

EIV47 The Theatre. Another Point of View on "The Land of Joy," 9 November. [Quoted as "Spanish Dancers Who Have Made New York Sit Up
and Take Notice" in Current Opinion, January 1918.]

1918

EIV48 Music. "Pelléas et Mélisande" with Mary Garden, 1 February.

EIV49   Music. Mary Garden's Transcendant Art, 6 February. [A7, A15]

EIV50   Music. Another View of Galli-Curci [a letter in response to the
        music editor's opinion of Amelita Galli-Curci], 28 February.

1919

EIV51   Marguerite d'Alvarez, 5 November.

V Contributions to Miscellaneous Newspapers

1915

EV1   [a letter to the editor about Algernon St. John Brennon], New York
        Morning Telegraph, 24 December. [EIV23]

1918

EV2   Readable Musical Criticism: A Talk With One Who Writes It—Carl Van
        Vechten [an interview with Theodora Bean who contributed only the
        first paragraph], Morning Telegraph, 24 February. [Quoted in "Cedar
        Rapids Finds the Bolshevik—Carl Van Vechten," Musical Courier, 11
        April 1918. EV4]

EV3   A Palm For Mary Garden, Chicago Daily News, 27 February.

EV4   How I Do It, Chicago News Book Review, 13 March. [EV2]

EV5   Should a Critic Know Interpreters?, Chicago Daily News Book Review,
        17 April.

1919

EV6   Edgar Saltus Again, Chicago Daily News Book Review, 16 April.

EV7   Lemon Pie [Gerald Cumberland, Set Down in Malice], Chicago Daily
        News Book Review, 16 July.

EV8   Oscar Hammerstein: An Obituary, New York Morning Telegraph, 17 Aug-
        ust. [A9, A17]

EV9   A Charming Book [Arthur Symons, Studies in Elizabethan Drama], Chi-
        cago Daily News Book Review, 17 September.

EV10   John McCormack's Book [John McCormack: His Own Life Story], Chicago
        Daily News Book Review, 24 September

EV11   Music [Sir George Henschel, Musings and Memories of a Musician],
        Chicago Daily News Book Review, 1 October.

EV12   A Book About Books [Old and New Masters], Chicago Daily News Book
        Review, 22 October.

EV13 More Light Essays [Philip Littell, Books and Things], Chicago Daily News Book Review, 5 November.

EV14 A Successful Biography [Don C. Seitz, Artemus Ward], Chicago Daily News Book Review, 12 November.

EV15 Hearn's Tropical Lilies [Lafcadio Hearn, Fantastics and Other Fancies], Chicago Daily News Book Review, 19 November.

EV16 A Book About Musicians [Frederick H. Martens, Violin Mastery], Chicago Daily News Book Review, 17 December.

1920

EV17 The Italian Drama [Lander MacClintock, The Contemporary Drama in Italy], Chicago Daily News Book Review, 18 February.

1921

EV18 Enrico Caruso [translated into Yiddish by Nathan Belkin], Die Zeit, 7 August.

EV19 A Note on American Letters [translated into Yiddish by Nathan Belkin], Die Zeit, 11 September.

EV20 The Prodigious Russian: Chaliapin, Singer and Actor, Revisits America, Boston Transcript, 5 November. [A6, A10]

EV21 A Belated Biography [Raymond M. Weaver, Herman Melville: Mariner and Mystic], New York Evening Press, 31 December. [C4]

1922

EV22 A Warning to Biographers, New York Tribune, 14 May.

EV23 Musk and Mortar [Edgar Saltus, The Ghost Girl], New York Tribune, 10 September.

1923

EV24 More Praise for Jane Cowl in "Romeo and Juliet," Chicago Evening Post, 14 February.

EV25 [a letter to "Kenelm Digby" (William Rose Benét) in "The Literary Lobby"], New York Evening Post, 19 April.

EV26 Medals for Miss Stein [Gertrude Stein, Geography and Plays], New York Tribune, 13 May.

EV27 "The Flower Beneath the Foot" by Ronald Firbank, New York Tribune, 24 June. [A17]

1925

EV28 The Dean of Jazz [Alexander Woollcott, The Story of Irving Berlin],
      New York Herald Tribune Books, 5 April.

EV29 The Great John L. [R.F. Dibble, John L. Sullivan], New York Herald
      Tribune Books, 3 May.

EV30 More Edgar Saltus [Uplands of Dreams; Purple and Fine Women; The
      Anatomy of Negation; Mr. Incoul's Misadverture], New York Herald
      Tribune Books, 16 August.

EV31 Edgar Saltus in His Socks [Marie Saltus, Edgar Saltus, The Man],
      New York Herald Tribune Books, 11 October.

EV32 The Songs of the Negro [The Book of American Negro Spirituals, Ed.
      James Weldon Johnson; Howard W. Odum and Guy B. Johnson, The Negro
      and His Songs; Dorothy Scarborough, On the Trail of Negro Folk-
      songs], New York Herald Tribune Books, 25 October. [A28]

EV33 Uncle Tom's Mansion [The New Negro, Ed. Alain Locke; Negro Work
      Songs, Street Cries and Spirituals, Ed. Mellows], New York Herald
      Tribune Books, 20 December. [A28]

1926

EV34 A Triumphant Negro Heroine [Walter White, Flight], New York Herald
      Tribune Books, 11 April. [A28]

EV35 A Virginia Lady Dissects a Virginia Gentleman [Ellen Glasgow, The
      Romantic Comedians], New York Herald Tribune Books, 12 September.
      [C7]

EV36 Mean Ole Miss Blues Becomes Respectable [Blues, Ed. W.C. Handy],
      New York Herald Tribune Books, 6 June. [A28]

EV37 Don't Let Dis Harvest Pass [The Second Book of Negro Spirituals, Ed.
      James Weldon Johnson; Seventy Negro Spirituals, Ed. William Arms
      Fisher; Howard W. Odum and Guy B. Johnson, Negro Workaday Songs;
      Newell Niles Puckett, Folk Beliefs of the Southern Negro], New York
      Herald Tribune Books, 31 October. [A28]

EV38 Nigger-himmel, Frankfurter Zeitung, 30 December 1926 through 27 Feb-
      ruary 1927. [A18q]

1927

EV39 Through the Eyes of Innocence [Isa Glenn, Little Pitchers], New
      York Herald Tribune Books, 2 January.

1929

EV40 Yesterday Book [Henry Handel Richardson, Maurice Guest], New York
      Herald Tribune Books [?], undated and unidentified clipping.

1930

EV41 L'Araignée Mâle, La Revue Hebdomadaire [Paris], 25 January through
      22 March. [A19k]

1932

EV42 L'Araignée Mâle, Le Journal du Cairo [Egypt], 19 March. [A19k]

1937

EV43 Some Cakewalks and Blues and Spirituals [J. Rosamond Johnson, Roll-
      ing Along in Song], New York Herald Tribune Books, 30 May.

1938

EV44 Born to Use a Lens [Walker Evans, American Photographs], New York
      Herald Tribune Books, 16 October.

1939

EV45 Neglected Genius of Fifty-seventh Street [William Schack, And He
      Sat Among the Ashes, a Biography of Louis M. Eilshemius], New York
      Herald Tribune Books, 12 November.

1940

EV46 [a letter to John Murray Anderson about Romeo and Juliet], New York
      Journal American, 22 May.

1941

EV47 W. C. Handy, Dean of Negro Composers [W.C. Handy and Arna Bontemps,
      Father of the Blues, An Autobiography], New York Herald Tribune
      Books, 6 July. [A28]

1943

EV48 Most Revealing Prefaces [Ellen Glasgow, A Certain Measure], New
      York Herald Tribune Books, 17 October.

1946

EV49 Choreography for Americans [Grace Roberts, The Borzoi Book of Bal-
      lets] New York Herald Tribune Books, 16 June. [A25]

EV50 Pigeons and Roses Pass, Alas! [an obituary for Gertrude Stein],
      New York Post, 9 December. [D169]

EV51 Gertrude Stein's Now Puzzling God [an unauthorized reprint of the foregoing obituary for Gertrude Stein, an undated and unidentified clipping].

1948

EV52 Gertrude Stein in Jaegers [W.G. Rogers, When This You See Remember Me: Gertrude Stein in Person], New York Post Home News, 9 July.

EV53 Soul of a People Lifted in Song [Roland Hayes, My Songs], New York Herald Tribune Books, 21 November. [A28]

1953

EV54 Stein's Mailbag Brilliant Grab Bag of Names, Talent [The Flowers of Friendship: Letters written to Gertrude Stein, Ed. Donald Gallup], New York Post, 16 August.

F.
EPHEMERA AND MISCELLANEA

1911

F1 New York Times review of "The Spring Maid" by Louis F. Werba and Mark
A. Lueschner, reprinted in the Liberty Theatre program, circa January:
12 pp., 23 X 15.3 cm., white coated stock printed in black and orange.
[EII565]

1914

F2 New York Press review of "Too Many Crooks" by Frank Craven, reprinted
in part in the Century Theatre program, circa February: 16 pp., 23 X
14.3 cm., white stock printed in black. [EIII134]

1916

F3 Advertising blurb for Music and Bad Manners dust jacket: salmon or
blue wrapper printed in green. [A5a]

1917

F4 Advertising blurb for Interpreters and Interpretations [A6]
a. dust jacket: yellow wrapper printed in green.
b. The New Borzoi Books, Fifth Season, Fall of 1917, orange and white
wrapper printed in blue, 12.7 X 7.7 cm., p. 30.
c. reprinted in F5b, p. 30; F7, p. [2].

1918

F5 Advertising blurb for The Merry-Go-Round [A7]
a. dust jacket: yellow wrapper printed in black.
b. The New Borzoi Books, Sixth Season, Spring of 1918, yellow wrapper
printed in green, 12.7 X 7.7 cm., pp. 13-14.

c. reprinted in The New Borzoi Books, Seventh Season, Autumn, 1918,
    blue wrapper printed in black, 12.7 X 7.7 cm., pp. 13-14; F7,
    p. [3].

F6 Advertising blurb for The Music of Spain [A8]
    a. dust jacket: yellow wrapper printed in red.
    b. reprinted in F7, p. [4].

1919

F7 Advertising brochure for Carl Van Vechten's books: [4] pp., 18.1 X
    13.7 cm.; ivory stock printed in brown: [1] photograph of Van Vech-
    ten by Mishkin and quotation from The Philadelphia Press; [2] blurb
    for Interpreters and Interpretations [F4] and publisher's note; [3]
    blurbs for Music and Bad Manners [F8] and The Merry-Go-Round [F5];
    [4] blurb for The Music of Spain [F6] and an order blank. Printed by
    Alfred A. Knopf, Inc., but not so indicated.

F8 Advertising blurb for Music and Bad Manners [A5b]
    a. dust jacket: orange wrapper printed in black.
    b. reprinted in F7, p. [3].

1920

F9 [Marguerite d'Alvarez] A Remarkable Tribute to a Remarkable Artist
    [D76]
    a. reprinted in facsimile from Musical Courier, 22 April, as an ad-
        vertising broadside, circa April, 39.5 X 27.7 cm., machine-finish
        commercial paper. According to Scott Cunningham's 1924 biblio-
        graphy, "The pages were reprinted for Miss d'Alvarez's use in
        publicity, and it is doubtful if more than a dozen copies still
        are in existence. It is nevertheless a legitimate Carl Van Vech-
        ten first edition."
    b. reprinted in an advertising brochure, [4] pp., 21.6 X 15.3 cm.,
        ivory stock printed in black, p. [2]

F10 Advertising blurb for In the Garret dust jacket: yellow wrapper
    printed in red. [A9]

F11 Advertising blurb for Interpreters dust jacket: yellow wrapper
    printed in black. [A10]

F12 Advertising blurb for The Tiger in the House [A11]
    a. Green paper label, 25.7 X 19 cm., with an illustration, Minette
        Washes, from a drawing by Gottfried Mind.
    b. Green paper label, 25.7 X 19 cm., with an illustration, Cat With
        Muff, from a drawing by Grandville.
    c. reprinted in New Borzoi Books, No. 18.
    d. reprinted on dust jacket for second edition: gray wrapper printed
        in blue.
    e. reprinted on dust jacket for Lords of the Housetops, F13a.
    f. reprinted on dust jacket for the English edition of The Tattooed
        Countess, A14e.

1921

F13 Advertising blurb for Lords of the Housetops [B3]
     a. dust jacket: yellow wrapper printed in brown.
     b. The New Borzoi Books, August, 1921, orange wrapper printed in
         black, 19.1 X 13.3 cm., p. 20.

1922

F14 Advertising blurb for Peter Whiffle: His Life and Works [A12]
     a. dust jacket, first state: light blue wrapper printed in dark
         blue.
     b. The New Borzoi Books, No. 13, Spring, red wrapper printed in
         black, 18.2 X 12.8 cm., p. 22.

F15 Advertising blurb for Kittens by Svend Fleuron [B4] dust jacket:
     orange wrapper printed in black and white.

F16 Advertising blurb for My Musical Life by Nikolai Rimsky-Korsakoff
     [B6]
     a. The New Borzoi Books, No. 14, Autumn, blue wrapper printed in
         black, 18.4 X 12.8 cm., p. 3.
     b. The New Borzoi Books, No. 14, Autumn, tall paper edition of 50
         copies; tan, blue, and green wrappers with lime green label
         printed in green; Japan Imperial vellum, 22 X 15.1. cm., p. 3.

F17 Advertising blurb for The Hill of Dreams by Arthur Machen
     a. dust jacket: blue wrapper printed in black.
     b. reprinted in F16.
     c. The New Borzoi Books, No. 15, Spring 1923, red wrapper printed
         in black, 18.4 X 12.7 cm., p. 9.
     d. The New Borzoi Books, No. 15, Spring 1923, tall paper edition of
         50 copies; tan and orange wrapper with tan label printed in
         orange, 21.9 X 15 cm.

F18 Advertising blurb for The Secret Glory by Arthur Machen
     a. dust jacket: green wrapper printed in black.
     b. reprinted in F16, p. 24.
     c. reprinted in Borzoi Broadside, Spring 1923, p. 24.

F19 Advertising blurb for The House of Souls by Arthur Machen
     a. dust jacket: blue wrapper printed in black.
     b. reprinted in F16.

1923

F20 Advertising blurb for Proud Lady by Neith Boyce
     a. Borzoi Broadside, January, pp. 6-7.
     b. reprinted in F17c.

F21 Advertising blurb for The Blind Bow-Boy [A13]
     a. dust jacket: white wrapper printed in blue, black, and green,
         with an illustration by Robert E. Locher on the front.
     b. Publishers' Weekly, 14 July, p. 8.

    c. dust jacket for <u>Peter Whiffle</u>, ninth printing only, pink wrapper
        printed in dark blue.
    d. <u>Borzoi Monthly List</u>, No. 6, August: ivory leaf, folded, 22.9 X
        14.8 cm.
    e. <u>The New Borzoi Books</u>, No. 16, Autumn: yellow wrapper printed in
        black, 18.2 X 12.6 cm., p. 3.

F22   Advertising blurb for <u>Things Near and Far</u> by Arthur Machen, dust
      jacket: yellow wrapper printed in black.

F23   Advertising blurb for <u>Three Imposters</u> by Arthur Machen, dust jacket:
      red wrapper printed in black.

F24   Advertising blurb for <u>Hieroglyphics</u> by Arthur Machen, dust jacket:
      green wrapper printed in black.

1924

F25   Endorsement for <u>Hickory Smoked Montgomery County</u> [Tennessee] Hams,
      distributed by Thomas Dabney Mabry in an advertising brochure: [4]
      pp., 21.6 X 14 cm.; white leaf, folded, containing a letter, signed
      by Van Vechten, 23 December 1923, p. [2].

F26   Advertising blurb for <u>Jennifer Lorn</u> by Elinor Wylie, <u>New York Evening</u>
      <u>Post</u>, 2 February.

F27   Advertising blurb for <u>Dog and Duck</u> by Arthur Machen
    a. dust jacket: yellow wrapper printed in black.
    b. <u>New York Evening Post</u>, 9 February.
    c. <u>The New Borzoi Books</u>, No. 19, Midwinter: pumpkin wrapper printed
        in black, 18.5 X 12.7 cm., p. 11.

F28   Advertising blurb for <u>Ornaments in Jade</u> by Arthur Machen
    a. dust jacket: green wrapper printed in black.
    b. <u>The New Borzoi Books</u>, No. 17, Spring: orange wrapper printed in
        black, 18.5 X 12.7 cm., p. 17.
    c. <u>The American Mercury</u>, May.
    d. <u>The New Borzoi Books</u>, No. 18, Fall: green wrapper printed in
        black, an edition of 1,000 copies for salesmen, p. 10.
    e. <u>The New Borzoi Books</u>, No. 18, Fall: orange wrapper printed in
        black, revised edition, p. 15.

F29   Advertising blurb for <u>London Adventure</u> by Arthur Machen
    a. dust jacket: orange wrapper printed in black.
    b. [titled, except on the dust jacket, <u>Machen in London</u>], <u>Borzoi</u>
        <u>Broadside</u>, July-August, p. 5.
    c. F28d, p. 34.
    d. F28e, p. 39.
    f. <u>Borzoi Broadside</u>, Autumn, p. 26.

F30   Advertising blurb for <u>The Lord of the Sea</u> by M. P. Shiel [B9]
    a. dust jacket: red wrapper printed in black
    b. F28d, p. 20.
    c. F28e, p. 23.
    d. F29e, p. 33.

F31 Advertising blurb for <u>The Fire in the Flint</u> by Walter White, <u>The</u>
<u>American Mercury</u>, November.

1925

F32 Advertising blurb for <u>Red</u> [A15]
a. dust jacket: yellow wrapper printed in red and black.
b. <u>The New Borzoi Books</u>, No. 20, Spring: pumpkin wrapper printed
in black, 18.5 X 12.7 cm.

F33 Endorsement for Taylor Gordon and J. Rosamond Johnson on a program
for a recital of Negro spirituals, 31.7 X 15.3 cm., ivory leaf
printed in black, April.

F34 Advertising blurb for <u>The Wooings of Jezebel Pettyfer</u> by Haldane
MacFall
a. dust jacket: white wrapper printed in black, blue, red, green.
b. <u>The New Borzoi Books</u>, No. 21, Fall: blue wrapper printed in
black, p. 16.
c. <u>Borzoi Broadside</u>, September, p. 16.

F35 Advertising blurb for <u>Fifty Drawings</u> by Alastair [B11]
a. F34b, a quotation from Van Vechten's "Introduction," p. 18.
b. F34c, pp. 19-20.
c. advertising brochure: [4] pp., 28.8 X 22.3 cm.; a single leaf
of Van Gelder paper from the text, folded, printed in black, with
a quotation from Van Vechten's "Introduction," p. [2].

F36 Advertising blurb for <u>Saïd the Fisherman</u> by Marmaduke Pickthall, in
F34b, pp. 16-17.

F37 Advertising blurb for <u>The Prince of Wales and Other Famous Americans</u>
by Miguel Covarrubias [B12]
a. F34b., p. 18.
b. <u>Borzoi Broadside</u>, October, p. 18.

F38 Advertising blurb for <u>Firecrackers</u> [A16]
a. dust jacket: yellow wrapper printed in red and green.
b. F34b, p. 18.
c. dust jacket for English edition: yellow wrapper printed in red
and blue.

F39 Advertising blurb for <u>The Venetian Glass Nephew</u> by Elinor Wylie, in
<u>Saturday Review of Literature</u>, 10 October.

F40 <u>Ten Favorite Books of Robert Benchley, Ernest Boyd, Philip Guedalla,</u>
<u>William McFee, Carl Van Vechten, Alexander Woollcott, Roland Young</u>;
French-fold brochure, 14.3 X 8.8 cm., issued by The Holiday Book-
shop, 49 East 49th Street, New York City.

1926

F41 Advertising blurb for <u>Gentlemen Prefer Blondes</u> by Anita Loos, in
<u>The New York Times</u>, 24 January.

F42   Advertising blurb — a quotation from Van Vechten's introduction —
      for The Weary Blues by Langston Hughes [B13]
      a. dust jacket: yellow wrapper printed in black and red.
      b. Borzoi Broadside, January, p. 2.
      c. Borzoi Broadside, Spring, pp. 55-56.
      d. The New Borzoi Books, No. 22, Spring: orange wrapper printed
         in black, pp. 55-56.

F43   Advertising blurb for Excavations [A17]
      a. dust jacket: red, blue, green, orange, or lavender wrapper
         printed in black.
      b. F42d, p. 26.
      c. dust jacket for the English edition of The Tattooed Countess,
         A14e, F12f.

F44   Advertising blurb for Lolly Willowes, or The Loving Huntsman by Syl-
      via Townsend Warner, in The New York Times, 14 May.

F45   Advertising blurb for Flight by Walter White, New York Tribune, 12
      April.

F46   Advertising blurb for The Book of American Negro Spirituals by James
      Weldon Johnson, in The Wasp [Brooklyn], 29 May.

F47   Advertising blurb for The House of Souls by Arthur Machen
      a. dust jacket: yellow wrapper printed in black.
      b. Saturday Review of Literature, 12 June.

F48   Advertising blurb for Blues by W. C. Handy, in New York Times, 27
      June.

F49   Advertising blurb — a quotation from Van Vechten's review — for
      The Romantic Comedians by Ellen Glasgow, New York Times, 26 Septem-
      ber. [C7, EV35]

F50   Advertising blurb for Nigger Heaven [A18]
      a. dust jacket: blue wrapper printed in white.
      b. The New Borzoi Books, No. 23, Fall: blue wrapper printed in
         black, p. 15.
      c. dust jacket for The Blind Bow-Boy, seventh printing

F51   Advertising endorsement for Ethel Waters, Pittsburgh Courier, 23
      October.

F52   Advertising blurb for Tropic Death by Eric Walrond, Saturday Review
      of Literature, 30 October.

                                  1927

F53   Advertising blurb for Three Lives by Gertrude Stein
      a. dust jacket for English edition [John Lane]: gray wrapper
         printed in black.

F54   Advertising blurb for Mr. Fortune's Maggot by Sylvia Townsend Warner,
      Saturday Review of Literature, 16 April.

F55   Advertising endorsement for the Ambassador Hotel in Hollywood,
      Chicago Tribune, 11 May.

F56   Advertising blurb for Son of the Grand Eunuch by Charles Pettit,
      New York World, 17 August.

F57   The "Favorite" Books of Famous People; [32] pp., 16.2 X 12.2 cm.,
      rust wrapper printed in black on stapled pamphlet; issued by the
      Atlantic Monthly Bookshop, 8 Arlington Street, Boston. Van Vech-
      ten's list and F58, p. [19].

F58   Advertising blurb for Peter Whiffle: His Life and Works [A12i]
      a. slipcase: cream paper printed in turquoise, pink, and black.
      b. F57, p. [19].

F59   Advertising blurb for God's Trombones by James Weldon Johnson, Satur-
      Review of Literature.

                                  1928

F60   Advertising blurb for Spider Boy [A19]
      a. dust jacket: white wrapper printed with full-color illustration.
      b. The New Borzoi Books, No. 26, Spring: blue wrapper printed in
          black, p. 12.

F61   Advertising blurb for Mr. Hodge and Mr. Hazard by Elinor Wylie, New
      York World, 19 July.

                                  1929

F62   Advertising blurb for Passing by Nella Larsen; a green strip printed
      in black, 47 X 7 cm., to wrap around the book.

F63   Advertising blurb for The Magic Island by William Seabrook, New York
      World, 15 January.

F64   Advertising blurb for Transport by Isa Glenn, New York Times, circa
      January.

F65   Advertising blurb for The Hell of Loneliness by Henry von Rhau, In-
      wood Press brochure, 29 February.

F66   Advertising endorsement for Stepin Fetchit in "Hearts in Dixie," New
      York Times, 20 March.

F67   Advertising blurb for Red Harvest by Dashiell Hammett, New York
      World, 23 March.

F68   Advertising blurb for The Innocent Voyage by Richard Hughes, New
      York Times, circa April.

F69   Advertising blurb for Cold Steel by M. P. Shiel, New York World, 25
      April.

F70   Advertising blurb for Black Magic by Paul Morand, New York Times, 5 May.

F71   Advertising blurb for Peter Arno's Parade, New York World, 21 December.

1930

F72   Advertising blurb for The Maltese Falcon by Dashiell Hammett, New York World, 8 March.

F73   Advertising blurb for Sweet Man by Gilmore Millen, Saturday Review of Literature, 6 September. [A28]

F74   Advertising blurb for Parties [A21]
      a.   dust jacket: green wrapper printed in dark green and silver.
      b.   green tags printed in black, 14 X 6.9 cm.; approximately 5,800 were distributed to booksellers for publicity.
      c.   The New Borzoi Books, No. 31, Autumn: gray wrapper printed in red and black, 18.8 X 11.8 cm., p. 34.
      d.   dust jacket for English edition: cream wrapper printed in black, magenta, and turquoise.

F75   Advertising blurb for Hullabaloo by Peter Arno, New York Times, 28 November.

F76   Advertising blurb for A Short History of Julia by Isa Glenn, New York Times, 14 December.

1931

F77   Advertising blurb for A Woman on Her Way by John Van Druten, New York World, 13 February

F78   Advertising broadside for The Negro Mother by Langston Hughes, The Golden Stairs Press, 20.7 X 16.2 cm.; cream leaf printed in brown and black, 24 September, unsigned.

1932

F79   Advertising blurb for Hindoo Holiday by J. R. Ackerly, New York Times, 10 July.

F80   Advertising blurb for Sacred and Profane Memories [A22]
      a.   dust jacket: white wrapper printed in purple, pink, and turquoise.
      b.   The New Borzoi Books, No. 34, Spring: white wrapper printed in red and blue, 20.3 X 13.2 cm., p. 17.

1933

F81   Introductory quotation from Parties in Going Somewhere by Max Ewing, New York: Alfred A. Knopf, Inc.

F82 Advertising blurb for <u>Going Somewhere</u> by Max Ewing
     a. green tags printed in black, 14 X 6.9 cm., distributed to book-
         sellers for publicity.
     b. <u>The New Borzoi Books</u>, No. 35, Winter; white wrapper printed in
         orange and green, 20.3 X 13.2 cm., p. 9.

F83 Advertising blurb [quotation from a letter to Alfred A. Knopf], for
     <u>The Thin Man</u> by Dashiell Hammett, <u>Borzoi Broadside</u>, February.

F84 Advertising blurb for <u>Man and Mask</u> by Feodor Chaliapin
     a. F82b., p. 23.
     b. F83, p. 23.

F85 Advertising blurb for <u>Along This Way</u> by James Weldon Johnson, <u>New</u>
     <u>York Times</u>, <u>circa</u> October.

                              1934

F86 Advertising blurb for <u>The Thin Man</u> by Dashiell Hammett, <u>New York</u>
     <u>Times</u>, 12 January.

F87 Advertising endorsement for <u>Come of Age</u> with Judith Anderson by
     Clemence Dane, <u>New York Times</u>, <u>circa</u> January.

F88 Advertising blurb for <u>The Ways of White</u> Folks by Langston Hughes,
     dust jacket. [A28]

F89 Advertising endorsement for <u>Stevedore</u> by George Sklar and Paul Pe-
     ters, in an advertising brochure issued by the Civic Repertory The-
     atre, 23.3 X 15.4 cm.; white leaf, folded, printed in red and black,
     19 April.

                              1935

F90 Advertising blurb for <u>Americans, What Now?</u> by James Weldon Johnson,
     unidentified clipping. [A28]

F91 Advertising blurb for <u>Jonah's Gourd Vine</u> by Zora Neale Hurston, <u>New</u>
     York Times, <u>circa</u> May.

F92 Advertising endorsement for Maurice Schwartz in <u>Yoshe Kalb</u>
     a. brochure issued by the Yiddish Art Theatre, 28 X21.8 cm.; white
         stapled pages printed in purple and half-tone, December.
     b. Actors' Fund Benefit program, 30.5 X 23.5 cm., white stapled
         pages printed in purple and half-tone, December., p. 22.

                              1937

F93 Advertising endorsement for Maurice Schwartz in <u>The Brothers Ashken-</u>
     <u>azi</u> by I. J. Singer, New York Times, 21 September.

F94 Advertising blurb for <u>Of Mice and Men</u> by John Steinbeck, in a bro-
     chure issued by Covici-Friede, 16 X 8 cm., folded to make [4] pp.;
     cream leaf printed in brown.

F95   Advertising blurb for Photo-Surrealism by Lewis Jacobs, in a brochure
      issued for an exhibition at the Rabinovitch Gallery, 40 West 56th
      Street, New York City, 16 X 14 cm.; white leaf, folded to make [4]
      pp., printed in halftone; 1—22 February.

F96   Advertising blurb for Everybody's Autobiography by Gertrude Stein,
      New York Times, 7 December.

                                    1938

F97   Advertising endorsement for Ram Gopal, in a brochure issued by Alek-
      sander Janta, 25 X 17.5 cm.; cream leaf folded to make [4] pp.,
      printed in brown. The text, including Van Vechten's endorsement, is
      in French.

F98   Advertising blurb for The Autobiography of an Ex-Coloured Man by
      James Weldon Johnson [a quotation from Van Vechten's introduction,
      B14], in a brochure issued by Viking Press, 18.4 X 13.5 cm.; cream
      leaf folded twice to make [6] pp., printed in brown, with a bio-
      graphical sketch by Walter White, reviewers' squibs and writers'
      blurbs for various books, and a list of lecture subjects.

                                    1939

F99   Advertising blurb for Eastward of Eden by I. J. Singer, Borzoi
      Broadside, March, p. 2.

F100 Second advertising blurb for Eastward of Eden by I. J. Singer, New
      York Times, March.

F101 Advertising blurb for The Young Cosima by Henry Handel Richardson,
      New York Times, 7 April.

F102 Advertising blurb for Young Man With a Horn by D. D. Baker, New York
      Times, 19 June.

F103 Advertising blurb for Scoop by Evelyn Waugh, New York Times, 17 July.

F104 Advertising blurb for The World is Round by Gertrude Stein
      a. [cover title] PRESS BOOK | for | GERTRUDE STEIN'S FIRST BOOK FOR
          CHILDREN | "THE WORLD IS ROUND" | William R. Scott, Inc., Pub-
          lisher | Joseph D. Ryle | 590 Madison Avenue | New York, N. Y.;
          16 pp., 29.2 X 22.9 cm.; light blue wrappers printed in black
          mimeograph.
      b. reprinted in a brochure issued by William R. Scott, Inc.: 1941/
          1942 Young Scott Books, North Bennington, Vermont and New York:
          [34] pp., 15.2 X 11.6 cm.; yellow wrapper printed in red.

F105 Advertising blurb for And He Sat Among the Ashes by William Schack,
      Art Digest, 15 October.

F106 Advertising blurb for The State of Music by Virgil Thomson, New York
      Times, 10 December.

1940

F107 THE PROPOSED | JAMES WELDON JOHNSON | MEMORIAL | By CARL VAN VECH-
TEN | Reprinted from Opportunity, Journal of Negro Literature,
March, 1940; 28.6 X 21.4 cm.; white leaf folded to make [4] pp. An
unknown number of copies were distributed to subscribers and poten-
tial contributors. [A28]

F108 Advertising blurb for The Ox-Bow Incident by Walter Van Tilburg
Clark, New York Times, 13 October.

F109 [contribution to a "gullet poll" of favorite foods] in Frank Case.
Do Not Disturb, New York: Frederick A. Stokes Company, p. 267.

1942

F110 "Some Views of View" [by Van Vechten, Karl Shapiro, and Henry Mc-
Bride], View, February-March, p. 9.

F111 Advertising blurb for My Lives and How I Lost Them by Countée Cullen (Harper), dust jacket.

F112 The J. W. Johnson Collection at Yale, reprinted from Crisis, July,
1942; 1 leaf, 29.6 X 22.3 cm. An unknown number of copies were reprinted from the magazine for advertising purposes. [A28]

F113 Advertising blurb [from Van Vechten's review, EV41] for In Certain
Measure by Ellen Glasgow, New York Herald Tribune Books, 16 June.

1946

F114 Advertising blurb for Winter of Artifice by Anaïs Nin, in a publisher's brochure, 22 X 14.2 cm.; cream leaf folded to make [4] pp.,
printed in black.

F115 Advertising blurb for The Borzoi Book of Ballets by Grace Roberts
[from Van Vechten's review, A25, EV42], New York Herald Tribune
Books, 16 June.

F116 Advertising blurb for The House on the Park by Marjorie Worthington, New York Times, circa October.

1947

F117 Advertising blurb for On These I Stand by Countée Cullen, Harper
publicity card, 22.6 X 15 cm. [A28]

F118 Advertising blurb for Lonely Crusade by Chester Himes, New York
Times, 21 September. [A28]

F119 Advertising blurb for Masterpieces of the World's Fine Literature
in Story Form, Ed. Frank McGill, dust jacket.

1948

F120 Advertising blurb for Cry the Beloved Country by Alan Paton, Ebony,
      March.

F121 Advertising blurb for Seraph on the Suwanee by Zora Neale Hurston,
      New York Times, 26 October. [A28]

F122 Advertising blurb for books by Abraham Walkowitz, Girard, Kansas:
      Haldeman-Julius Publications; white machine-finish leaf folded to
      make [4] pp.; a flyer with order blank.

1949

F123 Advertising blurb for Last of the Conquerors by William Gardner
      Smith, in Farrar Straus publisher's catalog, winter-spring.

F124 CARL VAN VECHTEN [an autobiographical resumé]: two typed leaves,
      28 X 21.5 cm., reproduced in blue, and issued with a covering let-
      ter by Leo Perper of Roger Kent, Inc., to advertise a Van Vechten
      photographic exhibition, 11 April—2 May.

F125 Advertising blurb for Cats in Our Lives by Pamela and James Mason,
      New York Times, 10 July.

1950

F126 [extracts from four letters from Van Vechten to Alfred A. Knopf]
      Alfred A. Knopf, "Reminiscences of Hergesheimer, Van Vechten, and
      Mencken," Yale University Library Gazette, 24:145-64 (April).

F127 PIERRE MONTEUX [an appreciation], in an RCA Victor Records adver-
      tisement, The New Yorker, 14 October. [C29]

F128 Advertising blurb for Bob Brown's 1450-1950 (Jargon Council), on a
      yellow leaf, 28 X 21.5 cm.

F129 Advertising blurb for A Long Day's Dying by Frederick Buechner,
      Knopf dust jacket: black wrapper printed in red and white.

1951

F130 Advertising blurb for Ti-Coyo and His Shark by Clément Richer, New
      York Times, 9 September.

1952

F131 GERTRUDE STEIN ON RECORDS [an endorsement], white leaf, 28 X 21.5
      cm., printed in brown, issued by Dorian Records, 465 West 57th
      Street, New York City.

1953

F132 [two letters from Van Vechten to Gertrude Stein], advance publicity
      brochure for THE | FLOWERS | OF | FRIENDSHIP [the foregoing in a
      broken-line box] | Letters | written to | Gertrude | Stein | EDITED
      BY DONALD GALLUP [in a broken-line box] | [borzoi] | To be pub-
      lished on August 17. | Price $5.00. Illustrated | Alfred A. Knopf
      PUBLISHER. [C43] [32] pp., numbered [i-vii], viii, 50-52, 57-64,
      [101]-102, 116-18, 223-25, 254-55, 288, 324; 21 X 14 cm.; stapled
      leaves, with an introduction not included in the published volume,
      by W. G. Rogers.

1955

F133 [a letter from Van Vechten to Alfred A. Knopf, circa 1920, about
      The Tiger in the House, and the first, second, and third drafts of
      the opening paragraph of Nigger Heaven], quoted in John D. Gordan:
      "Carl Van Vechten, Notes for an Exhibition in Honor of His Seventy-
      Fifth Birthday," Bulletin of the New York Public Library, 59:343,
      359-60 (July). [A28]

F134 Advertising blurb for The Black Prince by Shirley Ann Grau, uniden-
      clipping, probably from the New York Times.

1958

F135 Advertising blurb for Aromas and Flavors by Alice B. Toklas, New
      York Times, 16 November.

F136 Advertising blurb for And Promenade Home by Agnes De Mille, New York
      Times, 17 November.

F137 [Walter Arensberg] quoted in Fiske Kimball, "Cubism and the Arens-
      bergs," Art News Annual, 24:104.

1959

F138 Advertising blurb for Malcolm by James Purdy, New York Times, 20
      September.

F139 Advertising blurb for Secrets of Chinese Cooking by Tsuifeng Lin
      and Hsianju Lin, Prentice Hall dust jacket. [a quotation from Van
      Vechten's introduction to the earlier edition, Cooking With the
      Chinese Flavor, B29]

1960

F140 [Richard Banks], in a brochure issued by the Galax Gallery, Phoenix,
      Arizona; a white leaf French-folded to make [4] pp.

F141 Advertising blurb for Mr. Cat by George Freedley, Howard Frisch
      dust jacket.

1963

F142 [Richard Banks, once a composer of note], Twenty Portraits of Mem-
      bers of the New York City Ballet Co.; a white card printed in black,
      10.8 X 15.5 cm., announcing an exhibition, 12 March—21 April.

F143 Record album note for The Making of Americans and "Plays" from
      Lectures in America by Gertrude Stein, read by Marian Seldes, Folk-
      ways RA No. FL9742; red, white, and black cardboard cover.

F144 Advertising blurb for Emblems of Conduct by Donald Windham, Scrib-
      ners dust jacket.

1965

F145 Advertising blurb for Cotton Comes to Harlem by Chester Himes, New
      York Times, circa September. [an excerpt from a letter from Van
      Vechten to Himes written several years earlier; A28]

F146 "Ten Dullest Authors [C9, D100] quoted in Quarterly Newsletter,
      XXXI, Book Club of California, Winter issue

F147 Advertising endorsement for Mother Goose of Montmarnasse, Selec-
      tions from the Writings of Gertrude Stein, read by Addison M. Met-
      calf, Folkways RA No. FL9746; purple, mauve, and white cardboard
      cover. [a quotation from a letter from Van Vechten to Metcalf]

1966

F148 "Richard Banks" [B33] in EXHIBITION OF PAINTINGS BY | RICHARD BANKS
      | April 26 thru May 15, 1966 | BURGOS GALLERIES LTD | 127 East
      57th Street New York NY | TE8.0017; an advertising broadside,
      21.5 X 14 cm.

1969

F149 [selection from The Tiger in the House] used as an introductory
      quotation to One Hundred & Sixty Cat Proverbs and Proverbial Simi-
      les, compiled by Jane Grabhorn, San Francisco: Grabhorn-Hoyen.

1978

F150 [extract from a letter from Van Vechten to Igor Stravinsky], in
      Vera Stravinsky and Robert Craft, Stravinsky in Pictures and Docu-
      ments, New York: Simon and Schuster, p. 655.

1979

F151 [selections from The Tiger in the House], in Moonshine on Cats,
      British Broadcasting Corporation program, first broadcast, 7 May.

F152 [inscription in a copy of <u>Nigger Heaven</u> from Van Vechten to Bruce
Kellner] on dust jacket for <u>Keep A-Inchin' Along</u> [A28], 24.2 X 55.7
cm.; heavy white leaf printed in black, with a caricature of Van
Vechten by Covarrubias; limited to 26 copies lettered A through Z.

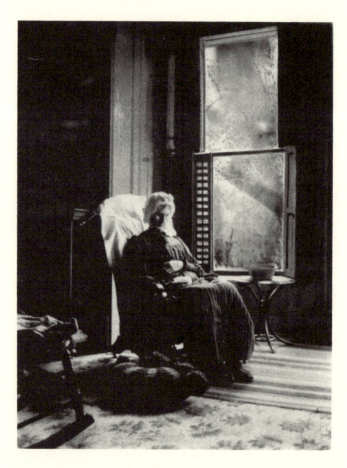

Grandmother Ilona Van Vechten, 1896 [G1275]

Ina Claire, 1932 [G243]

Ettie and Carrie Stettheimer, 1932 [G1198, G1197]. Courtesy of Yale University, Collection of American Literature.

Philadelphia Cheese Shop, 1933

Artificial Cave by Antoni Gaudí, Parque Guell, Barcelona, 1935

Domingo Ortega, El Soto, 1935 [G986]

Fania Marinoff, 1939 [G841]

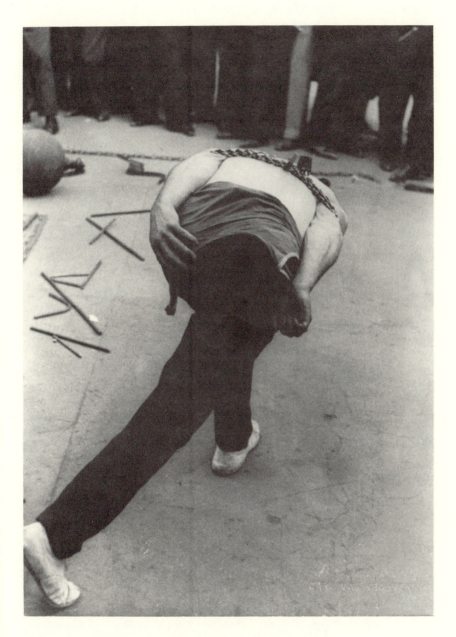

Strongman in Chains, Place de la Bastille, Paris, 1934 [G1377]

Columbus Circle, New York City, 1940. Courtesy of Yale University, Collection of American Literature.

Wystan Hugh Auden, 1939 [G51]. Courtesy of Yale University, Collection of
American Literature.

Alicia Markova's Hand, 1941 [G843]

Private Herbert Coburn, U.S. Army; Seaman Andy Mann, U.S. Navy; Seaman J.H. Keller, Canadian Navy—at the Stage Door Canteen, 1943 [G254, G833, G685]

Watching a Parade in Harlem, 1939. Courtesy of Yale University, Collection of American Literature.

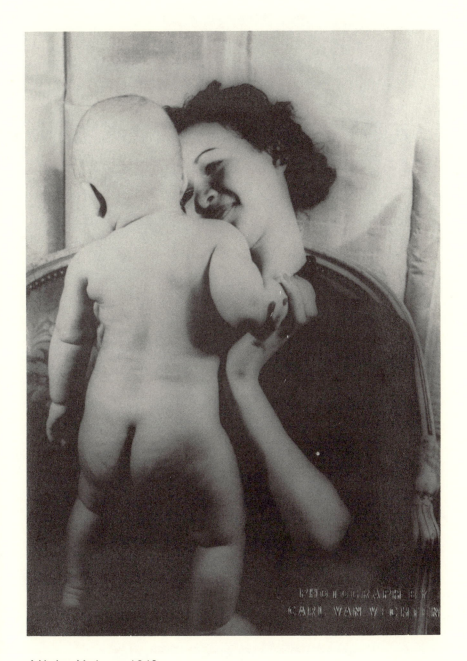

A Harlem Madonna, 1940

Sandy Campbell and Donald Windham, 1955 [G203, G1341]

Christopher Isherwood, 1950 [G622]

Isak Dinesen, the Baroness Karen Blixen, 1959 [G340]. Courtesy of Yale University, Collection of American Literature.

Pierre Olaf in *La Plume De Ma Tante*, 1960 (G975)

G.
PHOTOGRAPHY

G1 Berenice Abbott, 1937

G2 Bey Khaled Wahab Abdul, 1936

G3 Christabel Aberconway, 1950

G4 Gertrude Aberconway, 1950

G5 Peter Abrahams, 1955

G6 Eluba Okala Abutu, 1946

G7 Marina Ackerman, 1955

G8 Mercedes d'Acosta, 1935

G9 Louis Adamic, 1937

G10 Diana Adams, 1948

G11 Adele Addison, 1955

G12 Alvin Ailey, 1955
     [A25, A27, A28, H395]

G13 Anabid Ajemian, 1954

G14 George Ajemian, 1954

G15 Maro Ajemian, 1954

G16 Zöe Akins, 1935

G17 Edward Albee, 1961
     [A27, H395]

G18 Betty Allen, 1958

G19 James Allen, 1933

G20 Sanford Allen, 1964

G21 Sara Allgood, 1938
     [H276]
     Theatre Arts, April 1939

G22 Marguerite d'Alvarez, 1932
     [B31]
     New York Times, 28 October
     1956
     Marguerite d'Alvarez, Forsak-
     en Altars, London: Rupert
     Hart-Davis, 1958

G23 John Anderson

G24 Judith Anderson, 1932
     [A27, H276, H395]
     Town & Country, November 1932
     Theatre Arts, April 1939

G25 Marian Anderson, 1946
     [A27, A28, C35, H287, H380]

G26 Sherwood Anderson, 1933
     [A27]
     Shenandoah, Spring 1962

G27 Ann Andrews, 1932

G28 Donald Angus, 1932

G29   George Anthiel, 1933
      [H347]
      American Record Guide, May
          1968

G30   William Archibald, 1956

G31   Elsie Arden, 1933

G32   Argentinita, 1940
      [D158]

G33   John Arledge, 1932

G34   Harold Arlen, 1960
      Edward Jablonski, Happy With
          the Blues, Garden City:
          Doubleday, 1961

G35   Harry Armstrong, 1937

G36   Henry Armstrong, 1937
      [A27, A28, D161]

G37   Antony Armstrong-Jones, 1958

G38   Jacobus Arnoldus, 1961

G39   Martina Arroyo, 1961

G40   Chester Arthur, 1936

G41   Constance Askew, 1937

G42   Kirk Askew, 1937

G43   Gertrude Atherton, 1933

G44   Roy Atkins, 1934

G45   Brooks Atkinson, 1939

G46   Edward Atkinson, 1946

G47   Oriana Atkinson, 1939

G48   William Atkinson, 1939

G49   Lillian Attaway, 1941

G50   William Attaway, 1941

G51   Wystan Hugh Auden, 1939

G52   Gene Austin, 1938

G53   Gerald Ayres, 1957

G54   Ethel Ayler, 1957

G55   James T. Babb, 1955

G56   James T. Babb, Jr., 1955

G57   Don Bachardy, 1964

G58   Pearl Bailey, 1946
      [A27, A28]
      Black Magic, Ed. Langston
          Hughes, New York: Prentice
          Hall, 1967, uncredited
      Pearl Bailey, The Raw Pearl
          [dust jacket], New York:
          Harcourt, Brace and World,
          1968

G59   Josephine Baker, 1951
      [A27, A28]

G60   William Balash, 1954

G61   Hernán Baldrich, 1962

G62   James Baldwin, 1955
      [A27, A28]
      Arthur P. Davis, From the
          Dark Tower, Washington, D.
          C.: Howard University
          Press, 1975

G63   Ruth Baldwin, 1933

G64   Pierre Balmain, 1947

G65   Tallulah Bankhead, 1934
      [A27, H395]

G66   Danny Banks, 1963

G67   Richard Banks, 1951

G68   Theda Bara, 1939

G69   Samuel Barber, 1944
      [H347]

G70   J. Barbette, 1941

G71   Nelson Barclift, 1942
      Forward, November 1942
      Theatre Arts, March 1943

G72   George Gray Barnard, 1937

G73   Albert Coombs Barnes, 1937

G74   Djuana Barnes, 1933

G75   Natalie Clifford Barney, 1935

G76   Richard Barr, 1959

G77   Jean Louis Barrault, 1952
      [A27, with Madelaine Renaud]

G78   Evelyn del Barrio, 1938

G79   Joseph Barry, 1949

G80   Philip Barry, 1949

G81   Ethel Barrymore, 1942
      [A27, H276]
      Cedar Rapids [Iowa] Gazette,
         10 November 1947
      The Playbill, 5 February 1959

G82   Richmond Barthé, 1943
      [H380, with Fritzi Scheff]

G83   Richard Barthlemess, 1933

G84   Mandel Bass, 1940

G85   Ralph Bates, 1938

G86   Reginald Bean, 1938

G87   Romare Bearden, 1944

G88   Cecil Beaton, 1937
      [A27]

G89   Julian Beck, 1951

G90   John Beckett, 1934

G91   Frederic Beckman, 1935

G92   Harry Belafonte, 1954
      [A27, A28]

G93   Barbara Bel Geddes, 1955

G94   Norman Bel Geddes, 1935

G95   Louis Belson, 1950

G96   Jacob Ben-Ami, 1933

G97   Robert Benedusi, 1935

G98   Feral Benga, 1937

G99   Harry Bennett, 1949

G100 Martin Benson, 1935.

G101 Gladys Bentley, 1932

G102 Muriel Bentley, 1948

G103 Thomas Hart Benton, 1935
      [A27]

G104 Konrad Bercovici, 1933

G105 Roy Thompson Beresford, 1958

G106 Albert Berg, 1950

G107 Aline Bernstein, 1933
      [C49]
      Vanity Fair, October 1933
      Andrew Turnbull, Thomas
         Wolfe, New York: Scribners
      1968

G108 Eugene Berman, 1936

G109 Leonard Bernstein, 1944
      [A27, H347]

G110 Adolfo Best-Maugard, 1964

G111 Mary McLeod Bethune, 1949
      [A27]

G112 Christopher Bishop, 1949

G113 Helen Bishop, 1949

G114 John Peale Bishop, 1949

G115 Robert Bishop, 1949

G116 George Black, 1950

G117 Sidney Blackmer, 1932

G118 Charles Blackwell, 1955

G119 Claude Pierre Blanche, 1953

G120 Al Bledger, 1938

G121 Rudi Blesch, 1947

G122 Marc Blitzstein, 1947
      [H347]

G123 Malu Block, 1932

G124 Ralph Bloom, 1943

G125 Kermit Bloomgarten, 1943

G126 McHenry Boatwright, 1961

G127 Anna Roosevelt Boettiger,
      1935

G128 Charlotte Ives Boissevain,
      1943

G129 Todd Bolender, 1947
      [D158]

G130 Adolph Bolm, 1937
      [D158]

G131 Eugen Bonaccio, 1943

G132 Sudi Bond, 1951

G133 Margaret Bonds, 1957

G134 Arna Bontemps, 1938
      Harlem Renaissance Remem-
        bered, Ed. Arna Bontemps,
        New York: Dodd Mead, 1972,
        uncredited

G135 Shirley Booth, 1943
      Theatre Arts, March 1943,
        with Frank "Killer Joe"
        Piro

G136 Irene Bordoni, 1943

G137 Lewis Bouché, 1937

G138 Renée Bouché, 1937

G139 Margaret Bourke-White, 1938
      [A27]

G140 James Bourne, 1943

G141 Alexander Boutté, 1947

G142 Leni Bouvier, 1938

G143 Jane Bowles, 1951

G144 Paul Bowles, 1944
      Paul Bowles, Up Above the
        World, New York: Simon and

      Schuster, 1966, with James
        Purdy

G145 Neith Boyce, 1939
      Michael Marcaccio, The Hap-
        goods: Three Earnest Bro-
        thers, University of Vir-
        ginia Press, 1977

G146 Charles Brabin, circa 1943

G147 Tiny Bradshaw, 1942

G148 Edward R. Braithwaite, 1932

G149 William Stanley Braithwaite,
      1932
      Boston Public Library Bulle-
        tin, 1978

G150 Marlon Brando, 1949
      [A27]
      Bobbs-Merrill advertisements
        and Fall Catalog 1978 for
        A27

G151 Eric Braun, 1948

G152 Paul Brautigan, 1937

G153 Romney Brent, 1932

G154 John Breon, 1949

G155 Charles Bregler, 1938

G156 Honorable Dorothy Brett, 1958

G157 Joseph Brewer, 1935

G158 Oleg Briansky, 1955

G159 Carol Brice, 1947

G160 Jonathan Brice, 1953

G161 Bricktop [Ada de Congé Smith]
      1934
      [D161]

G162 Joseph Brockner, 1938

G163 Louis Bromfield, 1939

G164 Mary Bromfield, 1939

G165 Emerich Bronson, 1949

G166 Romaine Brooks, 1935
      Adelyn D. Breskin, Romaine:
      Thief of Souls, Washington
      D.C.: Smithsonian Insti-
      tute, 1971

G167 Anne Brown, 1948

G168 Debria Brown, 1958

G169 Gabriel Brown, 1935

G170 Irene Brown, 1937

G171 Marion Brown, 1942

G172 Roscoe Lee Browne, 1964

G173 Scoogie Browne, 1954

G174 Dave Brubeck, 1954
      [A27, with Paul Desmond]

G175 Robert Bruce, 1937

G176 Ferdinand Bruckner, 1937

G177 Mark Bruskin, 1964

G178 Doris Bry, 1950

G179 Joyce Bryant, 1953

G180 Bryher [Winifred Ellerman],
      1937
      W.G. Rogers, Ladies Bounti-
      ful, New York: Harcourt,
      Brace and World, 1968
      Bulletin of the New York
      Public Library, 79:461

G181 John Bubbles, 1935
      [B31]

G182 Pearl Buck, 1942

G183 Richard Buckle, 1950

G184 Ralph Buckman, 1935

G185 Frederick Buechner,,1950

G186 Robert Bührer, 1947

G187 Ralph Bunche, 1951
      [A27]

G188 Joseph Burk, 1940

G189 Henry Thatcher Burleigh, 1941

G190 Dan Burley, 1947

G191 Mary Burr, 1951

G192 Marian Burton, 1958

G193 Witter Bynner, 1933

G194 James Branch Cabell, 1935
      [D143]
      The Cabellian, Autumn 1971

G195 Priscilla Cabell, 1935

G196 Edmondo Cacciamani, 1934

G197 Paul Cadmus, 1937

G198 Roland Caillaux, 1949

G199 Nicholas Calas, 1940

G200 Alexander Calder, 1947
      [A27]

G201 Erskine Caldwell, 1934

G202 Cab Calloway, 1932
      [A27, H287]
      Detroit Free Press, 13 Jan-
      uary 1946
      Richmond Times Dispatch, 13
      January 1946
      Washington Sun Post, 13 Jan-
      uary 19466
      Jablonski, Happy With the
      Blues, 1961
      Black Magic, 1967, uncre-
      dited

G203 Sandy Campbell, 1955

G204 Richard Campbell, 1944

G205 Cora Canning, 1939

G206 Truman Capote, 1948
      [A27, H395]

G207 John Capsis, 1948

G208 John Carlis, 1958

G209 Kitty Carlisle, 1933

G210 Tullio Carminati, 1934

G211 Thelma Carpenter, 1949

G212 Joan Carr, 1932

G213 Diahann Carroll, 1955
      [A27]

G214 Paul Vincent Carroll, 1938

G215 Nat Carson, 1959

G216 Jo Carstairs, 1933

G217 Jack Carter, 1958

G218 Henri Cartier-Bresson, 1935
      [A27]

G219 Uriah Cartwright, 1942

G220 Rosemary Carver, 1936

G221 Frank Case, 1942

G222 Willa Cather, 1936
      [A27]

G223 Edward Caulfield, 1937

G224 Horace Cayton, 1947

G225 Ruby Cayton, 1947

G226 Vincenzo Celli, 1944

G227 Charles Cerbone, 1961

G228 Bennett Cerf, 1933
      [D161]

G229 Phyllis Fraser Cerf, 1940

G230 Marc Chagall, 1941
      [A27, H395]

G231 Elwyn Chamberlain, 1954

G232 Marc Chadourne, 1934

G233 Stewart Chaney, 1937

G234 Carol Channing, 1956
      [A27]

G235 Remy Charlip, 1951

G236 Ilka Chase, 1937

G237 Lucia Chase, 1941
      Inside Ballet Theatre, New
      York: Hawthorne Books,
      1977, with Agnes De Mille
      and Annabelle Lyons

G238 Carlos Chavez, 1937
      [H347]

G239 Giorgio de Chirico, 1936
      [A27]

G240 Lili Chookasian, 1964

G241 Walter Chrysler, Jr., 1937

G242 Jane Clabourne, 1946

G243 Ina Claire, 1932
      [H276]
      Theatre Arts, April 1939

G244 Terry Clare, 1943

G245 Alice Clark, 1933

G246 Emily Clark, 1933

G247 Omar Clay, 1962

G248 Duchesse de Clermont-Ton-
      nere [Elisabeth de Gra-
      mont], 1933

G249 Ladybird Cleveland, 1954
      Cedric Dover, American Negro
      Art, New York Graphic So-
      ciety, 1965

G250 Claude Cliff, 1936

G251 Patricia Johnson Clifford,
      1954

G252 Rosemary Clifford, 1954

G253 William Carl Clifford, 1948

G254 Herbert Coburn, 1943

G255 Jean Cocteau, 1949
      [A27]

G256 George M. Cohan, 1933
      [A27]
      Miniature Camera Work, Ed.
        Williard D. Morgan, New
        York: Morgan & Lester, 1938
      Theatre Arts, April 1939
      Cedar Rapids Gazette, 10 No-
        vember 1946

G257 Robert Cohan, 1955

G258 Jack Cole, 1937

G259 Louis Cole, 1934

G260 Leo Coleman, 1946

G261 Charles Ward Collier, 1935

G262 Constance Collier, 1932

G263 Durward Collins, Jr., 1962

G264 Janet Collins, 1949

G265 Horatio Colony, 1936

G266 Alvin Colt, 1952

G267 John Colton, 1935

G268 Padraic Colum, 1959

G269 Peggy Conklin, 1937

G270 Brian Connelly, 1954

G271 Marc Connelly, 1937

G272 Dennis Cooney, 1963

G273 Gladys Cooper, 1934

G274 Maurice Cooper, 1939

G275 Wyatt Cooper, 1964

G276 Aaron Copland, 1935
      [A27, H347]

G277 Clayton Corbin, 1954
      Black Magic, 1967, uncredited

G278 John Lawrence Cornell, 1955

G279 Katharine Cornell, 1933
      [A27]

G280 Lydia Cornell, 1955

G281 Peter Cornell, 1955

G282 Elezier Cortor, 1959
      Dover, American Negro Art,
        1965

G283 Staats Cotsworth, 1943

G284 Père Couturier, 1940

G285 Miguel Covarrubias, 1938

G286 Rose Covarrubias, 1938

G287 Henry Cowell, 1932

G288 Malcolm Cowley, 1963

G289 Helen Craig, 1937

G290 Robert Craig, 1937

G291 Vernon Crane, 1943

G292 Cheryl Crawford, 1938

G293 Pearl Creswell, 1957

G294 Helen Crosby, 1936

G295 James A. Cross, 1942

G296 Frank Crowninshield, 1937

G297 Countée Cullen, 1941
      [H287]
      Margaret Perry, A Bio-Bib-
        liography of Countée Cul-
        len, Westport, Connecti-
        cut: Greenwood Press, 1971
      Harlem Renaissance Remem-
        bered, 1972, uncredited
      Davis, From the Dark Tower,
        1975

G298 Constance Cummings, 1935

G299 Mina Kirstein Curtiss, 1949

G300 Robert Curtiss, 1955

G301 Roald Dahl, 1954
      [H395, with Patricia Neal]

G302 Irene Dailey, 1943

G303 Gala Dali, 1934

G304 Salvador Dali, 1934
      [A27; D161, with May Ray]

G305 Charles Dalmorés, 1907
      [H380]
      New York Times, 1 March 1908,
      uncredited

G306 Chester Dale, 1940

G307 Blythe Daly, 1937

G308 Clemence Dane, 1932

G309 Jimmie Daniels, 1937
      John Becker, The Negro in
      American Life, New York:
      Julian Messner, 1944 [with
      Dorothy Peterson]

G310 Alexandra Danilova, 1949
      [A27]

G311 Pierre Daninos, 1937

G312 Edward Darnell, 1946

G313 Lili Darvas, 1940

G314 Andrew Dasburg, 1934

G315 Marina Wister Dasburg, 1934

G316 Lucia Davidowa, 1932

G317 Jo Davidson, 1935
      [A27]

G318 Robert Davidson, 1948

G319 Christopher Davis, 1962

G320 Dee Davis, 1961

G321 Jimmie Davis, 1942

G322 Ossie Davis
      [A28, with Ruby Dee]

G323 Sammy Davis, Jr., 1956

G324 Gloria Davy, 1958

G325 William Dawson, 1934

G326 Lisa Dean, 1950

G327 Ruby Dee, 1952
      [A27; A28, with Ossie Davis]

G328 Beauford Delaney, 1953
      Dover, Negro American Art,
      1965

G329 Hap Delaney, 1935

G330 Carmen De Lavallade, 1955

G331 Alfred De Liagre, 1933

G332 Alice Delysia, 1949

G333 William Demby, 1956

G334 Agnes De Mille, 1944
      [A25, A27]
      Museum of Modern Art Bulle-
      tin, November 1943
      Agnes DeMille, Dance to the
      Piper, Boston: Little
      Brown, 1952
      Dance Perspectives, No. 17,
      1963
      Tanaquil LeClerq, The Ballet
      Cookbook, New York: Stein
      and Day, 1966
      Inside Ballet Theatre, 1977
      [with Lucia Chase and An-
      nabelle Lyon]

G335 Charles Demuth, 1932

G336 Roy Dennis, 1937

G337 Paul Desmond, 1954
      [A27, with Dave Brubeck]

G338 Crandall Diehl, 1954

G339 Hubert Dilworth, 1963

G340 Isak Dinesen [Baroness Karen
      Blixen], 1959
      [A27]

G341 Aland Dixon, 1935

G342 Dean Dixon, 1941

G343 Mattiwilda Dobbs, 1955

G344 Owen Dodson, 1942
      Owen Dodson, Come Home, Ear-
      ly Childhood, New York:
      Fawcett, 1978

G345 Anton Dolin, 1940
      [A25, D158]
      Theatre Arts, October 1943
      [with Alicia Markova]

G346 William Dollar, 1935
      LeClerq, The Ballet Cook
      Book, 1966

G347 Edward Donahue, 1933

G348 Marian Dorn, 1934

G349 Marie Doro, 1933

G350 Aaron Douglas, 1933
      [H413]
      New York Times, 2 January
      1972

G351 Mahalia Douglas, 1932

G352 Norman Douglas, 1935

G353 Evelyn Dove, 1935

G354 Cedric Dover, 1948

G355 Dorothy Dow, 1947

G356 Coleman Dowell, 1957

G357 Olin Downes, 1937

G358 Robert Downing, 1957

G359 Marian Doyle, 1937

G360 Alfred Drake, 1951

G361 Muriel Draper, 1932

G362 Paul Draper, 1932

G363 Saunders Draper, 1932

G364 Luba Drazovsky, 1959

G365 Theodore Dreiser, 1932
      [A27]
      W.A. Swanberg, Theodore Drei-
      ser, New York: Scribners,
      1975

G366 Michael Duane, 1948

G367 W. E. B. Du Bois, 1946
      [A27]

G368 Marcel Duchamp, 1933
      [A27]

G369 Bibi Dudensing, 1937

G370 Valentine Dudensing, 1937

G371 William Dufty, 1960

G372 Raoul Dufy, 1937
      [A27]

G373 Keir Dullea, 1961
      [A27]

G374 Rudolph Dunbar, 1946

G375 Todd Duncan, 1947

G376 Katherine Dunham, 1940
      [A25, A27, H291]
      Black Magic, 1967, uncredited

G377 Blanche Dunn, 1941

G378 Mildred Dunnock, 1955

G379 Walter Duranty, 1937

G380 Mrs. Thomas Eakins, 1938

G381 Bill Earl, 1961

G382 Eliana Krylenko Eastman,
      1934

G383 Max Eastman, 1934

G384 Roy Eaton, 1958

G385 John Edward, 1943

G386 Jon Edward, 1938

G387 Mary Edwards, 1941

G388 André Eglevsky, 1944
      [D158]

G389 Edward Ehrman, 1935

G390 Lillian Ehrhan, 1935

G391 Mary Ehrman, 1935

G392 Louis Michel Eilshemius,
      1937
      William Schack, And He Sat
      Among the Ashes, New York:
      Art Association Graphic
      Society, 1939
      New York Herald Tribune, 12
      November 1939
      New York Times, 10 December
      1939

G393 Eldon Elder, 1960

G394 Ruby Elzy, 1935

G395 Robert Emmett, 1960

G396 Gilbert Emery, 1932

G397 Lehmann Engel, 1956

G398 Jacob Epstein, 1934
      [A27]

G399 Ben Ericson, 1946

G400 Catherine d'Erlenger, 1940

G401 Morris Ernest, 1939

G402 Vincente Escuerdo, 1933

G403 Cisco Escobar, 1942

G404 Viola Essen, 1944

G405 Walter Estes, 1936

G406 Lillian Evanti, 1935

G407 Bobby Evans, 1942

G408 Marc Ettienne, 1952

G409 Judith Evelyn, 1952

G410 Max Ewing, 1932

G411 Mme. Alfred Fabre-Luce, 1933

G412 Barbara Fallis, 1948

G413 Mrs. James Farley, 1936

G414 Thomas Fast, 1937

G415 Charles Fatone, 1960

G416 William Faulkner, 1954
      [A27, H395]

G417 Trader Faulkner, 1951

G418 Bernard Fäy, 1934
      Virgil Thomson, Virgil Thom-
      son, New York: Alfred A.
      Knopf, 1966

G419 Peter Feibelman, 1958

G420 Edna Ferber, 1938

G421 José Fernandez, 1939

G422 Arthur Davison Ficke, 1937

G423 Gladys Brown Ficke, 1937

G424 Betty Field, 1948
      Richard Goldstone, Thornton
      Wilder, New York: Saturday
      Review Press, 1975

G425 Dorothy Fields, 1943

G426 Leonor Fini, 1936

G427 Robert Fisher, 1954

G428 Dwight Fiske, 1937

G429 Ella Fitzgerald, 1940
      [A27]

G430 F. Scott Fitzgerald, 1937
      [A27, H296, H395]
      Arthur Mizener, The Far Side
      of Paradise [dust jacket
      and order form], Boston:
      Houghton Mifflin, 1950
      Publishers' Weekly, 27 Jan-
      uary 1951
      Princeton Chronicle, Summer
      1951
      Esquire, October 1968
      Sheila Grahame, The Real F.
      Scott Fitzgerald, Garden
      City: Doubleday, 1976
      Native Voices: A Calendar
      of American Writing, 1977

G431 Arthur Fizdale, 1952

G432 Kirsten Flagstad, 1935

G433 Janet Flanner, 1940

G434 Martha Flowers, 1953

G435 Lynn Fontanne, 1932
      [A27]

G436 Countess Clarita de Force-
      ville, 1934

G437 Charles Henri Ford, 1934

G438 Helen Ford, 1943

G439 Ruth Ford, 1939

G440 Maureen Forrester, 1960

G441 Lucas Foss, 1962

G442 Gray Foy, 1950

G443 Janet Fox, 1943

G444 Esteban Francis, 1947

G445 Elda Frankau, 1934

G446 Lloyd Frankenberg, 1951

G447 Sidney Franklin, 1951

G448 Roy Franklyn, 1962
      advertising flyer for Nathan
      the Wise, 1962

G449 Margaret Freeman [Cabell],
      1937

G450 Claude Fredericks, 1951

G451 Pancho Freeto, 1955

G452 Olive Fremstad, 1907
      New York Times, 1 March 1908,
      uncredited

G453 Jared French, 1939

G454 Daniel Frohman, 1934

G455 Pierre Dominique Gaisseau,
      1962

G456 Paul Gallico, 1937

G457 Donald Gallup, 1951

G458 Elda Garbe, 1937

G459 Mariano Garcia, 1935

G460 Mary Garden, 1932
      [A27, H380]

G461 Benny Garland, 1948

G462 Robert Garland, 1934

G463 Eva Gauthier, 1938
      [B31]

G464 Madame B. Gay, 1933

G465 Thomas Gaydos, 1959

G466 Ben Gazzara, 1955
      [A27]

G467 George George, 1945

G468 George Gershwin, 1933
      [A27, B31, H347, H395]
      Miniature Camera Work, 1938
      David Ewen, A Journey to
         Greatness: The Life and
         Music of George Gershwin,
         Englewood Cliffs: Prentice
         Hall, 1956

G469 Maurice Gest, 1939

G470 Althea Gibson, 1958
      [A27]

G471 Ian Gibson, 1941

G472 Richard Gibson, 1959

G473 John Gielgud, 1936
      [A27, H436]
      Theatre Arts, April 1939

G474 Rosamond Gilder, 1938

G475 Dizzy Gillespie, 1955
      [A27, A28]

G476 Gin-Chin Kuo, 1940

G477 Margalo Gilmore, 1933

G478 Dorothy Gish, 1948

G479 Lillian Gish, 1933
      [A27]

G480 Ira Glackens, 1937

G481 William Glackens, 1937

G482 Harry Glynn, 1932

G483 Dagmar Godowsky, 1935

G484 Leopold Godowsky, 1935

G485 Dwight Godwin, 1942

G486 Robert Gold, 1952

G487 Emma Goldman, 1934

G488 Milton Goldman, 1941

G489 Nana Gollner, 1948
      Inside Ballet Theatre, 1977
          [with Hugh Laing]

G490 Vladimir Golschmann, 1937
      [H347]

G491 Eugene Goossens, 1945

G492 Ram Gopal, 1938
      [D158, F97]

G493 Taylor Gordon, 1933
      [B15c]

G494 John D. Gordan, 1951

G495 Phyllis Gordan, 1951

G496 Geoffrey Gorer, 1935

G497 Martha Graham, 1961
      [A25, A27, H395, with Bert-
          ram Ross]

G498 Shirley Graham, 1946

G499 Philip Grausman, 1961

G500 Gilda Gray, 1940

G501 Julian Green, 1932

G502 Lillian Green, 1942

G503 Diedre Greenway, 1958

G504 Marianne Greenwood, 1962

G505 Waylande Gregory, 1941

G506 Henry Wagstaff Gribble, 1937

G507 Stanton Griffis, 1937

G508 Emilie Grisby, 1937

G509 Reri Grist, 1959

G510 Chaim Gross, 1963

G511 Alice Guinzburg, 1935

G512 Harold Guinzburg, 1935

G513 Nicholas Guillen, 1949

G514 Brion Gysin, 1947

G515 Paul Haabon, 1932

G516 Sara Haardt [Mencken], 1932

G517 Dolly Haas, 1940

G518 Alice Halika, 1937

G519 Juanita Hall, 1949
      [A27]
      Black Magic, 1967, uncredited

G520 Lois Hall, 1938

G521 Monroe Hall, 1938

G522 Natalie Hall, 1932

G523 Mary Lee Hallaway, 1939

G524 Kay Halle, 1938

G525 Richard Halliday, 1938

G526 Oscar Hammerstein II, 1939
      [A27]

G527 Charles Hammond, 1937

G528 John Hammond, 1935

G529 Natalie Hays Hammond, 1944
      [A27]

G530 Percy Hammond, 1938

G531   Virginia Hammond, 1937

G532   Althayer Handforth, 1935

G533   Thomas Handforth, 1935

G534   William Christopher Handy,
       1932
       [A27, A28, EV47, H287, H347]
       Becker, The Negro in American
       Life, 1944
       Greenwood Press Catalog of
       Original Books, 1979, ad-
       vertisement for A27

G535   Barry Hankins, 1961

G536   Leonard Hanna, 1939

G537   Hutchins Hapgood, 1933

G538   Everson Harper, 1943

G539   Curtis Harrington, 1964

G540   Julie Harris, 1952

G541   Radie Harris, 1942

G542   Marsden Hartley, 1939
       [D161]

G543   Georgette Harvey, 1932

G544   Hurd Hatfield, 1951
       After Dark, October 1975

G545   Antonio Hatvany, 1939

G546   Robert Hawk, 1945

G547   William Hawkins, 1938

G548   William Hay, 1934

G549   Melissa Hayden, 1957
       [A25]

G550   Julie Haydon, 1939

G551   Marion Hayes, 1963

G552   Roland Hayes, 1954
       [A27]

G553   Eugene Hayes, 1947

G554   Godfrey Headley, 1959

G555   Frederic Hearn, 1938

G556   Michael Hedge, 1963

G557   Van Heflin, 1938

G558   Florence Vidor Heifetz, 1933

G559   Jascha Heifetz, 1933
       [A27, H347]

G560   Teresa Helburn, 1937

G561   Louise Hellström, 1933

G562   Robert Helpman, 1952

G563   W. J. Henderson, 1933

G564   Miguel Herroro, 1949

G565   George Herring, 1955

G566   John Hersey, 1958

G567   Gabriel Hess, 1934

G568   Dame Myra Hess, 1937
       [A27]

G569   Alan Hewitt, 1943

G570   Chippie Hill, 1947

G571   Leemar Hill, 1943

G572   Ruby Hill, 1946

G573   Chester Himes,11946
       [A27, A28]
       Chester Himes, The Quality
       of Hurt [dust jacket],
       Garden City: Doubleday,
       1972
       Davis, From the Dark Tower,
       1975

G574   Altonell Hines, 1934
       [H263]

G575   Al Hirschfeld, 1955
       [A27]

G576   Nina Hirschfeld,1963

G577 Edith Hoffenstein, 1936

G578 Samuel Hoffenstein, 1936

G579 Geoffrey Holder, 1954
      [A25, A27]

G580 Leo Holder, 1958

G581 Billie Holiday, 1949
      [A27, A28, D161, H395]
      Greenwood Press Catalog of
          Original Books, 1979

G582 Charlotte Hollomon, 1957

G583 Celeste Holm, 1943

G584 Libby Holman, 1935

G585 Nora Holt, 1937
      [A28]

G586 Hedda Hopper, 1934

G587 William Hopper, 1934

G588 Paul Horgan, 1942

G589 Harold Horn, 1956

G590 Juliet Hornblow, 1938

G591 Terry Hornblow, 1937

G592 Lena Horne, 1941
      [A27, A28]
      Jablonski, Happy With the
          Blues, 1961

G593 Marilyn Horne, 1961
      [H380]

G594 William Horne, 1947

G595 Elsie Houston, 1940

G596 Alice Howard, 1947
      Artist Life, April 1949

G597 Harry Howells, 1938

G598 Gerald Hoxton, 1935

G599 George Hoy, 1933

G600 George Hoyhingen-Heune, 1935

G601 Julia Hoyt, 1933

G602 S. I. Hsuing, 1935

G603 Richard Huey, 1944

G604 Franklin Hughes, 1938

G605 Langston Hughes, 1936
      [A27, A28; H395, with Stage
          Door Canteen servicemen]
      Harlem Renaissance Remem-
          bered, 1972, uncredited
      Davis, From the Dark Tower,
          1975
      Native Voices: A Calendar of
          American Writing, 1977

G606 Georges Hugnet, 1932

G607 James Hull, 1932

G608 Richard Hundley, 1964

G609 Robert Hunt, 1938

G610 Kim Hunter, 1960

G611 Dudley Huppler, 1951

G612 Fannie Hurst, 1932
      [A27]
      Bookman, February 1933

G613 Zora Neale Hurston, 1934
      [A28, H413]
      Harlem Renaissance Remem-
          bered, 1972, uncredited
      Davis, From the Dark Tower,
          1975
      Robert Hemenway, Zora Neale
          Hurston [also dust jacket
          and advertisment], Urbana:
          University of Illinois
          Press, 1977
      Historical Association of
          Southern Florida brochure,
          1977

G614 Clifton Hutchinson, 1934

G615 Earle Hyman, 1953

G616 Giuseppe Iadone, 1959

G617 Ilona [Royce-Smithkin], 1964

G618 William Inge, 1954

G619 Rex Ingram, 1934

G620 George Irwin, 1963

G621 William Irwin, 1963

G622 Christopher Isherwood, 1939
      Saturday Review, 12 April
         1952

G623 José Iturbi, 1933

G624 Burl Ives, 1955
      Burl Ives, Columbia Record
         album cover, 1956, un-
         credited

G625 Daniel Jablonski, 1956

G626 Ditta Jablonski, 1956

G627 Edward Jablonski, 1956
      [B31, dust jacket]

G628 Harold Jackman, 1932

G629 Charles Jackson, 1950

G630 Mahalia Jackson, 1962
      [A27, A28, H395, H438]

G631 Raymond Jackson, 1964

G632 Helen Jacobs, 1951

G633 Ivie Jahrman, 1962

G634 William Jahrman, 1962

G635 Charles James, 1955

G636 C. L. R. James, 1951

G637 Edward James, 1939

G638 Nancy Lee James, 1955

G639 Aleksander Janta, 1938

G640 Hans Jaray, 1940

G641 Robinson Jeffers, 1937

G642 Louise Jefferson, 1964

G643 Charles Joffe, 1939

G644 Mildred Joffe, 1936

G645 Phyllis Joffe, 1939

G646 Charles S. Johnson, 1948

G647 Donald Johnson, 1946

G648 Dots Johnson, 1948

G649 Grace Nail Johnson, 1932

G650 Hall Johnson, 1947

G651 J. Rosamond Johnson, 1933

G652 James Weldon Johnson, 1932
      [A28, H253]
      New York Times Book Review,
         15 October 1933, uncredited
      Yale University Library Ga-
         zette, October 1943

G653 Lamont Johnson, 1946

G654 Louis Johnson, 1955

G655 Margot Johnson, 1936

G656 Marie Johnson, 1948

G657 Mildred Johnson, 1937

G658 Philip Johnson, 1933
      [A27, H436]
      Thomson, Virgil Thomson,
         1971

G659 William Johnson, 1934
      Dover, American Negro Art,
         1965

G660 William Henry Johnson, 1944

G661 Klaus Jonas, 1954

G662 A. A. Jones, 1958

G663 James Earle Jones, 1961
      [A27]

G664 Lawrence Jones, 1955

G665 LeRoi Jones, 1962
      [A28]

G666 Marcel Jouhandeau, 1949

G667 Doris Julian, 1958

G668 Philippe Jullian, 1949

G669 William Justema, 1937

G670 Freda Kahloah, 1936

G671 Daniel-Henry Kahnweiler,
      1949

G672 Whitford Kane, 1938

G673 Barbara Karinska, 1940

G674 Maria Karnilova, 1943
      Inside Ballet Theatre, 1977
      ⌊with Anthony Tudor and
      Hugh Laing⌋

G675 Kieri Karnoski, 1944

G676 Karen Katzen, 1964

G677 E. McKnight Kauffer, 1934

G678 Beatrice Kauffman, 1934

G679 Alfred Kay, 1938

G680 Ulysses Kay, 1946

G681 Nora Kaye, 1944
      [A25, H355, H395]
      Cue, 16 April 1949
      Cue, 10 January 1952
      LeClerq, The Ballet Cook
      Book, 1966

      Dance Perspectives, No. 18,
      1963 ⌊with Anthony Tudor
      and Hugh Laing⌋
      Inside Ballet Theatre, 1977
      ⌊with Anthony Tudor and
      Hugh Laing⌋
      Charles Payne, American Bal-
      let Theatre, New York: Al-
      fred A. Knopf, 1978 ⌊also
      with Hugh Laing⌋

G682 Doris Keane, 1940

G683 Rhonda Keane, 1940

G684 Greta Keller, 1940

G685 J. H. Keller, 1943

G686 William Melvin Kelley, 1963

G687 Bruce Kellner, 1958
      [D165; H395, dust jacket]

G688 Margaret Wilcox Kellner, 1964

G689 William Kemper, Jr., 1940

G690 Lewanne Kennard, 1940

G691 Blanchard Kennedy, 1951

G692 Rockwell Kent, 1934
      [A27]

G693 Edna Kenton, 1934

G694 John O. Killens, 1954

G695 Alexander King, 1962

G696 Margie King, 1962

G697 Alex Kirkland, 1933

G698 Lincoln Kirstein, 1933
      [A27, H347]

G699 Rollin Kisby, 1937

G700 Moise Kisling, 1941

G701 Eartha Kitt, 1952
      [A27]

G702 Donald Klopfer, 1937

G703 Alfred A. Knopf, 1935
      [A27, C52]
      New York Times Book Review,
      15 May 1940
      Alfred A. Knopf Quarter Cen-
      tury, Ed. Elmer Adler,
      privately printed, 1940

G704 Alfred A. Knopf, Jr., 1933

G705 Blanche Knopf, 1932
      [C52]
      Borzoi Quarterly, 15 March
      1966

G706 Christopher Knopf, 1939

G707 Edwin Knopf, 1939

G708 Mildred Knopf, 1935

G709 Tom Koegh, 1949

G710 Ruth Ann Koesun, 1948

G711 Manuel Komroff, 1937

G712 Serge Koussevitsky, 1939
      [A27]

G713 Kuo Gin-Chiu, 1940

G714 Victor Kraft, 1935

G715 Nathalie Krassovska, 1948

G716 John Kriza, 1949
      [A25]

G717 Louis Kronenberger, 1955

G718 Joseph Wood Krutch, 1937

G719 Herbert Kubly, 1956

G720 Joseph Kusaila, 1946

G721 Kykunkor, 1936
      Theatre Arts, April 1942

G722 John Kysh, 1936

G723 Gaston Lachaise, 1933

G724 Jacques de Lacretelle, 1936

G725 Oliver Lafarge, 1933

G726 Hugh Laing, 1940
      [A25, with Janet Reed; H347,
        H395, with Alicia Markova]
      Theatre Arts, October 1943
      Theatre Arts, December 1944
      Dance Perspectives, No. 18,
        1963 [with Anthony Tudor
        and Nora Kaye]
      Inside Ballet Theatre, 1977
        [with Anthony Tudor and
        Maria Karnilova, with Nora
        Kaye and Anthony Tudor,
        with Nora Kaye, with Nana
        Gollner]
      American Ballet Theatre,
        1978 [with Nora Kaye]

G727 George Lamming, 1955

G728 J. R. Landis, 1939

G729 Lawrence Langner, 1934

G730 Philip Langner, 1932

G731 Phyllis Langner, 1938

G732 Nella Larsen [Imes], 1934
      [H413]
      Davis, From the Dark Tower,
        1975

G733 Elie Lascaux, 1949

G734 Steven Lasley, 1956

G735 Robert Latham, 1935

G736 John Latouche, 1940

G737 Charles Laughton, 1940
      [A27]

G738 Marie Laurencin, 1949

G739 Frieda von Richtofen Law-
        rence, 1950

G740 Jacob Lawrence, 1941
      Dover, American Negro Art,
        1965

G741 Jerome Lawrence, 1959

G742 Marie Lawrence, 1941

G743 Frank Lawton, 1934

G744 Richard Leach, 1938

G745 David Leavitt, 1941

G746 Francis Lederer, 1932

G747 Alyne Dumas Lee, 1953

G748 Canada Lee, 1941
      [A27]

G749 Everett Lee, 1948

G750 Janet Lee, 1961

G751 Robert Lee, 1959

G752 Robert E. Lee, 1961

G753 Lee Ya Ching, 1939

G754 Eva LeGallienne, 1937

G755 Fernand Leger, 1936

G756 Melchoir Lengyel, 1939

G757 Rosetta LeNoir, 1942

G758 Lotte Lenya, 1962
      [A27, H395]

G759 Leo Lerman, 1948
      [A27]

G760 Carlo Levi, 1947

G761 Joella Levy, 1936

G762 Marvin David Levy, 1961

G763 Henry Lewis, 1961

G764 Robert Lewis, 1939

G765 Sinclair Lewis, 1938
      [A27]
      Mark Shorer, Sinclair Lewis,
        New York: McGraw Hill,
        1961

G766 Goddard Lieberson, 1932

G767 Karl Light, 1949

G768 Lin Adet, 1939
      Time, circa September 1939
      [with Anor and MeiMei], un-
      credited

G769 Lin Anor, 1939
      Time, circa September 1939
      [with Adet and MeiMei], un-
      credited

G770 Lin Hsianju, 1936

G771 Lin MeiMei, 1939
      Time, circa September 1939
      [with Anor and Adet], un-
      credited

G771 Lin Yutang, 1936

G772 Howard Lindsay, 1944

G773 Edward Lineberry, 1950

G774 Duane Van Vechten Lineberry,
        1950

G775 Edward Livingston, 1935

G776 Fabyan Lloyd, 1937

G777 Alain Locke, 1941
      Davis, From the Dark Tower,
        1975

G778 Loh Tsei, 1939

G779 Avon Long, 1942
      [H287]
      Theatre Arts, April 1942
      Black Magic, 1967, uncredited

G780 Pauline Lord, 1933

G781 Lucille Lortel, 1955

G782 Joe Louis, 1941
      [A27, A28, H395, H438]

G783 Robert Morss Lovett, 1932

G784 Edmund Lowe, 1932

G785 James W. Lowe, 1963

G786 Mina Loy, 1937

G787 Claire Booth Luce, 1932
      [A27]

G788 Henry Luce, 1932

G789 Luigi Lucioni, 1938

G790 Edward Lueders, 1951
      [H318, dustjacket]

G791 Mabel Dodge Luhan, 1933
      [A27, D165]
      Mabel Dodge Luhan, Una and
        Robin, San Francisco: Ban-
        croft Library, 1976

G792 Sidney Lumet, 1940
      [A27]

G793 Alfred Lunt, 1932
      [A27]
      Theatre Arts, April 1939

G794 Philip Lyman, 1964

G795 Annabelle Lyon, 1941
      Inside Ballet Theatre, 1977
      [with Lucia Chase and Ag-
      nes DeMille]

G796 James Lyons, 1960

G797 Charles MacArthur, 1937

G798 Loren MacIvor, 1951

G799 Aline MacMahon, 1940
      [A27]

G800 Claudia MacNeill, 1957

G801 Robert MacNeill, 1958

G802 Robert McAfee, 1937

G803 Gervais McAuliffe, 1933

G804 Henry McBride, 1933
      [H367]

G805 Clifford McCarthy, 1938

G806 Rose McClendon, 1939

G807 Guthrie McClintic, 1935

G808 Wilbur McCormack, 1938

G809 Carson McCullers, 1959
      [A27]
      Virginia Spencer Carr, The
      Lonely Hunter, Garden City:
      Doubleday, 1975 [with Dr.
      Mary Mercer]

G810 Thomas McDermott, 1943

G811 Donald McDonald, 1938

G812 Robert McFerris, 1955

G813 Alemnia McKay, 1948

G814 Anthony McKay, 1948

G815 Claude McKay, 1934
      [H413]
      New York Times, 24 May 1948
      Time, 3 October 1969
      Harlem Renaissance Remem-
      bered, 1972, uncredited
      Davis, From the Dark Tower,
      1975

G816 Peter McKay, 1948

G817 Scott McKay, 1948

G818 Colin McPhee, 1935

G819 Jane Belo McPhee, 1934

G820 Kenneth McPherson, 1938

G821 Kenneth McTeer, 1942

G822 Ralph McWilliams, 1948

G823 Iris Mabry, 1954

G824 Thomas Mabry, 1935

G825 Donald Madden, 1961

G826 Charles Mahoney, 1955

G827 Norman Mailer, 1948
      [A27]

G828 MainBocher, 1941

G829 Gerri Major [Geraldyn Dis-
      mond], 1935
      New York Amsterdam News, 4
      April, 30 July 1938, 15
      April 1939, uncredited

G830 Judith Malina, 1951

G831 Eddie Malloy, 1941

G832 Rouben Mamoulian, 1935

G833 Andy Mann, 1943

G834 Thomas Mann, 1937
      [A27, H395]

G835 Katya Mann, 1937

G836 Jean Marais, 1949

G837 Frederic March, 1939
[A27]

G838 Claude Marchant, 1949

G839 Peter David Marchant, 1956

G840 Louis Marcoussis, 1935

G841 Fania Marinoff, 1932
[A27, H366, H395, H420]
advertising flyer for The
Temporary Mrs. Smith by
Jacqueline Susann and Bea-
trice Coll, September 1946
Janet Hobhouse, Everybody
Who Was Anybody, New York:
Putnam, 1975

G842 Jacob Marinoff, 1932

G843 Alicia Markova, 1940
[A25, with Milorad Misko-
vitch; A27; B33; H347,
H395, with Hugh Laing]
Theatre Arts, October 1943
[with Anton Dolin and with
Hugh Laing]
Agnes DeMille, Book of the
Dance, New York: Golden
Press, 1963
LeClerq, The Ballet Cook
Book, 1966
Opera News, 13 January 1958

G844 John Marquis, 1933

G845 Armina Marshall [Langner],
1948

G846 William Marshall, 1951

G847 John Martin, 1956
[H347]

G848 Mary Martin, 1949
[A27, H296]

G849 Nana Martin, 1963

G850 Giovanni Martinelli, 1939
[380]

G851 Burt Martinson, 1938

G852 Donald Marye, 1952

G853 Adolfo Mas, 1935

G854 Miranda Massacco, 1950

G855 Fritzi Massary, 1934

G856 Raymond Massey, 1953

G857 Thomas Masterson, 1955

G858 Edward Matthews, 1934
[H263]

G859 Henri Matisse, 1933
[A27]

G860 Pierre Matisse, 1933

G861 W. Somerset Maugham, 1934
[A27, D161]

G862 Michael Maule, 1954

G863 Saul Mauriber, 1943
[A27]

G864 André Maurois, 1949

G865 Elsa Maxwell, 1942

G866 Julian Mayfield, 1959
Davis, From the Dark Tower,
1975

G867 Dorothy Maynor, 1939

G868 Allen Juante Meadows, 1940

G869 Paul Meeres, 1932
New York Amsterdam News, 29
June 1952

G870 Lauritz Melchoir, 1935

G871 Henry Louis Mencken, 1932
[A27, D161, H395, H415]

G872 Gian Carlo Menotti, 1944
[H347]

G873 Georges Menozzi, 1943

G874 Alice de la Mer, 1932

G875 Mabel Mercer, 1963
[A27, A28]

G876   Mary Mercer, 1959
       Carr, The Lonely Hunter, 1975
         [with Carson McCullers]

G877   Burgess Meredith, 1939

G878   Philip Merivale, 1936

G879   Ethel Merman, 1935

G880   Alan Merrick, 1963

G881   Toni Merrill, 1946

G882   Oliver Messel, 1935

G883   Jan Meyerowitz, 1948

G884   Arthur Middlehurst, 1937

G885   Amy Laurie Jenks Mielziner,
         1937

G886   Jo Mielziner, 1937

G887   Barilli Milena, 1940

G888   Lizzie Miles, 1957

G889   Edna St. Vincent Millay, 1933
         [A27]

G890   Henry Miller, 1940
         [A27]
       Time, 13 December 1943

G891   Virginia Miller, 1937

G892   Carl Milles, 1941

G893   Russ Milton, 1943

G894   Joan Miró, 1935
         [A27]

G895   Milorad Miscovitch, 1954
         [A25, with Alicia Markova]

G896   Arthur Mitchell, 1955

G897   James Mitchell, 1952

G898   Kevin Mitchell, 1963

G899   Edgar Mittelhölzer, 1952

G900   Alan Mixon, 1963

G901   Philip Moeller, 1933

G902   Bent Mohn, 1955

G903   Benno Moisevitch, 1934

G904   Ferenc Molnár, 1941

G905   Francisco Moncion, 1944
         [A25]

G906   Lucy Monroe, 1943

G907   Felicia Montelegre, 1959

G908   Beni Montressor, 1964

G909   Mollie Moon, 1956

G910   Paul Moor, 1949

G911   Al Moore, 1936

G912   Grace Moore, 1933
         [A27, H378, H380]
       Chatanooga [Tennessee] Pines,
         30 April 1933 [with Val
         Parera]

G913   Leon Moore, 1939

G914   Marianne Moore, 1948
         [A27]
       The Days of Dylan Thomas,
         World Pictures, Inc.

G915   Lois Moran, 1932

G916   Suzanne Morand, 1949

G917   Arturo Moreno, 1943

G918   Helen Morgan, 1932
         [A27, H395, H401]

G919   Pat Morgan, 1932

G920   Willard Morgan, 1935

G921   Lenwood Morris, 1942

G922   Mackaye Morris, 1937

G923   Robert Morse, 1958

H924   Zero Mostel, 1958
         [A27, H395, H401]

G925 Etta Moten, 1934

G926 Willard Motley, 1947

G927 Michael Moylan, 1963

G928 Richard Mulligan, 1943

G929 Meg Mundy, 1948
      [H296]

G930 Paul Muni, 1932
      [A27]

G931 Ona Munson, 1932

G932 Nickolas Muray, 1939

G933 Blanche Muroff, 1963

G934 Ivor Muroff, 1963

G935 Merwin Muroff, 1963

G936 Dudley Murphy, 1949

G937 Samuel Murray, 1938

G938 John Musher, 1934

G939 Carmel Myers, 1933

G940 Nicholas Nabokoff, 1934

G941 Marguerite Namara, 1940

G942 Donaldo Nardona, 1956

G943 George Jean Nathan, 1933
      [A27]

G944 Robert Nathan, 1933

G945 Ramon Naya, 1941

G946 Patricia Neal, 1954
      [H395, with Roald Dahl]

G947 David Nelson, 1950

G948 Cathleen Nesbitt, 1952

G949 Theodore Newton, 1938

G950 Ada Neyland, 1937

G951 Robert Neyland, 1935

G952 Beverly Nichols, 1934

G953 Mariko Niki, 1955

G954 Anais Nin, 1940
      New York Times Book Review,
         26 April 1966
      Photographic Supplement to
         the Diaries of Anais Nin,
      New York: Harcourt, Brace
         and Jovanovich, 1974

G955 Harukuni Nishiwaza, 1964

G956 Marie Laure de Noalles, 1949

G957 Isamu Noguchi, 1935
      [A27]
      The New York City Ballet,
         New York: Alfred A. Knopf,
      1973, uncredited

G958 Charles Nolte, 1951

G959 Lee Nordness, 1946

G960 Louise Norton, 1932

G961 Ramon Novarro, 1934
      [A27]

G962 Bruce Nugent, 1936

G963 Geoffrey Nurse, 1959

G964 Marion Oates, 1937

G965 Vincent Obedencia, 1933

G966 Russell Oberlin, 1959

G967 Peter Francis O'Brien, S. J.,
         1964

G968 Erin O'Brien-Moore, 1934

G969 Denis O'Dea, 1933

G970 Clifford Odets, 1935
      [A27]

G971 Joseph O'Donahue III, 1937

G972 C. Patrick O'Donnell, 1936

G973 Inbona Ojike, 1946

G974 Georgia O'Keeffe, 1936
      [A27]

G975 Pierre Olaf, 1960

G976 Laurence Olivier, 1939
      [A27, H378]
      Michael Caine, The Films of
        Laurence Olivier [dust
        jacket], New York: Citadel,
        1978

G977 Oliver Elmer Olsen, 1956

G978 Rex O'Malley, 1937

G979 Carlotta Monterey O'Neill,
        1933
      [D161, with Eugene O'Neill]
      Inscriptions from Eugene
        O'Neill to Carlotta Mon-
        terey O'Neill, New Haven:
        Yale University Press,
        1953 [with Eugene O'Neill]

G980 Eugene O'Neill, 1932
      [A27; D161, with Carlotta
        Monterey O'Neill; H259,
        H395]
      Inscriptions from Eugene
        O'Neill to Carlotta Mon-
        terey O'Neill, 1953 [also
        with Carlotta Monterey
        O'Neill]
      Eugene O'Neill, Strange In-
        terlude, Columbia Records
        [album cover], 1959
      New York Times Book Review,
        15 March 1964
      Saturday Review, 21 March
        1964
      The New Yorker, 26 March
        1964
      Eugene O'Neill, More Stately
        Mansions [cover], New Ha-
        ven: Yale University Press,
        1970

G981 Eugene O'Neill, Jr., 1937

G982 Frederick O'Neill, 1958

G983 Stephen Ophiujsen, 1958

G984 Malvern Ore, 1937

G985 Piero Orioli, 1935

G986 Domingo Ortega, 1935

G987 Sono Osato, 1942

G988 Paul Osborn, 1938

G989 Lessa Origines, 1942

G990 Jon Ostrov, 1948

G991 Roi Ottley, 1943

G992 Earl Oxford, 1943
      Christian Science Monitor,
        20 November 1943 [with
        Philip Truex]
      Forward, November 1942
        [with Philip Truex]
      Theatre Arts, March 1943
        [with Philip Truex]

G993 Alfred Pach, 1937

G994 Paul Padgette, 1963
      [A25, dust jacket]
      Lost Generation Journal,

G995 Gennaro Palmese, 1945

G996 Val Parera, 1933
      Chatanooga [Tennessee]
      Pines, 30 April 1933 [with
      Grace Moore]

G997 Leonard de Paur, 1958

G998 Norma de Paur, 1958

G999 Beatrice Pearson, 1950

G1000 Ted Peckham, 1951

G1001 Brock Pemberton, 1943

G1002 Margaret Pemberton, 1943

G1003 Five Pennies, 1953

G1004 Eleanor Perenyi, 1947

G1005 Peter Perenyi, 1947

G1006 Kathleen Perper, 1949

G1007 Leo Perper, 1949

G1008 Esther Perkins, 1941

G1009 Julius Perkins, Jr., 1941

G1010 Lauretta Perkins, 1941

G1011 Mildred Perkins, 1937

G1012 Sammy Perkins, 1955

G1013 Charles Perry, 1962

G1014 Julia Peterkin, 1933

G1015 Carla Peterson, 1954

G1016 Donna Peterson, 1954

G1017 Dorothy Peterson, 1943
       Becker, The Negro in Ameri-
         can Life, 1944 [with Jim-
         mie Daniels]

G1018 Jane Peterson, 1954

G1019 Louis Peterson, 1960

G1020 Sidney Peterson, 1957

G1021 Ann Petry, 1948
       Davis, From the Dark Tower,
         1975

G1022 Irra Petina, 1948
       [H380]

G1023 Rita Piecenza, 1935

G1024 Phoebe Pierce, 1948

G1025 Horace Pippin, 1940
       Dover, American Negro Art,
         1965

G1026 Luigi Pirandello, 1935
       [A27]

G1027 Frank "Killer Joe" Piro,
         1943
       New York Post, 3 June 1943
         [with an unidentified
         dancing partner]
       Theatre Arts, March 1943
         [with Shirley Booth]

G1028 Evelyn LaRue Pittman, 1962

G1029 Christopher Plummer, 1959

G1030 Oscar Polk, 1937

G1031 Douglas Pollard, 1947

G1032 Anna Marble Pollock, 1934

G1033 Channing Pollock, 1934

G1034 Helen Channing Pollock,
         1934

G1035 Sherman Pollock, 1934

G1036 Marie Pollock, 1934

G1037 Lily Pons, 1942

G1038 Tyrone Power, 1953
       [A27]

G1039 Luba Pregarsky, 1959

G1040 Josephine Premice, 1955

G1041 Charles Prentice, 1937

G1042 Leontyne Price, 1951
       [A27, A28]

G1043 Vincent Price, 1939
       [H276]

G1044 Karl Priebe, 1948

G1045 Pearl Primus, 1943
       [A27]
       Black Magic, 1967, un-
         credited

G1046 Aileen Pringle, 1952
       [A27]

G1047 Frederic Prokosch, 1952

G1048 Jonathan Prude, 1951
       [D158]

G1049 James Purdy, 1957
       Bowles, Up Above the World,
         1966 [with Paul Bowles]

G1050 José Quintero, 1952

G1051 Muriel Rahn, 1944
       Black Magic, 1967, un-
         credited

G1052   Luise Rainer, 1937
        [A27, H378]

G1053   Ni Gusti Raka
        [A27]

G1054   Edith Ramsay, 1934

G1055   William Raney, 1943

G1056   David Raphael, 1943

G1057   Geronimo Rapre, 1959

G1058   Marjorie Kinnan Rawlings,
        1953

G1059   Man Ray
        [A27; D161, with Salvador
        Dali]

G1060   Bertice Reading, 1959

G1061   J. Saunders Redding, 1943

G1062   Janet Reed, 1944
        [A25, with Hugh Laing]

G1063   Susan Reed, 1945
        Theatre Arts, March 1946

G1064   Madeleine Renaud, 1952
        [A27, with Jean Louis Bar-
        rault]

G1065   Georges Rey, 1961

G1066   John Rhoden, 1937

G1067   Titania Riaboushinska, 1942

G1068   Elmer Rice, 1934

G1069   Rudy Rex Richards, 1948

G1070   Clément Richer, 1949
        Clément Richer, Son of Ti-
        Coyo, New York: Alfred A.
        Knopf, 1954

G1071   Arthur Richman, 1935

G1072   John Marshall Richman, 1939

G1073   Frank Riley, 1952

G1072   Diego Rivera, 1932
        [A27]

G1075   Frieda Kahlo de Rivera,
        1932

G1076   Barbara Robbins, 1943

G1077   Jerome Robbins, 1941
        [A25, A27]

G1078   Eslanda Robeson, 1933
        Gledhill Cameron, Paul Robe-
        son, New York: Viking
        Press, 1977

G1079   Paul Robeson, 1933
        [A27, H347, H378, H413]
        Theatre Guild Magazine,
        December 1929
        Theatre Arts, April 1942
        Shirley Graham, Paul Robe-
        son: Citizen of the World,
        New York: Messner, 1971
        Broadway Theatre Photo-
        graphs, Ed. William Stott,
        Austin: University of
        Texas Press, 1977

G1080   Paul Robeson, Jr., 1933

G1081   Bill "Bojangles" Robinson,
        1941
        [A25, A27; D158, with Carl
        Van Vechten; H87, H378]
        Theatre Arts, April 1942
        Black Magic, 1967 [dust
        jacket], uncredited

G1082   Mrs. Bill Robinson, 1941

G1083   Boardman Robinson, 1934

G1084   Francis Robinson, 1963

G1085   Emeline Roche, 1943

G1086   Guy Rogers, 1958

G1087   Percy Rodriguez, 1960

G1088   W. G. Rogers, 1937
        [H63]

G1089   Michael Rohman, 1938

G1090   Jules Romains, 1936

G1091   Harold Rome, 1950

G1092   Cesar Romero, 1934

G1093 Rita Romilly, 1933

G1094 Ned Rorem, 1956
       Ned Rorem, The Paris Diary,
          New York: George Brazil-
          ler, 1966

G1095 Sir Francis Rose, 1932

G1096 Stuart Rose, 1936

G1097 Marc Rosemberg, 1962

G1098 Jean Rosenthal, 1951

G1099 LeBelle Rosette, 1941

G1100 Bertram Ross, 1961
       [A25, A27, H395, with Mar-
          tha Graham]

G1101 Robert Ross, 1938

G1102 Beulah Roth, 1963

G1103 Selena Royle, 1943

G1104 Artur Rubinstein, 1937
       [A27, H347]

G1105 Nela Rubinstein, 1937

G1106 Richard Rutledge, 1951

G1107 Thomas Rutherford, 1943

G1108 Sabu [Walter Martin], 1942

G1109 Donald Saddler, 1943

G1110 Antonio Salemme, circa 1935

G1111 Salta Salemme, circa 1935

G1112 Sampih of the Keybar, 1952

G1113 Edith Sampson, 1949

G1114 Thomas Sand, 1955

G1115 Frank Sandiford, 1951

G1116 Diana Sands, 1963

G1117 William Saroyan, 1935
       [A27]

G1118 Charles Sarrell, 1963

G1119 Henri Sauget, 1949

G1120 Milton Saul, 1951

G1121 Archie Savage, 1942

G1122 Augusta Savage, 1942
       Dover, American Negro Ar-
          tists, 1965

G1123 Fritzi Scheff, 1943
       [H380, with Richmond Barthé]

G1124 George Schuyler, 1941
       Davis, From the Dark Tower,
          1975

G1125 Josephine Schuyler, 1941

G1126 Philippa Duke Schuyler, 1946

G1127 Arthur Schwartz, 1933

G1128 Maurice Schwartz, 19 3
       [F92]
       I.J. Singer, The Sinner,
          Apollo Theatre [Chicago]
          program, April 1933

G1129 Harold Scott, 1959

G1130 Henry Benjamin Scott, Jr.,
          1953

G1131 Shelley Scott, 1953

G1132 Zachary Scott, 1953

G1133 William Seabrook, 1933
       Marjorie Worthington, The
          Strange World of William
          Seabrook, New York: Har-
          court Brace Jovanovich,
          1966

G1134 Alan Searle, 1943

G1135 Amanda Seldes, 1932
       Marian Seldes, Bright Lights,
          Boston: Houghton-Mifflin,
          1978

G1136 Gilbert Seldes, 1932
       Seldes, Bright Lights, 1978

G1137   Marian Seldes, 1939
        Seldes, Bright Lights, 1978

G1138   Timothy Seldes, 1939

G1139   Tonio Selwart, 1932

G1140   Steven Semmelmeyer, 1961

G1141   Anne Seymour, 1938

G1142   Angevine Shaffer, 1937

G1143   Van Vechten Shaffer, 1937

G1144   Ravi Shankar, 1933
        [A27]

G1145   Irene Sharaff, 1940

G1146   Carl Van Vechten Shawber,
        1957

G1147   Lloyd Oberlin Shawber, 1957

G1148   Susan Shaffer Shawber, 1957

G1149   Vincent Sheean, 1958

G1150   Jimmie Sheldon, 1948

G1151   Hiram Sherman, 1943

G1152   George Shirley, 1961

G1153   Bobby Short, 1963
        [A28]

G1154   Louis Showers, 1933

G1155   Pearl Showers, 1933

G1156   Lawrence Sickman, 1935

G1157   Leonard Sillman, 1933

G1158   Beverly Sills, 1956
        [A27]

G1159   Lee Simonsen, 1933

G1160   Merton Simpson, 1959

G1161   Israel Joshua Singer, 1938
        Saturday Review, 9 October
        1965
        New York Times Book Review,
        25 October 1971

G1162   Noble Sissle, 1951

G1163   Jorma Jules Sjoblom, 1956

G1164   George Skibine, 1946

G1165   Bert Slaff, 1957

G1166   Mia Slavenska, 1948

G1167   Walter Slezak, 1934

G1168   Alexander Smallens, 1934

G1169   Bessie Smith, 1936
        [A27, A28, C64, D120, D141,
        H287, H296, H347, H395,
        H413, H438]
        Theatre Arts, March 1943
        The Bessie Smith Story, Col-
        umbia Records, Volumes I-
        IV, album covers, 1951
        Sunday Kensington [England]
        Times, 15 February 1959
        Paul Oliver, Bessie Smith,
        New York: A.S. Barnes,
        1961
        Black Magic, 1967, un-
        credited
        Personality Posters, Inc.,
        1970, uncredited
        The Negro in Music and Art,
        Ed. Lindsay Patterson, New
        York: Publisher's Company,
        1967-69
        American Record Guide, Feb-
        ruary 1971
        Chris Albertson, Bessie, New
        York: Stein and Day, 1972
        Bessie Smith, Empress of the
        Blues, Columbia Records,
        booklet and liner notes
        to five double albums,
        1972-1974
        Black Film Festival brochure
        issued by the Department
        of Education, Commonwealth
        of Pennsylvania, 1974, un-
        credited
        The Bessie Smith SongBook,
        New York: Schirmer, 1975
        Albert F. Murray, Stomping
        the Blues, New York: Mc-
        Graw Hill, 1976
        Tony Palmer, All You Need Is
        Love, New York: Grossman,
        1976

Cashbox, 6 August 1977, un-
credited
The 1979 Combined Humani-
ties Catalog, Berkeley:
University of California
Press, 1979, uncredited

G1170 Clarence Smith, Jr., 1950

G1171 Henry Templeton Smith, 1950

G1172 Muriel Smith, 1944
Black Magic, 1967, uncre-
dited

G1173 Oliver Smith, 1947

G1174 Queenie Smith, 1934

G1175 Russ Smith, 1943

G1176 William Gardner Smith, 1948

G1177 Wilson Smith, 1942

G1178 Zachary Solov, 1958

G1179 Ettore Sottsass, 1956

G1180 Fernanda Sottsass, 1956

G1181 Rawn Spearman, 1952

G1182 Louise Spencer, 1951

G1183 Bella Spewack, 1936

G1184 Sam Spewack, 1936

G1185 Arthur Spingarn, 1940

G1186 Spivey [Spivey LaVoe], 1944

G1187 Carl Sprinchorn, 1935

G1188 Hunter Stagg, 1932
[C59]

G1189 Kim Stanley, 1961
[H395]

G1190 Theodore Starkowsky, 1956

G1191 Muriel Starr, 1943

G1192 Gertrude Stein, 1934
[A27; B20a, dust jacket,

also with Alice B. Toklas;
B25; B27; B39, with Toklas;
C43; C64; C63; D161, D166,
with Toklas; D169; F143;
H103, H254, H263, H290,
H296; H318, with Toklas
and Van Vechten; H366, al-
so with Toklas and Fania
Marinoff; H395, H420, H422,
H423
Gertrude Stein, Lectures in
America, New York: Random
House, 1935
New York Times Book Review,
5 December 1937, uncre-
dited
New York Herald Tribune
Books, 12 December 1937,
uncredited
Publishers' Weekly, circa
January 1945, uncredited
New York Times Book Review,
4 March 1945
New York Herald Tribune
Books, 21 July 1946
Daily Times Herald [Dallas,
Texas], 9 November 1947
'47, October 1947
New York Amsterdam News,
24 July 1948
New York Amsterdam News,
25 July 1948
Dallas Morning News, 25 July
1948
Rosalind S. Miller, Form and
Intelligibility [also dust
jacket], New York: Exposi-
tion Press, 1949
flyer for Last Operas and
Plays by Gertrude Stein,
Straughan's Book Shop,
Greensboro, North Carolina,
1949
Saturday Review, 2 April 1949
Yes Is For a Very Young Man
by Gertrude Stein, Off
Broadway, Inc., program, 6
June 1949
Cue, 18 June 1949
Saturday Review, 6 August
1949
Flair, May 1949
Gertrude Stein Read by Ger-
trude Stein, Dorian Rec-
ords DR-331, album cover,
1952

flyer for Carl Van Vechten
and the Twenties, Univer-
sity of New Mexico Press,
1955 [with Alice B. Toklas
and Van Vechten]
Synapse [University of Cali-
fornia Medical Center], 5
April 1965, uncredited
Hi-Fi, May 1965
Gertrude Stein's First Read-
er, Polydor Records, 24-
7002, album cover, 1970,
uncredited
Gertrude Stein on Picasso,
Ed. Edward Burns, New York:
Liveright, 1970
Hockaday [Dallas, Texas],
Winter 1970
Cedar Rapids [Iowa] Gazette,
circa March 1971
MD, April 1971, uncredited
Folio KPFA [Berkeley, Cali-
fornia], September 1971
Faculty Exchange, Millers-
ville [Pennsylvania] State
College, 6 February 1974
Time, 4 March 1974 [with Al-
ice B. Toklas], uncredited
Lois Rather, Gertrude Stein
in California, San Fran-
cisco: Rather Press, 1974
"When This You See Remember
Me," University of Cali-
fornia at Los Angeles,
program for Gertrude Stein
centennial, 23 February
1974, uncredited
Bennett Cerf, At Random, New
York: Random House, 1977
20th Century Literature,
Spring, 1978
Bobbs-Merrill catalog and ad-
vertisement for Portraits
[A27], Fall 1978

G1193   Leo Stein, 1937
Leo Stein, Journey Into Self,
New York: Crown, 1950
John Malcolm Brinnin, The
Third Rose, Boston: Atlan-
tic Little Brown, 1959

G1194   Frances Steloff, 1964
[A27, D167]
W.G. Rogers, Wise Men Fish
Here [also dust jacket],
New York: Harcourt Brace
and World, 1965

Saturday Review, 6 February
1965
This World [San Francisco]
7 February 1965

G1195   G. B. Stern, 1932

G1196   Maurice Sterne, 1933

G1197   Carrie Stettheimer, 1932

G1198   Ettie Stettheimer, 1932

G1199   James Stewart, 1934
[A27]

G1200   Melvin Stewart, 1958

G1201   Dorothy Stickney, 1944

G1202   Alfred Stieglitz, 1935
[A27]

G1203   William Grant Still, 1949

G1204   McCleary Stinnett, 1933

G1205   Edward Stirling, 1938

G1206   Al Stokes, 1934

G1207   Christopher Stowkowski, 1959

G1208   Stanislaus Stowkowski, 1959

G1209   J. Strachey, 1939

G1210   Bryn Strandeness, 1940

G1211   Ronald Stratton, 1957

G1212   Billy Strayhorn, 1958

G1213   Maxine Sullivan, 1941

G1214   Charles Sultner, 1959

G1215   Clara Svensen, 1961

G1216   Howard Swanson, 1951
Black Magic, 1967, uncredited

G1217   Larry Swanson, 1951

G1218   Sandor Szabo, 1940

G1219   Mai Mai Sze 1935

G1220 George Szell, 1953

G1221 Ron-Dean Taffél, 1964

G1222 Harold Talbott, 1964

G1223 Olga Tamayo, 1945

G1224 Rufino Tamayo, 1945

G1225 Jessica Tandy, 1949

G1226 Ellen Tarry, 1950

G1227 Lilyan Tashman, 1934

G1228 Wesley Taun, 1962

G1229 Clyde A. Taylor, 1944

G1230 Deems Taylor, 1933

G1231 Laurette Taylor, 1933
[A27]

G1232 Paul Taylor, 1960
[A25]

G1233 Prentiss Taylor, 1933

G1234 Pavel Tchelichew, 1934

G1235 Valentine Tessier, 1949

G1236 Luisa Tetrazzini, 1910

G1237 Alonzo Thayer, 1935

G1238 Edna Thomas, 1932

G1239 Antonia Thompson, 1961

G1240 Claude Thompson, 1959

G1241 Harrison Thompson, 1947

G1242 Winifred Thompson, 1955

G1243 Virgil Thomson, 1947
[A27, H347, H395]

G1244 Alice B. Toklas, 1934
[A27; B20a, with Gertrude
Stein; B27; B39, with
Stein; C64; D161, D166,
with Stein; H263; H318,
with Stein and Van Vech-
ten; H366, and with Stein
and Fania Marinoff; H420,
H422, H423
Brinnin, The Third Rose,
1959
Alice B. Toklas, Verve Records, album cover, 15017,
1961
Linda Simon, The Biography
of Alice B. Toklas, Gar-
den City: Doubleday, 1963

G1245 Kristians Tonny, 1934

G1246 Marie Claire Tonny, 1934

G1247 Hugh Townley, 1955

G1248 Clavin Townsend, 1964

G1249 Trac [Gertrude Stein's and
Alice B. Toklas's Chinese
cook], 1934

G1250 Ivy Trautman, 1935

G1251 Philip Truex, 1942
Forward, November 1942
[with Earl Oxford]
Christian Science Monitor,
20 November 1942 [with
Earl Oxford]
Theatre Arts, March 1943
[with Earl Oxford]

G1252 Tsei Lott, 1939

G1253 Anthony Tudor, 1940
Inside Ballet Theatre, 1977
[with Nora Kaye and Hugh
Laing, and with Maria Karnilova and Hugh Laing]

G1254 Gene Tunny, 1934

G1255 Reginald Turner, 1935
Stanley Weintraub, Reggie
[dust jacket], New York:
George Braziller, 1965
Saturday Review, 18 Septem-
ber 1965

G1256 Andrew Turnbull, 1962

G1257 Robert Turney, 1936

G1258 Helen Twelvetrees, 1943

G1259 Parker Tyler, 1935

G1260 Veronica Tyler, 1961

G1261 Margaret Tynes, 1959
concert tour flyer for Margaret Tynes, circa 1960

G1262 Doris Ulman, 1933

G1263 Leonore Ulric, 1932

G1264 Sigrid Undset, 1941

G1265 Gladys Unger, 1934

G1266 William Valentine, 1940

G1267 Emily Vanderbilt, 1933

G1268 Gloria Vanderbilt, 1959
[A27]

G1269 Irita Van Doren, 1933

G1270 John Van Druten, 1932

G1271 Henry Van Dyke, 1961

G1272 Goetz Van Eyck, 1940

G1273 Henry Van Loon, 1933

G1274 Carl Van Vechten, 1934
[B37, with Gertrude Stein
and Alice B. Toklas; C64;
D158, with Ram Gopal and
with Bill Robinson; D169;
H318, with Stein and Tok-
las, and with Ethel Wat-
ers; H335; H360, with Waters; H370, H378; H382,
with Stein and Toklas;
H387, dust jacket; H395,
H413, H417, H429, H430]
New Haven Register, 13 January 1946
Richmond Times Dispatch, 13
January 1946
Washington Sun Post, 13 January 1946
flyer for Carl Van Vechten
and the Twenties, Univer-
sity of New Mexico Press,
1955 [with Gertrude Stein
and Alice B. Toklas]

G1275 Ilona Van Vechten, 1896
[A22]

G1276 Carmen Vasquez, 1949

G1277 Bayard Veiller, 1938
New York Times, 17 June 1943

G1278 Violette Verdy, 1961
[A25]

G1279 Shirley Verrett, 1961

G1280 André François Villon, 1961

G1281 Eugene Von Grona, 1938

G1282 Michael Wager, 1955

G1283 Bruce Wagner, 1963

G1284 Tommy Wales, 1944

G1285 Margaret Walker, 1942

G1286 Abraham Walkowitz, 1937

G1287 Emmett Wallace, 1943

G1288 Regina Wallace, 1939

G1289 Hugh Walpole, 1934

G1290 William Warfield, 1951
[H395]

G1291 Kate Warriner, 1941

G1292 Ben Washer, 1935

G1293 Fredi Washington, 1933
Bobby Short, Black and White
Baby, New York: Dodd Mead,
1971

G1294 Annie von Wasserman, 1934

G1295 Edward Wasserman, 1935

G1296 Ethel Waters, 1934
[A27, A28; H287; H318, with
Van Vechten; H347; H360, with
Van Vechten; H418]
Cue, 19 November 1938
Theatre Arts, April 1939
Theatre Arts, April 1942

Cedar Rapids [Iowa] Gazette,
11 March 1951
Lucien Mazenod, Les Femmes
Célèbres II, Paris: Édi-
tions d'Art, 1955
Jablonski, Happy With the
Blues, 1961
Black Magic, 1967, uncre-
dited
The Bessie Smith Song Book,
1975

G1297 Linda Watkins, 1938

G1298 Alec Waugh, 1936

G1299 Evelyn Waugh, 1948
       [A27]

G1300 Beatrice Robinson Wayne,
       1934
       [H263]

G1301 Clifton Webb, 1932
       [A27]
       The Spur, December 1932
       Theatre Arts, December 1944

G1302 Beveridge Webster, 1934

G1303 Charles Weidman, 1933

G1304 Paul Weiner, 1947

G1305 Shirley Weingarten, 1947

G1306 Karel Weiss, 1956

G1307 Elisabeth Welch, 1946

G1308 Orson Welles, 1937
       [A27]
       Bobbs-Merrill catalog and
         advertisement for Por-
         traits [A27], Fall 1978

G1309 Marguerite Wennergren, 1934

G1310 Franz Werfel, 1940

G1311 Glenway Wescott, 1936

G1312 Dorothy West, 1948

G1313 Rebecca West, 1934
       [A27]

G1314 M. Moran Weston, 1961

G1315 Helen Westley, 1938

G1316 Erik Wettergren, 1935

G1317 Gertrud Wettergren, 1935
       [H380]

G1318 Carl Darrow White, 1959

G1319 Jane White, 1943

G1320 Josh White, 1946

G1321 Miles White, 1943

G1322 Portia White, 1944

G1323 Walter White, 1938
       [A27]

G1324 Walter White, Jr., 1943

G1325 Raoul Whitfield, 1933
       The Candle [Las Vegas, Ne-
         vada], 11 July 1934

G1326 Alma Wiener, 1933

G1327 Thornton Wilder, 1948
       [A27]
       Goldstone, Thornton Wilder,
         1975

G1328 Roy Wilkins, 1958
       [A27]

G1329 Billy Dee Williams, 1963

G1330 Burton Williams, 1961

G1331 Camilla Williams, 1946

G1332 Dorothy Williams, 1940

G1333 Frances Leigh Williams

G1334 John A. Williams, 1962

G1335 Paul Williams, 1936
       Becker, The Negro in Amer-
         ican Life, 1944

G1336 Tennessee Williams, 1948
       [A27]

G1337 Maurice Williford, 1961

G1338 Ellis Wilson, 1948
       Dover, American Negro Art-
           ists, 1965

G1339 Gil Wilson, 1948

G1340 Dorothy Steven Wiman, 1933

G1341 Donald Windham, 1955

G1342 Thomas Wolfe, 1937
       [A27, H395]
       Native Voices, 1977

G1343 Anna May Wong, 1932
       [A27, H395, H401]

G1344 James Wong, 1950

G1345 Pearl Wong, 1950

G1346 Richard Wong, 1940

G1347 Peggy Wood, 1944

G1348 Alexander Woollcott, 1939
       [A27, D161]

G1349 F. J. Work, 1940

G1350 Marjorie Worthington, 1944

G1351 James Wright, 1933

G1352 Michael Wright, 1951

G1353 Richard Wright, 1939
       Yale University Association
           Newsletter, December 1976
       Richard Wright, Southern
           Media, Inc., filmstrip,
           1977

G1354 William Wyckoff, 1942

G1355 Olivia Wyndham, 1936

G1356 June Yalman, 1956

G1357 C. F. Yao, 1937

G1358 Hilda Yen, 1937

G1359 William Yen, 1937

G1360 Ossip Zadkine, 1936

G1361 Jerome Zerbe, 1939

G1362 Carl Zigrosser, 1937

G1363 Efrem Zimbalist, 1933

G1364 Vera Zorina, 1945

G1365 George Zoritch, 1940

G1366 Robert Zorn, 1960

G1367 Stefan Zweig, 1939

G1368 Two black children in front
           of the Harriet Beecher
           Stowe house, Cincinnati,
           Ohio, 1896
           [A28]

G1369 Café d'Harcourt, Paris, 1907
           [A12i]

G1370 Bronze head of Paul Robeson
           by Jacob Epstein, 1933
           [A28]

G1371 Fountain figure, 1936
           [H261]

G1372 Four Saints in Three Acts,
           44th Street Theatre mar-
           quee, New York City, 1934
           [B37]

G1373 Lucey Church, France, 1934
           [H263]

G1374 Students at Williamsburg,
           Virginia [obscuring Ger-
           trude Stein], 1934
           [H263]

G1375 "The Life of the Party at
           Finnegan's Wake," painting
           by Ruth Bower, 1938
           [C20, H167]

G1376 Four Saints in Three Acts,
           Broadway Theatre marquee,
           New York City, 1952
           [B37]

H.
BIOGRAPHY,
BIBLIOGRAPHY,
AND CRITICISM

H1   Wolfe, Rennold. "Chronicles of Broadway," <u>Green Book Album</u>, October.

1912

H2   Clark, Kenneth. "Interviewing the Interviewer," <u>Musical America</u>,
23 March.

1914

H3   Evans, Donald. "In the Gentlemanly Interest" and "Love in Patagonia,"
<u>Sonnets From the Patagonian</u>. New York: Claire Marie, 1914. Reprint-
ed, Philadelphia: Nicholas Brown, 1918.

1915

H4   "<u>Music After the Great War</u>," <u>Cedar Rapids</u> [Iowa] <u>Gazette</u>, 31 December.
[A4]

1916

H5   "<u>Music after the Great War</u>," <u>Boston Transcript</u>, 1 January. [A4]

H6   Lamarter, Eric De. "Suggestion from Grand Opera and Ballet," <u>Chicago
Tribune</u>, 2 January. [A4]

H7   Peyser, H. F. "<u>Music after the Great War</u>," <u>Musical America</u>, 29 January. [A4]

H8   Mencken, H. L. "The Tone Art," <u>Smart Set</u>, July. Reprinted as "Music
After the War," in <u>H. L. Mencken on Music</u>, Ed. Cheslock Louis. New
York: Alfred A. Knopf, Inc., 1961, pp. 158-62. [A4]

H9   Borowski, Felix. "New and Interesting Musical Essays," Chicago Herald, 3 December. [A5]

H10   Bellows, Henry Adams. "Musical Criticism and Readable English," Bellman, 23 December. [A5]

1917

H11   Ramsey, Russell. "Modern Tendencies in Music," Dial, 62;21-3 (11 January). [A5]

H12   Peyser, H. F. "Music and Bad Manners," Musical America, 17 February. [A5]

H13   Mencken, H. L. "Shocking Stuff," Smart Set, May. [A5]

H14   Jackson, Edna Barrett. "Interview with Carl Van Vechten," Cedar Rapids Gazette, 16 June.

H15   Sell, Henry Blackman. "Well, Well, A Readable Music Critic," Chicago Daily News, 17 October. [A6]

H16   "Other Books," New Republic, 17 November. [A6]

H17   "A Readable Book on Music," Musical Courier, 27 December. [A6]

1918

H18   Bean Theodora. "Readable Musical Criticism; A Talk with One Who Writes it—Carl Van Vechten," New York Morning Telegraph, 24 February. [EV2, EV4]

H19   Mencken, H. L. "The National Letters, Smart Set, February. [A6]

H20   Ross, Claire. "Interview with Carl Van Vechten: Cedar Rapids Finds the Bolshevik," Musical Courier, 11 April.

H21   "Van Vechten's Essays," New York Sun, 5 May. [A6]

H22   "Interpreters and Interpretations," Musical America, 13 July. [A6]

H23   Liebling, Leonard. "The Iconoclastic Carl," Musical Courier, 3 October.

H24   "The Stylist Who Created a Mythology of Manhattan," Current Opinion, October. [A7]

H25   Bourne, Randolph. "The Light Essay," Dial, 65:419-20 (16 November). [A7]

H26   "The Merry-Go-Round," Musical America, 23 November. [A7]

H27   De Casseres, Benjamin. "The Resurrection of Edgar Saltus," New York Sun, 1 December. [A7]

1919

H28 Mencken, H. L. "Nothing Much Here, Alas!" <u>Smart Set</u>, January. [A7]

H29 "Personalities," <u>New York Tribune</u>, 1 February.

H30 Mencken, H. L. "Mainly Fiction," <u>Smart Set</u>, March. [A8]

H31 Huneker, James Gibbons. "More Musical Fiction," <u>New York Times</u>, 17
     August. [A6]

H32 Hale, Philip. "Music of Spain and Master Violinists," <u>Boston Her-
     ald</u>, 20 September. [A8]

H33 Hergesheimer, Joseph. "Carl Van Vechten," <u>Chicago Daily News</u>, 4
     December.

1920

H34 Starrett, Vincent. "Carl Van Vechten," <u>Reedy's Mirror</u>, 29:29-30
     (8 January).

H35 Broun, Heywood. "<u>In the Garret</u>," <u>New York Tribune</u>, 16 January. [A9]

H36 "Music and Letters," <u>Times Literary Supplement</u>, 5 February. [A9]

H37 "A Book About Spanish Music," <u>Times Literary Supplement</u>, 19 Febru-
     ary. [A8]

H38 "In the Garret," <u>Argonaut</u> [San Francisco], 28 February. [A9]

H39 Terrill, Mary. "About Essays, and Three," <u>Bookman</u>, 51:192-95 (April).
     [A9]

H40 Mencken, H. L. "More Notes From a Diary," <u>Smart Set</u>, May. [A9]

H41 Preston, Keith, "Cats" [a poem], <u>Chicago Daily News</u>, 24 November.

H42 Edgett, Elwin Francis. "Harmless Egotism of the Necessary Cat,"
     <u>Boston Transcript</u>, 11 December. [A11]

H43 Moeller, Philip. "Van Vechten" [with a portrait by Harriet Furness],
     <u>The Borzoi 1920</u>, New York: Alfred A. Knopf, Inc., pp. 32-33 [and in-
     cluding a bibliography and notes about <u>The Tiger in the House</u> by Al-
     fred Knopf].

1921

H44 Krutch, Joseph Wood. "Cosmography and Cats," <u>Nation</u>, 112:243-44 (9
     April). [A11]

H45 Mencken, H. L. "A Soul's Adventures III," <u>Smart Set</u>, March. [A11]

H46 Garland, Robert. "Cat is Crowned King of Beasts by Van Vechten,"
     <u>Baltimore News</u>, 2 April. [A11]

H47   Hawthorne, Hildegarde. "Lord of the Housetops," New York Times, 28 August. [B3]

H48   "The Riddle of the Cat," London Times, 27 September. [A11]

H49   "The House Tiger," Times Literary Supplement, 13 October. [A11]

H50   "Natural History and Animal Books," New Statesman [London], 3 December. [A11]

H51   Minchin, H. C. "All About the Cat," London Times, 25 December. [A11]

H52   "The Tiger in the House," Bookman [London], December. [A11]

1922

H53   Ellis, S. M. "The Literature of 1921," Fortnightly Review [London], 3:163 (January). [A11]

H54   Walker, Henry. "Peter Whiffle," New York Herald Tribune, 16 April. [A12]

H55   Stagg, Hunter. "Refuge for Stray Cats," New York Tribune, 23 April. [A12]

H56   Hansen, Harry. "An Open Letter to Carl Van Vechten," Chicago Daily News, 26 April. [A12]

H57   Nathan, Robert. "Peter Truffle Meditates," The Reviewer, April. [A12, a parody of Peter Whiffle]

H58   Jones, Llewllyn. "Whiffle," Chicago Evening Post, 5 May. [A12]

H59   Van Doren, Carl. "The Roving Critic," Nation, 114:569 (10 May). Reprinted as "Invention and Veracity," The Roving Critic, New York: Alfred A. Knopf, Inc., 1923. [A12]

H60   Stagg, Hunter. "Books of the Month," The Reviewer, 3:540-41 (June). [A12]

H61   "Peter Whiffle," New York Times, 2 July. [A12]

H62   Walkup, Fairfax Proudfit. "Peter Whiffle: His Life and Works," Double Dealer, 4:49-50 (July). [A12]

H63   Stuart, Henry Logan. "Worldliness and Wordliness," Freeman, 13 September. [A12]

H64   Stein, Gertrude. "One: Carl Van Vechten," Geography and Plays, Boston: Four Seas Company, 1922, pp. 199-200. Reprinted, New York: Haskell House Publishers Ltd., 1967; New York: Something Else Press, Inc., 1968

1923

H65 Ewing, Max. "Carl Van Vechten," Michigan Daily Sunday Magazine (Ann Arbor), 14 January. Reprinted, Detroit Free Press, Literature Section, 4 February.

H66 Walpole, Hugh. "Six Best American Novels of 1922; an English Critic's View," International Book Digest, 1:70 (January). [A12]

H67 Mortimer, Raymond, "New Novels," New Statesman (London), 17 March. [A12]

H68 Gould, Gerald. "New Fiction," Saturday Review (London), 135;406 (24 March). [A12]

H69 Reid, Forrest. "Four American Novels," Nation and Athenaeum (London), 24 March. [A12]

H70 Harwood, H. C. "New Books: Novels," Outlook (London), 21 April. [A12]

H71 "Peter Whiffle," Challenge (London), 4 May. [A12]

H72 King, Richard. "With Silent Friends," Tatler (London), 16 May. [A12]

H73 Broun, Heywood. "The Blind Bow-Boy," New York World, 19 May. [A13]

H74 Hansen, Harry. "The Disillusioned Romantics," Chicago Daily News, 15 August. [A13]

H75 Pender, Horace. "The Blind Bow-Boy," New York Herald Tribune Books, 15 August. [A13]

H76 Liveright, Horace. "Carl Van Vechten's New Novel The Blind Bow-Boy," Philadelphia Public Ledger, 18 August. [A13]

H77 Jones, Llewellyn. "Ends in Themselves," Chicago Evening Post, 24 August. [A13]

H78 Eddy, Frederick B. "A Glittering Novel," New York Evening Post, 25 August. [A13]

H79 Rascoe, Burton. "The Blind Bow-Boy," New York Herald Tribune, 26 August. [A13]

H80 Bergengren, Ralph, "The Little God Eros as a Hero," Boston Evening Transcript, 1 September. [A13]

H81 Hoffenstein, Samuel, "The Dome," New York Tribune Book News, 2 September. Reprinted as The Tow-Headed Blind Boy, Cedar Rapids, Iowa: Laurance Press Co., 1923. [1-5] 6-19 [20] pp., 2 blank leaves; 17.7 X 11.2 cm.; stiff cream wrapper with glassine, patterned wrapper; 250 copies privately printed, none for sale. [A13, a parody]

H82 Boyd, Ernest. "Van Vechten's New York, Nation, 117:244-45 (5 September). [A13]

H83 Gould, Gerald. "New Fiction," Saturday Review [London], 136:474 (17 October). [A13]

H84 Flanner, Janet. "The Blind Bow-Boy," New Republic, 36:259-60 (31 October). [A13]

H85 Stagg, Hunter. "Some Literary Curiosities," The Reviewer, 4:58-60 (October). [A13]

H86 Van Doren, Carl. "The Blind Bow-Boy," Century, 106 (October). [A13]

H87 Wilson, Edmund. "Late Violets from the Nineties," Dial, 75:387-90 (October). Reprinted in The Shores of Light, New York: Farrar, Straus, 1952, pp. 68-72. [A13]

H88 "The Blind Bow-Boy," Times [London], 1 November. [A13]

H89 Harwood, H. C. "New Books: Novels," Outlook [London], 10 November. [A13]

H90 Mortimer, Raymond. "New Novels," New Statesman [London], 10 November. [A13]

H91 Kirkley, Donald. "Interview with Carl Van Vechten," Baltimore Evening Sun, 15 November.

H92 Reid, Forrest. "The Blind Bow-Boy," Nation and Athenaeum [London], 17 November. [A13]

H93 Bullett, Gerald. "Selected Novels," Challenge [London], 30 November. [A13]

H94 "The Blind Bow-Boy," [New York University] Arch, November. [A13]

H95 Wilson, Edmund. "The Atom, the Bow-Boy, and Tennyson," Vanity Fair, November. [A13]

H96 Markey, Gene. "Carl Van Vechten," Literary Lights, A Book of Caricatures, New York: Alfred A. Knopf, No. 32.

1924

H97 Johnson, Merle. "American First Editions, a Series of bibliographical checklists. No. 61: Carl Van Vechten," Publishers' Weekly, 105:524 (16 February). Reprinted, enlarged, in American First Editions, New York: Bowker, 1932, pp. 354-56.

H98 Ewing, Max. "Frosted Windows. Alchemy in Fairfax Arms. To and for Carl Van Vechten," Michigan Daily (Ann Arbor), 16 March. Reprinted in Sonnets from the Paronomasian, New York, 1925, p. 11; reprinted in Saturday Review of Literature, 14 March 1925.

H99 Johnson, Nunnally. "The Actress-Wife and Writer-Husband who Maintain one Home and two Professions," Brooklyn Eagle, 9 March.

H100 "Interview with Carl Van Vechten," Richmond News Leader, 31 March.

H101 Mencken, H. L. "Three Gay Stories," American Mercury, March. [A13]

H102 Bickley, Francis. "Surprise and Fantasy," Life and Letters [London]
      1:270 (19 April). [A13]

H103 Stein, Gertrude. "Van or Twenty Years After. A Second Portrait of
      Carl Van Vechten," The Reviewer, 4:176-77 (April). Reprinted in
      Morrow's Almanac for 1928, New York: Morrow, 1927, pp. 81-83; re-
      printed in Portraits and Prayers, New York, Random House, 1934; re-
      printed in Writings and Lectures 1911-1945, Ed. Patricia Meyerowitz,
      London: Peter Owen, 1967.

H104 Hoyt, Nancy. "A Literary Triangle," Vanity Fair, June. [A13, a
      parody]

H105 Knopf, Alfred A., dust jacket blurb for The Tattooed Countess [A14]

H106 Butcher, Fanny. "You'll Read This Eventually—Why Not Now?" Chicago
      Tribune, 16 August. [A14]

H107 "Mr. Van Vechten Tattooed a Countess in a New Novel," New York Times,
      17 August. [A14]

H108 "Books on Our Table," New York Evening Post, 20 August. [A14]

H109 Hansen, Harry. "Countess Amid Corn," Chicago Daily News, 20 August.
      [A14]

H110 Jones, Llewellyn. "Culture and Anarchy," Chicago Evening Post, 22
      August. [A14]

H111 Lewis, Sinclair. "'Ioway' and the Countess," Saturday Review of
      Literature, 1:75 (30 August). [A14]

H112 Krutch, Joseph Wood. "Artifice," Nation, 119:241 (3 September).
      [A14]

H113 Barton, Ralph. "The Inquiring Reporter," New Yorker, 5 September
      [a parody, with a caricature]

H114 Lovett, Robert Morss. "The Tattooed Countess," New Republic, 40:53
      (10 September). [A14]

H115 Markey, Gene. "Books and Bookmen," Chicago Tribune, 21 September.
      [A14]

H116 Niles, E. A. "The Tattooed Countess," Independent, 113:201 (27 Sep-
      tember). [A14]

H117 "The Tattooed Countess," Vogue, 1 October. [A14]

H118 Cushing, Edward. "Aphorisms for the New Spirit," Town Topics, 92:
      43-44 (9 October). [A12]

H119 Redman, Ben Ray. "Speaking of Books," Spur, 15 October. [A14]

H120 Arne, Gladys. "Interview with Carl Van Vechten," Cedar Rapids Ga-
      zette, 24 October.

H121 Atherton, Gertrude. "The Adventures of a Predatory Countess," Li-
      terary Digest, International Book Review, October. [A14]

H122 Rascoe, Burton. "The Tattooed Countess," Vanity Fair, October.
      [A14]

H123 Stagg, Hunter. "About Books. Pot-Luck," The Reviewer, 4:416-18
      (October). [A14]

H124 Muret, Maurice. "Une Satire Américaine: La Comtesse Tatouée,"
      Journal des Débats [Paris], 21 November. [A14]

H125 Barton, Ralph. "Heroes of the Week," New Yorker, 12 December. [a
      caricature]

H126 Fuller, Henry Blake. "The Duchess Visits Her Home Town," Bookman,
      60:413-16 (December). [A14, a parody]

H127 Baldwin, Charles C. "Carl Van Vechten," The Men Who Make Our Novels,
      New York: Dodd, Mead, pp. 523-29.

H128 Cunningham, Scott. A Bibliography of the Writings of Carl Van Vech-
      ten, Philadelphia: The Centaur Bookshop. [B8]

H129 Ward, Christopher. "The Blind Booby, by Carl Far Fechten," Twisted
      Tales, New York: Holt, pp. 55-64. [A13, a parody]

                              1925

H130 Newman, Ernest. "The World of Music," Sunday Times [London], 1 Feb-
      ruary. [A15]

H131 Boyd, Ernest. "Readers and Writing," Independent, 114:188 (14 Feb-
      ruary). [A15]

H132 Ward, Christopher. "The Tattooed Countess," Saturday Review of Li-
      terature, 1:558-59 (28 February). Reprinted as "The Tittatooed
      Countess," Foolish Fiction, New York: Holt, pp. 71-81. [A14, a
      parody]

H133 Maugham, W. Somerset. "Novelist or Bond Salesman. Letters to an
      Anxious Mother," Bookman, 60:685-86 (February). Reprinted in Char-
      les H. Towne, ed. William Somerset Maugham, New York: Doran, pp. 52-
      53. [A14]

H134 "New York of 1924 in a New Van Vechten Novel," New York Times, 9
      August. [A16]

H135 Cunningham, Scott. "Yellow-Jackets," Chicago Evening Post, 14 Aug-
      ust. [A16]

H136 Butcher, Fanny. "Firecrackers Called Best Yet of Van Vechten " Chi-
      cago Tribune, 15 August. [A16]

H137 Fuller, Henry B. "Crepitant Fantasy," Saturday Review of Literature, 2:39 (15 August). [A16]

H138 Van Doren, Carl. "Under Stained Glass," New York Herald Tribune Books, 31 August. Reprinted in Wayne Gard. Book Reviewing, New York: Alfred A. Knopf, 1927. [A16]

H139 Harper, Moses. "Americans All," New Republic, 44:105-7 (16 September). [A16]

H140 "The Always Scintillating Carl Van Vechten," Boston Transcript, 19 September. [A16]

H141 Curtis, William. "Firecrackers," Town and Country, 1 October. [A16]

H142 Terhune, Albert Payson. "Some are Firecrackers and Some are—Squibs," New York Evening Post, 3 October. [A16]

H143 Douglas, Donald. "Damp Powder," Nation, 121:491-92 (28 October). [A16]

H144 Pangborn, H. L. "Firecrackers," International Book Review, October. [A16]

H145 Mencken, H. L. "Fiction Good and Bad," American Mercury, 6:380-1 (November). [A16]

H146 Hall, Mordaunt. "Strange Parcel of Mirth Serves as Miss Negri's Latest Vehicle," New York Times, 20 December. [A14, A Woman of the the World, with Pola Negri]

H147 Covarrubias, Miguel. "Carl Van Vechten," The Prince of Wales and Other Famous Americans, New York: Alfred A. Knopf, No. 24. [B12, a caricature]

H148 Frankenstein, Alfred V. "Music after the Great War: A Review after Ten Years," Syncopating Saxophones, Chicago: Robert O. Ballou, pp. 89-103. [A4]

H149 Wylie, Elinor. "Carl Van Vechten" [with a caricature by Ralph Barton], The Borzoi 1925, New York: Alfred A. Knopf, pp. 232-34 [and including a bibliography].

1926

H150 Duncan, Thomas W. "The Unknown Van Vechten," Des Moines [Iowa] Register, 3 January.

H151 "Carl Van Vechten Collects Some Literary Strays," New York Times Book Review, 10 January. [A17]

H152 Davidson, Edward. "Peter Whiffle Incognito," Saturday Review of Literature, 2:507 (23 January). [A17]

H153 Redman, Ben Ray. "Men and Places 'Out of Season,'" New York Herald Tribune Books, 7 March. [A17]

H154   Curtis, William. "Excavations," Town and Country, 15 March. [A17]

H155   Shanks, Edward. "Reviews," Saturday Review [London], 142:4 (10 July). [A17]

H156   "Excavations," Nation, 123:135 (11 August). [A17]

H157   Jones, Llewellyn. "Across the Color Line," Chicago Post, 21 August. [A18]

H158   Yust, Walter. "Novels by Van Vechten and Pio Baroja," New York Evening Post Literary Review, 21 August. [A18]

H159   Clark, Edwin. "Carl Van Vechten's Novel of Harlem and Negro Life," New York Times Book Review, 22 August. [A18]

H160   Hansen, Harry. "Van Vechten's Harlem," New York World, 22 August. [A18]

H161   Maugham, W. Somerset. "The Creative Impulse," Harper's Bazaar, August. [Van Vechten's criticism of Mrs. Albert Forrester]

H162   Johnson, Charles S. "Nigger Heaven; a letter to Carl Van Vechten," Pittsburgh Courier, 4 September. [A18]

H163   Niles, Abbe. "Aunt Hagar's Children," New Republic, 48:162-3 (29 September). [A18]

H164   Mencken, H. L. "Three Novels," American Mercury, September. [A18]

H165   Thurman, Wallace. "Nigger Heaven," Messenger, September. [A18]

H166   Walrond, Eric. "The Epic of a Mood," Saturday Review of Literature 3:153 (2 October). [A18]

H167   Harrison, Hubert. "Nigger Heaven," Amsterdam News, 9 October. [A18]

H168   "Opinions," Times Literary Supplement, 14 October. [A17]

H169   Johnson, James Weldon. "Romance and Tragedy in Harlem," Opportunity, 4:316-17,330 (October). [A18]

H170   Kronenberger, Louis. "Nigger Heaven," International Book Review, October. [A18]

H171   Calvin, Floyd. "Nigger Heaven," Pittsburgh Courier, 6 November. [A18]

H172   Schuyler, George S. "Nigger Heaven," Pittsburgh Courier, 6 November. [A18]

H173   Bibb, Henry. "Nigger Heaven," Chicago Whip, 24 November. [A18]

H174   Benson, Elisabeth. "Some Contemporary Authors," Vanity Fair, November.

H175   Thurman, Wallace. "A Fire Burns," Fire, November. [A18]

H176   "Nigger Heaven," Times [London], 2 December. [A18]

H177   Harwood, H. C. "New Books: Nigger Heaven," Outlook [London], 4
        December. [A18]

H178   Du Bois, W. E. B. "Books," Crisis, December. [A18]

H179   Beach, Joseph Warren. "The Peacock's Tail," The Outlook for Ameri-
        can Prose, Chicago: University of Chicago Press, pp. 5,139-61.
        [critical essay about Van Vechten's style]

H180   Bodenheim, Maxwell. Ninth Avenue, New York: Boni and Liveright.
        [Van Vechten is "Paul Vanderlin," a character in the novel.]

H181   Kemp, Harry. More Miles, New York: Boni and Liveright. [Van Vech-
        ten is "Jarl Loring," a character in the novel.]

                                1927

H182   Clephane, Irene. "The Color Problem in an American Novel," London
        Daily Herald, 5 January. [A18]

H183   Pember, John E. "Race Amalgamation Will Settle American Problem:
        An Interview With Carl Van Vechten," Chicago Defender, 26 March.

H184   "Firecrackers," Times Literary Supplement, 21 April. [A16]

H185   Turner, W. S. "Writer Says There is No Such Thing as 'New Negro,'"
        Chicago Defender, 30 April. [interview about race problems]

H186   Ordynski, Ryszard. "Kilka nazwisk wrpolszesnej literatury amery-
        kanskiej," Wiadomości literackie [Warsaw], 8 May. [A18]

H187   Horgan, Paul. "Notes on Carl Van Vechten," [New Mexico Military
        Institute] Library, 15 May.

H188   Bradish, C. R. "Carl Van Vechten; the Author of Nigger Heaven,"
        Melbourne [Australia] Herald, 30 July. [biographical essay]

H189   "Neger-Himmel, Neger-Hölle," Frankfurter Zeitung, 25 August. [in-
        terview with Alain Locke]

H190   Riddell, John. "Eenie Meenie Minie Mo," Vanity Fair, September.
        [parody by Corey Ford of Van Vechten's Hollywood articles, D124,
        D125, D127, D128]

H191   "Tombstones: Epitaphs for Living Lions," American Sketch, 3:20 (Oc-
        tober). [epitaph for Van Vechten by James Weldon Johnson]

H192   Morand, Paul. "Sous Pavillon Noir," in Carl Van Vechten. Le Para-
        dis des Nègres, Paris: Simon Kra. [180]

H193   "Nominated for the Hall of Fame," Vanity Fair, March 1927. [bio-
        graphical sketch and photograph, C149]

1928

H194 "1927: The Van Vechten Award" [for the best signed contribution to
      Opportunity], Opportunity, 6:5 (January). [A28]

H195 "We Nominate for the Hall of Fame," Vanity Fair, 29:77 (February).
      [biographical sketch and photograph]

H196 Salpeter, Harry. "The First Reader. Van Vechten's Hollywood," New
      York World, 15 August. [A19]

H197 Glenn, Isa. "Real Life in Hollywood," New York Herald Tribune
      Books, 19 August. [A19]

H198 Gould, Bruce. "Books on Our Table," New York Evening Post, 20 Aug-
      ust. [A19]

H199 "Spider Boy," Times Literary Supplement, 23 August. [A19]

H200 Mann, Dorothea Lawrence. "Van Vechten Goes to the Movies," Boston
      Transcript, 25 August. [A19]

H201 Hartley, L. P. "Spider Boy," Saturday Review [London], 1 September.
      [A19]

H202 "Spider Boy," New Republic, 12 September. [A19]

H203 McHugh, Vincent. "Hollywood à la Carl Van Vechten," New York Post,
      15 September. [A19]

H204 "Fiction Shorts," Nation, 127:275 (19 September). [A19]

H205 Robbins, Frances Lamont. "Characters of Twentieth Century Style,"
      Outlook [London], 19 September. [A19]

H206 Motherwell, Hiram. "Angel Town," Theatre Guild Magazine, October.

H207 Fisher, Rudolph. The Walls of Jericho, New York: Alfred A. Knopf.
      [Van Vechten is "Conrad White," a character in the novel.]

H208 Riddell, John. "Hollywood Boy," Vanity Fair, November. Reprinted
      in Meaning No Offense, New York: John Day, 1928. [a parody of Spi-
      der Boy by Corey Ford, with a caricature by Miguel Covarrubias]

H209 Marble, Annie Russell. "Carl Van Vechten," A Study of the Modern
      Novel, British and American, Since 1900, New York: Appleton, pp.
      397-98.

1929

H210 Seldes, Gilbert. "Back From Utopia," Saturday Evening Post, 6 July.

H211 "Perfect Setting for an Anglo-American Novel," Boston Transcript,
      13 July. Reprinted, Illustrated London News, 25 October; Town and
      Country, 15 July 1931. [photograph of Hugh Walpole and Van Vechten]

H212 Baker, Gladys. "An Eye on Father Knickerbocker," Birmingham [Alabama] News, 13 October.

H213 Draper, Muriel. Music At Midnight, New York: Harpers, pp. 120-31. [Van Vechten in Florence, Italy, 1913]

H214 Gordon, Taylor. Born To Be, New York: Covici-Friede, pp. 185-86. Reprinted, Seattle: University of Washington Press, 1975. [B15]

H215 Posselt, Erich. "Carl Van Vechten," On Parade, New York: Coward-McCann, pp. 165-65. [with a caricature by Eva Hermann]

H216 Wickham, Harvey. "The McKay and Van Vechten Blues," The Impuritans, New York: Dial, pp. 282-90. [with a caricature by Sheel]

H217 Carl Van Vechten, an advertising brochure, distributed by Alfred A. Knopf, Inc., 18.5 X 12.7 cm., with biography, bibliography, list prices, and a photograph.

1930

H218 Delatte, F. F. "Littérature Anglo-Américaine," Le Thyrse [Brussels], 1 January. [A18]

H219 Chamberlain, John. "The Negro as Writer," Bookman, February. [A18]

H220 Massock, Richard G. "The Daybook of a New Yorker: Introducing Carl Van Vechten," Columbus [Ohio] Dispatch, 9 May.

H221 Britten, Florence Haxton. "Those Tired Sophisticates," New York Herald Tribune Books, 12 August. [A21]

H222 Gannett, Lewis. "Books and Other Things," New York Herald Tribune, 15 August. [A21]

H223 Hansen, Harry. "The First Reader," New York World, 15 August. [A18]

H224 McFee, William. "Life in the Speakeasies," New York Sun, 15 August. [A21]

H225 Soskin, William. "Books on Our Table," New York Evening Post, 15 August. [A21]

H226 Butcher, Fanny. "Drys and Wets Sure to Shake 'Parties' Well," Chicago Tribune, 16 August. [A21]

H227 "Cocktail in Hand," New York Times, 17 August. [A21]

H228 Yust, Walter. "Of Making Many Books," Public Ledger [Philadelphia], 18 August. [A21]

H229 Jones, Llewellyn. "Parties," Chicago Post, 22 August. [A21]

H230 Kruger, Bernhard. "Van Vechten in Berlin; der Autor des Negerhimmels," 8 Uhr-Abendblatt [Berlin], 26 August.

H231   Jackson, Joseph Henry. "The Grim Forgetters," Argonaut [San Francisco], 6 September. [A21]

H232   Simpson, Clinton. "So This is New York," Saturday Review of Literture, 6 September. [with a caricature by Sheel]

H233   "Parties," Times Literary Supplement, 11 September. [A21]

H234   Dangerfield, George. "Parties," Bookman, 72:71-72 (September). [A21]

H235   "Carl Van Vechten," Bookman, 72:140 (October). [photograph by Doris Ulman]

1931

H236   Perdeck, A. "Amerikaansche Lettran," Nieuwe Rotterdamsche Courant, 18 February.

H237   Chesnutt, Charles W. "Post-Bellum—Pre-Harlem," Colophon, II, Part 5 (February). [A18]

H238   Lewis, D. B. Wyndham. "Dark Party," New Yorker, 7:23-25 (7 March). [a parody of Parties]

H239   Perdeck, A. "Carl Van Vechten," Critisch Bulletin [Rotterdam], pp. 123-26. (April).

H240   Clark, Emily. "Carl Van Vechten," Innocence Abroad, New York: Alfred A. Knopf, pp. 129-45

H241   Dilly Tante [pseudonym]. "Carl Van Vechten," Living Authors, New York: H.W. Wilson, pp. 420-21.

1932

H242   Benson, E. M. "Re-edited Articles," New York Sun, 15 April. [A22]

H243   Butcher, Fanny. "Title of Book by Van Vechten May Fool You," Chicago Tribune, 15 April. [A22]

H244   Hansen, Harry. "The First Reader," New York World Telegram, 16 April. [A22]

H245   Soskin, William. "Reading and Writing," New York Evening Post, 16 April. [A22]

H246   Ross, Virgilia Peterson. "On the Thread of Memory," New York Herald Tribune Books, 17 April. [A22]

H247   Dodd, Lee Wilson. "The Years of Our Past," Saturday Review of Literature, 8:743 (21 May). [A22]

H248   Delatte, F. F. "Lettres Anglo-Américaines. Déchéance," Le Thyrse [Brussels], 34:364-65 (1 December). [A21]

H249 Cullen, Countée. <u>One Way To Heaven</u>, New York: Harper. [Van Vechten is "Walter Dervent," a character in the novel.]

H250 Marcellini, Giovanni. "Nota Introduttiva," in Carl Van Vechten. <u>Il Romanzo d'Hollywood</u>, Giuseppe Carabba, Editore Lanciano, pp. 9-10. [A19]

H251 Marks, Percy. "Carl Van Vechten," <u>The Craft of Writing</u>, New York: Harcourt, Brace, pp. 165,172.

1933

H252 <u>Bergdorf-Goodman Exhibition of New York Beauty</u>, a catalog, January. [3 Van Vechten photographs]

H253 Johnson, James Weldon. [Carl Van Vechten], <u>Along This Way</u>, New York: Viking Press.

H254 Stein, Gertrude. [Carl Van Vechten], <u>The Autobiography of Alice B. Toklas</u>, New York: Harcourt, Brace, 1933; Literary Guild, 1933. Reprinted, London: John Lane, 1933; Weekend Library, 1935; New York: Random House, 1946 [B20], 1955; London: Arrow Books, 1960; Penguin, 1966; New York: Modern Library, 1962, 1972 [B20]

1934

H255 Schwartz, Harry W. "Carl Van Vechten," <u>Racket</u>, Part 2, Milwaukee: Casanova Press, p. 13.

H256 <u>First Leica Exhibition Catalog</u>. [4 Van Vechten photographs]

1935

H257 Adams, Franklin P. <u>The Diary of Our Own Samuel Pepys</u>, 1926-1934, New York: Simon and Schuster.

H258 McBride, Henry. "The Leica Exhibition," <u>New York Sun</u>, 30 November. [critical assessment of Van Vechten's photography]

H259 <u>Second Leica Exhibition Catalog</u>. [14 Van Vechten photographs]

1936

H260 Lawrence, D. H. "<u>Nigger Heaven</u>," <u>Phoenix: The Posthumous Papers of D.H. Lawrence</u>, New York: Viking Press, pp. 361-63. [A18]

H261 <u>Third Leica Exhibition Catalog</u>. [12 Van Vechten photographs]

1937

H262 Jack, Peter Monro. "The James Branch Cabell Period," <u>New Republic</u>, 89:323-36 (13 January).

H263 Stein, Gertrude. Everybody's Autobiography, New York: Random House. Reprinted, Vintage Books, 1973.

1938

H264 Stonier, C. W. "Cats," New Statesman and Nation [London], 15:884-86 (21 May). [All]

H265 Polly and Dolly [pseudonym]. "The Tiger in the House," Now and Then [London], 59:25-26 (Spring). [All]

1939

H266 Wolfe, Thomas. The Web and the Rock, New York: Harper. [Van Vechten is "Van Vleeck," a character in the novel.]

1940

H267 Anderson, John. "Van Vechten Defends Olivier-Leigh Romeo," New York Journal American, 22 May. [EV46]

H268 Hughes, Langston. "When Harlem Was in Vogue," Town and Country, 95:49,64-66 (July).

H269 _____. [Carl Van Vechten], The Big Sea, An Autobiography, New York: Alfred A. Knopf, pp. 216-17,251-55.

H270 Millet, Fred B. "Carl Van Vechten," Contemporary American Authors, New York: Harcourt, Brace, pp. 35,626-28.

H271 Wolfe, Thomas. You Can't Go Home Again, New York: Harper. [Van Vechten is "Stephen Hook," a character in the novel.]

1941

H272 Beach, Joseph Warren. The Twentieth Century Novel, 1920-1940, New York: Macmillan.

H273 Cargill, Oscar. "The Intelligentsia: Carl Van Vechten," Intellectual America, New York: Macmillan, pp. 507-11.

1942

H274 Pearson, Norman Holmes. "The Gertrude Stein Collection," Yale University Library Gazette, 16:45-47 (January).

H275 The Theatre Through the Camera of Carl Van Vechten, 18 November to 11 January, Museum of the City of New York catalog for an exhibition of 104 photographs, 25.5 X 20 cm., white folder printed in green.

H276 [5 photographs and information about H275], New York Times Magazine, 15 November, p. 38.

H277 Martin, John. "The Dance: Van Vechten," New York Times, 19 November. [D135]

H278 Kazin, Alfred. "The Exquisites: Coda," On Native Grounds, An Interpretation of Modern American Prose Literature, New York: Reynal & Hitchcock, pp. 244-46.

1943

H279 Bontemps, Arna. "The James Weldon Johnson Memorial Collection of Negro Arts and Letters," Yale University Library Gazette, 18:19-26 (October).

1944

H280 "Carl Van Vechten," The Princeton University Library Chronicle, 5: 79-80 (February). [Van Vechten's photographs of Eugene O'Neill]

H281 "Not to Newcastle," Time, 43:75 (6 March). [Van Vechten's collections at Yale and Fisk Universities]

H282 Frankenstein, Alfred V. "1915-1945: Progress or Decline?" Musical Courier, 130:4-5 (September-October). [A4]

1945

H283 Carter, Michael. "Van Vechten Explains Racial Views," AFRO-American [Baltimore], 54:1,9 (24 November).

H284 Gloster, Hugh M. "The Van Vechten Vogue," Phylon [Atlanta], 6:310-14 (Fourth Quarter). Reprinted in Negro Voices in American Fiction, Chapel Hill: University of North Carolina Press, pp. 157-63.

H285 Vaucher-Zananiri, Nelly. "Carl Van Vechten et le Monde Noir de Harlem," Voix d'Amérique: étude sur la littérature américaine d'auhourd'hui, Le Caire: Schindler, pp. 73-76. [A18]

H286 American Negro Exhibit, Syracuse University Library catalog. [B21]

1946

H287 "Carl Van Vechten's Gallery of Negro Notables," Negro Digest [Chicago], 5:53-62 (December).

H288 Graham, Shirley. [Carl Van Vechten], Paul Robeson: Citizen of the World, New York: Julian Messner, pp. 146-58.

H289 "Time Capsule of Negro Culture; Carl Van Vetchen [sic] Preserves Satchelmouth and Black Boy for the Ages," Ebony [Chicago], 1:9-10 (January). [4 photographs of Van Vechten and Grace Nail (Mrs. James Weldon) Johnson at Yale]

1947

H290 Gallup, Donald. "The Gertrude Stein Collection," Yale University Library Gazette, 22:21-32 (October).

H291 Bontemps, Arna. "Foreword," Selected Items from the George Gershwin Memorial Collection of Music and Musical Literature, Nashville: Fisk University; 32 pp. 21.6 X 14 cm., pamphlet with blue wrapper.

1948

H292 Scott, Lillian. "James W. Johnson honored by Yale University: Carl Van Vechten Donates Noted Author's Works," Chicago Defender, 24 April.

H293 Vidal, Gore. The City and the Pillar, New York: Dutton. [Van Vechten is "Nicholas Rollonson," a character in the novel.]

1949

H294 Mr. Leo Perper | President ROGER KENT | invites you | to view an exhibition of | Documentary | Photographs | By | Carl VAN Vechten | PERSONALITIES | OF OUR | TIMES | April 11—May 2 | Rockefeller Plaza. Cream French-fold brochure, printed in blue, 25.5 X 10.5 cm., with a portrait of Van Vechten by Harrison Thompson.

H295 "Attractions at the Galleries," New York Sun, 15 April. [Roger Kent exhibition]

H296 Lewis, Emory. "Carl Van Vechten: Novelist of the Twenties is now a Superb Portrait Photographer," Cue, 9 April, pp. 18-19. [biographical sketch, with photographs]

H297 Stettheimer, Florine. "Carl," "He Photographs," "Dear Carlo," "Carlo," "To Carl Van Vechten," "Houpla Carlo!" "To Carl," Crystal Flowers, Pawlet, Vermont: The Banyan Press. [privately printed poems]

H298 [Peterson, Dorothy]. Jerome Bowers Peterson Memorial Collection of Photographs of Celebrated Negroes by Carl Van Vechten, Wadleigh High School, New York City, exhibition catalog. [B24]

1950

H299 Frankenstein, Alfred V. "Art and Music—a Review of Music Trends during the Last Fifty Years," San Francisco Chronicle, 13:9 (1 January). [A4]

H300 Johnson, Charles Spurgeon. "Literature and the Practice of Living," Exercises Marking the Opening of the James Weldon Johnson Memorial Collection of Negro Arts and Letters, Yale University, 7 January, pp. 9-15, in program.

H301 "Yale Collection of Negro Life is Inaugurated," New York Herald Tribune, 8 January, p. 38.

H302 "Fisk University dedicates Alfred Stieglitz Collection," Crisis, 57:157-59 (March). [in the Carl Van Vechten Gallery of Fine Arts]

H303 Knopf, Alfred A. "Reminiscences of Hergesheimer, Van Vechten, and Mencken," Yale University Library Gazette, 24:145-64 (April). [an address delivered at the time of a Cabell-Hergesheimer-Mencken-Van Vechten exhibition in the Sterling Memorial Library at Yale University]

H304 Rockwell, Kenneth. "Carl Van Vechten, King of the Cats," Daily Times Herald [Dallas, Texas], 21 May.

H305 McFee, William. "Yesterday They Wrote Best Sellers," New York Times Book Review, 2 July, p. 10.

H306 Toklas, Alice B. "They Who Came to Paris to Write," New York Times Book Review, 6 August, p. 1.

H307 Schuyler, George S. "The Van Vechten Revolution," Phylon [Atlanta], 11:362-68 (Fourth Quarter). Also issued as a pamphlet, "especially prepared for private distribution with independent pagination," in gray wrappers.

1951

H308 Langner, Lawrence. The Magic Curtain, New York: Dutton.

H309 Lueders, Edward George. "Music Criticism in America," American Quarterly (Minneapolis), 3:142-51 (Summer).

H310 Morris, Lloyd. "Carl Van Vechten and the Negro Renaissance," High Life and Low Life of the Last Hundred Years, New York: Random House, pp. 336-37.

H311 Philadelphia Museum of Art photographic exhibition brochure for Adrian Siegel, Carl Van Vechten, and Harry Wright, October-November.

H312 Schuyler, George S. "A Critical Commentary," in Carl Van Vechten. Nigger Heaven, New York: Avon Publishing Co., pp. [191-94]. [A181]

H313 Waters, Ethel. [Carl Van Vechten], His Eye Is On the Sparrow, An Autobiography, New York: Doubleday, pp. 193-96.

1952

H314 Gallup, Donald. "Carl Van Vechten's Gertrude Stein," Yale University Library Gazette, 27:77-86 (October).

H315 O'Connor, William. An Age of Criticism, 1900-1950, Chicago: Regnery, pp. 19,32.

1954

H316 Hoffman, Frederick. The Twenties, New York: Viking Press.

H317 Marchant, Peter David. "Carl Van Vechten: Novelist and Critic. A
      Study in the Metropolitan Comedy of Manners," Master of Arts thesis,
      Columbia University, New York, unpublished.

1955

H318 Lueders, Edward. Carl Van Vechten and the Twenties, Albequerque:
      University of New Mexico. [a revised version of Lueders's Phd dis-
      sertation, University of New Mexico]

H319 _____. "Mr. Van Vechten of New York City," New Republic,
      132:20,36-37 (16 May).

H320 Bontemps, Arna. "Public Oration for Carl Van Vechten," delivered
      by Charles S. Johnson, President of Fisk University on the occasion
      of Van Vechten's honorary doctor of literature degree, unpublished.

H321 Evans, Amon. "Carl Van Vechten, Author, Gets Honorary Fisk Degree,"
      Nashville Tennessean, 31 May.

H322 "Talk of the Town: Good Egg," New Yorker, 31:18 (18 June).

H323 MDH, "Carl Van Vechten, Critic, Novelist, Photographer," Exhibi-
      tion of Photographs by Carl Van Vechten from the Countee Cullen
      Memorial Collection, Trevor Arnett Library, Atlanta University, 6
      May—3 June, a mimeographed brochure, 4 pp.

H324 Starrett, Vincent. "Books Alive," Chicago Sunday Tribune Magazine
      of Books, 5 June, p. 8. [H318]

H335 Gordan, John D. "Carl Van Vechten: Notes for an Exhibition in
      Honor of His Seventy-Fifth Birthday," Bulletin of the New York Pub-
      lic Library, 59:331-66 (July).

H336 Gallup, Donald. "The Carl Van Vechten Exhibition," Yale University
      Library Gazette, 30:83-84 (October). [an exhibition of Van Vech-
      ten's gifts to Yale, including 300 photographs]

H337 Jonas, Klaus W. Carl Van Vechten: A Bibliography with a Preamble
      ["Bouquet for Carlo"] by Grace Zaring Stone, New York: Alfred A.
      Knopf. [an edition of 400 copies]

H338 Barret, John Townsend. "Analysis and Significance of Three Ameri-
      can Critics of the Ballet: Carl Van Vechten, Edwin Denby, and Lin-
      coln Kirstein," Master of Fine Arts thesis, Columbia University,
      New York, unpublished.

1957

H339 Stein, Gertrude, [Van] in "To Do," Alphabets and Birthdays, Ed.
      Donald C. Gallup, New Haven: Yale University Press, pp. 61-65.

1958

H340 Glasgow, Ellen. [fourteen letters to Van Vechten], Letters of Ellen Glasgow, Ed. Blair Rouse, New York: Harcourt, Brace and World.

H341 Smith, Hugh L. "Jazz and the American Novel," English Journal, November.

1959

H342 Benkovitz, Miriam J. "Ronald Firbank in New York," Bulletin of the New York Public Library, 63:247-59 (May).

H343 Dreiser, Theodore. [letter to Van Vechten], Letters of Theodore Dreiser, Ed. Robert H. Elias, Philadelphia: University of Pennsylvania Press.

1960

H344 [Kellner, Bruce]. Carl Van Vechten: A Biographical Exhibition, Coe College, Cedar Rapids, Iowa, March; French-fold brochure, 14 X 9.2 cm., of which ten copies, signed, were distributed in Japanese woodcut envelopes.

H345 Gallup, Donald. 80 | WRITERS whose books and letters | have been given over the past twenty years to the | Yale University Library by Carl Van Vechten, | compiled in honor of his 80th birthday, | 17 June 1960. | New Haven: Yale University Library 1960; [1-12] pp., including cover title printed in brown on a pink wrapper, 21.7 X 14.1; caricature by Miguel Covarrubias, p. [5]; facsimile of a note from James Weldon Johnson, p. [12]; 1,250 copies printed June.

H346 Chapman, Gilbert. "Citation of Carl Van Vechten on His Eightieth Birthday," Bulletin of the New York Public Library, 64:[349] (July). [on the occasion of Van Vechten's name being incised in the Library lobby as one of the New York Public Library's principle benefactors]

H347 Jablonski, Edward. "Carlo Patriarch: An Appreciation" and James Lyon. "Evviva Carlo," American Record Guide, June [with 20 photographs; D160]

H348 Hurst, Fannie. "Zora Neale Hurston: A Personality Sketch," Yale University Library Gazette, 35:17-22 (July).

1961

H349 O'Connor, Jim. "Old Film Bows As Musical," Journal American, 2 May. [The Tattooed Countess by Coleman Dowell; A14]

H350 Crist, Judith. "First Night Report," New York Herald Tribune, 4 May. [A14]

H351 Taubman, Howard. "Theatre: Corn in Ioway," New York Times, 4 May. [A14]

H352 Coleman, Robert. "Tattooed Countess is Sketchy," <u>New York Mirror</u>,
      5 May. [A14]

H353 Lewis, Emory. "The Tattooed Countess," <u>Cue</u>, 13 May. [A14]

H354 Jonas, Klaus. "Additions to the Bibliography of Carl Van Vechten,"
      <u>Papers of the Bibliographical Society of America</u>, 55:42-45 (First
      Quarter). Also issued as a pamphlet in tan wrapper, stapled, 23.3
      X 15.6 cm.

H355 National Institute of Arts and Letters and American Academy program
      and exhibition catalog, No. 17, 24 May. [manuscript and photograph
      exhibit of new members' work, including Van Vechten]

H356 Lerman, Leo. "Dance: June Walk," <u>New York Times</u>, 18 June.

H357 [Six letters to Van Vechten], <u>Letters of H. L. Mencken</u>, Ed. Guy J.
      Forgue, New York: Alfred A. Knopf.

                              1962

H358 Atkinson, Brooks. "Critic at Large," <u>New York Times</u>, 23 November.
      [EII859]

H359 Kramer, Jane. "A Room for an Astonished Muse," <u>The</u> [Greenwich]
      <u>Villager</u>, 16 August. [interview with Martha Graham and Van Vechten]

H360 Schneider, John, "A World of Whiffles: The Novels of Carl Van Vech-
      ten," <u>Wagner</u> [College] <u>Literary Magazine</u>, No. 3 (Fall).

H361 [Two letters to Van Vechten from Cabell], <u>Between Friends: Letters
      of James Branch Cabell and Others</u>, New York: Harcourt, Brace and
      World. [B34]

                              1963

H362 "Talk of the Town: Van Vechten," <u>New Yorker</u>, 38:47,21-22 (12 Janu-
      ary).

H363 McDonald, Paul. "Bring Back Van Vechten," <u>Esquire</u>, 39:2 (February).

H364 Cowley, Malcolm. "Last of the Lost Generation," <u>Esquire</u>, 40:177-79
      (July).

H365 [Five letters to Van Vechten], <u>Letters of F. Scott Fitzgerald</u>, Ed.
      Andrew Turnbull, New York: Scribners.

H366 Toklas, Alice B. <u>What Is Remembered</u>, New York: Holt, Rinehart,
      Winston.

H367 Tyler, Parker. <u>Florine Stettheimer: A Life in Art</u>, New York: Far-
      rar Straus and Company. [B37]

1964

H368 Gallup, Donald. "The Yale Collection of American Literature," Yale University Library Gazette, 384:151-59 (April).

H369 "Van Vechten Dies; Critic and Author," New York Post, 21 December.

H370 "Writer Carl Van Vechten Dies at 84," New York World Telegram and Sun, 21 December.

H371 "An Author Others Wrote About" (Associated Press), New York Daily News, 22 December.

H372 "Carl Van Vechten is Dead at 84; Author, Critic and Photographer," New York Times, 22 December.

H373 Price, Jo-Ann. "Van Vechten: Prodigious Creativity," New York Herald Tribune, 22 December.

H374 "Private Rites for Novelist Van Vechten," New York Journal American, 22 December.

H375 "Carl Van Vechten," Variety, 23 December.

H376 Hogan, William. "Carl Van Vechten and the Jazz Age," San Francisco Chronicle, 31 December.

1965

H377 " "Milestones," Time, 85:68 (1 January).

H378 "The Connoisseur," Newsweek, 65:62-63 (4 January).

H379 Martin, John. "Carl Van Vechten, 1880-1964," New York State Theatre program, Lincoln Center, 15 January.

H380 [Obituary with nine photographs], Opera News, 29:4 (13 February).

H381 Knopf, Alfred A. [Carl Van Vechten], Borzoi Broadside, The Second Quarter, April.

H382 K[olodin], I[rving]. "Vale Van Vechten," Philharmonic Hall Program, Lincoln Center, 15 February.

H383 Clark, John Whitbeck. "Re Van Vechten," Saturday Review, 48:13 (27 March). [A10]

H384 Kirstein, Lincoln. "Carl Van Vechten, 1880-1964," Yale University Library Gazette, 39:157-62 (April). [In a slightly different form, this eulogy was given by Kirstein at Van Vechten's memorial service, 23 December 1964.]

H385 Hughes, Langston. "Carl Van Vechten, 1880-1964," Proceedings of the American Academy of Arts & Letters and National Institute of Arts & Letters, Second Series, 15:504-6. [A28]

H386   CARL VAN VECHTEN | 1880 — 1964 | A MEMORIAL EXHIBITION OF | HIS
        LIFE AND WORK | FROM THE COLLECTION OF | PAUL PADGETTE | SAN FRAN-
        CISCO PUBLIC LIBRARY | JUNE 1965 [the foregoing in a decorative
        border. 8 leaves, 1-22 pp., 1 leaf, 23.8 X 15.5 cm.; stapled pages
        in stiff red wrapper with facsimile signature on front. "Commemor-
        ative Accolades; Ruminations; Laudans Omniumgatherum" by Padgette,
        pp. 1-3; bibliography, pp. 5-9; catalog, pp. 13-22; limitation note,
        recto last leaf: 300 copies | printed in Garamond type | by Frank
        Westlake at | The Bindweed Press, | San Francisco | [stamped number]
        | COPIES ONE THROUGH FIFTY NUMBERED

H387   Lueders, Edward. Carl Van Vechten, New York: Twayne Publishing Co.
        [C54]

H388   Ingénue Among the Lions: Letters of Emily Clark to Joseph Hergeshei-
        mer, Ed. Gerald Langford, Austin: University of Texas Press.

H389   Padgette, Paul. "New Focus on a Neglected Writer," San Francisco
        Chronicle, 6 June. [H387]

                                1966

H390   [Four letters to Van Vechten], Letters of Wallace Stevens, Ed. Holly
        Stevens, New York: Alfred A. Knopf.

                                1967

H391   Zug, Mrs. Richard C. and Anne C. Pearson. "Photographs of Carl Van
        Vechten Given by Mark Lutz," Philadelphia Museum of Art catalog No.
        P/M/VECHT/P544p of 12,299 photographs. [unpublished]

H392   Gallico, Paul. "Carl Van Vechten and Fania Marinoff" in Nickolas
        Muray, The Revealing Eye: Portraits from the 20's and 30's, New
        York: Atheneum.

H393   Kellner, Bruce. "Introduction" to Carl Van Vechten, "The Origin of
        the Sonnets from the Patagonian," Hartwick Review, 3:50-51 (Spring).
        [D165]

H394   Paluka, Frank. "Carl Van Vechten," Iowa Authors: A Bio-Bibliography,
        Iowa City: Friends of the [University of Iowa] Library.

                                1968

H395   Kellner, Bruce. Carl Van Vechten and the Irreverent Decades, Nor-
        man: University of Oklahoma Press. [C58]

H396   Van Dyke, Henry. Blood of Strawberries, New York: Farrar, Straus &
        Giroux. [Van Vechten is "Max Rhode," a character in the novel.]

H397   "The Lens of Carl Van Vechten," Hammond Museum catalog of 370 photo-
        graphs, 28 August—29 December. [unpublished]

H398   Padgette, Paul.. "Out of Obscurity," San Francisco Chronicle, 12
        January. [H395]

H399   Wagenknecht, Edward. "The Book Parade," Waltham, Massachusetts
        Tribune, 11 February. [H395]

H400   Larson, Charles R. "Three Harlem Novels of the Jazz Age," Criti-
        cism, 2:66-78. [A18]

H401   Rogers, W. G. "Carl Van Vechten and the Irreverent Decades," New
        York Times Book Review, 16 February. [H395]

H402   Foote, Edward. "Driving Nihilism," Hartford [Connecticut] Courant,
        30 March. [H395]

H403   Ringo, James. "A Three-Quarter Length Portrait of Carl Van Vech-
        ten," The Cabellian, 1:68-70 (April). [H395]

H404   _____. "A Big Bon Bon for Carlo, and Cheers for Three Ca-
        reers," American Record Guide, 35:852-58 (May). [H395]

H405   Benkovitz, Miriam. Ronald Firbank, New York: Alfred A. Knopf.

H406   Russell, Nina. "A la Recherche de Carl Van Vechten," After Dark,
        November 1970. [H395]

H407   Thurman, Wallace. The Blacker the Berry, New York: Arno Press,
        first published by Macaulay Publishers, 1929. [Van Vechten is
        "Campbell Kitchen," a character in the novel.]

                                  1971

H408   Andrews, Clarence. "Le Comte de Cedar Rapids," The Iowan, 19:12-
        14,48-50 (March).

H409   Kellner, Bruce. "HLM and CVV: Friendship on Paper," Menckeniana,
        39:2-9 (Fall).

H410   "Fania Marinoff, Actress, 81, Dead," New York Times, 17 November.

H411   Simbro, William. "Van Vechten Estate Aid for 3 C[edar] R[apids]
        Institutions," Des Moines [Iowa] Register, 1 December.

H412   Robinson, Clayton. "Gilmore Millen's Sweet Man Neglected Classic
        of the Van Vechten Vogue," University of Houston Forum, 8:32-35.

H413   Huggins, Nathan Irvin. [Carl Van Vechten], Harlem Renaissance,
        New York: Oxford University Press, pp. 93-118. [A18]

H414   Bradbury, Malcolm. "Carl Van Vechten," The Penguin Companion to
        American Literature, New York: McGraw Hill, p. 256.

H415   Padgette, Paul. "Carl Van Vechten and the Irreverent Decades,"
        Fitzgerald-Hemingway Annual 1971. [H395]

H416   Churchill, Allen. [Carl Van Vechten], The Literary Decade, New
       York: Prentice Hall.

                                 1972

H417   Andrews, Clarence. [Carl Van Vechten], A Literary History of Iowa,
       Iowa City: University of Iowa Press, pp. 186-92.

H418   Kirby, Richard. "Mask and Community: Behavioral Revolt in the
       Novels of Carl Van Vechten and Some of His Contemporaries," PhD
       dissertation, University Sussex, England, unpublished.

H419   Mills, George. "The Tattooed Countess," Rogues and Heroes from
       Iowa's Amazing Past, Ames: Iowa State University Press. [This is
       a biographical sketch, not a review of the novel.]

H420   Waters, Ethel. To Me It's Wonderful, New York: Harper and Row, pp.
       54-59.

                                 1973

H421   Hart, Robert C. "Black and White Literary Relations in the Harlem
       Renaissance," American Literature, 44:612-18. [A18]

H422   [Thirty-seven letters to Van Vechten], Staying on Alone: Letters
       of Alice B. Toklas, Ed. Edward Burns, New York: Liveright.

                                 1974

H423   Coleman, Leon Duncan. "Carl Van Vechten Presents the New Negro,"
       Studies in the Literary Imagination, 7:85-104 (Fall). [excerpted,
       with revisions, from "The Contributions of Carl Van Vechten to the
       Negro Renaissance: 1920-1930," University of Minnesota PhD disser-
       tation, 1969, unpublished]

H424   Mellow, James R. Charmed Circle, Gertrude Stein & Company, New
       York: Praeger Publishers

                                 1975

H425   "Front Matter," Bulletin of the New York Public Library, Spring,
       268-70. [Gertrude Stein centennial exhibition, including a letter
       from Stein to Van Vechten]

H426   Kellner, Bruce. "Alfred Kazin's Exquisites: An Excavation," Ill-
       inois Quarterly 38:45-62 (Fall). [H278]

H427   [Six letters to Van Vechten], Letters of James Branch Cabell, Ed.
       Edward Wagenknecht, Norman: University of Oklahoma Press.

H428   Padgette, Paul. "Introduction" and notes, The Dance Writings of
       Carl Van Vechten, Brooklyn: Dance Horizons. [A25]

H429   Vaughn, David. "The Dance Writings of Carl Van Vechten," Dance
       Magazine, November. [A25]

1976

H430   Berry, Faith. "Did Van Vechten Make or Take Hughes' Blues?" Black
       World, February, 18-20.

H431   Helbling, Mark. "Carl Van Vechten and the Harlem Renaissance,"
       Negro American Literature Forum, July, 39-47 [A18]

H432   Shirer, William L. [Carl Van Vechten], Growing Up in Iowa, 1913-
       1925, New York: Harcourt Brace Jovanovich, pp. 184-86.

1977

H433   Kellner, Bruce. "Baby Woojums in Iowa, Books at Iowa, 26:3-18
       (April). [Gertrude Stein and Van Vechten, EV50]

H434   Padgette, Paul. "Twentieth Century Books: A Collector's Guide,"
       Book Collector's Market, 3:11-12 (January-February)

H435   [Two letters to Van Vechten], The New Mencken Letters, Ed. Carl
       Bode, New York: Dial.

H436   Austin, Roger. Playing the Game: The Homosexual Novel in America,
       Indianapolis: Boobs-Merrill.

1978

H437   Dean, Phillip Hayes. [Carl Van Vechten], Paul Robeson, Garden
       City: Doubleday, pp. 29-30.

1979

H438   Berlin, Brigid. "Leo Lerman on Carl Van Vechten," Interview, 9:
       65-67 (April).

H439   Kellner, Bruce. "Introduction" and notes, "Keep A-Inchin' Along":
       Selected Writings of Carl Van Vechten about Black Arts and Letters,
       Westport, Connecticut: Greenwood Press, Inc. [A28]

H440   _____. "Carl Van Vechten," Great Writers of the English
       Language, London: St James Press Ltd., New York: St. Martin's Press.

H441   Seidler, Lawrence Martin. "Van Vechten birth," Cedar Rapids [Iowa]
       Gazette, 17 June.

H442   Kellner, Bruce. Friends and Mentors: Richmond's Carl Van Vechten
       and Mark Lutz, Richmond, Virginia: Friends of the Boatwright Memor-
       ial Library, December 1979.

I.
COLLECTIONS

a. Carl Van Vechten Collection, Manuscript and Archives Division

Established by Van Vechten in 1941 and added to until his death in
1964, this collection contains copies of his books in all editions and
translations as well as copies of books to which he contributed; the
typescripts — usually in three drafts each — galley and page proofs
for his published works; unpublished manuscripts, notebooks, diaries,
juvenilia, college themes, plays, musical compositions; all periodicals to which he contributed and complete files of several of them;
file cases labelled "Opera" containing peripheral material connected
with his career; eighteen large scrapbooks of his newspaper writing and
clippings about his books; publishers' and book-sellers' catalogs; all
family papers, including his letters to his second wife, Fania Marinoff, and her letters to him, all letters from all correspondents
dealing with his published work, correspondence about all collections
he established, family and personal photographs, records of stocks,
copyrights; business correspondence; inventories of possessions. Following Van Vechten's death, his color slides and other photographs
dealing with the Stage Door Canteen, the 1939 World's Fair, his apart-
ments and objets d'art were deposited in the collection.

b. Henry W. and Albert A. Berg Collection

To the Berg Collection, Van Vechten gave his collections of books and
letters of English writers, Ronald Firbank, Arthur Machen, W. Somerset
Maugham, "Ouida," Matthew Phipps Shiel, Philip Thicknesse, and Hugh
Walpole, as well as his collection of Eugene O'Neill's work, a substantial number of photographs and two manuscripts. [B5, D118]

c. Lincoln Center Library for the Performing Arts

To the theater archive, Van Vechten donated his collection of programs which he had begun circa 1888, early autograph books of opera

singers, musicians, and actors; his collection of cigarette picture cards of popular turn-of-the-century actresses; a number of his photographs of people connected with the theater. To the dance archive, he presented The Fania Marinoff Collection of Dance Photographs.

I 2   Beinecke Rare Book and Manuscript Library, Yale University

a. Collection of American Literature

Van Vechten deposited his personal correspondence — by 1960, it had filled five four-drawer filing cabinets — including extensive letters from James Branch Cabell, Ellen Glasgow, Joseph Hergesheimer, Chester Himes, Langston Hughes, James Weldon Johnson, Mabel Dodge Luhan, H. L. Mencken, Henry Miller, James Purdy, Gertrude Stein, and Alice B. Toklas; early collections of autographs; inscriptions from several hundred of his photographic subjects, each accompanied by a Leica print of the subject; copies of his published works; several thousand photographs; and substantial manuscript material, much of it unpublished. In addition to the books of those writers listed among his correspondents, Van Vechten gave his collections of other American writers, most notably Herman Melville, but also Theodore Dreiser, Henry Blake Fuller, Edgar Saltus, and many others accounted for in Donald Gallup's checklist, 80 [H345]. Following Van Vechten's death, the negatives for his photographs were deposited at Yale, and shortly before her own death, his widow, Fania Marinoff, gave her scrapbooks and diaries to the Van Vechten Archive. . Van Vechten was instrumental in encouraging other gifts as well: the Arthur Stieglitz Archive from Georgia O'Keeffe, the Theatre Guild Collection from Lawrence Langner, Theresa Helburn, and Armina Marshall, and the papers of Max Ewing, Arthur Davison Ficke, Mabel Dodge Luhan, Gertrude Stein, Alice B. Toklas, and the Stettheimer sisters, Ettie ("Henrie Waste") and Florine.

b. The James Weldon Johnson Memorial Collection of Negro Arts and Letters

Founded by Van Vechten in 1941, this collection is administered by the Collection of American Literature. In addition to Van Vechten's private collection of black literature and some of his own manuscript materials, it includes manuscripts and correspondence of nearly every important black writer of the first half of the century, notably Langston Hughes, James Weldon Johnson, Chester Himes, Zora Neale Hurston, Claude McKay, and Walter White; programs and clippings; phonograph records; and photographs and Kodachrome slides of celebrated black artists and writers. Having added annually to the endowment fund for the collection, Van Vechten specified in his will that any income realized from his work be donated to it.

c. The Anna Marble Pollock Memorial Collection of Books About Cats

Founded by Van Vechten in 1948, this collection is also administered by the Collection of American Literature. It includes graphic materials as well as books, and the cat library of Hettie Gray Baker was added to it through the courtesy of Dartmouth College.

I 3   Fisk University

a. The George Gershwin Memorial Collection of Music and Musical Litera-
    ture

    Van Vechten founded this collection in 1946. It includes autograph
    letters by Charles Gounod, Giacomo Meyerbeer, Richard Wagner, and
    Carl Maria von Weber, among other musicians; manuscripts by several
    modern American composers, notably Leonard Bernstein, Aaron Copland,
    Gershwin, and Virgil Thomson; inscribed books, scores, programs, and
    pamphlets; an archive of Russian music; inscribed photographs from
    singers and composers; a selection of his own photographs of music-
    ians.

b. The Florine Stettheimer Memorial Collection of Books About the Fine
    Arts

    Van Vechten founded this collection in 1948. The title is self-ex-
    planatory, although it also includes a selection of photographs as
    well as various graphic materials.

I 4   Museum of the City of New York

    Van Vechten gave about a thousand photographs of theater luminaries
    in 1942, when a selection of them was exhibited; a decade later, he
    gave a large selection of celebrated black artists and writers and
    his collection of post cards and greeting cards.

I 5   Museum of Modern Art

    Van Vechten gave the illustrations for a projected edition of Nigger
    Heaven, by E. McKnight Kauffer, in 1942, and the largest single col-
    lection of his ballet and dance photographs in 1945.

I 6   Philadelphia Museum of Art

    Mark Lutz, a friend to whom Van Vechten sent prints of nearly all his
    photographs, donated 13,000 of them in 1967. This is the largest
    single collection of Van Vechten photographs extant.

I 7   Minor Collections

a. Atlanta University: The Countée Cullen Memorial Collection of Photo-
    graphs of Celebrated Negroes by Carl Van Vechten, donated by Harold
    Jackman

b. Brandeis University: 1,600 photographs, donated by Fania Marinoff
    Van Vechten

c. Detroit, Michigan, Free Public Library: The E. Azalia Hackley
    Memorial Collection of Photographs of Celebrated Negroes by Carl Van
    Vechten, donated by Van Vechten

d. Hammond Museum, North Salem, New York: 2,000 photographs, donated by
    Saul Mauriber

e. Howard University: The Rose McClendon Memorial Collection of Photo-
    graphs of Celebrated Negroes by Carl Van Vechten, donated by Van
    Vechten

f. Iowa, University of: a nearly complete run of Van Vechten's books,
    from the collection of his cousin, Mary Pickney, and a manuscript
    [D169, EV50], both donated by Van Vechten; also a large selection of
    photographs

g. New Mexico, University of: The James Bowers Peterson Memorial Col-
    lection of Photographs of Celebrated Negroes by Carl Van Vechten,
    originally donated by Van Vechten to Wadleigh High School in New York
    City and subsequently donated to the University of New Mexico

h. Richmond, Virginia, University of: a nearly complete run of Van
    Vechten's books, pamphlets, and ephemera, manuscripts [B9, B12, B13,
    C14] and photographs, through the bequest of Mark Lutz; also a selec-
    tion of photographs

i. Other minor manuscripts are at the University of Texas [B6] and the
    University of Virginia [A11d]; other substantial photographic col-
    lections are at the Cedar Rapids, Iowa, Arts Center, Princeton Uni-
    versity, and Tulane University

INDEX

Abbot, Bessie, 122, 123, 132, 135, 149
Ackerly, J.R., 176
Adams, Franklin P., 35, 231
Adams, Maude, 129, 157
Adams, Robert K., 29
Adler, Elmer, 89
Aguglia, Mimi, 9, 12, 110, 157
Aiken, Conrad, 49
Ailey, Alvin, 56, 59, 100
Alastair [Hans Henning Voight], 68, 173
Albani, Emma, 144
Albéniz, Isaac, 12, 33
Alda, Frances, 136, 141, 147
Aldrich, Richard, 90
Alfred Knopf at Sixty, 96
Alice B. Toklas Cookbook, The, 97, 98.
Allan, Maud, 56, 95, 134
All Cats Go to Heaven, 99
Allen, William G. [Van Vechten pseudonym], 162
Alvarez, Marguerite d', 110, 111, 116, 164, 170
Ambassador Hotel, 175
American Negro Exhibit, 74
American Weekly Jewish News, 109, 110
Anderson, John Murray, 167
Anderson, Marian, 59, 94, 116
Anderson, Sherwood, 241, 242
Andrews, Clarence, 241, 242
Anglin, Margaret, 8, 9, 129, 159, 160, 163

Appia Adolphe, 6, 108
Arensberg, Walter, 181
Armstrong, Henry, 59
Arno, Peter, 176
Arnould, Sophie, 33, 60
Art From Life to Life, 95-96
Artzybasheff, Boris, 64
Atherton, Gertrude, 30, 52, 112, 181
Atkinson, Brooks, 152, 238
Austin, Roger, 243
Autobiography of an Ex-Coloured Man, The, 70
Autobiography of Alice B. Toklas, The, 76

Baker, D.D., 178
Baker, Josephine, 59
Banks, Richard, 79, 181, 182
Barrett, John Townsend, 236
Barrie, Sir James, 141, 146, 151, 158
Barrymore, Ethel, 141, 146, 154
Barrymore, John, 138
Barthé, Richmond, 59, 73, 74
Barton, Ralph, 20, 21, 26, 27, 29, 223, 224
Bates, Blanche, 158
Bauer, Harold, 145
Bauermeister, Mathilda, 124
Bayes, Nora, 142
Beach, Joseph Warren, 227, 232
Bean, Theodora, 164, 218
Beecham, Sir Thomas, 144
Beecroft, John, 99

Belasco, David, 131, 140
Bel Geddes, Norman, 112
Benchley, Robert, 173
Benét, William Rose, 36, 49, 112
Benkovitz, Miriam, 102, 241
Berkovitz, Alexander, 125
Berlin, Irving, 166
Bernhardt, Sarah, 140
Bernstein, Henri, 126
Bernstein, Leonard, 246
Berry, Faith, 243
Best Cat Stories, 96
Between Friends, 79
Bibliography of the Writings of
  Carl Van Vechten, 66, 67
Blech, Leo, 146
Blind Bow Boy, The, 19, 22-25, 102,
  171, 221-222, 223
Blinn, Holbrook, 158
Blixen, Baroness Karen, 100
Bodenheim, Maxwell, 227
Bolton, Guy, 159
Bonci, Alessandro, 119, 121, 139,
  146
Bontemps, Arna, 59, 167, 233, 234,
  236
Boon, Miels, 144
Born to Be, 70-71
Borrow, George, 10
Borzoi 1920, The, 14, 83
Borzoi 1925, The, 84
Borzoi Reader, The, 88
Bouché, Louis, 111
Bourne, Randolphe, 218
Boyce, Neith, 171
Boyd, Ernest, 19, 24, 35, 86, 111,
  173, 221, 224
Bradbury, Malcolm, 241
Bragdon, Claude, 7, 61
Brandt, Sophie, 138
Brawley, Benjamin, 114
Breaking Into Print, 89
Brennon, Alternon St John, 162,
  164
Brice, Fannie, 159
Bricktop [Ada de Congé Smith], 59
Bromfield, Louis, 33, 45, 49
Broun, Heywood, 219
Brown, Lawrence, 59, 68
Bryan, William Jennings, 124
Buechner, Frederick, 180
Burke, Billie, 157, 160
Burleigh, Henry T., 143
Burt, Evelyn [Van Vechten pseudo-
  nym], 162
Burrian, Carl, 121

Butcher, Fanny, 19, 33, 223, 224,
  229, 230
Butler, Nicholas Murray, 125
Bynner, Witter, 42

Cabell, James Branch, 30, 32, 54,
  79, 115, 231, 238, 243, 245
Cabell, Margaret Freeman, 79
Calvé, Emma, 121, 122, 142, 149
Campanari, Leandro, 120, 150
Campau, Francis Denis, 3
Canepa, Giuseppe, 143
Cantatance, Mme., 145
Capote, Truman, 51
Carl Van Vechten, 101, 240
Carl Van Vechten and the Irrever-
  ent Decades, 55, 102, 240
Carl Van Vechten and the Twen-
  ties, 236
Carpenter, John Alden, 149
Carr, Thomas, 125
Caruso, Enrico, 120, 126, 132,
  139, 140, 142, 143, 145, 147,
  148, 151, 165
Case, Frank, 179
Castle, Vernon, 129
Cats and Cats, 89
Cats: A Personal Anthology, 101
Cavallieri, Lina, 120, 133, 134,
  145
Chadell, Georges, 138
Century Cyclopedia of Names, 82
Chaliapin, Feodor, 8. 13, 109,
  122, 123, 165, 177
Chanler, Robert, 71, 145
Cheatham, Kitty, 90, 122, 124,
  134, 140, 142, 144
Chesnutt, Charles W., 230
Chesterton, G.K., 156
Chiapilli, Francesco, 41, 42
Chicago American, 118-19
Chronicles of the American Dance,
  94
Cincinnati Symphony Program, 82
Cisheros, Eleanora de, 148
Clappé, Arthur A., 147
Clark, Emily, 86, 230, 240
Clark, Kenneth, 217
Clark, Walter Van Tilburg, 179
Clarke, Frances E., 89, 98
Cohan, George M., 121, 153, 156
Coleman, Leon Duncan, 242
Collings, Pierre, 29
Colum, Padraic, 79
Columbia Oral History, 101, 102

Concert Life in New York 1902-1923, 90
Confidence Man, The, 103
Congreve, William, 3
Conklin, Chester, 29
Conreid, Heinrich, 120, 121, 122, 123, 128
Copland, Aaron, 246
Cooking With the Chinese Flavor, 77
Covarrubias, Miguel, 32, 69, 70-71, 112, 173, 183, 225, 228, 237
Coverley, Roy de, 43
Cowl, Jane, 165
Craft, Robert, 182
Craig, Gordon, 6, 108
Craven, Frank, 159, 169
Crosman, Henrietta, 156
Crothers, Rachel, 156
Crowther, Bosley, 152
Cullen, Countée, 58, 112, 179, 231, 246
Cumberland, Gerald, 164
Cunningham, Scott, 14, 18, 22, 31, 66, 161, 170, 224
Cushing, Mary Watkins, 116

Dalmores, Charles, 123, 135, 136, 141
Damrosch, Walter, 121, 133, 138, 144, 148, 150, 151
Dance 62, 99-100
Dance Writings of Carl Van Vechten, The, 55-56
Dane, Clemence, 49, 177
D'Annunzio, Gabrielle, 143, 158
Darktown Follies, The, 156, 161
Davis, Richard Harding, 153
Dearborn, Willie [Van Vechten pseudonym], 118
Debussy, Claude, 129
Defranne, Hector, 134
DeKoven, Reginald, 145, 148, 153, 154
Delibes, Leo, 33, 56, 112
Delna, Marie, 130, 134, 135
Delys, Gaby, 144, 160
DeMille, Agnes, 56, 116, 117, 181
Demuth, Charles, 111
DeReszke, Jean, 120, 149
Destinn, Emmy, 139, 140, 147
Dibble, R.F., 166
Dickinson, Edward, 143
Dickinson, G. Lowes, 135
Dippel, Andreas, 121, 123, 124, 132, 133, 136, 137, 144

Doctor Faustus Lights the Lights, 96
Dowell, Coleman, 29, 237-38
Drake, Alexander Wildon, 163
Draper, Muriel, 70, 117, 229
Dreiser, Theodore, 49, 54, 115, 237, 245
Drew, Elisabeth, 86-87
Drew, John, 153, 154
DuBois, W.E.B., 39, 226
Duncan, Isadora, 56, 91-92, 93-94, 110, 125, 133, 141
Dunreith, Effie, 143
Dupee, F.W., 73

Eames, Emma, 121, 144, 146
Ediss, Connie, 122
Edwards, Ellen, 37
Eilshemius, Louis M., 167
Eliot, Gertrude, 154
Ellis, Havelock, 12, 29, 109
Elman, Mischa, 141
Et Cetera, 84
Evans, Donald, 108, 117, 217
Evans, Walker, 167
Ewing, Max, 176, 177, 221, 222, 245
Excavations, 27, 33-34, 174, 225-26

Fairchild, Blair, 147
Farley, Dot, 29
Farrar, Geraldine, 8, 13, 109, 122, 123, 126, 134, 140, 141, 150, 151
Fauset, Jessie, 112
Faversham, William, 158, 159
Favorite Cat Stories, 98
Feathers, 48-49, 86-87, 96, 98, 99
Fetchit, Stepin, 175
Ficke, Arthur Davison, 101, 245
Field, Anna T.L., 163
Fields, Lew, 155
Fifty Drawings by Alastair, 68, 173
Firbank, Ronald, 65, 102-3, 104-5, 111, 165, 241, 244
Firecrackers, 30-33, 173, 224, 225, 227
First List of Books, A, 74
Fisher, Rudolph, 228
Fisher, William Arms, 166
Fiske, Minnie Maddern, 136, 137
Fitch, Clyde, 107, 154, 160

Fitch, Morgan Lewis, 61
Fitzgerald, F. Scott, 103-4, 112, 238
Five Old English Ditties, 3
Flanner, Janet, 75, 222
Fleuron, Svend, 62, 170
Flood, W.H. Grattan, 147
Florine Stettheimer, 92
Florine Stettheimer: A Life in Art, 81
Flowers of Friendship, The, 97, 181
Foote, F. Varrington, 143
Forbes-Robertson, Johnston, 8, 154, 156
Ford, Corey, 227, 228
Fornia, Rita, 124, 138
Foster, May, 29
Four Saints in Three Acts, 72, 87, 117, 151
Foy, Eddie, 146
Fragments from an unwritten auto-biography, 54
Frankenstein, Alfred V., 225, 233, 234
Franklin, Sir John, 132
Franko, Sam, 119
Freedley, George, 80, 182
Fremstad, Olive, 8, 13, 109, 116, 120, 122, 123, 138, 139, 145, 147
Fuller, Henry Blake, 33, 85, 111, 224, 225, 245
Fuller, Loie, 56, 128, 131, 133
Fyfe, H. Hamilton, 150
Gadski, Johanna, 141, 147
Galli-Curci, Amelita, 164
Gallup, Donald, 97, 168, 181, 234, 235, 236, 237, 238, 245
Galston, Gottfried, 150
Garden, Mary, 8, 9, 10, 13, 109, 115, 122, 123, 124, 126, 133, 134, 135, 136, 137, 139, 141, 141, 143, 145, 148, 163, 164
Gatti-Casazza, Giulio, 123, 124, 125, 136, 138, 148
Geltzer, Katerina, 146
Genee, Adeline, 150
Gentlemen Prefer Blondes, 112
Gerhardt, Elena, 146
Gershwin, George, 36, 78, 112, 246
Gershwin Years, The, 78
Gielgud, Val, 101
Gilbert, Charles, 139
Gilbert, W.S., 143
Girl of the Golden West, The, 137, 140, 143, 145

Giselle and I, 78-79
Glasgow, Ellen, 35, 84-85, 165, 167, 174, 179, 237, 245
Glaspell, Susan, 153
Glenn, Isa, 166, 175, 176, 228
Gloster, Hugh, 233
Gluck, Alma, 149
Glyn, Elinor, 125
Godowsky, Leopold, 145
God's Trombones, 78
Goldman, Emma, 130, 131
Gopal, Ram, 178
Gordan, John D., 181, 236
Gordin, Jacob, 129
Gordon, Taylor, 59, 70-71, 173, 229
Gotham Book Mart, 81, 89
Gounod, Charles, 246
Granville-Barker, Harley, 155
Grau, Shirley Ann, 181
Graves, Charles L., 147
Great Gatsby, The, 103-4, 112
Greece 1821-1941, 90
Gregory, Walter Leon, 3, 4
Grippon, Eva, 131
Guedalla, Philip, 173
Guilbert, Yvette, 8, 13, 76, 109
Gunbourg, Raoul, 126
Gunther, Charles, 120

Hackett, E. Byrne, 8
Hackley, E. Azalia, 247
Hadley, Henry, 139
Haddon, J. Cuthbert, 143
Hammerstein, Oscar, 12, 33, 119, 120, 121, 122, 123, 125, 130, 132, 133, 134, 135, 136, 137, 138, 139, 140, 141, 142, 143, 146, 148, 149, 150, 151, 163, 164
"Hammerstein, Oscar" [Van Vechten as ghostwriter], 149
Hammett, Dashiell, 175, 176, 177
Hanako, 122
Handy, W.C., 59, 115, 166, 167, 174
Hansen, Harry, 39, 220, 221, 223, 226, 229, 230
Harbach, Otto, 156
Hart-Davis, Rupert, 116
Hartley, L.P., 228
Hayes, Roland, 168
Hearn, Lafcadio, 165
Heighton, Percy, 163
Helbling, Mark, 243
Helburn, Theresa, 245

Hemenway, Robert, 71
Henderson, W.J., 143
Henschel, Sir George, 164
Herbert, Holmes, 28
Herbert, Victor, 122, 139, 144,
    151, 153
Hergesheimer, Joseph, 12, 54, 115,
    219, 240, 245
Hertz, Alfred, 139
Hervey, Arthur, 144
Hichens, Robert, 144
Hill, J. Leubrie, 156
Himes, Chester, 59, 179, 182, 245
Hinshaw, William, 143
Hirschfeld, Al, 78
Hodge, Helen Hale, 129
Hoffenstein, Sam, 221
Hoffman, Gertrude, 144
Hofmann, Josef, 9, 10, 146, 162
Hofmannsthal, Hugo von, 157
Holiday, Billie, 59
Hollander, Victor, 147, 149
Holt, Henry, 147
Holt, Nora, 59
Homer, Louise, 134, 138
Hopwood, Avery, 9, 109
Horgan, Paul, 227
Houdini, Harry, 149
Housman, Laurence, 154
Howard, Bronson, 157
Huffo, Tito, 146
Huggins, Nathan I., 241
Hughes, Langston, 36-39, 40, 41-43,
    44, 58, 59, 69-70, 112, 152, 174,
    176, 177, 232, 239, 243, 245
Hughes, Richard, 175
Humperdinck, Englebert, 90, 140
Hundley, Richard, 81
Huneker, James T., 219
Hurston, Zora Neale, 58, 177, 180,
    237, 245

Improvisations of New York, 95
In a Winter City, 62
In His Own Time, 103-4
Innocence Abroad, 86
Interpreters, 13, 93, 170
Interpreters and Interpretations,
    7-9, 13, 61, 93, 169, 170, 218
In the Garret, 11-12, 22, 170, 219
Isadora Duncan, 93
Isadora Duncan in Her Dances, 91-
    92
Isak Dinesen, 100-1

Jablonski, Edward, 78, 237
Jackman, Harold, 59, 246
Jacobi, Josephine, 136
Jacobs, Lewis, 178
Janis, Elsie, 146
Jeritza, Marie, 111
Johnson, Constance, 3
Johnson, Edward, 124
Johnson, Guy B., 166
Johnson, Grace Nail, 59
Johnson, J. Rosamond, 167, 173
Johnson, James Weldon, 36, 39, 45,
    52, 58, 59, 70, 78, 89, 112,
    166, 174, 175, 177, 178, 179,
    226, 227, 231, 237, 245
Johnson, Merle, 222
Johnson, Nunnally, 24, 222
Jonas, Klaus, 107, 236, 238
Joseph, Michael, 86-87, 96

Kahn, Otto, 134, 144
Kalich, Bertha, 131, 156
Kauffer, E. McKnight, 45, 246
Kazin, Alfred, 233, 242
"Keep A-Inchin' Along", 58-59,
    183
Kellner, Bruce, 55, 56, 58, 102,
    183, 237, 240, 241, 242, 243
Kellog, Clara Louise, 141
Kemp, Harry, 227
Kenton, Edna, 14, 17
Kern, Jerome, 155
Kimball, Fiske, 181
King, Hettie, 122
Kirby, Richard, 242
Kirstein, Lincoln, 239
Kittens, 62, 170
Knopf, Alfred A., 8, 14, 17, 18,
    20, 24, 26, 40, 45, 96, 100,
    111, 180, 181, 235, 239
Knopf, Blanche, 10, 11, 16, 45
Knote, Heinrich, 123
Kreisler, Fritz, 133
Kronenberger, Louis, 226
Krutch, Joseph Wood, 219, 223
Kubelik, Jan, 145

Langner, Lawrence, 49, 245
Larsen, Nella, 175
Last Operas and Plays, 75
LaTouche, John, 115
Lawrence, D.H., 231
LeBlanc, Georgette, 146
Lehar, Franz, 145, 150, 159
Leoncavallo, Ruggerio, 120

Lerman, Leo, 238, 243
Leschetizky, Theodor, 151
Lewis, D.B. Wyndham, 230
Lewis, Sinclair, 223
Lhévinne, Josef, 122
Lindemann, Kelvin, 43
Lin Hsianju, 77, 181
Lin Tsuifeng, 77, 181
Liszt, Franz, 144
Littel, Philip, 165
Lloyd, Marie, 122, 154, 161
Locher, Robert, 22, 65, 171
Locke, Alain, 166, 227
Loos, Anita, 36, 112, 173
Lord of the Sea, 67, 68
Lords of the Housetops, 7, 161-
    62, 171, 220
Lovett, Robert Morss, 223
Lueders, Edward, 101, 235, 236,
    240
Lueschner, Mark A., 169
Luhan, Mabel Dodge, 245
Lunn, Louisa Kirkby, 120
Lussan, Zéliede, 124
Lutz, Mark, 246, 247
Lyly, John, 3
Lynes, George Platt, 98

Mabry, Thomas Dabney, 172
Machen, Arthur, 33, 111, 112, 171,
    174, 244
Mack, Charles Emmett, 28
Maeterlinck, Maurice, 127
Magrill, Paul, 93, 94
Mahler, Gustav, 123, 124, 136
Maitland, J.A. Fuller, 143
Mann, Dorothea Lawrence, 85, 228
Manners, J. Hartley, 159
Mannes, David, 147
Manning, Irene, 28, 237, 238
Marchant, Peter David, 236
Marinoff, Fania, 5, 7, 13, 17, 35,
    58, 109, 110, 157, 222, 241, 244,
    245, 246
Markova, Alicia, 56, 78, 79, 116
Marlowe, Julia, 129, 154
Marshall, Armina, 49, 245
Martin, John 233, 239
Martin, Ricardo, 142, 146
Martens, Frederic H., 165
Mascagni, Pietro, 139
Mason, James, 98, 152, 180
Mason, Pamela, 98, 152, 180
Massenet, Jules, 6, 107, 133
Matisse, Henri, 126
Matzenauer, Marguerite, 145

Maugham, W. Somerset, 27, 31, 35,
    132, 157, 224, 226, 244
Mauriber, Saul, 57, 247
Maxwell, Mary Mortimer, 126
May, Florence, 147
Mazarin, Mariette, 8, 109, 135
Melba, Nellie, 120, 121, 124, 137,
    138, 140
Melis, Carmen, 134
Melville, Herman, 33, 83, 103,
    111, 165, 245
Mencken, H.L., 19, 33, 54, 115,
    217, 218, 219, 225, 226, 238,
    241, 243, 245
Merry-Go-Round, The, 9-10, 94,
    169-70
Metcalf, Addison M., 182
Meyerbeer, Giacomo, 246
Millen, Gilmore, 176
Miller, Henry, 245
Moby Dick as Dubloon, 103
Modern American Prose, 88
Modjeska, Helena, 130
Moeller, Philip, 9, 60, 109, 219
Molnár, Ferenc, 153
Monteux, Pierre, 180
Moore, George, 11, 53, 107, 108,
    154
Morales, Pedro, 10, 11
Morand, Paul, 40, 176, 227
Mordkin, Mikhail, 144
More Mr. Cat, 80
Morehouse, Dr. C.L., 130
Morgan, Anna, 85
Morton, Dr. Rosalie, 130
Music After the Great War, 5-6,
    217, 218
Music and Bad Manners, 6-7, 169,
    170, 218
Music of Spain, The, 9, 10-11, 18,
    170
My Musical Life, 63-65, 171

McBride, Henry, 92, 179, 231
McClendon, Rose, 247
MacClintock, Lander, 165
McCord, David, 85
McCormack, John, 133, 164
MacDowell, Edward, 123
MacFall, Haldane, 173
McFee, William, 173, 229, 235
MacIntosh, Francis, 20
McKay, Claude, 39, 229, 245
MacKaye, Percy, 157
McRae, Ronald, 45, 175

Nathan, George Jean, 111
Nathan, Robert, 220
Naughty Marietta, 139
Nazimova, Alla, 131
Negri, Pola, 28, 225
Neruda, Wilma, 136
Nethersole, Olga, 140, 154
Newman, Ernest, 84, 112, 224
New York City Ballet, 98
New York Globe, 161-64
New York Press, 152-61
New York Times, 119-53
Nichols, Beverly, 31
Nielsen, Alice, 132
Nigger Heaven, 32, 34-45, 58, 101,
    166, 174, 181, 183, 226, 227,
    229, 231, 246
Nijinsky, 93
Nijinsky, Waslav, 8, 13, 56, 93,
    109
Nïn, Anais, 179
Nordica, Lillian, 119, 122, 123,
    130, 137, 141, 150
Noria, Jane, 132, 138
"Noria, Jane" [Van Vechten as
    ghostwriter], 138
Novel of Thank You, A, 77
Novello, Clara Anastasia, 140
Nugent, Bruce, 43

Odum, Howard W., 166
Of Cats and Men, 98
O'Keeffe, Georgia, 245
Oliver, Guy, 29
Once and For All, 85
Ornstein, Leo, 7, 141
Orridge, Theodora, 144
Ouida [Louise de la Ramé], 62, 33,
    244
Overton, Grant, 83
Owl, The, 91

Paccielfantica, Teresa Lina, 142
Pachmann, Vladimir de, 124, 145
Packard, Mrs. Harriet Dement, 4
Paderewski, Ignace, 128
Padgette, Paul, 20, 55, 238, 240,
    241, 242
Palmer, Mrs. Potter, 119
Paluka, Frank, 240
Pankhurst, Emmeline, 163
Paris We Remember, The, 91
Parker, Horatio, 143, 147
Parlow, Kathleen, 140, 162

Parties, 20, 50-52, 176, 229, 230
"Pastiches et Pistaches," 111,
    112
Paton, Alan, 180
Paul, Elliot 91
Pavlova, 94
Pavlova, Anna, 56, 94, 112, 135,
    136, 139, 142, 146, 161, 162
Payne, Windham, 24, 25
Perper, Leo, 180
Peter Whiffle: His Life and Works,
    12, 17-22, 27, 88, 91, 171, 175,
    220, 221
Peters, Paul, 177
Peterson, Dorothy, 75, 234
Peterson, Jerome Bowers, 75, 247
Pettit, Charles, 175
[Photography], 56
Pickney, Mary, 247
Pickthall, Marmaduke, 173
Pierné, Gabriele, 140
Pink Lady, The, 142
Pitcairn, Robert, 130
Plain and Fancy Cats, 98-99
Pohlig, Carl, 148
Polacco, Giorgio, 149
Polaire, 137, 155
Pollock, Anna Marble, 4, 48, 54,
    245
Pollock, Channing, 107, 145, 154,
    160
Portrait of a Publisher, 100
Portraits, 57-58
Portraits by Robert Chanler, 71
Powell, Maud, 147, 148
Prancing Nigger, 65
Prince of Wales and Other Famous
    Americans, 69, 173
Puccini, Giacomo, 121, 139
Puckett, Newell Niles, 166
Purdy, James, 181, 245
Puss in Books, 86-87
Pygmalion, 107, 160

Rachmaninoff, Sergei, 133, 134,
    139
Rains, Leo, 150
Rascoe, Burton, 24, 36, 45, 221,
    224
Red, 29-30, 173, 223
Redman, Ben Ray, 223, 225
Reicher, Hedwig, 145
Reinhardt, Max, 151
Rémon, Maurice, 27, 48
Renaud, Maurice, 120, 123, 146

Rhau, Henry von, 175
Richards, Grant, 20, 24
Richardson, Henry Handel, 166, 178
Richer, Clément, 180
Rimsky-Korsakoff, Nicolai, 63-65,
     171
Ring, Blanche, 129
Ringo, James, 241
Roberts, Grace, 167, 179
Robeson, Paul, 36, 59, 68
Robillard, Norbert, 130
Rodin, Auguste, 127, 128
Rogers, W.G., 168, 181, 241
Rolland, Romains, 145
Romberg, Sigmund, 158
Roosevelt, Theodore, 125
Rosenkavalier, Der, 141, 144
Rostand, Edmond, 126, 151
Ruffo, Titta, 150
Russell, Lillian, 131
Russell, Nina, 241

Sacred and Profane Memories, 51-
     54, 89, 176
Saint Clair, Malcolm, 29
Saint-Saëns, Camille, 120, 121
Salome, 106, 110, 121, 127, 128,
     134, 137, 143, 157
Saltus, Edgar, 9, 33, 86, 110, 164,
     165, 166, 245
Sanborn, John Pitts, 161
Sands, G.W., 125
Sardou, Eugene, 160, 161
Satie, Erik, 8, 33, 82, 109
Scarborough, Dorothy, 166
Schack, William, 167, 178
Schauffler, Robert Haner, 147
Sheel, Fritzi, 121
Scheff, Fritzi, 116
Schmidt, André Jaeger, 144
Schnitzler, Arthur, 158
Schumann-Heink, Ernestine, 123
Schuyler, George, 38-39, 226, 235
Schwartz, Maurice, 177
Scott, Harold, 78
Scotti, Antonio, 163
Seabrook, William, 175
Seguin, Zelda, 143
Seitz, Don C., 165
Seldes, Gilbert, 228
Seldes, Marian, 182
Selected Writings of Gertrude
     Stein, 73-74
Selections from the Gutter, 105
Sembrich, Marcella, 149
Seven Keys to Baldpate, 153

Shakespeare, William, 129, 153,
     154, 156, 159, 160, 163, 165,
     167, 232
Shapiro, Karl, 179
Shaw, Anna, 129
Shaw, George Bernard, 107, 108,
     143, 155, 156, 157, 159, 160
Sherwin, Louis, 161
"Sherwin, Louis" [Van Vechten as
     ghostwriter], 162
Shiel, Matthew Phipps, 33, 67-68,
     172, 175, 244
Shoenberg, Arnold, 151
Singer, I.J., 178
Sklar, George, 177
Slezak, Leo, 133, 146
Smirnoff, Dimitri, 147
Smith, Bessie, 59, 105, 113, 115
Smith, Clara, 59, 113
Smith, William Gardner, 180
Snyder, Anna Elizabeth, 3
Sophie, 60
Sophocles, 160
Southern, Edward, 129, 154
Spider Boy, 45-49, 167, 175, 228,
     231
Spring Maid, The, 140, 169
Stagg, Hunter, 220, 222, 224
Stallings, Lawrence, 24
Stanford, Sir Charles, 147
Starrett, Vincent, 84, 219, 236
Stein, Gertrude, 10, 72, 73, 75,
     76, 77, 80, 96, 97, 104, 107,
     117, 151, 165, 167, 168, 174,
     178, 180, 181, 182, 220, 223,
     231, 232, 234, 236, 242, 243,
     245
Steinbeck, John, 177
Stern, Herbert F., 102
Stettheimer, Carrie, 53
Stettheimer, Ettie, 53, 245
Stettheimer, Florine, 53, 81, 92,
     111, 115, 234, 245, 246
Stevens, Wallace, 102, 116, 240
Stewart, John, 29, 237, 238
Stewart, Lawrence D., 75
Stieglitz, Alfred, 93, 245
Stieglitz Memorial Portfolio, 93
Stone, Grace Zaring, 236
Stransky, Josef, 162
Strauss, Richard, 106, 110, 121,
     127, 128, 137, 134, 135, 137,
     141
Stravinsky, Igor, 6, 108, 163,
     182
Stravinsky, Vera, 182
Sullivan, Sir Arthur, 12

Sullivan, John L. 166
Sweethearts, 153
Sylva, Marguerite, 130, 132
Symonds, Arthur, 164
Symphony Society Bulletin, 4

Tanguay, Eva, 111, 130
Tattooed Countess, The, 26-28, 223,
    224, 237, 238
Taylor, Laurette, 159
Taylor, Loomis H., 147
Taylor, Prentiss, 53, 55, 102, 176
Tempest, Marie, 138
Tempest, Walter [Van Vechten
    pseudonym], 107
Ternina, Milka, 135
Tetrazzini, Luisa, 107, 122, 123,
    124, 125, 133, 137, 139, 140,
    141, 142, 147, 162
"Tetrazzini, Luisa" [Van Vechten
    pseudonym], 107
Teyte, Maggie, 145, 148
Theatre Annual 1943, 91
Thénevaz, Paul, 111
Thicknesse, Philip, 12, 33, 244
Thomas, Elisabeth Finley, 91
Thompson, Denman, 122
Thomson, Virgil, 178, 246
Thousand Years Ago, 157
Three Lives, 72, 174
Thuille, Ludwig, 145
Thurman, Wallace, 226, 241
Tiger in the House, The, 13, 14-17,
    27, 89, 98, 99, 101, 170, 182,
    219, 220, 232
Toklas, Alice B., 76, 97-98, 181,
    235, 238, 242, 245
Too Many Crooks, 159, 169
Torrence, Ridgely, 160
Towndrow, C. Romney, 27
Trentini, Emma, 138
Trigg, Emma Gray, 117
Two: Gertrude Stein and Her Bro-
    ther, 75
Tyler, Parker, 81, 238

Underhill, John Garrett, 11

Valverde, Joaquin, 9, 109, 163
Van Doren, Carl, 19, 31, 33, 49,
    88, 220, 222, 225
Van Druten, John, 176
Van Dyke, Henry, 59, 240

Van Vechten, Ada Amanda Fitch, 18
Van Vechten, Ralph, 33
Varèse, Edgar, 82
Vedder, Enoch R., 137
Veiller, Bayard, 149, 153
Vidal, Gore, 234

Wagenknecht, Edward, 241, 242
Wagner, Richard, 7, 108, 147, 246
Walker, A'lelia, 59
Walker, Edith, 139
Walker, George, 59
Walker, Sarah, 148
Walkowitz, Abraham, 91, 92, 95,
    96, 181
Walpole, Hugh, 19, 26, 27, 31,
    221, 228, 244
Walrond, Eric, 174, 226
Ward, Artemus, 165
Ward, Christopher, 224
Ward, Lucille, 28-29
Warner, Sylvia Townsend, 174
Waste, Henrie [see Stettheimer,
    Ettie]
Waters, Ethel, 59, 113, 114, 152,
    174, 235, 242
Waugh, Evelyn, 178
Weary Blues, The, 69-70, 174
Weaver, Raymond, 165
Weber, Carl Maria von, 246
Wedekind, Frank, 126
Weingartner, Felix, 150
We Moderns, 90
Werba, Louis, F., 69
West, Rebecca, 49
When Winter Comes to Main Street,
    83
White, Nelson, 32
White, Walter, 36, 58, 59, 166,
    173, 174, 245
Why and What, 5
Wilde, Oscar, 106, 157, 160
Wilkinson, Louis, 112
Williams, Bert, 59, 111, 157
Williams, Hattie, 130
Wilson, Edmund, 222
Wilson, Robert A., 76
Windham, Donald, 182
Winter, William, 163
With Formality and Elegance, 55
Wobert, Dorothea, 29
Wolf-Ferrari, Ermanno, 146, 147
Wolfe, Rennold, 145, 154, 217
Wolfe, Thomas, 232
Woman of the World, A, 28-29

Woollcott, Alexander, 173
Words and Music, 92
Worthington, Marjorie, 179
Wylie, Elinor, 35, 67, 87, 111,
    112, 172, 173, 173, 225
Wylie Elinor, The Collected Prose
    of, 87

Yaw, Ellen Beach, 124
Young, G.W., 141, 144
Young, Roland, 173

Zenatello, Giovanni, 121
Zimbalist, Efrem, 145, 149, 151

ABOUT THE COMPILER

Bruce Kellner is an associate professor of English at Millersville State College in Pennsylvania. His essays have appeared in *Menckeniana, Western Humanities Review, Contemporary Poetry, Illinois Quarterly, Opera News,* and in *Great Writers of the English Language.* He is the author of *Carl Van Vechten and the Irreverent Decades*, the editor of *"Keep A-Inchin' Along": Selected Writings of Carl Van Vechten About Black Arts and Letters* (Greenwood Press, Inc.), and, presently, the compiler of selections from Van Vechten's uncollected newspaper and periodical writings and of his correspondence.